CW01203555

Military Adaptation in War

Military Adaptation in War addresses one of the most persistent, yet rarely examined, problems that military organizations confront: namely, the problem of how to adapt under the trying, terrifying conditions of war. This work builds on the book that Dr. Williamson Murray edited with Allan Millett on military innovation (a quite different problem, although similar in some respects). In Clausewitzian terms, war is a contest, an interactive duel, which is of indeterminate length and presents a series of intractable problems at every level, from policy and strategy down to the tactical. Moreover, that the enemy is adapting at the same time presents military organizations with an ever-changing set of conundrums that offers no easy solutions. As the British general James Wolfe suggested before Quebec: "War is an option of difficulties." Dr. Murray provides an in-depth analysis of the problems that military forces confront in adapting to these difficulties.

Williamson Murray is Professor Emeritus of History at The Ohio State University. At present he is a defense consultant and commentator on historical and military subjects in Washington, D.C. He is co-editor of *The Shaping of Grand Strategy* (with Richard Hart Sinnreich and James Lacey, Cambridge, 2011) and *The Making of Peace* (with James Lacey, Cambridge, 2008); *The Past as Prologue* (with Richard Hart Sinnreich, Cambridge, 2006); *The Dynamics of Military Revolution, 1300–2050* (with MacGregor Knox, Cambridge, 2001); *Military Innovation in the Interwar Period* (with Allan R. Millett, Cambridge, 1996); and *The Making of Strategy* (with Alvin Bernstein and MacGregor Knox, Cambridge, 1994).

Military Adaptation in War

With Fear of Change

WILLIAMSON MURRAY

CAMBRIDGE UNIVERSITY PRESS
Cambridge, New York, Melbourne, Madrid, Cape Town,
Singapore, São Paulo, Delhi, Tokyo, Mexico City

Cambridge University Press
32 Avenue of the Americas, New York, NY 10013-2473, USA

www.cambridge.org
Information on this title: www.cambridge.org/9781107006591

© Williamson Murray 2011

This publication is in copyright. Subject to statutory exception
and to the provisions of relevant collective licensing agreements,
no reproduction of any part may take place without the written
permission of Cambridge University Press.

First published 2011
Printed in the United States of America

A catalog record for this publication is available from the British Library.

Library of Congress Cataloging in Publication data
Murray, Williamson.
Military adaptation in war : with fear of change / Williamson Murray.
p. cm.
Includes bibliographical references and index.
ISBN 978-1-107-00659-1 (hardback)
1. Strategic culture – Case studies.   2. Tactics – Case studies.   3. Adaptability
(Psychology) – History.   4. Military art and science – Decision making – Case studies.
5. Operational art (Military science) – Case studies.   6. Organizational effectiveness –
Case studies.   7. Military history, Modern – Case studies.   I. Title.
U21.2.M88   2011
355.3–dc23   2011025078

ISBN 978-1-107-00659-1 Hardback

Cambridge University Press has no responsibility for the persistence or accuracy of URLs
for external or third-party Internet Web sites referred to in this publication and does not
guarantee that any content on such Web sites is, or will remain, accurate or appropriate.

Dedicated to

Lieutenant General Paul K. Van Riper, USMC (ret.)
Marine, educator, intellectual

Colonel Richard H. Sinnreich, USA (ret.)
Soldier, educator, historian

And to the members of the Class of 1957, U.S. Naval Academy
for their commitment to strategic
education and military history

Contents

Preface		*page* ix
1	Introduction: The Background to Military Adaptation	1
2	The Historical Framework of Adaptation	37
3	Complex Adaptation: The Western Front: 1914–1918	74
4	Flawed Adaptation: German Adaptation: The Opening Battles of World War II	119
5	The Battle for the British Isles: June 1940–May 1941	153
6	Adaptation in the Air War: RAF Bomber Command and the *Luftwaffe*'s Air Defenses (15 May 1940–7 May 1945)	196
7	The 1973 Yom Kippur War	262
8	Conclusion: Adaptation and the Future	305
Index		329

Preface

Innumerable people have helped with this effort to suggest the extent of the problems associated with the adaptation that military institutions involved in the conduct of combat operations invariably must confront. In particular, I must thank Andrew Marshall for the trust he showed in my work by providing the funding for much of the research and writing of the manuscript on which this book rests. I must also thank my colleagues at the Institute for Defense Analyses, who read and commented extensively on all of the chapters in their various iterations. In particular, I am grateful for all the work and hours that Karl Lowe, Jim Lacey, Kevin Woods, Jim Kurtz, and, in particular, Katy-Dean Price put in in attempting to whip ill-formed thoughts and syntax into a presentable whole. Outside of the Institute for Defense Analyses, I am particularly grateful for the succinct, sharp, and intelligent comments that Richard Sinnreich provided as he read through various drafts. I also need to thank Shimon Naveh, Dov Tamari, and Ofra Gracier for all their work in arranging, translating where necessary, and supporting my research efforts in Israel. I would be remiss if I were to not also thank the Class of 1957 of the United States Naval Academy for the Chair that the members endowed at the academy and which they allowed me to hold for two years. Finally, I must thank my long-suffering wife, Dr. Lesley Mary Smith, who patiently read and reread chapter after chapter and who attempted to force me to support my suppositions with real arguments and real facts. In the end though, whatever mistakes exist in this work are mine and mine alone.

I

Introduction
The Background to Military Adaptation

The problem of adaptation in war represents one of the most persistent, yet rarely examined problems that military institutions confront. As Michael Howard has suggested, military organizations inevitably get the next war wrong, mostly for reasons that lie beyond their control.[1] Consequently, one of the foremost attributes of military effectiveness must lie in the ability of armies, navies, or air forces to recognize and adapt to the actual conditions of combat, as well as to the new tactical, operational, and strategic, not to mention political, challenges that war inevitably throws up.[2] This observation has proven increasingly true throughout the course of the twentieth century, in small wars as well as major conflicts, and there is every reason to believe it will continue to be true in the twenty-first century.

This work begins by examining what it and its case studies mean by *adaptation*. In Clausewitzian terms, war is a contest, a complex, interactive duel between two opponents. It is a phenomenon of indeterminate length, which presents the opportunity for the contestants to adapt to their enemy's strategy, operations, and tactical approach. But because it is interactive, both sides have the potential to adapt to the conflict at every level, from the tactical to the strategic. Thus, the problems posed by the

---

[1] Michael Howard, "The Uses and Abuses of Military History," in *The Causes of War and Other Essays* (Cambridge, MA, 1983), pp. 188–197.
[2] For an examination of the problems involved in the effectiveness of military institutions, see Allan R. Millett, Williamson Murray, and Kenneth Watman, "The Effectiveness of Military Institutions," in Allan R. Millett and Williamson Murray, eds., *Military Effectiveness*, 3 vols. (London, 1988, reprint Cambridge, 2010), chap. 1.

battle space do not remain constant; in fact, more often than not, they change with startling rapidity. Moreover, war in the past two centuries has seen an increasing pace of adaptation, as military organizations confront not only the problems posed by their adaptive opponent but also the reality that technology is changing and advancing.

Admittedly, military organizations must also change in peacetime, which a series of studies in which the author has participated have termed as innovation.[3] While there are similarities between the processes of innovation and adaptation, the environments in which they occur are radically different. Simply put, one cannot replicate in peacetime the conditions of war. In the case of innovation, there is always time available to think through problems, whatever their nature, but peacetime invariably lacks the terrible pressures of war as well as an interactive, adaptive opponent who is trying to kill us. In the case of war, on the other hand, there is little time, but there is the feedback of combat results, which can suggest necessary adaptations, but only if lessons are identified *and* learned, the latter representing a major "if."

Why adaptation to the challenges of war has proven difficult is the result of a number of complex factors. Ironically, for much of history until the nineteenth century, adaptation was rarely a part of the military equation. Before the European "way of war" emerged in the sixteenth century, military adaptation in war, much less innovation during times of peace, was simply not a part of the military landscape.[4] Even after the reinvention of the Roman legionary system of civic and military discipline in the seventeenth century, military adaptation in Europe took place at a glacial pace, most usually in tactics but occasionally in the operational sphere. It was not until technological and sociological changes of the Industrial Revolution began to interfere with the processes of war in the mid-nineteenth century that adaptation to an increasingly complex battle space became a major element in military effectiveness. By the twentieth century, military organizations confronted the problem of adapting not only to the technological changes occurring during peacetime, the consequences of which have often been difficult to estimate in terms of their

---

[3] On innovation, see Williamson Murray and Allan R. Millett, *Military Innovation in the Interwar Period* (Cambridge, 1996).

[4] See, in particular, MacGregor Knox and Williamson Murray, eds., *The Dynamics of Military Revolution, 1300–2050* (Cambridge, 2000). See also Geoffrey Parker, *Military Innovation and the Rise of the West* (Cambridge, 1996); and Clifford Rogers, ed., *The Military Revolutions Debate* (Boulder, CO, 1995).

impact on operations, but also to the fact that war itself has inevitably turned up the speed of technological change.[5]

History suggests that military organizations have been more committed to the ethos of the past than to preparing to meet the future. There is a good reason for this: the effectiveness of military institutions in the Western tradition has depended on their ability to inculcate discipline through the means of what the British Army terms "square bashing" – the regimen of drilling recruits endlessly on parade fields.[6] Yet, the demand of discipline and rigid respect for one's superiors – on which cohesion in battle depends – are antithetical to the processes of adaptation, which require a willingness on the part of subordinates to question the revealed wisdom of their superiors. It is this inherent tension between the creation of disciplined, obedient military organizations, responsive to direction from above, and the creation of organizations adaptive to a world of constant change that makes military innovation in peacetime and adaptation in war so difficult. And one should not forget that adaptation and innovation often require military organizations to abandon proved equipment, organizations, and methods in favor of untested alternatives. Nor is that reluctance entirely unjustified. Adaptation, for example, inevitably incurs risks when the test of battle is difficult to approximate.

As a result, for most of the historical record, at least until the early twentieth century, adaptation depended on the imaginative interventions of a few great generals. This was particularly true in Western military history beginning in the seventeenth century through the Industrial Revolution in the mid-nineteenth century. After the adaptations of a few

---

[5] Here the fact that both sides of the war were now involved in a desperate race to bring more effective weapons to the battlefront inevitably increased the pressure for new and better adaptation. See Chapter 3 of this book for further elaboration on this issue.

[6] The British military pundit B. H. Liddell Hart criticized such training as entirely antithetical to the needs of modern soldiers without understanding that the most important attributes of trained soldiers are discipline and cohesion, best inculcated in a soldier's early days on parade fields. The reinvention of Roman military discipline in the late sixteenth century depended on learning how to use the Roman marching commands as a two-step pattern of commands – preparatory and execution – for organized formations both on the march and standing. For the importance of this as the first step in creating disciplined, organized military formations, see William H. McNeill, *The Pursuit of Power: Technology, Armed Force, and Society since A.D. 1000* (Chicago, 1982), pp. 128–133. For the insight in which Maurice of Orange's innovators recognized that the Roman march commands must be two steps, preparatory and execution, see Hans Delbruck, *History of the Art of War*, vol. 4, *The Dawn of Modern Warfare*, trans. by Walter J. Renfoe, Jr. (Lincoln, NE, 1985), p. 159.

military geniuses had spread throughout the corpus of military understanding in the West, usually a relatively quick process, matters generally settled back to "business as usual."[7]

But the increasing pace of technological change in the mid-nineteenth century added considerably to the complexity of combat as well as to the need to combine various weapons systems. During the American Civil War, technological and societal changes forced the pace of tactical and operational adaptation.[8] World War I saw the invention of modern war, as the trends marking the Industrial Revolution and the French Revolution merged. Throughout the twentieth century and into the twenty-first, those processes have accelerated, and the need for tactical adaptation has increased with improvements in technology that have made combat increasingly lethal. Moreover, that lethality has made it more difficult and dangerous for military leaders to see with their own eyes what is actually happening at the sharp end of combat as well as easier to hold on to the illusions that peacetime and the past have constructed.[9] Not surprisingly, then, military institutions have proven resistant to change throughout the twentieth century even during times of conflict, and more often than not, they have paid for adaptation with the blood of their maimed and dead rather than through the exercise of their minds and mental agility.

This chapter aims to provide the larger context of military adaptation to examine why military adaptation has proven difficult. In fact, the growing technological complexity of war has made adaptation an increasingly important facet of military effectiveness. It has also reduced the time available to get it right. Yet, psychological factors, as well as the nature of war itself, have made adaptation an intractable problem – at least in terms of most of the levels of war. After the Introduction has delineated the problem, this book turns first to the historical patterns of military adaptation and then to a series of case studies to examine in greater depth the complex problems associated with adaptation under the trying conditions of combat as well as cultural change. Finally, it ends with general comments of what the past suggests about the future.

In the twentieth century, adaptation to the realities of combat has reflected how well military institutions have, or have not, innovated in

---

[7] See Chapter 2 for a discussion of the parameters of adaptation throughout history.
[8] See Mark Grimsley, "Surviving Military Revolution: The U.S. Civil War," in Knox and Murray, *The Dynamics of Military Revolution*.
[9] I am indebted to Alec Wahlman of the Joint Advanced Warfighting Division of the Institute of Defense Analyses for this point.

peacetime to change their concepts and understanding of what future combat might look like. Successful innovation has depended on the organizational culture, the imagination and vision of senior leaders, and the seriousness with which military organizations have taken the intellectual preparation of future leaders through an honest and intelligent study of the past. Barry Watts and this author suggested in an earlier study for the Office of Net Assessment that there was a direct correlation between the willingness of military institutions to emphasize empirical evidence in the processes of peacetime innovation and their ability to recognize the actual conditions of war, the first step to serious adaptation.[10]

In peacetime, those military institutions that have not attempted to relate empirical evidence to their concept and doctrine development invariably have run into difficulty in adapting to the combat realities they confronted. Those that did innovate intelligently and with open minds had at least a reasonable chance of adapting to the actual conditions of war. As we suggested: "A related hypothesis... is that military organizations which have trouble being scrupulous about empirical data in peacetime may have the same difficulty in time of war. The RAF's failure before and during the early years of World War II to deal with the problem of locating targets, much less accurately bombing them, would appear to be a graphic instance of this sort of intellectual 'bad habit' carrying over from peacetime to wartime."[11] The evidence would also indicate that serious intellectual effort during peacetime in thinking through what the past and present suggest about the future plays an important role in how well military organizations are able to adapt in conflict. Without that effort, there is unlikely to be a baseline from which to plot out intelligent courses for adaptation.

The evidence presented in this book suggests a consistent pattern of behavior on the part of military organizations. Inevitably, senior leaders, even the most effective, build a picture of what they think future war will look like and then confront combat realities that differ substantially from their assumptions. The magnitude of the disparity can vary. The more realistic military organizations are about future war, and the more honest their evaluations of peacetime exercises, the quicker they will adapt.

---

[10] Barry D. Watts and Williamson Murray, "Military Innovation in Peacetime," in Williamson Murray and Allan R. Millett, eds., *Military Innovation in the Interwar Period* (Cambridge, 1996).
[11] Ibid., p. 414. This last chapter in *Military Innovation in the Interwar Period* was written at the express request of Andrew Marshall, Director of Net Assessment in the Pentagon.

In some cases, the difference between vision and reality is not so great as to obviate prewar concepts. But adaptation will have to take place.[12] Effective military organizations adapt their prewar assumptions and concepts to reality. However, most military organizations and their leaders attempt to impose prewar conceptions on the war they are fighting, rather than adapt their assumptions to reality. In this case they adapt only after great losses in men and national treasure.

There is every indication that war in the future will be as messy, uncertain, and complex as it has been in the past. Certainly, American experiences in Iraq and Afghanistan would suggest this to be the case.[13] Of all human endeavors, war places the greatest psychological pressures on its human participants. It is invariably a milieu of fear, horror, and deep anxiety. The resulting combination of adrenalin, fatigue, angst, and horrific impressions makes it difficult for even those possessing the clearest of minds to gain, much less present, a clear picture of what they and their subordinates have experienced. What this book aims to elucidate is not a simple, clear answer to the problem of adaptation but rather to suggest how military organizations and their leaders might think more coherently about adaptation at the various levels of war both before and during combat.

By way of introduction, this first chapter examines several distinct issues that delineate the inherent problems in adaptation to the ever-changing conditions of war. The greatest difficulty clearly has to do with the fundamental nature of war itself. Second, human nature – especially when the egos of leaders at the highest levels become involved – places considerable difficulties in the path to understanding the tactical and operational issues military organizations confront. Without that understanding, adaptation to the actual conditions of conflict simply cannot take place or, even worse, will follow the wrong path.

Over the past century, the effective incorporation of change is what war has increasingly been about. Making change more difficult is the

---

[12] For example, the German commander of the XIX Panzer Corps, Heinz Guderian, at Sedan in May 1940 held his tanks concentrated and not as part of the combined-arms team in the initial battles. Within three days he had altered his approach and included panzers along with his infantry in the attacks on Stonne – an important adjustment.

[13] For the Iraq War and its complex and ambiguous nature, even before the postconflict stage, see particularly the last chapter of Williamson Murray and Robert H. Scales, Jr., *The Iraq War: A Military History* (Cambridge, MA, 2003); for a similar view of the war in Afghanistan, see Sean Naylor, *Not a Good Day to Die: The Untold Story of Operation Anaconda* (New York, 2005).

harsh fact that incompetence, rather than competence, lies at the heart of man's character.[14] Inevitably, a few individuals possess the clarity of vision, the self-discipline, the imagination, and the toughness of mind to understand the daunting problems that war creates. Moreover, effective performance at one level of war rarely guarantees success at the next level. A good company commander does not necessarily make a good battalion commander; nor a good brigade commander, a good division commander; nor a good corps commander, a good army commander.

That is why there have been so few great captains in military history. The Marlboroughs, Napoleons, Wellingtons, Jacksons, Grants, Marshalls, Kings, and Zhukovs stand out in the historical landscape because they are anomalies among a vast number of lesser figures. The few competent can see the forest and the wider landscape of war; most, however, see only the details and the irrelevant. As Sherman noted in comparing himself to Grant, "Whereas I see issues in all their complexity, Grant sees them in all their simplicity."[15] Exacerbating the difficulties that military institutions face is the fact that, more often than not, they reach decisions by corporate agreement. And there are few institutions in human life more dysfunctional in reaching clear, distinct, purposeful direction than committees. If true for life in general, the terrible challenges of war multiply the fundamental flaws inherent in human nature and character.

Finally, and perhaps most daunting, is the fact that war inevitably involves issues at the political, strategic, operational, and tactical levels. That spread of perspective invariably presents contradictory choices to military leaders. Moreover, the qualities that provide for excellence at one level may prevent adaptation at the other levels. No other military organization displayed greater ability to adapt at the tactical level than did the German Army during the course of two world wars. Yet, at the operational level, the Germans displayed far less ability, while their performance at the strategic level was appallingly incompetent and resulted in national catastrophe not once, but twice.[16] And in the second great

---

[14] For an examination of the dominant place of incompetence in human affairs and its effect on the course of events, see Williamson Murray, *The Change in the European Balance of Power, 1938–1939: The Path to Ruin* (Princeton, 1984), chap. 11.

[15] Conversation with Professor Jay Luvaas of the Army War College in the early 1990s, in which he provided me with this quotation of Sherman. I am indebted to Professor Leonard Fullencamp of the Army War College for reminding me of the quotation, but neither one of us has, as of yet, managed to track it down.

[16] For an examination of the inherent contradictions in German military effectiveness, see Williamson Murray, *German Military Effectiveness* (Baltimore, MD, 1992), chap. 1.

war, the German military's leadership ensured that the conflict would be fought to the "bitter end." The result was an even greater catastrophe for the German people.[17] So much for the legend of German military effectiveness.[18]

The Problem of War Itself

To understand the problems involved in adapting to war, one must first come to grips with the complexities, ambiguities, and nature of war itself. Of all mankind's endeavors, war confronts human beings not only with the greatest physical demands but also with the greatest psychological pressures. For those who command in war, it also presents the most complex and difficult intellectual problems. It is the combination of these pressures as well as the constraints of time that make decision making at every level of war so difficult. As the Germans insistently pointed out to their officers, better a bad decision taken in time than a perfect decision taken too late.[19] Again, it is the interactive nature of war that presents those who engage in it with the greatest difficulties. The enemy always gets a vote.

The great advantage that military organizations enjoy over other human pursuits is that they only episodically have the opportunity to practice their profession. The great disadvantage that military organizations confront is that they only episodically have the opportunity to practice their profession.[20] Unlike other human organizations, military forces in peacetime must prepare for a war that (1) will occur at some indeterminate point in the future, (2) is against an opponent whom they may not yet have identified, (3) is in an arena of brutality and violence, which they cannot replicate in peacetime, (4) involves a range of new

---

[17] For the terrible catastrophe of the last six months of the Second World War and the responsibility of Germany's military leaders for the disasters by their obdurate fanaticism in continuing the war "to the bitter end" as their Führer decreed, see the extraordinary work by Max Hastings, *Armageddon: The Battle for Germany, 1944–1945* (New York, 2004).

[18] In regard to the strategy of the German military in the Second World War, see particularly the brilliant essay by Wilhelm Deist, "The Road to Ideological War: Germany, 1918–1945," in Williamson Murray, MacGregor Knox, and Alvin Bernstein, eds., *The Making of Strategy: Rulers, States, and War* (Cambridge, 1996). See also Gerhard L. Weinberg, *A World at Arms, A Global History of World War II* (Cambridge, 1994).

[19] For the nature of officership and its responsibilities in the German Army, see Martin van Creveld, *Fighting Power: German and U.S. Army Performance, 1939–1945* (Westport, CT, 1982).

[20] This is less true for navies than for armies, because the former must always contend with the sea, which represents a major factor in their ability to perform in war.

technologies, employed by all the combatants and adapted to the conditions of the battlefield in different ways, and (5) is under political and sociological conditions which they may not be able to predict. These factors together inevitably present military organizations with a set of intractable and difficult challenges. But it is the last factor that makes their task especially difficult.

In a lecture in the early 1960s, Sir Michael Howard, himself a highly decorated veteran of the Second World War, pointed out:

> There are two great difficulties with which the professional soldier, sailor, or airman has to contend in equipping himself as a commander. First his profession is almost unique in that he may only have to exercise it once in a lifetime, if indeed that often. It is as if a surgeon had to practice throughout his life on dummies for one real operation; or a barrister appeared only once or twice in court towards the end of a career; or a professional swimmer had to spend his life practicing on dry land for an Olympic Championship on which the fortunes of his entire nation depended. Secondly the complex problem of running a [military service] at all is liable to occupy his mind and skill so completely that it is easy to forget what it is being run for.[21]

Only the discipline of peacetime intellectual preparation can provide the commanders and those on the sharp end with the means to handle the psychological surprises that war inevitably brings.

What the remainder of this chapter aims to do is to provide a general framework for examining the conditions of war that not only make human decision making within their context difficult but also contribute to the complexities and uncertainties of adaptation under these most trying of conditions. Without intellectual preparation, the adaptation that is always necessary will come at a far higher expenditure of the lives of those on the sharp end.

Psychology and Decision Making in War

No other human endeavor presents such consistent and ferocious challenges for the human psyche as does war. Clausewitz, that most perceptive of all the theorists of war, delineates the pressures that confronted the armies of his time in a section of his classic *On War* dealing with "Danger in War":

> Let us accompany a novice to the battlefield. As we approach the rumble of guns grows louder and alternates with the whir of cannonballs, which begin to attract his attention. Shots begin to strike close around us. We

---

[21] Howard, "The Use and Abuses of Military History."

hurry up the slope where the commanding general is stationed with his larger staff. Here cannonballs and bursting shells are frequent, and life begins to seem more serious than the young man had imagined. Suddenly someone you know is wounded; then a shell falls among the staff. You notice that some of the officers look a little oddly; you yourself are not as steady and collected as you were; even the bravest can become slightly distracted. Now we enter the battle raging before us, still almost like a spectacle, and join the nearest division commander. Shot is falling like hail, and the thunder of our guns adds to the din. Forward to the brigadier, a soldier of acknowledged bravery but he is careful to take cover behind a rise, a house, or a clump of trees. A noise is heard that is a certain indication of increasing danger – the rattling of grape shot on roofs and on the ground. Cannonballs tear past, whizzing in all directions, and musket balls begin to whistle around us. A little further we reach the firing line, where the infantry endures the hammering for hours with incredible steadfastness. The air is filled with hissing bullets like a sharp crack, if they pass close by one's head. For a final shock, the sight of men being killed and mutilated moves our pounding hearts to awe and pity.

The novice cannot pass through these layers of increasing intensity of danger without sensing that here ideas are governed by other factors, that the light of reason is refracted in a manner quite different from that which is normal in academic speculation.[22]

It is in this atmosphere of deadening fear and dread that men must not only make decisions on which their lives and the lives of their subordinates depend but also must gather the impressions and pattern recognition on which successful adaptations in both the short and the long term depend. As Clausewitz continues, under the immense psychological pressures that combat entails, "[i]t is an exceptional man who keeps his powers of quick decision intact."[23] Earlier in *On War*, Clausewitz underlines that point:

In the dreadful presence of suffering and danger, emotion can easily overwhelm intellectual conviction, and in this psychological fog it is so hard to form clear and complete insights that changes of view become more understandable and excusable. Action can never be based on anything firmer than instinct, a sensing of truth. Nowhere, in consequence, are differences of opinion so acute as in war, and fresh opinions never cease to batter at one's convictions. No degree of calm can provide enough protection: new impressions are always too powerful, too vivid, and always assault the emotions as well as the intellect.[24]

[22] Carl von Clausewitz, *On War*, trans. and ed. by Michael Howard and Peter Paret (Princeton, 1976), p. 113. This is a quotation to which political scientists who write about war, national security, and military issues should pay much closer attention.
[23] Ibid., p. 113.
[24] Ibid., p. 108. On the field at Waterloo, the Duke of Wellington saw the leg of one of his aides ripped off by a cannonball. Historians have tended to miss the point of Wellington's icy calm at that point. The duke simply could not afford to allow his

But here one must note an additional problem. If it is difficult to keep one's "powers of quick decision intact" under the pressures of combat, as John Keegan and a number of others have clearly pointed out, it is even more difficult to re-create in one's mind and then in some written form a clear picture of what one has seen and experienced.[25] When one adds the psychological pressures of combat to the fact that few individuals – and here soldiers are no exception – actually possess analytic powers, much less the ability to express them in a coherent, clear form, it is not surprising that military adaptation has proved difficult to accomplish, even without including the problems of technological change.

It is interesting to note how deeply the psychological effect of combat affects those involved in the fighting in the twentieth century. The fact is that the simple adaptation to a tactical situation in the midst of combat carries with it immense difficulties in conveying basic information, even in the case of one unit relieving another under fire. As S. L. A. Marshall and David Hackworth noted in a report on command practices at the tactical level in Vietnam in 1966:

> When [a] unit, having had a hard go in combat, is relieved or reinforced by another which must continue the fight, very rarely does the commander going out tell the full story, giving the details of the situation, to the incoming commander. Just as rarely does the latter insist on having it. This is an understandable human reaction, since both men are under the pressure of the problem immediately facing their units in a moment of high tension, the one withdrawing and worrying about extricating casualties, the other bent on deploying under fire without loss of time. But the danger of not having a full and free exchange as the relief begins is that the second unit, left uninformed, will at unnecessary cost attack on the same line and repeat the same mistakes made by the first unit. The record shows unmistakably that lessons bought in blood too frequently have to be repurchased.[26]

If the problem that Clausewitz eloquently characterized in describing the experience of combat applied to generals during the Napoleonic era,

---

emotions to influence his control of the battle. Similarly, over the course of the first night at Shiloh in the middle of a pouring rain, Grant left the only shelter available because it was also being used as a hospital; with another day of terrible fighting in front of him, Grant could not allow the scenes of human suffering to distort his ability to make the hard decisions that were going to be required on the morrow. Ulysses S. Grant, *Personal Memoirs of U.S. Grant*, vol. 1 (New York, 1885), p. 188.

[25] All military historians are in the debt of John Keegan for the extraordinary contribution that his book *The Face of Battle* (London, 1976) made toward reminding the profession about the nature of combat, which must be central to any understanding of war itself.

[26] Brigadier General S. L. A. Marshall (retired) and Colonel David Hackworth (U.S. Army, retired), "Vietnam Primer," Department of the Army, 1967, copy in the possession of the author.

it has become even more important in the twenty-first century, when independent command has devolved down to the level of captains and lieutenants – and, in some cases, sergeants – with the appearance of decentralized command and control on modern battlefields. If it is difficult for individuals to maintain their powers of decision under the psychological pressures of combat, it is obviously even more difficult for them to maintain and recount accurately a picture of what they have seen and experienced. It is the ability to pass along experiences that must be the product of peacetime training and education.

There is a corollary to this point. Adding to the psychological pressures on commanders in war is the loneliness of command. In his brilliant memoirs, Ulysses S. Grant best caught the nature of the problem. In 1861, given his first independent command, Grant found himself worrying about the myriad things his opponent might spring on him and the small force he was leading:

> My sensations as we approached what I supposed might be "a field of battle" were anything but agreeable.... As we approached the brow of the hill from which it was expected we could see Harris' [the Confederate commander] camp and possibly find his men ready formed to meet us, my heart kept getting higher and higher until it felt to me as though it was in my throat. I would have given anything then to have been back in Illinois but I had not the moral courage to halt and consider what to do; I kept right on. When we reached a point from which the valley below was in full view I halted. The place where Harris had been encamped a few days before was still there and the remains of a recent encampment were plainly visible but the troops were gone. My heart resumed its place. It occurred to me at once that Harris had been as much afraid of me as I had been of him. This was a view of the question I had never taken before; but it was one I never forgot afterwards. From that event to the close of the war, I never experienced trepidation upon confronting an enemy, though I always felt more or less anxiety. I never forgot that he had as much reason to fear my forces as I had his.[27]

What makes Grant such an interesting figure in military history was his ability to see and then understand the larger import of the terrible events he observed both at the time and two decades later, when he undertook to write his extraordinary memoirs.[28] His perception and understanding

---

[27] Grant, *The Personal Memoirs of U.S. Grant*, vol. 1, pp. 131–132.
[28] From the point of view of this author, Grant was by far the greatest of all the generals in the Civil War. Moreover, his memoirs present an honest view of the war that is quite extraordinary in comparison to the memoirs of virtually all other generals in all different ages. Only Field Marshal Viscount Slim (commander of the British Fourteenth Army in Burma during World War II) produced memoirs rivaling those of Grant for their honesty

shine not only in his memoirs but also in the clarity and eloquence of his dispatches to subordinates and superiors alike throughout the Civil War.[29]

In the twentieth century, as military organizations increasingly had to disperse their forces across expanding battlefields, their forces had to devolve command to lower and lower levels. During the American Civil War, it was rare for a division, much less a regimental, commander to confront a situation in which he had to make a major military tactical decision without reference to his superiors. Colonel Joshua Chamberlain's decision to order his regiment, the 20th Maine, as it was running out of ammunition, to fix bayonets and charge superior Confederate forces at the Battle of Gettysburg, was much the exception.

Yet, 55 years later in 1918, the whole basis of the German revolution in tactics, which emphasized decentralized command and control, rested on company and platoon commanders making tactical decisions on their own.[30] If anything, the history of tactics in the twentieth century through the war in Iraq in 2003 has been a story of dispersal – one in which the increasing lethality of the battlefield has forced armies to spread their soldiers and marines over ever greater distances.[31] That in turn has forced the more effective military organizations involved in the ground battle to push decision-making authority ever lower in the chain of command. As the former commandant of the U.S. Marine Corps, General Chuck Krulak, has noted, the corporals of the future are going to be involved in a "'three-block' war," in which their decisions may well carry strategic as well as tactical implications.[32]

---

and insight as well as their literary qualities. See Field Marshal Viscount Slim, *Defeat into Victory* (London, 1956).

[29] In this regard the reader should consult Grant's instructions to Major Generals George Meade and William Tecumseh Sherman on Grant's overall conception of how the 1864 campaign should unfold and what their tasks were to be. Grant, *The Personal Memoirs of U.S. Grant*, vol. 2, pp. 368–387, 389–390.

[30] There are a large number of works on this tactical revolution. Among others, see Timothy Lupfer, *The Dynamics of Doctrine: The Changes in German Tactical Doctrine during the First World War* (Fort Leavenworth, KS, 1984). See also Bruce I. Gudmundsson, *Stormtroop Tactics: Innovation in the German Army, 1914–1918* (New York, 1989).

[31] For the implications of this factor on military operations in the twenty-first century, particularly on the ground, see Major General Robert H. Scales, Jr., *Yellow Smoke: The Future of Land War for America's Military* (Lanham, MD, 2003).

[32] The three-block war, according to General Krulak, consists of major combat operations, operations against elusive guerrillas, and humanitarian operations – all often occurring at the same time. The offensive against Fallujah in the postconflict phase of military operations in Iraq in November 2004 by marines and soldiers very much reflected Krulak's vision of what future war would look like.

This phenomenon of dispersal has had the obvious effect of distancing military leaders from contact with the battlefield. Wellington was a direct observer of virtually all of the action that occurred at Waterloo. Napoleon at Austerlitz could stand on the Pratzen Heights and watch his greatest victory unfold.[33] He could also gain immediate feedback on battlefield experience, because he was, for the most part, an observer of what was happening. Even with the telegraph, much the same conditions persisted in the early years of the Civil War, although there were exceptions at the operational level. By 1864, however, both sides had begun to expand the killing zone; hence, they were making the battle space too large for any single commander to observe or control.[34]

By World War I, the combination of technology and tactics had reached the point where few generals above brigade level saw the battlefield.[35] Increasingly, they relied on reports from below to gain their understanding of what was happening. But the technologies of the time, as well as the nature of their military bureaucracies and cultures, resulted in the generals' receiving information too late, or receiving reports that bore little relationship to what was happening on the battlefield. In the first years of World War II, one of the major advantages the Germans enjoyed was the fact that their best division and corps commanders led from the front.

The issue here, however, is much more than simply that of good as opposed to bad leadership. The confusion and horror of combat make it difficult for those involved to put together a coherent picture of what

---

[33] Marshal Soult, who was to lead the decisive blow at the Allied center, approached Napoleon and asked whether it was time for French forces to attack. Looking at the immediate tactical situation, Napoleon replied that Soult should wait another five minutes before launching the decisive blow. David Chandler, *The Campaigns of Napoleon* (London, 1966), pp. 425–426.

[34] The campaigns in 1864 were not nearly as satisfactory for either men: for Lee, because Thomas "Stonewall" Jackson was no longer available after his death at Chancellorsville in 1863; for Grant because his subordinate commanders in the Army of the Potomac throughout the battles in northern Virginia in 1864 in no fashion resembled the superior subordinates, such as William T. Sherman and James McPherson, whom he had commanded in the 1863 campaigns in the west. For the campaign in Northern Virginia, see Mark Grimsley, *And Keep Moving On: The Virginia Campaign, May–June 1864* (Lincoln, NE, 2002).

[35] It is worth noting that in the Iraq War, both commanders of the lead divisions, Major General Buff Blount of the 3rd Infantry Division and Major General James Mattis of the 1st Marine Division, believed that they and a small operational headquarters had to remain at the leading edge of the battlefield, so that they could understand what was really happening. See Murray and Scales, *The Iraq War*, p. 116.

has happened. It took the British nearly a year of fighting in the deserts of North Africa to figure out that Rommel was setting out screens of lethal 88-mm Flak/antitank guns and then luring their armor into killing zones. The few survivors of the resulting slaughter of British armor, in which tankers had watched their friends blow up one after the other, were hardly in a position to present a coherent picture to their superiors.[36]

Moreover, without a coherent system of analyzing what is actually happening, military organizations have no means of adapting to the conditions they face except doggedly to impose assumptions on reality or, even more dubiously, to adapt by guessing. To a certain extent, the training revolution through which the U.S. military progressed in the 1970s and 1980s has mitigated the difficulties that confront military organizations at the tactical level.[37] Lessons-learned analysis teams now sprinkle every aspect of American training and form an integral part of the U.S. military all the way up to the joint level of command.[38] But beyond the problem of psychological pressure and the inherently flawed perceptions of human beings lie the problems of friction, chance, and strategic decision making – all of which make the problems involved in adaptation ever more complex and challenging.

The Problems of Friction and Chance

Perhaps Clausewitz's greatest contribution lies in his formulation and analysis of the concept of friction – an understanding that informs his analyses of conflict throughout *On War*.[39] He poses to his readers the

---

[36] For the British Army in the North African campaigns against Rommel, see among others: Samuel W. Mitcham, Jr., *Rommel's Greatest Victory: The Desert Fox and the Fall of Tobruk, Spring 1942* (Novato, CA, 1998); Ronald Lewin, *Rommel as Military Commander* (London, 1968), and *The Life and Death of the Afrika Korps* (London, 1977); and Erwin Rommel, *The Rommel Papers*, ed. by B.H. Liddell Hart (London, 1953).

[37] This is, of course, much in the conventional wisdom concerning Operation Iraqi Freedom. Nevertheless, one should note that there were aspects of how the Iraqis fought during the conventional phase of the conflict that did catch U.S. forces by surprise.

[38] In fact one of the most impressive aspects of the Iraq War of 2003 was the creation of a major lessons-learned team by Joint Forces Command at the direction of Admiral Edmund Giambiastiani. Members of that team, under the command of Brigadier General Robert Cone, were inserted throughout the various headquarters responsible for waging the war against Saddam's regime. The results of that effort – at least in terms of the lessons dealing with the conduct of joint operations – were judicious, honest, and forthright. Whether they have been learned is a matter that only time will tell.

[39] For a discussion of the contemporary relevance of this term, see Barry D. Watts, *Clausewitzian Friction and Future War* (Washington, DC, 1996).

straightforward paradox: "Everything in war is very simple but the simplest thing is difficult."[40] He then explains why this is so:

> Friction is the only concept that more or less corresponds to the factors that distinguish real war from war on paper. The military machine – the army and everything related to it – is basically very simple and therefore seems easy to manage. But we should bear in mind that none of its components is of one piece; each part is composed of individuals, every one of whom retains his potential of friction.... A battalion is made up of individuals, the least important of whom may chance to delay things or somehow make them go wrong. The dangers inseparable from war and the physical exertions war demands can aggravate the problem to such an extent that they must be ranked among [friction's] principal causes.[41]

In the 1990s, a number of pundits, including several senior officers in the U.S. military, began arguing that modern technologies, particularly the computer, had created a situation in which fog and friction would no longer remain significant factors in war – at least from the American point of view.[42] Their views exercised considerable influence on how the U.S. military thought about future war in the 1990s. The first joint vision statement, "JV2010," postulated a capability that it called "information superiority" – the ability of U.S. forces to amass so much information that they would be able to dominate America's opponents. Reality, however, has proven to be somewhat more difficult to manage. A recent book on the conduct of the Iraq War by marine units notes: "On this, the 'high' side of the digital divide, there was, arguably, too much information available. It was difficult to know which data stream to enter, how to extract what was relevant, and how to combine streams."[43] In other words, information superiority has often equaled information overload, with commanders drowning in too much information. What really matters – real knowledge of the enemy's intentions, potential, and future actions – remains largely unknowable, because such factors remain locked within the minds and character of human beings.[44]

---

[40] Clausewitz, *On War*, p. 119.
[41] Ibid., p. 119.
[42] For the most recent exposition of this argument, see Admiral Bill Owens with Ed Offley, *Lifting the Fog of War* (New York, 2000).
[43] Col. Nicholas E. Reynolds, *Basrah, Baghdad, and Beyond: The U.S. Marine Corps in the Second Iraq War* (Annapolis, MD, 2005), p. 103.
[44] One of the clearest examples of this factor is one in which the intelligence was 100 percent correct but, at the same time, turned out to be completely wrong. In January 1941, General Erwin Rommel arrived in North Africa with the direct order from the German Army's high command that he was to remain on the defensive. Enigma decrypts

The largest problem with such assumptions about technology's supposed ability to remove friction from the battlefield lies in the fact that they fly in the face of what modern science suggests about the natural world in which man lives – a world of chaos, uncertainty, and ambiguity. Chance and unforeseen factors can and do play an incalculable role in the world of nature. Not surprisingly, those factors tend to dominate in human life as well.[45] It is not that man lives in a completely incalculable world. Calculation about the future is possible but always uncertain. However, effective military organizations and commanders must mix prediction and calculation with intuition, cultural understanding, previous patterns of behavior, and a sense of the fact that war "is an unchartered sea, full of reefs."[46]

Exacerbating the influence of friction is chance. One of the dominant themes in Thucydides' history of the Peloponnesian War is the role he assigns to *tyche* – often translated as "chance" but in fact possessing a subtler and more complex meaning, suggesting that aspects of life are often inexplicable by any rational calculus.[47] It is not surprising, then, that Clausewitz should suggest that "No other human activity [other than war] is so continuously or universally bound up with chance. And through the element of chance, guesswork and luck come to play a great part in war."[48] At its heart, war is not only about the psychological pressures of combat, it is also about the unexpected. The Thebans possessed a near-perfect plan to seize the small polis of Platea at the beginning of the Peloponnesian War, but on the night their relieving army crossed the mountain range, a huge rainstorm occurred, which obscured their path, and the main force arrived too late.[49] The American dive bombers arrived over the Japanese carriers at Midway in June 1942 at exactly the right moment, when the suicidal attack of U.S. torpedo aircraft had pulled the

of these orders were then passed to senior British commanders. Rommel, however, immediately proceeded to disobey his orders and went over to the offensive, thus making the intelligence irrelevant.

[45] For an outstanding examination of the implications of nonlinearity and Clausewitz's writings, see Alan Beyerchen, "Clausewitz, Nonlinearity, and the Predictability of War," *International Security*, vol. 17, no. 3, Winter 1992/1993.
[46] Clausewitz, *On War*, p. 120.
[47] I am indebted to Professor Donald Kagan of Yale for this insight.
[48] Clausewitz, *On War*, p. 85.
[49] As John Keegan indicates at the beginning of his book *The Face of Battle*, Thucydides is one of the few historians to capture the reality of war on the sharp end. His account of the ill-fated Theban attack on Platea at the beginning of the war represents as brilliant a study of chance and human psychology as any historian has ever written. Thucydides, *History of the Peloponnesian War*, trans. by Rex Warner (London, 1954), pp. 124–128.

defending Japanese Zero fighters down to low altitudes where they could not intervene. Such incidents are incalculable, but they have happened in the past, and they will continue in the future.

It is this interplay of the factors of friction and chance that make much of combat incalculable and uncertain. Did we get it right? Or did our soldiers, through an extraordinary piece of luck, hit the one weak point in the enemy's defenses? Are the events that have just occurred an anomaly or part of a coherent pattern? Can one possibly calculate chance into the patterns of combat from which we must sketch our adaptations to the conditions of war? These are all questions that commanders and staffs must address – questions, moreover, to which no clear answer may exist, at least in terms of the combat operations.

Finally, there is the inherent problem that as one side adapts to the conditions it faces, so, too, do its opponents. In other words, "the enemy also gets a vote." The harsh fact is that the enemy is a community of living, breathing human beings who may be able to adapt to the conditions of war as fast, if not faster, than we will, or at least develop responses that lie outside our conceptions and assumptions. Thus, as Chapter 3 suggests, one can only clarify the nature of the First World War by examining the adaptations and changes occurring on both sides of the trench lines – in effect, understanding the war as a complex adaptive system. Understanding how the enemy might adapt represented, in the end, one of the most intractable problems that military organizations confronted in the twentieth century – a problem exacerbated by the general superficiality with which they have addressed that question.

Organizations, Bureaucracies, and Military Culture

One of the most serious impediments to effective adaptation is that human institutions, particularly the bureaucracies that run them on a day-to-day basis, do not exist for the purpose of adapting to a changing and uncertain world. They aim at imposing order and form on a world that is inherently disorderly and ambiguous. They exist to act as a brake on significant changes that upset current patterns of behavior. In fact, most bureaucracies oppose change, because it represents a direct threat to their position. MacGregor Knox has noted the following in respect to the nature of bureaucracies. While his remarks focus on the relationship of bureaucracies to the problem of making strategy, they are generally applicable to the problem that all bureaucracies pose to intelligent adaptation to the external world:

> Bureaucracies are neatly zweckrational: swift and precise – in theory and surprisingly often in practice – in executing orders.... They are happiest with established wisdom and incremental change. They cherish the myth that virtually all strategic [and military] problems are soluble in and through their own element – be it diplomacy, economic power, covert knowledge and action, naval supremacy, or air bombardment – and that problems not thus soluble are not problems. When faced with the incommensurate or unquantifiable alternatives that are the stuff of strategy [and war], they usually retreat to incoherent compromise with their fellows or take flight into... intuition – unless the structure of... decision-making forces them to defend all choices in rational terms. And in the absence of driving political leadership, even structured debate may produce only paralysis.[50]

The comments of Sir Robert Vansittart, a senior official in the British Foreign Office in the late 1930s, underline the capacity of bureaucratic systems to stand in the way of effective action, in this case, as Britain confronted Nazi Germany:

> It seems clear that all the machinery here contemplated will involve the maximum delay and accumulation of papers. We surely do not want any more written 'European Appreciations.' We have been snowed under with papers from the Committee of Imperial Defense for years. Moreover, this procedure by stages implies a certain leisureliness which is not what we want at the present moment.[51]

If this is true in times of peace, it is even truer in war. Here the performance of the Coalition Provisional Authority and its bureaucrats in Iraq over the 2003–2004 period – or for that matter the Pentagon and service bureaucracies during the same time period – represents an example that requires little amplification.[52] But the problem of military bureaucracy is a relatively new one. Military bureaucracies are creatures of the nineteenth and twentieth centuries. To a considerable extent, they have resulted from the onrush of technological change. The Duke of Wellington in the Peninsula Campaigns could complain about the interference of a few bureaucrats in London, but in fact his famous rejoinder that he and his officers could either campaign against the French or attend to "the mass of futile correspondence" issuing forth from the capital represented only a minor

---

[50] MacGregor Knox, "Conclusion: Continuity and Revolution in the Making of Strategy," in *The Making of Strategy: Rulers, States, and War*, pp. 615–616.
[51] PRO FO 371/22922, C 1545/281/17, Minute by Sir Robert Vansittart, 10.2.38, criticizing CP 40 (39), "Staff Conversations with France and Belgium."
[52] See, among others, James Fallows, "Blind into Baghdad," *The Atlantic Monthly*, January/February, 2004; and George Packer, *The Assassins' Gate: America in Iraq* (New York, 2005).

irritant compared with what poured out of twentieth-century bureaucracies to commanders in the field.[53] To all intents and purposes, Wellington and his army represented an independent force, which depended on a minuscule War Office bureaucracy in London with only a few clerks to provide for a smattering of supplies, money, and rations to support the great duke's campaigns in Spain and Portugal.

One hundred years later, everything had undergone great changes. Field Marshal Sir Douglas Haig commanded armies in northwestern France and Belgium, an order of magnitude more complex in terms of size and requirements than Wellington's Peninsula forces. In effect, Haig's claim to competency lies almost exclusively in his organizational abilities, which provided the framework for supplying and deploying those massive forces.[54] The problem with Haig's generalship, however, lay in the fact that his focus on the organizational and bureaucratic aspects of command largely prevented him from gaining a sense of the tactical and operational realities of the Western Front. Moreover – and perhaps most damaging to his reputation – he failed to create the staff mechanisms that would have allowed the British Expeditionary Force in France to absorb and then transmit the lessons of its current battlefield experiences throughout its structure.[55] Ironically, even effective military organizations require

---

[53] Arthur Bryant, *Years of Victory: 1802–1812 (London, 1945)*, p. 419. On one occasion, the great duke commented in exasperation to the authorities in London: "Whilst marching to Portugal to a position which commands the approach to Madrid and the French forces, my officers have been diligently complying with your request which has been sent to H.M. ship from London to Lisbon and then by dispatch rider to our headquarters. We have enumerated our saddles, bridles, tents and tent poles, and all manner of sundry items for which His Majesty's Government holds me accountable. Each item and every farthing has been accounted for, with two regrettable exceptions for which I beg your indulgence. Unfortunately, the sum of one shilling and ninepence remains unaccounted for in one infantry battalion's petty cash, and there has been hideous confusion as to the number of jars of raspberry jam issued to one cavalry regiment during a sandstorm in western Spain. This reprehensive carelessness may be related to the pressure of circumstances since we are at war with France, a fact which may have come as a bit of a surprise to you gentlemen in Whitehall." Quoted in *Parameters*, Spring 2004, inside back cover.

[54] For why he does not deserve credit for competency in the running of military operations, see two brilliant studies of major battles on the Western Front involving the British Expeditionary Force (BEF): Robin Prior and Trevor Wilson, *Passchendaele: The Untold Story* (New Haven, 1996); and *The Somme: The Story of a Battle* (New Haven, 2004).

[55] Among others dealing with the broad spectrum of how Haig addressed the tactical problems confronting the BEF on the Western Front, see Tim Travers, *The Killing Ground: The British Army, the Western Front, and the Emergence of Modern Warfare, 1900–1918* (London, 1978). See also Prior and Wilson, *Passchendaele* and *The Somme* for enlightening discussions of the problems with Haig's generalship.

functioning bureaucracies, but such bureaucracies require close watching in war if they are to achieve their purpose, which is to support the sharp end, not maintain their comfortable peacetime practices.

In the twentieth century, because of the lethality of the battlefield, generals increasingly had to rely on their bureaucracies to report accurately what was happening on the battlefield. In the First World War, "chateau generalship" dominated the Western Front, although less so with the German Army.[56] Thus, generals lost touch with what their men were confronting. Moreover, with the exception of the Germans, military organizations in the 1914–1918 conflict simply did not possess the means to gather and analyze combat experience in a coherent fashion. The Germans did but failed to make good use of that system until the arrival of Field Marshal Paul von Hindenburg and his chief of staff (holding the position of quartermaster general) Erich Ludendorff in the supreme command in August 1916.[57] Perhaps the most important advantage the Germans enjoyed with their general staff system was the willingness of their staff officers to maintain close ties with the front line, while executing their staff responsibilities.

There is a double irony here, because a bureaucratic system is an absolute necessity for successful adaptation. Nevertheless, at the same time, the rhythms and culture of most bureaucracies are antithetical to successful adaptation. They are the product of peacetime practices and measures of effectiveness. They are more about efficiency than effectiveness. Above all, they are the prisoners of prewar assumptions and perceptions. Theirs is the view of war as "it should be," not as it really is. The supposed comment by a British brigadier at the end of World War I that "the army could now get back to the real business of soldiering" may be apocryphal but reflects an attitude all too prevalent among the regular officers in that army. Such attitudes can drive military organizations into disastrous behavior patterns.

The cultural norms that drove the British military bureaucracy and its senior officers were not responsible for the initial heavy casualties suffered

---

[56] The Germans at least ensured that staff officers went to the front lines to discover what was happening. Immediately upon arrival at his new headquarters in September 1915, Colonel von Lossberg, chief of staff to the Third Army, visited the front lines to survey the terrain his forces would defend against the French fall offensive. Captain G. C. Wynne, *If Germany Attacks: The Battle in Depth in the West* (London, 1939), pp. 91–92.

[57] For the adaptation of the German Army to the tactical conundrums of the Western Front after Ludendorff took over in 1916, see particularly Lupfer, *The Dynamics of Doctrine*. See also Chapter 3 of this book.

on the Western Front in 1914 and 1915; there were basic realities that all the armies, including the German, had to learn in the war's first months.[58] But those norms were responsible for the catastrophe of 1 July 1916, the first day of the Somme, and particularly for the terribly botched battle of Passchendaele in late summer and fall of 1917.[59] Some British generals learned faster than others, but the bureaucratic framework and the culture of the prewar period ensured that learning took an inordinate amount of time. The same was the case with the French.[60] For the Germans, the military bureaucracy at times stood steadfastly against providing support for change. Nevertheless, the general staff provided a means of short-circuiting the bureaucracy, although it is worth noting that Ludendorff could not get the artillery expert Bruckmüller promoted to colonel because of opposition from the Prussian War Ministry.[61]

There is the fact that adaptation in times of war – unlike innovation in times of peace – carries with it the reality that bureaucratic mistakes or obfuscations can have all too noticeable results. Here, civil or military leaders can, and often do, overrule their bureaucracies, when essential matters are at stake and come to the attention of those who can act. That is, of course, presupposing they are not a part of the bureaucratic problem. Churchill was the enemy of bureaucratic groupthink. His "action this day" memos underlined the necessity he saw to energize the bureaucracy, military as well as civilian. But that system also contributed to the considerable unpopularity that Churchill's methods occasioned throughout the war among all those who found themselves the target of his ire.[62] And in some cases, such as the provision of an effective tank for the British Army, all of Churchill's efforts were for naught when they came up against the apathy of bureaucratic obfuscation that consistently

---

[58] For a discussion of these issues, see particularly Travers, *The Killing Ground*. Travers' is one of the few studies of a military institution that deals with the cultural framework within which it works.

[59] For how badly the Battle of Passchendaele was botched, see particularly Prior and Wilson, *Passchendaele*.

[60] In regard to the French failure to learn at anything faster than a snail's pace and the resulting slaughter of their troops in the first three years of World War I, see Robert Doughty, *The French Army in the First World War* (Cambridge, MA, 2005).

[61] Nevertheless, such was the prestige of the general staff that Ludendorff could provide Bruckmüller, a mere lieutenant colonel, with sufficient authority to order senior generals to manage their artillery fire plans in accordance with his wishes. For Bruckmüller's career, see David T. Zabecki, *Steel Wind, Colonel Georg Bruckmüller and the Birth of Modern Artillery* (Westport, CT, 1994).

[62] In this regard, see particularly Field Marshal Lord Alanbrooke, *War Diaries, 1939–1945*, ed. by Alex Danchev and Daniel Todman (Berkeley, CA, 2001).

made the wrong choices in tank development from 1940 through 1944.[63]

R. V. Jones was the extraordinarily competent scientific adviser to the Air Ministry during the Second World War, who attracted considerable attention to himself by being right about a number of complex and crucial intelligence problems in the face of opposition from senior officers and civilians. Jones commented on his resulting unpopularity: "Despite any unpopularity, I survived because war is different from peace: in the latter fallacies can be covered up more or less indefinitely and criticism suppressed but with the swift action of war the truth comes fairly quickly to light – as Churchill said, 'In war you don't have to be polite, you just have to be right!'"[64] In the end the bureaucracy struck back in the only fashion it was able, given Jones's relations with Churchill and Lord Cherwell. The prime minister had nominated Jones for a CB (the highest award for a civilian) for his contribution to the Battle of the Beams and the location of a crucial radar site at Bruneval (see Chapters 5 and 6 of this book). The head of the British civil service, Sir Horace Wilson, a major architect of Chamberlain's policy of appeasement and a bureaucrat of the highest order, "threatened to resign" if Jones received the award. Wilson's argument was that Jones "had been merely a scientific officer and... could not possibly have done work of such merit in [his] lowly position." Jones did not receive a CB at that time.[65]

By their nature, bureaucrats are loath to make decisions, especially when the results may in the end be attributable to them. Far better to reject proposals coming from below and thus not expose oneself to opprobrium on the part of their superiors. The wise commander recognizes this penchant of those in his organization and acts to counter it. Air Marshall Sir Arthur "Bomber" Harris, commander of the RAF's Bomber Command during the Second World War, infuriated by the failure of his bureaucracy to forward ideas and concepts up the chain of command, finally decreed that any staff officer turning down a proposal had to write an explanation of why he was rejecting the idea and then forward the proposal and rejection up the chain of command.[66]

---

[63] For a discussion of the appalling course of British tank design and production during the Second World War, see A. J. Smithers, *Rude Mechanicals: An Account of Tank Maturity during the Second World War* (London, 1987).
[64] R. V. Jones, *The Wizard War: British Scientific Intelligence, 1939–1945* (New York, 1978), p. 139.
[65] Ibid., p. 248.
[66] Interview of Sir Arthur Harris by Wing Commander Tony Mason, RAF Staff College Library, Bracknell, late 1970s.

The Issue of Competence

In the largest sense, of course, bureaucracies reflect the human hands that guide them. In this respect, their behavior reflects human nature itself. There is little in history to suggest that imagination, intelligent leadership, or innovative minds are characteristics shared by the great mass of humanity. In fact, the opposite would seem to be the case. The MacClellans, Haigs, and Westmorelands are far more typical of senior leaders than the Grants, Slims, and Eisenhowers.

Much of the writing about history aims to explain the causes of disaster. An underlying theme is often that incompetence, rather than competence, is the exception and that the latter lies at the heart of human behavior and actions.[67] Yet, the historical spectrum of human activity suggests the opposite. In war the results of incompetence by military institutions are graphically displayed for even the most obtuse to see in terms of the wreckage of dead and maimed, not to mention physical destruction. However, incompetence is not just a matter of military institutions. Its various manifestations such as shortsightedness, close-mindedness, and institutional rigidity – among a host of others – seem endemic in human affairs. It was, after all, human beings who produced the Great Depression, 60 years of planned agricultural disaster in the Soviet Union, "the Great Leap Forward," and myriad other disasters during the course of the twentieth century.

Nevertheless, there has been a tendency to regard military institutions as particularly prone to incompetence, as an entry in the index of David Lloyd George's memoirs suggests. Under the entry "Military mind" one finds the following: "narrowness of, 3051; stubbornness of, not peculiar to America, 3055; does not seem to understand arithmetic, 3077; its attitude in July 1918, represented by Sir Henry Wilson's fantastic memorandum of 25/7/18, 3109; obsessed with North West Frontier of India, 3119; impossibility of trusting, 3124; regards thinking as a form of mutiny, 3422."[68] Lloyd George's attitude toward the military finds more

---

[67] The unwillingness of many historians to recognize this harsh reality that lies at the heart of human performance on and off the battlefield helps to explain the popularity of conspiracy theories.

[68] These are all legitimate entries. David Lloyd George, *The Memoirs of David Lloyd George*, 6 vols. (London, 1936), vol. 6, p. 34. This author replied in kind to Lloyd George's swipe at the military mind with the following entry in *The Change of the European Balance of Power*, p. 482. "Civilian mind: narrowness of, not confined to universities, 358–59; appoints diplomatic mediator on the basis of complete unfamiliarity with the issues, 185; bases diplomatic estimate on comments of German butler,

than sufficient supporting evidence in the disasters British arms suffered at Gallipoli, Loos, the Somme, Passchendaele, and the battles of spring 1918, all of which he observed from the position of either a senior cabinet minister or prime minister. Yet, Lloyd George also played a significant role in the disaster at Passchendaele and the defeats of 1918 by his consistent unwillingness to confront Haig over the major issues dealing with British strategy on the Western Front.[69]

Still, for whatever reasons, the record of military institutions has been all too dismal, suggesting a pattern of incompetence in their failure to innovate and adapt. In looking at a series of essays examining the military effectiveness of national military organizations in the first half of the twentieth century, an eminent retired soldier commented in the following terms: "[I]n the spheres of operations and tactics, where military competence would seem to be a nation's rightful due, the twenty-one [essays by historians] suggest for the most part less than general military competence and sometimes abysmal incompetence. One can doubt whether any other profession in these seven nations during the same periods would have received such poor ratings by similarly competent outside observers."[70]

If the record on the other side of the ledger in civilian affairs is no more impressive, it is perhaps more difficult to discern. General Motors has been on a slow but steady slide toward oblivion over the past two decades, and it will perhaps take another two decades before it finally disappears. At the macro level, there are numerous indications of the impact of corporate incompetence. Of the 200 leading corporations in the United States in 1900, fewer than a dozen were still in the top ten at the end of the twentieth century – hardly a ringing endorsement for competence in the business world. Because the collapse of a major corporation takes decades to work its way out and the results appear less obtrusive than military defeat, the level of incompetence in the business world appears less obvious to historians, much less the casual observer. In the end, the nature of human beings, as well as the societies and cultures they create,

---

307–308; believes good shooting a primary requirement for diplomatic appointment, 60; cannot find fortifications on a map, 196; and infinite capacity for self-delusion, 284–85; mediating conflict 'in a dingy in mid-Atlantic,' 185; thinks that horses and violins have similarities, 87."

[69] For a clear discussion of Lloyd George's responsibilities with regard to the battle, see particularly Prior and Wilson, *Passchendaele*, pp. 143–155.

[70] Lieutenant General John H. Cushman, U.S. Army (retired), "Challenge and Response at the Operational and Tactical Levels, 1914–1945," in Allan R. Millett and Williamson Murray, eds., *Military Effectiveness*, vol. 3, *The Second World War* (London, 1988), pp. 320–340.

represents a major contributor to the failure to adapt to the changing landscape of politics, warfare, and economics.

Incompetence springs from any number of factors. Sheer human stupidity is an obvious contributor, and one should not underestimate the role that a lack of intelligence has played in pushing human institutions into disastrous failures. But other factors appear as equally important drivers behind incompetence. After all, stupid people rarely rise to the top of major corporations or military institutions, particularly in the modern world. Rather, the political, cultural, and ideological frameworks within which men and women adapt to the world's changing conditions, as well as their particular and peculiar personalities, represent the most important factors in the decision-making and organizational processes that determine competence or incompetence.

In the end intelligence is only one of a number of factors that figures into competence. In fact, in some cases, it inhibits competent performance. No one would deny that General Maurice Gamelin was an extraordinarily intelligent man.[71] The fact that he was a member of the Académie Française should underline his intelligence. But his catastrophic handling of the French Army's preparations for war as well as his disastrous handling of the 1940 campaign hardly suggests anything other than the grossest incompetence. In his case, his intelligence undoubtedly contributed to his belief that he need not listen to others.

On the other hand, there is no doubt that Napoleon possessed one of the most extraordinary minds in history.[72] Undoubtedly, it was the combination of his mental acuity with other attributes of his personality that made Napoleon history's greatest battlefield commander. Interestingly, Clausewitz does not use Napoleon – or Alexander or Caesar, the latter two who also possessed extraordinary mental capabilities – in his discussion of military genius. There are several explanations. The most obvious is that Napoleon was such an anomaly in historical terms that Clausewitz felt that to discuss the emperor was to mislead his readers as to what obtainable competence might represent. On the other hand, Napoleon's

---

[71] Astonishingly, three major studies by historians have defended Gamelin's reputation against the charge of incompetence. See Robert J. Young, *In Command of France: French Foreign Policy and Military Planning* (Cambridge, MA, 1978); Jeffery Gunsburg, *Divided and Conquered: The French High Command and the Defeat in the West, 1940* (Westport, CT, 1979); and Martin Alexander, *The Republic in Danger, General Maurice Gamelin and the Politics of French Defence, 1933–1940* (Cambridge, 2003).

[72] For a description of Napoleon's extraordinary mental capabilities, see Chandler, *The Campaigns of Napoleon*, part 3.

skills were so out of the ordinary that they inevitably led to megalomania. Believing that his tactical and operational capabilities could make up for France's strategic vulnerabilities in 1813 and 1814, Napoleon disregarded the favorable terms offered by the Allies and wagered all in attempting to achieve an unobtainable "decisive" victory.[73]

Of course, it is the cultural and political framework that allows genius either to flourish or wither. Tyrannical regimes have a particular penchant for removing the competent at the higher levels because of the threat that they might represent to the regime.[74] The story about the ancient Greek tyrant of Miletus related by Herodotus is particularly relevant. The new tyrant of Athens, Periander, sought counsel from Thrasybulus, who had remained in power for a number of decades, as to the secret of his success. The tyrant simply took the messenger from Athens out into a wheat field and cut off all the sheaves of wheat that stuck out above the rest. As Herodotus recounts: "Periander seized the point at once; it was perfectly clear that Thrasybulus recommended the murder of all the people in the city who were outstanding in influence or ability."[75]

Certainly that was the principle by which Joseph Stalin lived in his massive purges of the Red Army's officer corps in the late 1930s, purges that liquidated substantial numbers of the most competent and effective officers in the Red Army.[76] From a Western perspective, the results led to gross incompetence and military ineffectiveness – a bill paid with the blood of millions of Soviet soldiers and citizens in the disastrous events in the opening months of Operation Barbarossa in summer and fall 1941.[77] However, from Stalin's perspective, even after the Second World War

---

[73] See particularly Steven Ross, *European Diplomatic History, 1789–1815: France against Europe* (Malabar, FL, 1981), chap. 10.
[74] The Iraqi Perspectives Project, in which this author participated as a team member at the Institute of Defense Analyses, indicates that Saddam Hussein consistently and deliberately aimed at eliminating the competent and the intelligent from the senior levels of his government and military. See Kevin M. Woods with Michael R. Pease, Mark E. Stout, Williamson Murray, and James G. Lacey, *Iraqi Perspectives Project: A View of Operation Iraqi Freedom from Saddam's Senior Leadership* (Washington, DC, 2006).
[75] Herodotus, *The Histories*, trans. by Aubrey de Sélincourt (London, 1954), pp. 376–377.
[76] But not all, as the survival of Georgy Zhukov underlines.
[77] A number of Western commentators and historians have attempted to argue that the purges improved the quality of the Soviet officer corps. Such arguments reveal the grossest general ignorance of military history and the nature of military institutions, not to mention the nature of tyranny. For the price the Soviet Union paid for Stalin's purge of many of the most competent Soviet officers and the difficulty the Red Army had in overcoming the resulting weaknesses, see David. H. Glantz, *Colossus* (Lawrence, KS, 2005).

was over, the purge of so many competent officers made eminently good sense, because once completed, the purges ensured that there were no alternatives to the dictator, a fact that everyone at the senior levels of the Soviet bureaucracy fully understood in October 1941, when defeat stared the Soviets in the face and serious troubles broke out in Moscow. Much the same pattern of incompetence in tyrannical regimes has echoed throughout history, the most recent case being that of Saddam Hussein's Ba'athist regime in Iraq, in which the dictator made a practice of removing the most competent to ensure there were no alternatives near the throne.[78]

Such patterns of behavior are endemic in bureaucracies and military organizations, in which senior officers or officials get rid of the "best and the brightest" in one fashion or another, because of the threat that they represent. Lieutenant General Courtney Hodges, Bradley's replacement as First Army commander in August 1944, either consciously or unconsciously, made a practice of removing those subordinates who by their competence might represent a threat to his position.[79] Henry Halleck made every effort in the first two years of the Civil War to eliminate Grant from command and, when that was no longer possible, to minimize Grant's potential contribution to the war. In the largest sense, the nature of civil and military bureaucracies in democracies limits the competition for place by their rules and processes. In effect, they produce a higher level of competence than what tyrannies are, for the most part, able to produce.[80] At the same time, they are rarely able to control for the vagaries of human nature and the individual idiosyncrasies of their members.

Complicating any examination of the problem of competence of human affairs is the fact that the same attributes that in one individual may contribute to effectiveness, in another may lead to the most egregious incompetence. Some great commanders have been fanatical workers; others, like Admiral Raymond Spruance, followed a path marked by the most

---

[78] For a discussion of these issues, see Woods, *Iraqi Perspectives Project*.
[79] I am indebted to Dr. Allan R. Millett, professor emeritus at The Ohio State University and dean of American military historians for this point.
[80] The one exception to this rule is Nazi Germany, where Hitler encouraged a competition based on battlefield performance. I am indebted to Professor MacGregor Knox of the London School of Economics for this point. His current research on Nazi Germany should eventually clarify how it actually functioned in such an effective manner in the military sphere despite the chaotic manner with which the Führer exercised his powers. For his initial findings, see MacGregor Knox, *Common Destiny: Dictatorship, Foreign Policy, and War in Fascist Italy and Nazi Germany* (Cambridge, 2000), chap. 2.

relaxed of behavior. Yet diligence can prove as dangerous to the effective functioning of a military organization as indolence. Frederick the Great's topology of officers provides a hint of how one might best think about the issue of military competence. The Prussian king suggested that there were four types of officers. First were the brilliant but lazy. He suggested such officers had the attributes to function at the highest levels of command. Second were the brilliant, but diligent. They made the best staff officers. Third were the less intelligent but lazy. They made good battalion officers. Finally, there were the less intelligent and the diligent. They were the most dangerous to the proper functioning of any military organization, in both peace and war, because of their penchant for confusing process and work for product. Frederick's typology is, of course, overdrawn, but it does suggest that there are complex factors in the making of military competence. The problem is, as we shall suggest in the next section, that the qualities that go into an officer's success at the tactical and operational levels are not necessarily those that will make him successful at the strategic level.

Levels of War: The Problems of Adaptation and Strategy

The focus of the following chapters is on the difficulties that military institutions face in adapting at the operational and tactical levels of war. But it is crucial to examine at least in passing the problems associated with adaptation at the strategic level. It is here that statesmen and military leaders have found the greatest difficulties, not necessarily because it is difficult to perceive that the course of national strategy is flawed, but rather because the costs associated with strategic adaptation, not only in political terms but in personal terms as well, often represent too high a price.

The classic case is, of course, World War I, during which many statesmen and generals could not help but recognize the flawed nature of their prewar assumptions within the first months of the conflict, but, for the most part, the price to be paid for altering the disastrous courses on which they had embarked appeared too great for consideration. In the end, Europe's leaders maintained their course to the bitter end, and the smashups of 1917 (the Russian Revolution) and 1918 (the collapse of the German, Austro-Hungarian, and Ottoman Empires) were the direct result.

One of the classic myths to come out of the Vietnam War is that the U.S. military won all the battles but lost the war because of its failures at the political and strategic levels.[81] In fact, it hardly won all the battles, as the battle at "Landing Zone Albany" in November 1965 suggests.[82] But there is a germ of wisdom in the myth, because it is at the strategic level where wars are won or lost. And it was at the strategic and political levels that the United States lost the war.[83] In an essay summing up the lessons of the military effectiveness project sponsored by the Office of Net Assessment, Allan Millett and the author commented on the importance of intelligent political and strategic decision making in wartime in the following terms:

> No amount of operational [or tactical] virtuosity... redeemed fundamental flaws in political judgment. Whether policy shaped strategy or strategic imperatives drove policy was irrelevant. Miscalculations in both led to defeat, and any combination of politico-strategic error had disastrous results, even for some nations that ended the war as members of the victorious coalition. Even the effective mobilization of national will, manpower, industrial might, national wealth, and technological know-how did not save the belligerents from reaping the bitter fruits of severe mistakes [at this level]. This is because it is more important to make correct decisions at the political and strategic level than it is at the operational and tactical level. Mistakes in operations and tactics can be corrected but political and strategic mistakes live forever.[84]

What makes the Vietnam War such a depressing case study is that senior leaders in the Johnson administration recognized early in the major commitment of U.S. forces that the war was unwinnable, at least in the terms on which they were willing to fight it. About the best that Robert McNamara's undersecretary of defense Robert McNaughton could come up with was the argument that staying the course, even if it meant defeat, would serve to persuade America's allies that the United States was loyal and faithful.[85] Nevertheless, as the United States sank deeper and deeper into a morass of its own strategic assumptions, the president and his advisers refused to consider a fundamental reassessment

---

[81] This claim is made at the beginning of Harry Summer's book, reassessing the Vietnam War. *On Strategy: A Critical Analysis of the Vietnam War* (Novato, CA, 1995).

[82] For the battle of Landing Zone Albany, see Lieutenant General Harold G. Moore and Joseph L. Galloway, *We Were Soldiers Once... and Young, Ia Drang: The Battle That Changed the War in Vietnam* (New York, 1992).

[83] For the role of the military as well as the politicians in the incredibly flawed decision-making processes that led to America's intervention into the Vietnam War in summer 1965, see H. R. McMaster, *Dereliction of Duty: Lyndon Johnson, Robert McNamara, the Joint Chiefs of Staff, and the Lies That Led to Vietnam* (New York, 1996).

[84] Allan R. Millett and Williamson Murray, "Lessons of War," *The National Interest*, Winter 1988.

[85] McMaster, *Dereliction of Duty*, pp. 184, 189, 237.

until after the Tet Offensive had persuaded significant numbers of Americans that the Johnson administration had no coherent idea about what it hoped to achieve or how it planned to extract the United States from Vietnam.

Similarly, the emerging picture of events in Iraq makes it clear that the political and civilian leaders at the top believed there would be few problems during the postconflict phase after the collapse of Saddam Hussein's evil regime.[86] Thus, when the insurgency emerged in the conflict's aftermath, the initial response was denial of what was happening, a denial that Secretary of Defense Donald Rumsfeld persisted in through winter 2006. For those on the scene, it was apparent as early as June 2003 that the political and strategic assumptions were badly askew. In fact, one brigade commander at the time suggested to the author that a fundamental reassessment in early July 2003 of the political and strategic assumptions driving U.S. actions might well have nipped the insurgency in the bud.[87] No such reassessment took place. Apparently, senior leaders were either oblivious to what was happening or had too much political capital invested in their prewar assumptions to dare alter course. But the immediate political costs of admitting strategic error either overwhelmed or suppressed the growing reality perceived by soldiers and marines on the ground that things were going south.

An examination of the processes of how different nations form grand strategy suggests that unspoken and unwritten assumptions, intimately associated with the national heritage and history, form and guide how statesmen, military leaders, and policy makers understand and address the external world.[88] If there have been few great generals in the landscape of history, there have been even fewer great statesmen capable of seeing beyond the horizons of their own cultural and political framework. Those few not only could see the forest as it was but could also dimly perceive it as it might be tomorrow. The challenge all confront is that in an ever-changing and fluid world, even the greatest edifices of strategic policy rest on a base of sand.

---

[86] In this regard, see particularly Fallows, "Blind into Baghdad," and Packer, *The Assassins' Gate*.

[87] Conversation with Colonel Peter Mansoor, Institute of Defense Analyses, Alexandria, Virginia. Colonel Mansoor was a brigade commander in Iraq in the 1st Armored Division in summer and fall 2003.

[88] For a discussion of the various factors – geography, history, ideology, religion, among others – that go into the making of strategy, see Williamson Murray and Mark Grimsley, "Introduction: On Strategy," in Murray, Knox, and Bernstein, *The Making of Strategy*, chap. 1.

Prussia's Iron Chancellor, Otto von Bismarck, understood the limits as well as the advantages that Prussia possessed in the mid-nineteenth century but failed to convey to his successors any recognition that the new Imperial German state was, and would remain, vulnerable within the context of European politics, particularly if it attempted to make changes to the status quo. Within less than a decade of Bismarck's removal from office, Wilhelm II and his advisers had dismantled Bismarck's carefully balanced alliance system and replaced it with a militant foreign policy, one that soon united the rest of Europe against Imperial Germany. Astonishingly, in 1917 the Germans, already engaged in a desperate struggle against the European powers, launched an unrestricted submarine campaign against the British despite knowing such an effort would bring the United States into the conflict.[89]

Even when it occurs, the adaptation of strategy to the actual conditions of war is invariably a contentious and painful process. Sometimes it occurs. In the year before the Japanese attack on Pearl Harbor, America's military leaders developed a strategy that focused on "Germany first."[90] In the end, that was what occurred with the American war effort. But for much of 1942 and well into 1943, the United States deployed substantially greater forces to the Pacific than to Europe. This was in response both to political pressure from the American people and the rapidly deteriorating situation in the Pacific war.[91]

Notwithstanding, in July 1942, President Franklin Roosevelt ordered U.S. commanders to execute major landings in fall 1942 against French

---

[89] A reality they dismissed in the belief that they would win the war before the United States could build military forces and ship them to Europe.

[90] The foremost example of this was the "Plan Dog" memorandum by the chief of naval operation Admiral "Betty" Stark, which, in a major turn from interwar U.S. naval strategy, with its emphasis on Japan as America's premier enemy, argued that only Germany could win a war against the Allies, and therefore, the latter rather than the former should be the main focus of the American effort.

[91] One could argue that the situation on the Eastern Front in summer 1942 appeared to be deteriorating even more rapidly than that in the Pacific, as German forces advanced toward Stalingrad and the Caucasus. Nevertheless, there was relatively little that American military power as it existed at the time could do to help the Soviets. American military planners, at the urging of President Roosevelt, did draw up tentative plans for a suicidal landing on the coast of France, should the Soviets appear to be collapsing. Those plans did not have to be executed, however, because the Soviets were not in as desperate a situation in 1942 as they were suggesting at the time to their British and American "allies." For a discussion of the strategic issues, see Williamson Murray and Allan R. Millett, *A War to Be Won: Fighting the Second World War* (Cambridge, MA, 2000).

North Africa to support British efforts in the Mediterranean. The army's chief of staff, General George Marshall, argued vociferously that such a commitment would delay the strategic goal of achieving a major amphibious landing on the coast of northern France – the heart of the "Germany first" strategy – by at least a year. Marshall proved correct in his military estimate of the impact of Operation Torch, but what he missed was the political necessity of keeping the attention of the American people focused on the war against Germany – a conflict which held little interest for most of them, especially given the enormous anger that the Japanese attack on Pearl Harbor had occasioned.

Perhaps the most successful case of political and strategic adaptation came during the American Civil War, when Abraham Lincoln addressed a fluid and dynamic situation in which few of the initial assumptions proved accurate.[92] In the largest sense, the North's political objective in the war's first year remained entirely focused on reestablishing the Union. Only a small group of abolitionists in the northeast argued for freeing the slaves. But the events of 1861 and 1862 clearly indicated the Union assumption that secession had the support of only a small percentage of the Southern population was wrong. In his memoirs, Grant caught much of what that recognition entailed:

> Up to the Battle of Shiloh, I, as well as thousands of other citizens, believed that the rebellion against the Government would collapse suddenly and soon, if a decisive victory could be gained over any of its armies. Donelson and Henry were such victories. An army of more than 21,000 men was captured and destroyed. Bowling Green, Columbus and Hickman, Kentucky, fell in consequence, and Clarkesville and Nashville, Tennessee, the last two with an immense amount of stores, also fell into our hands. The Tennessee and Cumberland rivers from their mouths to the head of navigation were secured. But when Confederate armies were collected which not only attempted to hold a line further south, from Memphis to Chattanooga, Knoxville and on to the Atlantic but assumed the offensive and made such a gallant effort to regain what had been lost, then, indeed, I gave up all idea of saving the union except by complete conquest.[93]

By late summer, the course of the war had convinced Lincoln that he had to extend the North's grand strategy to include the abolition of slavery. Thus, after the Battle of Antietam, he issued the Emancipation Proclamation, a step aimed not only at the heart of the South's culture but

---

[92] In this case on both sides but Lincoln and the North adapted, while Jefferson Davis showed little willingness to recognize a changing political and strategic landscape.

[93] Grant, *The Personal Memoirs of U.S. Grant*, vol. 1, p. 368.

at its economic foundation as well. The Emancipation Proclamation was only the opening shot of what was to turn into a strategy of war against the South's economy and political structure. It was a war that in some ways resembled the RAF Bomber Command's "dehousing" campaign of the Second World War, except that advancing Union troops allowed the inhabitants to exit their dwellings. Sherman's soldiers were soon to refer to the Southern towns they passed as "Chimneyvilles." By 1864 the Union had embarked on what its leaders termed the "hard war."[94] Sherman encapsulated the approach that Union armies would take in the last years of the war in a letter to the assistant adjutant general of the Department of Tennessee:

> The government of the United States has in North Alabama any and all rights which they choose to enforce in war – to take their lives [those of the inhabitants], their lands, their everything – because they cannot deny that war exists there, and war is simply power unconstrained by constitution or compact. If they want eternal war, well and good; we accept the issue and will dispossess them and [put] our friends in their place.... To those who submit to the rightful law and authority all gentleness and forbearance but to the petulant and persistent secessionist, why, death is mercy and the quicker he or she is disposed of the better. [Satan] and the rebellious saints of Heaven were allowed a continuous existence in hell merely to swell their just punishment.[95]

Grant's orders for Sheridan as to how he should treat the Shenandoah Valley were simply to render the area "a barren waste... so that crows flying over it for the balance of this season will have to carry their provender with them."[96]

Adaptation at the strategic level, of course, presupposes that a nation has a strategy or at least a strategic concept. That was certainly not the case with Imperial Germany throughout the First World War. The Reich's civilian leaders, as suggested earlier, abdicated all responsibility and turned the conduct of the war over to the military.[97] Thus, Imperial

---

[94] For the hard war, see particularly Mark Grimsley, *The Hard Hand of War, Union Military Policy toward Southern Civilians, 1861–1865* (Cambridge, 1995).

[95] *Official Records of the Union and Confederate Armies*, series I, vol. 32, part 2 (Washington, DC, 1891), pp. 280–281.

[96] Quoted in Bruce Catton, *Grant Takes Command* (New York, 1968), p. 347.

[97] This did not only happen in Imperial Germany. The British politicians, despite clear knowledge of what was happening on the Western Front, refused to intervene and force a confrontation with Field Marshal Sir Douglas Haig. This was particularly true during the course of the Passchendaele battles in Flanders in summer and fall 1917. For a clear discussion of this abdication, see particularly Prior and Wilson, *Passchendaele*.

Germany fought the First World War with no strategy but rather as a series of distinct campaigns, which its leaders failed to connect to any strategic vision.⁹⁸ The Germans took virtually all of their decisions on the basis of immediate tactical utility without regard to the strategic or operational consequences – perhaps the most bizarre case being the use of poison gas in Flanders in April 1915. At the operational level, that decision made no sense because the prevailing winds on the Western Front blew from west to east, toward the German front lines. Worse yet, at the strategic level it helped convince the majority of Americans that Germany was indeed the dangerous power the Allies were portraying it as, a view which the sinking of the *Lusitania* in May 1915 only served to confirm.

A recent study of the cultural framework within which the German civilian and military leadership operated notes the following:

> The structural and institutional barriers to strategic planning meant that military viewpoints were not coordinated with or subordinated to political-economic-legal calculations but were free to develop according to their own unexamined logic. The longer the war continued the more the power discrepancy tipped to Germany's disadvantage. Genuine strategic planning would have been forced to acknowledge that Germany was too small to become a world power, or to win a world war. For those who wanted to avoid this conclusion, purely military thinking was attractive. For the German military had developed its culture on the very premise of over-achievement, of using quality, daring, and tactical proficiency to overcome strategic disadvantage. By acquiescing to German military culture, civilians could conveniently deny the discouraging truth of Germany's situation.⁹⁹

Adaptation in the Twenty-First Century

Sir Michael Howard has suggested that the military profession is not only the most difficult of all the professions in terms of its physical demands but that it is also the most demanding in terms of its intellectual challenges. Making those challenges more difficult is the reality that military organizations are only episodically able to practice the business for which they are established. The humdrum, bureaucratic business of sustaining those organizations in peacetime makes it all too easy for military leaders

---

⁹⁸ I am indebted to a former graduate student, Brad Meyer, now of the USMC's School of Advanced Warfighting at Quantico, for this insight.
⁹⁹ Isabel V. Hull, *Absolute Destruction, Military Culture and the Practices of War in Imperial Germany* (Ithaca, NY, 2005), p. 2006.

to forget Clausewitz's warning: "The end for which a soldier is recruited, clothed, armed, and trained, the whole object of his sleeping, eating, drinking, and marching *is simply that he should fight at the right place and the right time.*"[100]

Adding to the intractable problems war has always raised has been the fact that military organizations confronted an increasing pace of technological change in the twentieth century. Not only does technological change occur in peacetime but the very nature of conflict, where the enemy gets a vote, inevitably increases the demand for change and adaptation. And soldiers and marines in particular must recognize that the enemy may well fight within an entirely different cultural and intellectual framework than that which guides their actions. That simple fact is one of the enduring lessons of history – one that Americans find all too easy to forget.

Yet the very nature of the modern battlefield, whether one is dealing with the rapid conventional advance on Baghdad in March 2003 or the interminable insurgencies that followed, presents all the ambiguities, uncertainties, and frictions that have characterized war in the past. How to make sensible adaptations in a world dominated by chance, horror, misperceptions, and human frailty is the hard question that military institutions, no matter how sophisticated their technology, will confront for the remainder of this century and beyond – in fact for as long as the human race fights wars.

[100] Clausewitz, *On War*, p. 95.

2

The Historical Framework of Adaptation

Over the course of the past century and a half, adaptation in one form or another has been a characteristic of successful military institutions and human societies under the pressures of war. Yet, before the onslaught of technological change that began in the early nineteenth century, military adaptation proceeded at what appears a snail's pace to the modern observer.[1] It was not until the Industrial Revolution that adaptation became a crucial factor in the effectiveness of military institutions in the conduct of war. But military innovation and adaptation have always conferred advantages on military organizations, even before the Industrial Revolution.

Nevertheless, the Industrial Revolution stepped up the pace of change, and over the course of the past 150 years, that pace has steadily accelerated. In the modern period, when machines and technology have become crucial enablers for those who do the fighting, the concepts and innovations of peacetime invariably get much of the next war wrong. Two factors are significant here: first, how well one estimates the impact of new technologies on the battlefield, and second, how well one closes the gap between the initial estimates and assumptions and what turns out to be reality. The first factor has proven particularly difficult in the twentieth century, because multiple technologies and tactical conceptions

---

[1] A clear example of the snail's pace of change in the ancient world is the fact that the Marian legion, based on the cohort and developed into its early-first-century BC form by Gaius Marius, still formed the basis of the Roman military system at the beginning of the third century AD – nearly four centuries later. Recruitment patterns may have changed over that period, but discipline, organization, and weapons remained largely the same.

have come into play simultaneously, while multiple actors are adapting at the same time. Military organizations have had to estimate not only the impact of technology but also the synergy of multiple technologies as well as how their opponents will utilize them.

Those military organizations that have adapted to the actual conditions of combat are those that perform the best in war. In the modern world, technological improvements and tactical and operational learning on both sides make adaptation a major factor in the conduct of war. Thus, it would seem useful to sketch out the overall pattern of adaptation in history as a means of understanding the factors and the difficulties that have confronted military institutions, commanders, and statesmen as they have struggled to adapt to the realities of war, before turning to case studies in the problems of military adaptation. As then–Major General James Mattis, USMC, suggested in 2004 about the importance of history to the military profession:

> Ultimately, a real understanding of history means that we face nothing new under the sun. For all the 'Fourth Generation of War' intellectuals running around today saying that the nature of war has fundamentally changed, the tactics are wholly new, etc., I must respectfully say: 'Not really.' Alex the Great would not be in the least perplexed by the enemy that we face right now in Iraq, and our leaders going into this fight do their troops a disservice by not studying (studying, vice just reading) the men who have gone before us. We have been fighting on this planet for 5,000 years and we should take advantage of their experience. 'Winging' it and filling body bags as we sort out what works reminds us of the moral dictates and the cost of competence in our profession.[2]

The Ancient and Medieval World

It is difficult to talk about military adaptation in the ancient world, largely because technological development was minimal – at least in terms of weapons technology. There were only two prominent systems of warfare in the history of the Mediterranean world from 700 BC through AD 300, the Greek phalanx and the Roman legion. Each underwent only one major tactical innovation over its history – the period of each spanning multiple centuries. That alone suggests how little military adaptation affected war in the ancient world. Because the technological framework remained stable, there was little need to alter military organizations and systems, which consistently were able to defeat internal and, from the point of view of the Roman Empire, external enemies.

---

[2] Unpublished e-mail, quoted by permission of General Mattis.

The Greek phalanx, which depended on the discipline provided by cultural integration, which the Polis (city-state) imbued in its citizens, dominated war in the Aegean for a period of more than 300 years without significant adaptations or innovations.[3] The most significant tactical innovation with the phalanx came only at the beginning of the fourth century BC with its radical alteration by the Thebans. At the Battle of Leuctra in 371 BC, their general, Epaminondas, hit on the relatively simple adaptation of overloading the Theban phalanx on its left wing.[4] As a result, the Thebans overwhelmed the Spartan right wing, the heart of the Spartan Army. For the first time in more than 300 years, a Spartan hoplite force went down to defeat at the hands of an opponent on the open field.[5]

Epaminondas's tactical change ushered in a period of significant innovations in the phalanx that lasted approximately 50 years. A young Macedonian prince by the name of Philip was in Thebes at that time as a hostage. After his return and assumption of the Macedonian kingship, what he had observed eventually led him to reorganize the Macedonian phalanx and include cavalry as an integral part of a combined-arms team. Unlike the Greek city-states, the Macedonians now combined the strength of the phalanx with significant improvements in weaponry along with the maneuverability of cavalry forces that possessed discipline and training.

The result was a series of devastating victories over the Greeks that established Macedonian hegemony over the entire Aegean. Philip's son, Alexander, then took his father's military system and conquered most of the known world, including the Persian Empire, in barely a decade.[6] From that point, however, significant military adaptations in the Greek

---

[3] For one of the greatest works of scholarship as well as of intuitive and counterintuitive thinking in the field of military history, see Victor Davis Hanson, *The Western Way of War: Infantry Battle in Classical Greece* (Oxford, 1989).

[4] The Thebans tried something similar at the Battle of Delium, when they also overloaded one of their wings but thereafter appear to have returned to a balanced line, at least until Leuctra caught the attention of everyone in the Greek world. Thucydides, *History of the Peloponnesian War*, p. 321.

[5] A small force of Spartans had been defeated and captured by the Athenians on the island of Spactaria in the late fifth century BC, but the battle was, to a considerable extent, an anomaly in Spartan history over the course of the history of that city-state. Moreover, the Spartans had not been able to fight the Athenians in their typical phalanx formation. Thucydides, *History of the Peloponnesian War*, pp. 265–290.

[6] Alexander, like Julius Caesar and Napoleon, provided a distorted model of generalship, largely because he, like the other two, was a natural – a phenomenon and an aberration of such enormous ability and instinct that even the competent can never hope to copy. For the best biography of Alexander, see Robert Lane Fox, *Alexander the Great* (London, 1973).

world largely ceased except in siege war. As a result, the eastern Mediterranean world soon went down to defeat before a superior military system – namely, the legions of Rome.

The Romans had begun their military conquests in central Italy with formations that looked much like Greek phalanxes.[7] But by the early fourth century BC, because much of their fighting occurred in the mountainous terrain of central Italy, the Romans had evolved a new and more flexible tactical formation. The heart of their legions was a tactical unit called the maniple – approximately 120 to 150 soldiers – each of which consisted of two centuries. The new legions proved superior to every army the Romans confronted over the next two and a half centuries, including, eventually, the mixed formations that Hannibal brought to the field during the Second Punic War.[8] That superiority rested not only on Rome's willingness "to pay any price, bear any burden" and the toughness of the legionnaires but also on the combination of flexibility with steadfastness that the manipular legion provided its soldiers.

However, at the end of the second century BC, a massive migration by two German tribes, the Teutons and the Cimbri, threatened Rome directly. The tactical problem confronting the Romans was the fact that, while the manipular legion provided considerable tactical flexibility and sufficient staying power against the phalanxes of Greece and Macedonia, as well as the barbarian tribes which had hitherto threatened the Mediterranean, the system failed to work against the Germans. Confronting the massed rush of the *furor Teutonicus*, the coherence of manipular legions broke down, with a resulting collapse in cohesion.

The masses of German warriors overwhelmed the legions' maniples with their first rush. At the Battle of Arausio – for the second time in eight years – a German charge overwhelmed a Roman army (this one consisting of 80,000 legionnaires). Arausio represented a defeat as big as any that Hannibal had inflicted on the Romans during the Second Punic War, but defeat by the Carthaginians had come at the hands of conventional military forces. As in the war against the Carthaginians, the survival of the Roman Republic hung in the balance. While the Romans and their military institutions were by nature conservative and slow to change, they now had to adapt to new conditions in a short period of

---

[7] They were undoubtedly influenced by watching how the Greek city-states that populated southern Italy were fighting their battles.
[8] For the Second Punic War, see Polybius, *On Roman Imperialism: The Histories of Polybius*, ed. by Alvin Bernstein (Lake Bluff, IL, 1987).

time, something the Romans had rarely been required to do in their history.

Confronting a dangerous challenge, the Romans adapted in the midst of war. One of the republic's great generals, Gaius Marius, reorganized the legions as the Germans moved to invade Italy and advance on Rome. Within a relatively short period, Marius executed a massive change in the Roman tactical system. He formed the maniples into cohorts, thus greatly increasing the legion's basic tactical formation. The new legions now possessed ten cohorts, each with a strength of approximately 500 to 600 men.[9] The new Marian legions still provided considerable tactical flexibility on the battlefield – much more than the Greek phalanx – but its staying power in meeting the shock of the Germans' first charge maximized the advantages of Roman discipline and training in combat.

The result was that Marius and his subordinate commander Cornelius Sulla destroyed the Teutons and Cimbri in two great battles. The Marian legion proved that it could maintain its cohesion in halting the first onrush of the barbarians, and then discipline and training would take over. Over the long term, the Roman legion based its tactical mobility on the cohort; it offered a system that on almost every occasion crushed the Germans and other barbarians for the next *four centuries*.[10] The genius of the Romans was that they were able to institutionalize the cohort-legion system and build the defense of their vast empire on the superlatively trained formations of that system.

By the reign of the first emperor, Caesar Augustus, the Romans had completed that process. If there were one great advantage the Romans enjoyed over their opponents in the centuries after Marius, it had little to

---

[9] The cohort system would form the model for European innovators at the beginning of the seventeenth century, when they developed the regimental system. See William McNeil, *The Pursuit of Power: Technology, Armed Force, and Society since AD 1000* (Chicago, 1982), p. 86.

[10] There was, of course, the defeat in the Teutobergwald during the reign of Augustus, but the defeat was largely the result of the incompetence of the Roman commander Publius Quinctilius Varus, who marched his three legions to their winter quarters in peacetime formation. Thereafter, for the next three centuries, the Romans consistently defeated the Germans in battle and ravaged their lands, when behavior on the right bank of the Rhine occasioned the need for a Roman response. For the most part, the Romans were content to manage the German problem through a combination of bribery, diplomacy, and political intrigue that aimed with considerable success at encouraging the Germans to fight among themselves rather than against the Romans. When necessary, however, they were willing to launch major campaigns onto German territory and slaughter the Germans in enormous numbers. By the end of the second century AD, the Romans controlled most of southern Germany and all of Austria.

do with their ability to adapt.[11] In fact, given the weight of Roman conservatism, the word *change* simply did not exist in their Weltanschauung. Nevertheless, the advantage in their discipline that the Roman legionnaires enjoyed is quite similar to that which U.S. soldiers and marines enjoyed in Iraq throughout the 2003 campaign.[12] Roman military superiority rested on a ruthless, rigorous system of training. So regularized was that system that at the height of the empire – a period of more than 200 years – the four legions deployed in Britain would have trained, looked, and fought in a fashion similar to the legions stationed in Syria on the Euphrates frontier or in the desert sands of North Africa, thousands of miles away and in entirely different geographic conditions.

In his examination of the reasons contributing to the defeat of the Jewish rebellion, the historian of the Roman-Jewish War of AD 66–70, Flavius Josephus, emphasized that the Romans' greatest advantage lay in their training regime:

> And, indeed, if anyone does but attend to the other parts of [the Romans'] military discipline, he will be forced to confess, that their obtaining so large a dominion hath been the acquisition of their valour, and not the bare gift of fortune: for they do not begin to use their weapons first in time of war, nor do they put their hands first into motion, having been idle in times of peace; but, as if their weapons were part of themselves, they never have any truce from warlike exercises; nor do they stay till times of war admonish them to use them; for their military exercises by no means fall short of the tension of real warfare, but every soldier is every day exercised, and that with real diligence, as if they were in time of war, which is why they bear the fatigue of battles so easily; ... nor would he be mistaken that would call those their exercises unbloody battles, and their battles bloody exercises.[13]

In the sense of technological innovation or adaptation, the Romans were even more conservative than the Greeks. In the first century AD, the Roman general Frontinus commented in a military treatise that "I leave aside siege works and engines, human invention having been exhausted

---

[11] For the Roman Army during the period of the empire, see particularly B. Campbell, *The Roman Army, 31 BC–AD 235* (Oxford, 1984); Adrian Goldsworthy, *In the Name of Rome: The Men Who Won the Roman Empire* (London, 2003); Graham Webster, *The Roman Imperial Army of the First and Second Centuries A.D.* (New York, 1979); Michael Grant, *The Army of the Caesars* (New York, 1974); and Laurence Keppie, *The Making of the Roman Army: From Republic to Empire* (Norman, OK, 1984).

[12] For a discussion of discipline in that campaign, see Williamson Murray and Robert H. Scales, Jr., *The Iraq War: A Military History* (Cambridge, MA, 2003).

[13] Flavius Josephus, *The Great Roman Jewish War: A.D. 66–70*, trans. by William Whiston and revised by D. S. Margoliouth (New York, 1960), p. 121.

in that realm long ago: I see no basis for further improvement."[14] From the Roman perspective, he was, of course, right, because their system of disciplined, trained military forces gave them an immense advantage over their barbarian enemies on the frontiers of the empire. Quite simply, the Romans did not have to innovate or adapt, and without an incentive for change, human beings and their institutions will rarely, if ever, alter the proven methods of the present in favor of the uncertain in the future. As long as they possessed that advantage, the Romans could hold their opponents at bay at relatively small cost.[15]

The Roman system, however, began to break down in the third century AD, when economic problems, civil and political strife involving the legions, and disease combined to erode the empire's strength and the army's discipline. That discipline had represented the glue essential to Roman military superiority for a span of more than six centuries.[16] When the glue began to fail, Roman military superiority evaporated with it. The degeneration of discipline, and hence Roman military superiority, appears to have been a process that took centuries rather than decades. In the late fourth century, the Romans suffered a series of devastating defeats against their enemies – the first under Emperor Julian at the hands of the Parthians; the second at the hands of the Goths at Adrianople, which finished off the remnants of the legionary system. The cultural biases of the ancient world appear to have pushed later emperors to risk their fragile armies in the fashion of a Caesar or Alexander, when the context of war and their ability to recruit had fundamentally changed. The price paid was the collapse of Roman civilization and power in the western empire and a long degenerative collapse in the east that took more than a millennium.[17]

---

[14] Quoted in J. E. Lendon, *Soldiers and Ghosts: A History of Battle in Classical Antiquity* (New Haven, CT, 2005), p. 7.

[15] At its height, the Roman Empire, which ranged from Portugal to the Euphrates and Tigris and from Scotland to Morocco, was defended by 30 legions and a number of auxiliary cohorts – approximately 150,000 legionaries – and 150,000 auxiliaries. That number was about the maximum an empire based on subsistence agriculture could bear without running into serious economic difficulties. Both economic difficulties and the size of the threat significantly increased in the third century with a disastrous impact on the empire. Nevertheless, the Romans were able to hold out in the west for another century, while the Eastern Roman Empire's decline lasted until the fifteenth century, when Constantinople finally fell to the Turks.

[16] No other polity in history has managed to equal the extent and time over which the Romans exercised their military superiority.

[17] I am indebted to Lendon, *Soldiers and Ghosts*, chap. 13 for this point.

What followed the collapse of the Roman Empire was a period of tribal warfare in Europe during which neither innovation nor adaptation took place, given the chaos and the inability to develop and maintain a sufficient resource base. A warrior society dominated the Western world; the results of the basing of military power on feudal levies of arrogant, willful nobles, no matter what their individual prowess, were armed mobs. In such circumstances adaptation was a matter for the individual warrior, and his actions only occasionally affected the preparation for war and the conduct of others on the battlefield.

Thus, it is difficult to talk about a consistent pattern of innovation in peacetime or adaptation in war during the Middle Ages. To a certain extent, Edward III of England, with his use of English archers and the *chevauchée,* occasioned both tactical and operational-strategic adaptation to the battlefields of the Hundred Years' War. The advantages that accrued from those adaptations provided the English, who possessed barely one-third the population of France, with a battlefield effectiveness sufficient to defeat their opponents on a consistent basis for more than 100 years.[18] The English warrior kings came close to conquering France. In the end they failed – just – but others could not copy their adaptations, because use of the long bow depended on the peculiar social and political culture of the English border areas with Wales and Scotland. Moreover, social and economic changes in their society in the sixteenth century made it impossible for the English to maintain the culture of the Welch marches, and, with that decline, archers who could handle the longbow were no longer available.[19]

In the late Middle Ages, the Swiss adapted their cultural habits to a military system quite similar to the Greek phalanx. The resulting cultural

---

[18] For the changes in medieval war that the English instituted, see particularly Clifford J. Rogers, *War Cruel and Sharp, English Strategy under Edward III, 1327–1360* (Woodbridge, UK, 2000); see also his article: "'As If a New Sun Had Risen:' England's Fourteenth Century RMA," in MacGregor Knox and Williamson Murray, eds., *The Dynamics of Military Revolution, 1300–2050* (Cambridge, 2003).

[19] The advantage the English enjoyed with the long bow could not be copied by the French, because the combination of archer and long bow represented a cultural weapon – one that demanded the archer be trained in the use of the weapon from his earliest years. It was not a weapon that could be given to a French peasant upon being called up to join the feudal levies. The result of childhood acculturation on the border areas, particularly those between Wales and England, was an archer who was armed with a bow that possessed a drawstring pull of somewhere between 100 and 140 pounds – an almost unbelievable capacity compared with modern competition bows. The ability to use that weapon with skill provided English archers with unheard of killing power on the French and Scottish battlefields of the fourteenth and fifteenth centuries.

and military system, based on the cohesion of relatives and friends, allowed the Swiss to defeat the armies of Hapsburg knights on a number of occasions. But again, others could not copy their system, dependent as it was on a cultural cohesion developed in the villages of the Swiss cantons, with much effectiveness.

There were, of course, evolutionary changes in the Middle Ages. The artisans who fashioned armor moved from mail to plate. The quality of steel improved throughout the period. And in the fourteenth century, gunpowder weapons made their appearance, aided and abetted, ironically, by improvements in metallurgy achieved in the casting of bronze bells for the great cathedrals.[20] That development provided European monarchs with a means to curb the power of the great nobility. Since bronze was enormously expensive, only the monarchies of Europe could maintain significant artillery forces; those in turn allowed them to destroy the castled walls of the nobility in a matter of days. Thus, sieges no longer had to last months or involve great expense to those who were hiring and maintaining the besiegers.

Nevertheless, the slow pace of change makes it difficult to see innovation and adaptation taking place – at least in terms that would be familiar to those who live in the twenty-first century. In 1346, French knights on horseback went down to disastrous defeat at Crecy at the hands of the English archers. Ten years later at Poitiers, they went down to another disastrous defeat under the arrow storm – this time on foot. Approximately 70 years later, using both cavalry and infantry, they suffered another major defeat at Agincourt. Like too many subsequent French armies, they appear "to have learned nothing and forgotten everything."[21] There was clearly neither adaptation in war nor innovation in peacetime taking place within the French monarchy's military institutions.

Adaptation and the Military to the Nineteenth Century

The first great waves of military innovation and change in the West came in the sixteenth and seventeenth centuries, particularly the latter. Those innovations played a major role in the creation of the

---

[20] McNeil, *The Pursuit of Power*, p. 86.
[21] The phrase was first used to describe the Bourbons on their return to France in 1814 after the overthrow of Napoleon. Their incompetent political actions allowed Napoleon to return to power for 100 days and again threaten Europe's stability – at least until the Duke of Wellington and Field Marshal Blücher solved the problem of Napoleon for Europe at Waterloo.

modern state and its military institutions. Those "new model" armies and navies, like the legions of the Roman Empire, possessed both civil and military discipline.[22] Like legionaries, beginning with the Swedes, they wore a common uniform. More important, they were subordinate to state authority in both internal and external matters and, therefore, obeyed its dictates. The most important step came with the deliberate reinvention of the Roman legion, now equipped with gunpowder weapons.[23]

At the end of the sixteenth century, Maurice of Orange had the Roman marching and organizational commands translated from Latin into Dutch so that he could drill his soldiers according to Roman tactical patterns.[24] These processes of innovation and adaptation were important because generals could now thin out their battle lines with better disciplined and drilled formations of the new pattern armies.[25] Thus, their armies could maximize the potential of gunpowder weapons. Gustavus Adolphus, particularly, drew out this innovation to its full potential and won a series of devastating victories over the armies of the Catholic Hapsburgs in northern and central Germany before his death at the Battle of Lützen in November 1632.[26]

---

[22] For a discussion of the role of military revolutions and revolutions in military affairs in the military history of the West, see particularly Williamson Murray and MacGregor Knox, "Thinking about Revolutions in Warfare," in Knox and Murray, eds., *The Dynamics of Military Revolution*. Among the many books dealing with various facets of this crucial aspect of Western military history, see particularly McNeil, *The Pursuit of Power*; Geoffrey Parker, *Military Innovation and the Rise of the West* (Cambridge, 1996); and Clifford J. Rogers, ed., *The Military Revolutions Debate* (Boulder, CO, 1995).

[23] For a first-rate examination of the development of war in the Renaissance, see Thomas F. Arnold, *Renaissance at War* (London, 2001).

[24] Hans Delbrück, *History of the Art of War*, vol. 4, *The Dawn of Modern Warfare*, trans. by Walter J. Renfroe, Jr. (Lincoln, NE, 1985), pp. 157–159.

[25] What one may be dealing with here is adoption of ancient practices rather than the adaptation and innovation, although once the Europeans had adopted the Roman approach to discipline, adaptation and innovation then took over. I am indebted to my colleague Jim Kurtz for this point.

[26] In his groundbreaking 1956 lecture, Michael Roberts pointed to the innovations of Gustavus Adolphus as representing a military revolution. See Michael Roberts, *The Military Revolution, 1560–1660* (Belfast, 1956). The historian Clifford Rogers was the first to point out – in a talk at the Association of Military Historians in spring 1991 – that there was a larger pattern of revolutions throughout Western military history than just a military revolution in the sixteenth and seventeenth centuries. For the published version of Rogers's talk, see C. J. Rogers, ed., *The Military Revolution Debate* (Boulder, CO, 1995).

Tactics and techniques stabilized at the end of the seventeenth century as technological change ebbed.[27] The last technological innovation came with the invention of the ring bayonet, which allowed the musket to serve as both a gunpowder weapon and a pike. The vast changes of the seventeenth century allowed the European powers to contest with each other for control of the globe from the forests of North America, to the jungles of India, to the spice islands of the Indies. Yet, between 1700 and 1815, there were few changes in the weapons with which the Europeans fought.[28] More than a century later, Wellington's troops on the Peninsula were still using the "Brown Bess" musket, a weapon similar to the muskets which Marlborough's troops had used against the French at Blenheim in 1705.[29]

Innovations and adaptations did take place, however, in the organization of military forces, as well as in how states paid for the wars they fought. With respect to the latter, the British gained a major advantage over the French when they radically altered how they paid for the wars of the eighteenth century – in effect inventing the first modern system of finance.[30] That system rested on a far more coherent framework of both taxation and borrowing on the nation's wealth to meet the expenses of major conflicts. The failure of the French monarchy to create a similar system eventually led to its financial collapse and revolution in 1789. With respect to the former, the division and corps system developed by French Revolutionary armies – further refined by Napoleon – represented

---

[27] These revolutions involved, among other factors, the technological (artillery), the tactical and organizational (the reinvention of the cohort in the battalion), the psychological (the imposition of civil and military discipline), and the architectural (the angled-bastion fortress).

[28] Nor did naval technology change much during this period; the great adaptations and developments in ships occurred over the course of the seventeenth century.

[29] The best account of the War of Spanish Succession, which was the first global war, remains Winston S. Churchill's *The Duke of Marlborough*, 4 vols. (London, 1932–1937); for a modern history of the conflict, see David Chandler's excellent *The Campaigns of Marlborough* (London, 1973).

[30] The invention of modern governmental financing emerged from the British need for consistent funding and large sums of money to keep a naval fleet, as well as to support military operations on the continent. In fact, this innovation was one of the major factors in Britain's success in the great wars for European and world supremacy that raged between 1700 and 1815. In this regard, see, among others, John Brewer, *The Sinews of Power: War, Money, and the English State, 1688–1783* (New York, 1989), and D. W. Jones, *War and Economy in the Age of William III and Marlborough* (Oxford, 1988).

a major change in the operational framework within which the Europeans fought.

The most truly revolutionary change in the "European way of war" since the creation of the modern state came in the domestic political context within which wars were fought in the last decade of the eighteenth century. The French Revolution upset the social and political framework within which European states had conducted their wars since the Treaty of Westphalia in 1648.[31] When the revolutionaries in Paris, confronting military defeat in the field with Prussian and Austrian armies invading northern France, decreed the *levée en masse*, they were executing the most fundamental adaptation – namely, in the basic nature of the relationship between the individual and the state in wartime. The French Assembly explicitly decreed that everyone was now at the service of the nation:

> From this moment, until our enemies have been driven from the territory of the Republic, the entire French nation is permanently called to the colors. The young men will go into battle; married men will forge weapons and transport supplies; women will make tents and uniforms, and serve in the hospitals; children will make old cloth into bandages; old men will have themselves carried to the public squares to rouse the courage of the warriors and preach hatred of kings and the unity of the Republic.[32]

As Clausewitz suggested in *On War*, the French revolutionaries radically altered the price of admission to European wars by hugely increasing its cost in economic resources and lives, as well as financial resources. Ironically, the French forced even the most conservative regimes of Europe eventually to adapt their political and military systems to confront new realities:

> Suddenly war again became the business of the people – a people of thirty millions, all of whom considered themselves to be citizens.... The people became a participant in war; instead of governments and armies as heretofore, the full weight of the nation was thrown into the balance. The resources and efforts now available for use surpassed all conventional limits; nothing now impeded the vigor with which war could be waged, and consequently the opponents of France faced the utmost peril.[33]

---

[31] For an examination of the military impact of the French Revolution, see MacGregor Knox, "Mass Politics and Nationalism as Military Revolution: The French Revolution and After," in Knox and Murray, eds., *The Dynamics of Military Revolution*.
[32] Quoted in Stanley Chodorov and MacGregor Knox, *The Mainstream of Civilization since 1660* (6th edition, New York, 1994), p. 595.
[33] Clausewitz, *On War*, p. 592.

Furthermore, it was "[n]ot until [Europe's] statesmen had at last perceived the nature of the forces that had emerged in France" that they could meet the French on an even footing – at least when Napoleon was not present.[34] That adaptation at the strategic and political levels, however, took nearly 20 years, as well as innumerable humiliations and military defeats at the hands of the armies of the French Revolution and Napoleon, before the opponents of France finally altered their systems to handle the political and social dictates of a life-and-death struggle. Yet, these adaptations occurred only at the highest levels of policy and strategy. As suggested earlier, the British soldiers, who met and defeated the final charges of Napoleonic fury at Waterloo, represented in their drill and performance no technological and little tactical improvement over the British soldiers and units who had fought at Blenheim, Ramilles, Oudenarde, and Malplaquet 110 years earlier in the War of Spanish Succession.[35]

Nevertheless, if changes in technology exercised little influence over the battlefields of this period, they did play a crucial part in winning the war for the Allies. At the same time the terrible wars against the French were occurring, the Industrial Revolution was changing the way the British economy worked in fundamental ways. By revolutionizing the means of production, it altered the basis on which human economic activity had rested since the dawn of time – namely, human and animal muscle power. In effect, the economic and financial gains that this revolution in economic affairs and technology provided to the British allowed their government to provide the financial subsidies that supported the great coalitions against the French, including the last one that brought Napoleon's empire to destruction.

The Invention of Modern War: The Crimea, the Civil War, and the German Wars of Unification

At the midpoint of the nineteenth century, technology intervened on the battlefield. This time, by forcing radical reassessments of hoary tactical assumptions that had held true for the previous century and a half, it demanded that adaptation take place. That requirement should have become clear in the Crimean War. Unfortunately for those involved, the

---

[34] Ibid., p. 609.
[35] These battles had represented devastating defeats for the armies of Louis XIV. For the nature of Marlborough's victories, see Chandler, *Marlborough as Military Commander*.

armies that fought in the Crimea proved incapable of recognizing the need for major adaptations.[36]

In only in a few instances did adaptations take place. The British and French armies possessed rifled muskets with the ability to reach out and kill Russians at ranges reaching up to 300 yards because of the invention of the Minié ball. The Russians, on the other hand, still equipped their soldiers with old-fashioned smooth-bore muskets that could only strike back at ranges well under 100 yards. The result, particularly at the Battle of Alma, was that the British Army's "thin red line" took on and destroyed massed columns of Russian infantry. In such a one-sided conflict, there appears to have been little tactical adaptation on either side. Thereafter, the war degenerated into the brutal siege of Sevastopol that lasted through the winter, as the Russians no longer dared to take on the Anglo-French armies directly.

A failure to adapt was certainly not the case in the American Civil War.[37] Here the two great military-civil revolutions of the late eighteenth century came together in a fashion they had not done in the wars between 1792 and 1815.[38] The Industrial Revolution with its technological impact forced the contending sides to adapt – although relatively slowly. Moreover, the impact of popular nationalism resulted in the mobilization of societies and economies in both North and South.[39] Here the North enjoyed an important advantage because its progress in industrialization was far in advance of what had occurred in the Southern states before the war. Moreover, the war occurred over continental distances, which helps to explain why it lasted for four bloody years.[40] In conceptualizing the extent of adaptation during the Civil War, it is not a stretch to suggest that the armies of 1861 were closer to the armies of Revolutionary France in 1793 than they were to those of 1865. Likewise, the military power the

---

[36] For the Crimean War, see, among others: Christopher Hibbert, *The Destruction of Lord Raglan: A Tragedy of the Crimean War, 1854–1855* (London, 1961); Cecil Woodham Smith, *The Reason Why* (New York, 1960); and Andrew D. Lambert, *The Crimean War: British Grand Strategy against Russia, 1853–1856* (Manchester, 1996).

[37] In this regard, see Mark Grimsley, "Surviving Military Revolution, The U.S. Civil War," in Knox and Murray, eds., *The Dynamics of Military Revolution*.

[38] In the introduction to *The Dynamics of Military Revolution*, MacGregor Knox and this author termed the combination of the French Revolution with the fruits of the Industrial Revolution as the third great military revolution that changed the calculus within which Western military institutions would wage war. See ibid., chap. 1.

[39] This was less true in the North than the South.

[40] See Williamson Murray, "Why It Took the North So Long to Win," *Military History Quarterly*, Autumn 1989.

The Historical Framework of Adaptation

North projected in 1865 was closer to that of Europe's military in 1914 than it was to the armies that fought at Bull Run in 1861. The North's military power that crushed the rebellion rested on a mobilization of popular will and immense industrial power that undergirded a logistical infrastructure built around the railroad and steamboat that allowed the projection of the North's armies over continental distances.

The first problem – and the most intractable – to confront the opposing sides was the raising of great mass armies with which to fight the conflict. In fact, there was no basis of experience on either side on which to establish the kind of military power the war would require. The frontier constabulary that was the U.S. Army provided little more than the glimmerings of how to organize and discipline bodies of troops.[41] As for tactics and operations, irrelevant historical lessons drawn from the myths of Napoleonic warfare provided what little guidance there was.[42] Certainly service on the frontier did little to prepare the eventual commanders of Civil War armies for the operational and logistical tasks that the war presented. Given the fact that rifled weapons now possessed at least three times the range and accuracy of Napoleonic muskets, there

---

[41] Bruce Catton recounts the following incident that suggests the difficulties that many regular officers faced in dealing with volunteer troops in the first years of the Civil War. "The army had been pushing along for days and the men were dead on their feet. Near midnight one exhausted column dropped by the roadside for a short breather.... [The corps commander, Major General Charles C.] Gilbert saw the men and was offended that nobody bothered to call them to attention and offer a salute so he collared the first officer he saw...and angrily demanded: 'what regiment is this ?'... 'who in the hell are you?' 'Major General Gilbert, by God sir. Give me your sword, sir, you are under arrest.' The racket roused the regiment's colonel, who came up to defend his captain. Gilbert turned on him furiously, saying that he should have had the regiment lining the road at present-arms when the corps commander rode by. The colonel replied with some heat:... he 'would not hold a dress parade at midnight for any damn fool living.'" Bruce Catton, *This Hallowed Ground, The Story of the Union Side of the Civil War* (New York, 1956), p. 174.

[42] The Swiss commentator and theorist Baron de Jomini, although largely faulty in his analysis of Napoleonic warfare, provided what little guidance there was to the generals on both sides in 1861, but by 1862, those who were in leadership positions were forging their own view of war. The Israeli historian of military thought Azar Gat has commented on Jomini in the following terms: "Jomini claimed that all military history from Scipio and Caesar to Napoleon had been guided by the principles he had extracted from Napoleonic warfare, and referred to all periods of history that clearly contradicted this claim as undeveloped or degenerate.... Rather than understanding Frederick [the Great's] strategy against the background of the political and military conditions of the time, Jomini maintained that Frederick had not been operating according to Napoleonic principles because military thought had not yet developed enough to recognize these principles." Azar Gat, *A History of Military Thought: From the Enlightenment to the Cold War* (Oxford, 2001), p. 124.

was a clear mismatch between the tactical framework and the new reality of greater battlefield lethality.

At Shiloh in the west in April 1862 and Antietam in the east in September 1862, the opposing sides stood in the open waiting for the enemy's attack and then blasted each other to pieces.[43] This was indeed the crudest sort of learning on the battlefield. Yet, the difference between Antietam in September 1862 and Fredericksburg, which occurred three months later, was stark. By December 1862 the Confederates were entrenching themselves in positions which overlooked the town of Fredericksburg and provided them maximum protection to slaughter attacking Union formations – a complete change from their defensive approach at Antietam three months earlier, when they had stood out in the open from the beginning to the end of the battle.[44]

By 1864, it had become standard practice for the armies on both sides to throw up entrenchments to protect themselves against an attack immediately upon halting. In 1864 a Union officer observed at the beginning of one of Hood's ferocious attacks on Union forces encircling Atlanta that one-third of the surprised troops appeared immediately to run away. In reality, they were not fleeing but gathering rocks and fencing material to build a palisade in front of the firing line that their comrades had already formed to meet the onrushing Confederates.[45] By 1864, the armies on both sides had become so skilled at constructing defensive positions quickly that attacks on prepared positions rarely, if ever, succeeded.

---

[43] The paintings at the visitor's center at Antietam indicate that the Confederates simply stood out in the open waiting for Sedgwick's divisional attack to reach them. The same approach was used by both sides at the Battle of Shiloh in the west in April 1862. After those seminal experiences, the armies on the opposing sides recognized at the lowest levels that modern firepower was simply too lethal to receive an enemy's charge in the open. The result was the rapid construction of defensive positions when advances came to a halt. By 1864, Civil War troops were able to construct fortified lines in a matter of hours that could not be taken by direct assault. See Grant, *The Personal Memoirs of U.S. Grant*, vol. 2, pp. 204–205.

[44] In one section of the Confederate defenses on the right flank of Lee's Fredericksburg position, Confederate troops dug zigzag trenches – they had been one of the units outflanked in the sunken road and slaughtered by the Union troops, who had lapped their flank in the early afternoon of the Battle of Antietam, where the Antietam tower is presently located. I am indebted to Professor Jay Luvaas, formerly of the Army War College, for this story.

[45] This episode is cited in Philip Sheiman's senior history thesis at Yale University, "The Defensive Offense: A Military Analysis of the Siege of Atlanta," 1983.

In his memoirs U.S. Grant describes the defensive preparations of the soldiers of the Army of the Potomac, when on the march, in the following terms:

> In every change of position or halt for the night, whether confronting the enemy or not, the moment arms were stacked the [soldiers of the Army of the Potomac] intrenched themselves. For this purpose they would build up piles of logs or rails if they could be found in their front, and dig a ditch, throwing the dirt forward on the timbers. Thus the digging they did counted in making a depression to stand in, and increased the elevation in front of them. It was wonderful how quickly they could in this way construct defenses of considerable strength.[46]

Like the Roman legionnaires who dug themselves in every night in the great march camps, the soldiers of the Civil War sought to protect themselves by digging. Well might historians comment that "the more things change, the more they stay the same." One of the few occasions where a direct attack succeeded in the last year of the war occurred at Spotsylvania Courthouse, where Emory Upton launched a massed brigade column at dawn's first light. He succeeded largely because his attack caught the Confederates by surprise. The attack created a breakthrough in the center of Lees's line. But that success was much the exception.

The result of the difficulties involved in tactical adaptation was a war of attrition that inflicted horrendous casualties on the opposing sides. Only Sherman's brilliantly executed campaign of 1864, which devastated the South's heartland, eventually led to the Confederacy's collapse and Union victory.[47] In retrospect, tactical adaptation was slow and uncertain throughout the conflict – perhaps largely because of the extraordinary nature of the problems of mobilizing and creating military instruments, where nothing similar had existed before. Moreover, those institutions had to fight over continental distances. In other respects, however, adaptations such as the creation of the Union's riverine navy, so important in Grant's campaign to open the Mississippi, were extraordinary for their technological and tactical adaptations to the problems the war raised in the western theater.

---

[46] Grant, *The Personal Memoirs of U.S. Grant*, vol. 2, p. 205.
[47] For the adaptations that took place in how the Union Army treated civilians during the course of the war, see Mark Grimsley, *The Hard Hand of War: Union Military Policy toward Southern Civilians, 1861–1865* (Cambridge, 1995).

So, too, eventually with field fortifications. The trench systems that enveloped Petersburg and Richmond in late 1864 and early 1865 certainly presaged what was to happen during the First World War. One might also note the extraordinary adaptation of railroads to the movement and supplying of troops over great distances. The movement in September 1863 of two corps from the Army of the Potomac to redress the strategic results of the Union defeat at the Battle of Chickamauga is a case in point. Forty hours after Lincoln and Stanton had made the decision to move the two corps (20,000 men, their horses, wagons, and artillery), the first trains left Culpepper, Virginia, on the way to Bridgeport, Tennessee, a distance of 1,233 miles. Eleven days later, the final portion of the movement arrived at the base camp near the Tennessee River.[48] Finally, the telegraph allowed the coordination of armies over continental distances, a factor that the Union would not take full advantage of until 1864. Both the railroad and the telegraph proved to be essential enablers to the projection of the Union's military power into the South's heartland.

In 1864, Prussia and Austria-Hungary went to war with Denmark, ostensibly to uphold the rights of Germans who lived in the duchy of Schleswig-Holstein. This conflict certainly looked much more like the European conception of war than the messy and lengthy, ill-disciplined bloodbath taking place in the United States. But unlike most of the European wars over the previous two centuries, the war with Denmark occurred within a brilliant strategic framework – one created by the Prussian chancellor, Otto von Bismarck. For the three wars that Prussia fought between 1864 and 1871, the "Iron Chancellor" isolated his country's enemies politically and strategically, so that they had to fight alone against the Prussian Army.

A first-class military organization buttressed Bismarck's strategy. The army, under the military genius of the chief of the Prusso-German general staff, Graf Helmut von Moltke, took advantage of the strategic framework that Bismarck created. In the period before 1864, its leaders, particularly Moltke, had prepared the army by seeking to turn the technological revolution to Prussia's advantage.[49] Thus, the Prussians possessed

---

[48] Thomas Weber, *The Northern Railroads in the Civil War, 1861–1865* (Bloomington, IN, 1952), pp. 181–184.

[49] For the Prussian innovations during the period before the wars of unification, see Dennis Schowalter's brilliant, groundbreaking study: *Railroads and Rifles, Soldiers, Technology, and the Unification of Germany* (Hamden, CT, 1975).

the only army in Europe capable of fully utilizing the transportation revolution that railroads had created.[50] On the opposing sides, the armies Moltke confronted remained ensconced in conceptions of war rooted in the first decade of the nineteenth century.

Thus, the Prussians went to war in 1864 (against Denmark), 1866 (against Austria), and 1870–71 (against France) with enormous strategic and operational advantages over their opponents. In 1866 their possession of the bolt-action needle gun provided a tactical advantage over their Austrian opponents. In the war's early skirmishes as well as at the Battle of Königrätz, the Prussians slaughtered their Austrian opponents by the thousands.[51] Nevertheless, it was Bismarck's brilliant strategy that isolated Austria and its allies among the German states from the other major powers. Then, when Prussian arms had achieved a signal victory, he brought the war to a successful and immediate conclusion and, to the outrage of the Prussian generals, prevented them from celebrating their victory with a march down the boulevards of Vienna.

However, in 1870, the French *chassepôt* rifle was superior to the Prussian needle gun. Yet, the operational performance of the Prussians was so superior to that of the French that within two months Moltke's Prusso-German armies had encircled the two main French armies in Metz and Sedan, where both eventually surrendered. Without trained cadres, the French were then unable to put together a successful resistance despite a *levée en masse*. The result was that the Prusso-German Army had defeated the French in the opening moves of the conflict, victories that the peace of 1871 solidified – at least until 1945.[52]

---

[50] This author was asked in fall 1980 by a scholar at the Militärgeschichtliche Forschungsamt whether the American railroads had been laid out for their military utility similar to the way the Prussians had laid out their railroads. The question and the answer – that they had not been laid out in the American case with their military utility in mind – speak volumes for the differences between the European and the American Industrial Revolutions. It is worth noting that the chief of the Prussian Great General Staff, Count Helmut von Moltke, played a major role in the construction of Prussia's railroad system. See Schowalter, *Railroads and Rifles*, pp. 19–74.

[51] For the Seven Weeks' War, see Geoffrey Warrow, *The Austro-Prussian War: Austria's War with Prussia and Italy in 1866* (Cambridge, 1996).

[52] The war would burble on into the spring of 1871 as the Prusso-German armies besieged Paris, and the French attempted to drive them away from the capital. But with the loss of most of their officer corps and cadres in the Battles of Sedan and Metz, where virtually the entire French Imperial Army found itself besieged by the Prusso-Germans, the French, despite massive mobilization of their population and resources, were never able to put together effective military forces. The best book on the Franco-Prussian

The Run-up to World War I

The startling suddenness with which Moltke's armies achieved their victories had unfortunate consequences. First, it persuaded most of the senior Prusso-German military leaders to believe that military force alone had achieved victory and that Bismarck's strategic policies had played only a subsidiary role in Prussia's successes. Second, it convinced most of Europe's military leaders that short, decisive wars still remained a real possibility. Thus, from their perspective, there were few lessons to be learned from the American Civil War, in which, as Moltke suggested, ill-trained and ill-disciplined militias had bashed each other to pieces because of their lack of serious professional leadership and training.[53]

The third impact was to push the other European armies to establish staff colleges and create staffs similar to those the Great General Staff the Prussians had possessed during the wars of unification. But they copied the form rather than the substance of the Prussian general staff system.[54] The latter emphasized the early identification and education of the brightest officers to serve as future planners *and* commanders. Their imitators among the other armies in Europe established staff colleges without the emphasis on identifying intellectual excellence and military character. As a result, staff colleges became training rather than educational institutions, not only in Europe but in the United States as well. The emphasis outside of Germany was simply on producing officers who knew how to perform good staff work, mostly by rote.

That said, the Prussian general staff remained narrowly focused on planning for mobilization, deployment, and campaigns, while the study of strategy – not to mention the wider issues of war, politics, and

---

war remains Michael Howard, *The Franco-Prussian War: The German Invasion of France, 1870–1871* (London, 1961). Geoffrey Warrow's *The Franco-Prussian War: The German Conquest of France in 1870–1871* (Cambridge, 2003) and Alistair Horne's *The Fall of Paris, The Siege and the Commune, 1870–1871* (New York, 1965) are also worth consulting.

[53] It was not just the Europeans who drew such lessons. The Union general Emory Upton argued in his postwar writings that the high losses both sides suffered during the war had been the result of a lack of a large professional army in the United States before the war broke out. His attitudes were to remain embedded in the U.S. Army throughout the course of the twentieth century and significantly affected many of the choices that that organization was to make in that period, and also poisoned the relations between the army and its reserve components, especially the National Guard, well into the twentieth century.

[54] This was also true of the American Army's Command and General Staff College and the Naval War College at Newport, where performance in the classroom translated into promotion in the officer corps.

strategy – failed to appear in the curriculum of the *Kriegsakademie*. The panzer general Leo Geyer von Schwepenburg commented in a letter to the British military pundit Basil Liddell Hart about his educational experiences at that institution immediately before the First World War. "You will be horrified to hear that I have never read Clausewitz or Delbrück or Haushofer. The opinion on Clausewitz in our general staff was that [he was] a theoretician to be read by professors."[55] The lack of a more systematic study of war at the strategic and political levels goes far toward explaining why the Germans were to do so badly in adapting to the problems at the strategic and political levels that they were to encounter in both world wars. Thus, the Germans repeated every mistake in World War II they had made in World War I (with a few additional ones thrown in – a record of strategic ineffectiveness hardly worthy of emulation).[56]

During the interwar period between 1871 and 1914, not even the German Army possessed the ability to analyze what had happened on the battlefields of the last war and its implications for the future development of combat capabilities. This factor reflected the deeply inbred conservative cultures of Europe's military institutions. On one hand, they were attempting to develop a modern sense of professionalism, while on the other they were grappling with the ever-increasing pace of technological change.

Much of what might have been learned from a careful analysis of the Wars of Unification disappeared in the smoke thrown up by the desire of the Prusso-German victors to create new myths. The terrible casualties borne by the Prussian infantry at battles such as St. Privat and Gravellotte became the heroic story of Prussian infantry overcoming the horrific difficulties of the battlefield. The dismal performance of the Prussian cavalry throughout the war against the French soon became the heroic story of brilliant, colorful charges that swept the French away in a cloud of dust. Thus, in the immediate decades after the Franco-Prussian War, the Prusso-Germans seem to have drawn romantic, but wrong, lessons from their last war.[57]

---

[55] Letter from Leo Geyer von Schweppenburg to Basil Liddell Hart, 1948, BHLH Archives, King's College Archives, London, 9/24/61, p. 32.

[56] For a discussion of this issue, see Williamson Murray, "The Problem of German Military Effectiveness, 1900–1945," in *German Military Effectiveness* (Baltimore, MD, 1992), chap 1. One might also note the peculiar military culture that the Kaiser Reich developed. In this regard, see the brilliant study by Isabel V. Hull, *Absolute Destruction: Military Culture and the Practices of War in Imperial Germany* (Ithaca, NY, 2005).

[57] In this case, as with so much of the history of other military institutions during the course of the twentieth century, the Germans studied the last war and learned the

If the Germans, who at least possessed a real staff system, drew the wrong lessons, the other European armies developed even faultier pictures. As the comment by Geyer von Schwenburg suggests, European military cultures were not only ahistorical but anti-intellectual as well. Thus, European armies entered the long 43-year period of peace following the Franco-Prussian War with little understanding of the potential capabilities modern technology and industrialization were raising. Nor were they capable of recognizing, despite the brutal warnings of the Boer War and the Russo-Japanese War, the implications of the drastic changes that were occurring in combat capabilities.

None, including the Germans, possessed the mechanisms to adapt or innovate in the face of the greatest period of technological change the world had ever seen. In the period between 1871 and 1914, revolutionary changes in technology occurred at a dizzying pace, not just in terms of weapons systems but in the form and structure of European and American societies and their economic systems. In the largest sense, the medical revolution and the rapid pace of industrialization led to huge increases in the manpower available to armies. Moreover, modern industrialized societies possessed staying power that would allow them to wage war almost indefinitely without the danger of financial or economic collapse.[58]

For the military the changes represented a revolution of immense proportions. Armies replaced the primitive bolt-action rifles of 1871 with

---

wrong lessons – those that made the various branches feel good about their increasingly faulty assumptions about the nature of future war. For an important book about this period, see Eric Dorn Brose, *The Politics of Military Technology in Germany during the Machine Age, 1870–1918* (Oxford, 2001), p. 224. See also Antulio J. Echevarria, II, *After Clausewitz: German Military Thinkers before the Great War* (Lawrence, KS, 2000). Echevarria focuses on the few thinkers who attempted to grapple with the problems raised by the accelerating pace of military technology that was altering the face of the world. But it is also clear that those thinkers had relatively little influence in shaping the attitudes of the great mass of officers. For an understanding of the culture of the German Army and its pernicious impact on the course of German history in the first half of the twentieth century, see Hull, *Absolute Destruction*, one of the most important scholarly works on the German Army to appear in the past several decades.

[58] Ironically, most of the so-called experts argued that modern industrialized society was incapable of standing up to the pressures of prolonged conflict. Moreover, conservative officer corps argued that city-bred youths would not possess the psychological or physical stamina to stand up to the demands of modern war – a reflection of the Social Darwinism that passed for serious social science in the early twentieth century. The German Army, for example, drafted fewer of the urban working population because of a pervasive belief in the officer corps that youths drawn from such a background were ill disciplined compared with youths drawn from the peasant population of Germany's farms. All of this was sheer and utter nonsense.

magazine-fed weapons that could kill at distances up to 1,000 yards. The *mitrailleuse* found itself replaced by rapid-fire machine guns; soldiers no longer had to re-lay howitzers with recoil mechanisms after each firing and could aim them indirectly from defilade positions; artillery could now reach out far into enemy rear areas; nitroglycerine provided unheard of explosive potential for bombarding enemy positions: smokeless powder hid defenders from observation; the radio possessed the potential to replace the telegraph; the internal combustion engine made its appearance with implications not only for ground transportation but manned flight as well; steam power combined with increasingly sophisticated turbine and ship design to revolutionize the weight and speed of naval vessels; and finally the submarine made its baleful (at least to admirals) appearance.

In naval terms alone, the experiences of the admirals who led the navies to war in 1914 in the course of their careers, many of which had begun in the early 1880s, suggest the extent of the revolution. When they had entered their respective navies, their ships still had sails, could barely reach speeds of ten knots, and possessed smooth-bore guns, which barely reached out to targets 1,000 yards distant and weighed under 5,000 tons. By 1914 they were commanding fleets of huge battleships. The most modern British and German *Dreadnoughts* were approaching 30,000 tons, could reach speeds of 25 knots, and possessed main gun armament of 15 inches that could hit enemy ships at distances on the order of 25,000 yards.[59] These great behemoths possessed supporting casts of cruisers, destroyers, and torpedo craft that could reach speeds in excess of 30 knots. And finally, the appearance of the submarine suggested entirely new directions for the conduct of naval war.

Surely, part of the explanation for the failure to adapt with sufficient speed during the First World War had much to do with the lack of hands-on experience in combat with the new weapons among the military leaders and general staffs who went to war in 1914.[60] But that is not the only explanation. To put it bluntly, the officer corps of Europe's armies and navies enthusiastically substituted a bureaucratized focus on the peacetime routines of soldiering, or the naval equivalent, at the expense of seriously coming to grips with the technological revolution that was swirling around them. Europe's military organizations also forgot much of the relevant historical past in peacetime pursuits of parades and polishing brass.

---

[59] For a discussion of the implications, see Holger H. Herwig, "The Battlefleet Revolution, 1885–1914," in Knox and Murray, eds., *The Dynamics of Military Revolution*.

[60] For further discussion of these issues, see the next chapter of this work.

The Royal Navy still lionized Admiral Horatio Nelson. It had, however, almost completely forgotten the tactics, leadership qualities, and initiative that had marked Nelson's decentralized, aggressive combat philosophy. It was the Royal Navy's tactical initiative that resulted in the devastating victories the British won over the French at the Battles of the Nile and Trafalgar. A century later, the Royal Navy's admirals displayed little of that quality at Dogger Bank (1915) or Jutland (1916), as those sea battles unfolded.[61]

In terms of the armies, not surprisingly, the British led the way with their contempt for "inky-fingered" officers – those who read books.[62] Leo Amery's description of the British Army between the Crimean War and World War I may have been unfair, but only slightly:

> [The British army's role was] less as an instrument for war... than as a state established institution to be maintained and perpetuated for its own sake. Regarded as an institution or society, the British Army of 1899 was undoubtedly a success.... As a fighting machine it was a sham. The number of full-grown efficient soldiers was small, the military training of all ranks inadequate, and the whole organized on no definitely thought out principle of Imperial defence, and prepared for no eventualities.[63]

Admittedly, the British Army's role only shifted to a serious commitment to the European continent in the first decade of the twentieth century. Nevertheless, it was an army that valued form over substance, birth and connection over competence, and glitter over professionalism.

If the British were openly contemptuous of serious study, the Germans were not much better. The period following the Franco-Prussian War represented a flight from reality with the various combat branches engaging in a search for the irrelevant. Not until immediately before the outbreak of the First World War did the Germans return to a more reasonable approach to the tactical problems raised by advances in military technology. As one historian has suggested about the German army: "The prewar reforms and innovations... were not 'too little,' but they came 'too late' to completely root out the effects of decades of interservice rivalry and conservative, sometime technophobic thinking."[64]

---

[61] See particularly, Andrew Gordon, *The Rules of the Game: The Royal Navy and the Battle of Jutland* (London, 1998).
[62] I am indebted to Major General Jonathan Bailey, British Army, for this wonderful phrase that was common throughout his army at the beginning of the twentieth century.
[63] Brian Bond, *The Victorian Army and the Staff College, 1854–1914* (London, 1972), p. 181.
[64] See particularly Brose, *The Kaiser's Army*, p. 224.

Nevertheless, as one of the recent histories of German military thought after Clausewitz has suggested:

> On the whole, military theorists of the turn of the century, though not without their faults and shortcomings, appear to have been exceptional in many ways. No more than a few score existed in each army, and they were more reflective and usually more well-read than their colleagues. However, such attributes could work against them in a [military] culture that placed more value on action than on deliberation. In many ways, it is a pity that the armies that went to war in 1914 did not have more of them, or did not pay attention to their ideas at least. Had they done so, the lethality and intensity of the military operations of the First World War might not have come as such a surprise.[65]

It was not as if the European armies had not received a salient warning that many, if not all, of their assumptions about the nature of the future battlefield were faulty. The Boer War gave the British firsthand experience as to the lethality of the modern weapons – at least in the period of conventional military operations. But the period of "postconflict" guerrilla warfare allowed too many senior officers to forget the dark days at the Modder River, Magersfontein, and Spion Kop.[66] At least the British did take away from South Africa the importance of disciplined, aimed rifle fire. In the 1914 battles, their troops fired at such a rapid rate and with such accuracy that German officers believed their enemies had equipped themselves with twice to three times the number of machine guns they actually possessed.[67]

If the Boer War provided some warning, it was nothing compared with what Manchuria in 1904 and 1905 should have suggested. Virtually every major difficulty that emerged in the first years of the First World War was apparent in the desperate fighting in Manchuria. Moreover, the European observers identified those difficulties in their reports back to London, Paris, Berlin, and Moscow. Yet the war offices and armies in Europe remained largely deaf to what was happening in Asia.[68] One of the more unfortunate lessons was that because of the combination of the

---

[65] Echevarria, *After Clausewitz*, p. 224.
[66] The experiences in South Africa made an indelible impression on some of the junior officers. Swinton, who would go on to become one of the inventors of the tank in the First World War, wrote one of the great classics of military history, *The Defence of Duffer's Drift* (London, 1907), to convey his thoughts on the war.
[67] Which may explain why the Germans were to increase so drastically the number of machine guns per battalion in 1915.
[68] For an examination of what was not learned, see Jonathan Bailey, "Military History and the Pathology of Lessons Learned: The Russo-Japanese War, A Case Study," in Williamson Murray and Richard Hart Sinnreich, eds., *The Past as Prologue: The Importance of History to the Military Profession* (Cambridge, 2006).

supposed political and financial need for a short war and the lethality of modern war, armies in a future war in Europe would need to display an almost Kamikaze-like spirit to achieve victory.[69] That appeared to be the lesson with Czarist Russia's collapse into revolution in 1905, while the Japanese victories on the battlefield were ascribed to the willingness of their soldiers to charge into the face of machine guns. To many generals in the prewar period, defeat of the enemy would require throwing the last battalion into the slaughter and, by staying the tactical course, winning the victory that the theories of short, decisive war had promised.

World War I

The record of military organizations in adapting to the realities of war has been even more difficult – and dismal – in the twentieth century than was the case in earlier centuries. Because the case studies in this volume involve military institutions and the adaptation processes in the modern period, there is little reason to examine in detail here the problems of adaptation, their origins and causes, their impact on the various levels of war, and the likelihood of their persistence. Instead, the last section of this chapter makes a number of general comments about the historical problems of adaptation in the twentieth century.

What is clear is that the onrush of technological development that increasingly marked the last century – and which has every prospect of continuing in our new century – has exacerbated and increased the difficulties confronting military institutions in adapting to war. At certain levels and in certain forms of combat, military organizations have improved their ability to adapt to tactical conditions. But the record is spotty and particularly underlines the point made in the last chapter: without the intellectual and educational preparation of the officer corps before war, military institutions have found it exceedingly difficult to adapt to the demands of war on the new battlefields.

In the First World War, both sides spent the first two years killing huge numbers of their soldiers without coming to grips with the fundamental tactical problems that combined arms and the lethality of modern weapons presented. In retrospect, much of the slaughter could have been

---

[69] One of the bizarre themes in the prewar period – with echoes that persist through to the twenty-first century – is that modern societies are fragile and unable to absorb heavy blows. In fact, the exact opposite is true, as the resiliency that American society displayed in the aftermath of 9/11 suggests. In 1914, Europe's ability to mobilize its industrial and manpower resources and then sustain the war over four terrible years of bloodletting underlines the strength of the modern state.

avoided had European armies put serious effort into the intellectual side of their profession.[70] But they had not. Thus, without having developed the systemic processes required to analyze the social, technological, and psychological dimensions of their rapidly changing world, they were not prepared for the even greater demands war presented.

To a considerable extent, European armies aggravated their difficulties in World War I by pushing the frontiers of developing technology. This helped to solve some of the immediate problems confronting front-line troops. But new technological developments only added to the dimension of the problem. In the end, modern war began to emerge from the slaughter, but technology played a relatively minor role in the solutions. Technology may well have been the source of the war's tactical and operational difficulties, but by itself, it could not provide answers. The processes of adaptation finally reached the point in 1918 where commanders, their staff, and those on the sharp end could return maneuver to the war's tactical and operational environment. Nevertheless, casualties in 1918 were the heaviest of any year of the war. But the revolution was not complete, and the war ended only because the Germans destroyed their army in their "successful" offensives of spring 1918.[71]

The road to 1918 was a difficult one indeed. Only in late 1916, as the losses at Verdun and the Somme sank in, did the Germans set in motion a real effort to learn the larger tactical lessons of the battlefield.[72] The great advantage they possessed was the fact that they had an effective organization – namely, the general staff for systematic reporting and then learning the lessons of combat.[73] Throughout the first two years of the struggle on the Western Front, the military leadership of the Reich,

---

[70] For a general examination of the state of Europe's armies before the First World War, see particularly David Hermann, *The Arming of Europe and the Making of the First World War* (Princeton, 1996).

[71] For the role of the British Army in defeating the Germans, see Tim Travers, *How the War Was Won: Command and Technology in the British Army on the Western Front, 1917–1918* (London, 1992); and J. P. Harris with Niall Barr, *Amiens to the Armistice: The BEF in the Hundred Days' Campaign, 8 August–11 November 1918* (London, 1988). For the German side of the equation, see the brilliant work by David Zabecki, *The German 1918 Offensive: A Case Study in the Operative Level of War* (London, 2006).

[72] For the German development of lessons-learned processes and their impact on the defensive and offensive battles in the First World War, see G. C. Wynne, *If Germany Attacks: The Battle in Depth in the West* (London,1940); and Timothy Lupfer, *The Dynamics of Doctrine: The Changes in German Tactical Doctrine during the First World War* (Fort Leavenworth, KS, 1981).

[73] The best work on the role of the general staff in learning and then promulgating the tactical lessons of the 1916–1917 battlefields on the Western Front remains Wynne, *If Germany Attacks*.

in particular, General Erich von Falkenhayn, provided the general staff with little latitude in adapting to the changing face of battle in the west.[74] But in 1916 Eric Ludendorff assumed the key position in the army, and he set in motion a revolution in tactics.

The fashion in which the German general staff system functioned provided feedback loops that analyzed information flowing from front-line experiences as to what was relevant and what needed to be discarded in tactical doctrine. Moreover, the general staff accorded its officers every opportunity to gain combat experience on the front lines, although compared with line officers, their time at the front remained limited. Ludendorff was willing to use and push the general staff system into providing the means and impetus for major changes in doctrine. Thus, for the last two years of the war, the Germans adapted faster at the tactical level than their opponents. But that ability only kept the war going for an additional year and made the conflict's impact on Europe and Germany that much the worse. This was because the Germans failed to solve the problem of exploitation at the operational level, when the mode of movement was muscle power – man and horse.[75]

On the other side of the line, matters did not go so well. While the British did create a series of tactical notes they passed around various headquarters, the commander of the British Expeditionary Force, Field Sir Marshal Douglas Haig, failed to establish a center for lessons-learned analysis for much of his tenure in command. Tactical adaptation thus devolved on the various army headquarters in the British Expeditionary Force. Some did it well, others did not. The French seem to have attempted to learn the lessons of the war in a more coherent fashion than the British. The great problem they confronted, however, was that they were on the forward edge of the learning curve on the Western Front for adaptation in offensive war. As a result, they consistently suffered the heaviest casualties. But they also ran into the extraordinarily bad luck of having their innovative adaptations of late 1916 run into the massive reformation of the German defensive system that Ludendorff had set in motion over the winter of 1916–1917. The resulting defeat of the Nivelle offensive came close to breaking the French Army and losing the First World War for the Allies before the Americans could arrive.

Similar patterns of learning – or not learning – from experience continued into the postwar period. The Germans did extraordinarily well

[74] See Chapter 3 of this book for further discussions of these issues.
[75] This point is drawn from Zabecki, *The German 1918 Offensive*.

at learning the lessons of the World War I battlefield about combined-arms tactics.[76] They failed entirely, however, to absorb the political and strategic lessons of their defeat.[77] The British, on the other hand, failed to establish a lessons-learned analysis of what had happened on the battlefields during 1918; consequently, they failed to develop a coherent approach that integrated the various combat arms – a situation that the persuasive military pundits B. H. Liddell Hart and J. F. C. Fuller further exacerbated.[78] The crucial point is not that the British failed to understand the value of the tank during the interwar period. Rather, it was that they failed to establish a system through which they could absorb and then effectively promulgate the lessons of the last war.

World War II

Unfortunately for their future opponents, the Germans refined the whole lessons-learned process throughout the interwar period.[79] The result was that they were able to absorb the tactical and operational lessons of the Polish campaign. They identified a number of significant weaknesses that had appeared in that campaign and then, in a rigorous and thorough program, retrained the whole army in the months before they launched *Fall Gelb* ("Case Yellow"), the invasion of Western Europe. Those processes continued through to the end of the war. The Germans proved throughout the war to have the most thorough system of learning the lessons of combat – at least of the ground war.[80]

---

[76] See particularly James S. Corum, *The Roots of Blitzkrieg: Hans von Seeckt and German Military Reform* (Lawrence, KS, 1990).

[77] Simply put, the strategic and political lesson of the Reich's defeat in World War I should have been that Germany should not again attempt to take on the whole world; instead the Germans persuaded themselves that defeat in 1918 had largely resulted from the army's having been stabbed in the back by communist revolutionaries and the Jews. For an examination of this massive effort at self-deception, see Holger Herwig, "Clio Deceived," *International Security*, Spring 1988.

[78] For a particularly perceptive examination of the British failures in the interwar period, see J.P. Harris, *Men, Ideas, and Tanks, British Military Thought and Armored Forces, 1903–1939* (Manchester, 1995).

[79] For the processes through which the German Army proceeded, see Williamson Murray, "Armored Warfare: The British, French and German Experiences," in Williamson Murray and Allan R. Millett, eds., *Military Innovation in the Interwar Period* (Cambridge, 1996).

[80] The situation in terms of the naval and air war was not so positive. Particularly in regards to technological and tactical adaptation to the demands of the U-boat war, the Germans proved to be slow learners.

At the strategic level, however, the Germans could not adapt, because neither the senior military leadership nor Adolf Hitler had the breadth of knowledge or requisite understanding of the external world to adapt to the conditions that their actions had set in train during the first two years of the war. No one in Germany besides the Führer was willing to address the larger strategic issues of the war – a situation quite similar to what had occurred in the last war. In effect, the Germans set disastrous strategic conditions for the war they were waging in 1941 by their invasion of the Soviet Union on 22 June 1941 and then by their declaration of war on the United States on 11 December 1941.[81]

The fact that the *Kriegsmarine* enthusiastically supported the declaration of war on the United States in summer 1941, while no general in either the army or the *Luftwaffe* appears to have had the slightest qualms about Hitler's decision to declare war on the United States, underlines how little the Germans were prepared to adapt to the changing strategic conditions of the war.[82] Those two strategic decisions made Nazi Germany's defeat inevitable no matter how well the *Wehrmacht* performed at the operational and tactical levels – and even in those areas, the Germans, confronting overwhelming numbers, began to lose their superiority on the battlefields of World War II.

There are a number interesting factors in the interwar period from 1920 to 1939 that set the basis for how well military organizations did or did not adapt to the actual conditions of combat in the next conflict. In the case of British and American airmen in the prewar period, a pervasive dismissal of the lessons of history – not only military history in general but the experiences of World War I as well – allowed them to create a distorted picture of future war that was to have a serious impact on the Combined Bomber Offensive.[83]

---

[81] For a discussion of these issues, see Williamson Murray and Allan R. Millett, *A War to Be Won: Fighting the Second World War* (Cambridge, MA, 2000), chap. 6.

[82] The chief of the army's general staff, Generaloberst Franz Halder, admittedly deeply concerned with events that were transpiring in Russia, hardly mentioned the events in the Pacific or Hitler's disastrous decision to declare war on the United States in his diary: Generaloberst Franz Halder, *The Halder War Diary, 1939–1942*, trans. and ed. by Charles Burdick and Hans-Adolf Jacobsen (Novato, CA, 1988), diary entries for December 1941, pp. 584–596. But then the German Navy, having learned nothing from World War I, had been encouraging Hitler to declare war on the United States over the course of summer 1941. For the navy's role, see Holger H. Herwig, *Politics of Frustration, The United States in German Naval Planning, 1889–1941* (Boston, 1976), pp. 228–234.

[83] See Murray and Millett, *A War to Be Won*, chap. 12.

On the other hand, in terms of thinking through the larger implications of World War I and the failures of the U.S. government and its military to prepare for a full economic mobilization of the American government, the U.S. Army, despite – or perhaps because of – the paucity of funding during the interwar years, took the trouble to found what is today known as the Industrial College of the Armed Forces. In many ways, those intellectual and organizational preparations for World War II provided the basis for America's most important contribution to the winning of the war against the Axis.[84]

In the largest sense, America's adaptation to the actual conditions of the Second World War underlined the importance of prewar conceptual innovation and education to the preparation of the next war's leaders. Here the U.S. Navy and the U.S. Marine Corps displayed a willingness to innovate that was truly extraordinary. War gaming at the Naval War College in Newport in the early 1920s provided the key insights into the potential that the aircraft carrier might possess at a time *when the navy did not possess a single carrier*.[85] The innovators in the navy then translated those conceptual insights into actual capabilities through experiments on board the first carriers, fleet exercises, additional war games, and consistent, intelligent debate.[86]

Similarly, in 1931, the Marines took their entire minuscule educational system and concentrated on the development of a doctrine for amphibious war, at a time when virtually the rest of the world's military organizations had flatly rejected the utility as well as the possibility of major amphibious operations in future warfare.[87] The point here is that the intellectual capital created within the officer corps of the navy and the marine corps would go far in furthering the adaptations that allowed the Western Powers to return to the European Continent and capture the island bases that led to the defeat of Imperial Japan. Equally significant was the fact

---

[84] For a discussion of the contribution that American industry made to the winning of the war, see ibid., pp. 533–538.

[85] After the war, Admiral Chester Nimitz, CINCPAC (commander in chief Pacific) for virtually the entire war, credited Newport as having foreseen everything that was to happen in the Pacific except the Kamikazes.

[86] For a discussion of how the United States stretched the possibilities offered by the carrier while the Royal Navy minimized that potential, see the superb study by Thomas C. Hone, Mark Mandeles, and Norman Freedman, *American and British Carrier Development, 1919–1941* (Annapolis, MD, 1999).

[87] For the development of amphibious operations during the interwar period, see Allan R. Millett, "Amphibious War: The American, British, and Japanese Cases," in *Military Innovation in the Interwar Period*, ed. by Murray and Millett, chap. 2.

that America's civilian and military leaders got the strategic framework right before the war with the "Germany first strategy," and then modified that strategy in 1942 and 1943 in accordance with the political and military framework within which the United States had to fight the war.[88]

Other military organizations proved less able or willing to grapple with the serious intellectual business of preparing for war, and whether they were able to adapt successfully or not, the price they paid in blood and treasure for their failure to encourage serious and honest intellectual preparation was invariably high.[89] The most tragic case came in the Soviet Union, where through 1937, the senior leadership of the Red Army was in many respects the most innovative and forward thinking in the world.[90] But Stalin's grim purge of the military that began in May 1937 ravaged the Red Army's officer corps, killing off most of the brightest and imaginative. At the same time, the dictator and his murderous secret police demanded that all traces of new ideas and innovations be suppressed. In this effort, they were all too successful.

The result was that Barbarossa, the German invasion of June 1941, caught the Soviets with the effects of the purges still deeply embedded throughout the officer corps, while the theoretical and practical concepts surrounding "deep battle" that the Red Army's great theorists and military reformers Triandafillóv and Tukhachevsky had been developing in the early to mid-1930s were only distant echoes in an officer corps brought to slavish obedience. Nevertheless, those echoes gradually emerged as the Soviets adapted to the terrible conditions involved in fighting an ideological war against the Germans, if not openly, then in the minds of the senior leaders of the Red Army responsible for the great victories of 1944 and 1945.[91] But the cost of adapting in 1941 and 1942 represents a bill that

---

[88] Throughout the war, the American people exhibited a strong inclination to pursue the war with Japan with far less interest in the war in Europe. That was one of the major factors that led Roosevelt to overrule his senior military advisers and order the invasion of French North Africa in November 1942. Murray and Millett, *A War to Be Won*, pp. 272–273.

[89] This work will deal with the experiences of British airmen and the conduct of their portion of the Combined Bomber Offensive in Chapter 6.

[90] The collapse of the Soviet Union has resulted in a virtual flood of first-class works dealing with the Red Army in the interwar period, as well as the impact of the purges on the Red Army's officer corps. Among the more interesting, see Shimon Naveh, *In Pursuit of Military Excellence: The Evolution of Operational Theory* (London, 1997); and Mary Habeck, *Storm of Steel: The Development of Armor Doctrine in Germany and the Soviet Union, 1919–1939* (Ithaca, NY, 2003).

[91] David M. Glantz, *Colossus Reborn: The Red Army at War, 1941–1943* (Lawrence, KS, 2005).

is almost unimaginable to those who live in the West at the beginning of the twenty-first century.

The Cold War

The surviving powers almost immediately embarked on a period they termed the Cold War. On one side stood the Soviet Union, on the other the United States and its allies. From its inception, the struggle between East and West represented an ideological contest, perhaps as deeply felt as the ideological war that had made World War II such a horrendous event in human history. By every standard of the past, it should have resulted in World War III. Ironically, the extraordinary technological developments of the two sides in effect made war too dangerous to wage. By the mid-1950s, the continuing deaths in Hiroshima and Nagasaki from the radiation poisoning that had resulted from the use of the atomic bombs had begun to percolate into the consciousness of the leaders of both sides. The explosive power as well as the contaminating potential of fission and then fusion weapons only exacerbated the problem.

The result, luckily for the human race, was a standoff. The U.S. Air Force's Strategic Air Command had as its motto "Peace is our profession." Nevertheless, the stasis at the highest levels did not prevent smaller wars from occurring. In the Korean War and especially the Vietnam War, U.S. military forces found themselves waging conflicts that resembled at the tactical level the conventional conflict of World War II. Yet, the political constraints that leaders in Washington placed around the conduct of air and ground operations represented a relatively new factor – at least to the American military.

Most surprising was the unwillingness or inability to pass along lessons throughout the military bureaucracy. Many of the hard lessons of World War II had to be relearned in Korea, in the air as well as on the ground. To a considerable extent, the attitude, at least among senior leaders in the U.S. Air Force, appears to have been that Korea was an anomaly in the world of nuclear weapons. One of the marks of the period of the Cold War was the disappearance of serious professional military education throughout the American services. The general feeling among U.S. military leaders seems to have been that the staff and war colleges were places for officers to rest in their busy careers.[92] Ironically, the business of thinking about

---

[92] As late as 1990, the dean of the Army War College stated in an interview with the press that he would rather see his officers out on the golf course than in the library.

a future war was turned almost entirely over to civilian theorists, who developed theories such as "mutually assured destruction."

However, such theories proved virtually useless when the United States confronted the problem of the Vietnam War. The inability and unwillingness of the American military to seriously examine a war it did not want to fight turned the field over to civilian theorists. Theories of "signal sending" and "rational actors" were completely inapplicable against an opponent motivated by a combination of ideological and nationalistic fervor.[93] Without a coherent intellectual framework, the military was incapable of framing the debate over national security and intervention in the Vietnam War in a fashion in which they could influence policy.[94] That intellectual framework had not existed before the war, and thus it took too long to develop during the course of the war itself, especially because of the personnel policies of one-year rotations.

One of the major weaknesses of the American military during Vietnam was the inability to adapt to the actual conditions of the war. As the army's official history of the period after Tet notes somewhat offhandedly, Military Assistance Command Vietnam (MACV) had no means of passing along the successful methods employed by a brigade of the 101st Airborne Division in trapping and then destroying concentrations of Viet Cong guerrillas in cordon operations in 1969.[95] It simply did not possess an effective lessons-learned mechanism nearly four years after major combat operations had begun.

In other words, just as in the case of Haig's British Expeditionary Force (BEF), there was no systematic means to pass adaptations throughout the structure of U.S. forces operating in Vietnam. Without a clear concept or understanding of the war it was fighting, MACV proceeded to apply tactics and procedures that had little to do with a guerrilla war and far more with fighting a Soviet opponent on the plains of Europe.[96] General William Westmoreland, like Haig in 1916 and 1917, attempted to fight the war in Vietnam according to his prewar conceptions and experiences, rather than adapting to the actual conditions he confronted.

---

[93] Here it is worth underlining that Ho Chi Minh's North Vietnamese were the true descendants of Robespierre and the revolutionaries of 1793.

[94] For the failures of the American military to address the question they should have raised, see H. R. McMasters, *Dereliction of Duty: Lyndon Johnson, Robert McNamara, the JCS, and the Lies That Led to Vietnam* (New York, 1996).

[95] Ronald H. Spector, *After Tet, The Bloodiest Year in Vietnam* (New York, 1994).

[96] For an examination of this approach, which involved fighting the plan for a European-style conflict, see Andrew Krepinevich, *The Army in Vietnam* (Baltimore, MD, 1988).

One might also note that in the immediate period after World War II, Westmoreland had turned down an assignment to the Army War College with the comment that he would only accept a position on the faculty. He suggested his attitude toward the intellectual preparation for war in his memoirs: "Beside my bed at home I kept... several books: a Bible; a French grammar; Mao Tse-tung's little red book on theories of guerrilla warfare; a novel, *The Centurions*, about the French fight with the Viet Minh; and several works by Dr. Bernard Fall, who wrote authoritatively on the French experience in Indochina and provided insight into the enemy's thinking and methods. I was usually too tired in late evening to give the books more than occasional attention."[97]

But the situation was even worse in the air, if that is possible. Operation Rolling Thunder, the air campaign against North Vietnam from 1965 through summer 1968, aimed at dissuading the north from aiding the guerrilla war in the south that it had started and was supporting. From its onset, the air effort of the Navy and Air Force underlined that the air forces of the United States had prepared themselves almost exclusively for the great nuclear war against the Soviet Union.[98] The conduct of the air war over North Vietnam suggests that the North Vietnamese, with considerable support from the Russians, learned faster than the Americans.

While the bombing inflicted enormous damage on the North Vietnamese, it appeared to have little effect on their willingness to continue the war. Nevertheless, that damage came at great cost. The ridge to the northwest of Hanoi soon became known as "Thud Ridge," after the large number of F-105s shot down in the area. Moreover, American air capabilities with conventional weapons systems hardly proved impressive. After three years of bombing, the Than Hoa Bridge still stood. Even more depressing was the fact that the exchange ratio between North Vietnamese MiGs and U.S. fighters was 2 to 1 – the worst exchange ratio in American air-power history.[99]

---

[97] William C. Westmoreland, *A Soldier Reports* (New York, 1976), p. 364. Westmoreland is accurate in his remarks about not having time to read: except for the first chapter, *The Centurions* is about the war in Algeria.

[98] The best book about the grossly incompetent conduct of the air war against North Vietnam at the operational and tactical level is Marshall L. Michell, III, *Clashes: Air Combat over North Vietnam, 1965–1972* (Annapolis, MD, 1999). See also Wayne Thompson, *To Hanoi and Back: The U.S. Air Force and North Vietnam, 1966–1973* (Washington, DC, 2000).

[99] For the exchange ratios throughout the war, see Michell, *Clashes*.

Between summer 1968 and spring of 1972, American airmen in both the navy and the air force had nearly four years to mull over the failures of their campaigns against North Vietnam, while they continued to support ground operations in South Vietnam and attack the North Vietnamese logistical infrastructure in Laos and Cambodia.[100] The adaptations that did or did not occur make an interesting comment on the different service cultures and their ability to adapt to the conditions of the war. The air force focused on the lack of accuracy of its bombing efforts and by 1972 had reequipped a portion of its fighter bombers with the first versions of laser-guided bombs. On the other hand, the navy, dominated by its fighter pilot community, revisited virtually everything that had to do with the training and preparation of fighter pilots.

The results showed clearly in the two Linebacker campaigns. Over their course, the air force dropped approximately 27,000 laser-guided munitions. The accuracy that the new precision weapons provided broke the back of the North Vietnamese Easter Offensive. Moreover, air force attacks placed much greater pressure on the enemy's logistical capabilities; the Than Hoa Bridge was dropped on the second attack. However, the exchange ratio between air force aircraft and North Vietnamese fighters remained at the same dismal ratio of one American aircraft shot down for every two MiGs. But the navy, which was still dropping dumb bombs, upped its ratio to 12 to 1 – twelve MiGs shot down for every navy jet shot down – because it had instituted the Top Gun program to reinvigorate the approach of its fighter pilots to air-to-air combat.

Conclusion

At the beginning of the twenty-first century, America's military forces with their awesome array of computerized simulations and instrumented training areas would seem no longer to confront the problem of adaptation. That was certainly the argument promulgated by a number of military pundits in the 1990s.[101] And certainly from the short-term perspective, the conventional war against Iraq in 2003 would suggest that the American military has largely provided a base for adapting to the

---

[100] The plural of "campaign" is used here deliberately because there was nothing joint about the U.S. Air Force and Navy efforts. Each service ran its own efforts entirely independent of the other's.

[101] For the foremost example of this line of argument, see Admiral Bill Owens, with Bill Offley, *Lifting the Fog of War* (New York, 2000).

problems associated with the immediate tactical and operational conditions of combat.[102] In every respect, American commanders seemed able to adapt to surprisingly new and different circumstances, as their soldiers and marines drove into the heart of Iraq.

A closer look might suggest otherwise. While the adaptation of American soldiers and marines to the immediate tactical situations they confronted in the immediate aftermath of the war was effective, the performance of their more senior leaders in handling a growing insurgency at the operational and political levels was, to put it bluntly, inept and at times incompetent. The events in Iraq in the four years after conventional combat operations indicated a direct connection between a general lack of intellectual preparation before the invasion of Saddam Hussein's Iraq and the troubles that almost immediately flowed in its aftermath. One could, of course, point to the fact that the American military adapted to conditions in Southwest Asia more quickly than in South Vietnam, 40 years earlier. Nevertheless, this is cold comfort to the parents, husbands, and wives of those killed on the highways and in the towns of Iraq – especially when too many senior military leaders largely ignored the lessons of Vietnam, Panama, and Somalia during the first year of the postconflict phase.

Thus, the problem of military adaptation remains alive and well. Over the course of the past two-and-a-half millennia, the pressures on military organizations for rapid adaptation have grown considerably. Clearly, the introduction of technology into the equation of war has speeded up the demands for adaptation. Ironically, in view of the claims of many technomonists, technology has in fact placed greater intellectual demands on the military profession. It is not likely that this condition will change. Moreover, the political, religious, and ideological problems that now confront the developed world, in what Major General Robert Scales has so accurately described as the coming "cultural wars," make it more rather than less likely that adaptation will confront military organizations in the execution of their duties.

---

[102] For a short account of the campaign at the operational level, see Williamson Murray and Robert H. Scales, Jr., *The Iraq War: A Military History* (Cambridge, MA, 2003). For later works on the conduct of operations, also see Thomas Ricks, *Fiasco: The American Military Adventure in Iraq* (New York, 2006); and Michael R. Gordon and General Bernard E. Trainor, *Cobra II: The Inside Story of the Invasion and Occupation of Iraq* (New York, 2006).

3

Complex Adaptation

The Western Front: 1914–1918

The First World War has the justified reputation as one of the most brutal wars in history. It also possesses the reputation as a war of stagnation and military incompetence. The fact that the Western Front remained virtually stationary for four years, despite the slaughter at Verdun, the Somme, and Passchendaele, appears to provide the evidence of general military stupidity. Not surprisingly, historians have tended to depict the war as one in which the "donkeys" of the general staffs drove Europe's youth through the slaughter pens of the Western Front to their death.[1] In the bleak words of the great British war poet Siegfried Sassoon:

> If I were fierce, and bald, and short of breath
> I'd live with scarlet Majors at the base
> And speed glum heroes up the line to death....
> And when the war is done and youth stone dead
> I'd toddle safely home and die – in bed.[2]
> – Siegfried Sassoon, "Base Details"
> *Collected Poems of Siegfried Sassoon*

Reinforcing such bitter attacks on the war's leadership has been the belief that solutions to the war's tactical problems were obvious and that

---

[1] In this regard, see particularly Alan Clark, *The Donkeys* (New York, 1965), for one of the foremost examples of this genre. Even Barbara Tuchman's *The Guns of August* (New York, 1962), generally a highly respected work, contains a strong element of contempt for the war's military leaders and their inability to see what she regarded as the obvious.
[2] Siegfried Sassoon, "Base Details," in John Silkin, ed., *First World War Poetry* (New York, 1984), p. 131. Copyright 1918, 1920 by E.P. Dutton. Copyright 1936, 1946, 1947, 1948 by Siegfried Sassoon. Used by permission of Viking Penguin, a division of Penguin Group (USA) inc.

armies could easily have developed the means to deal with the battlefield stalemate.³ Since the late 1920s, this has been a prevailing theme in the war's historiography until recently. In his admirable novel on the First World War, *The General*, C. S. Forester likened the war's tactical difficulties to those confronted by a tribe of South Sea islanders who had come across a board with a large screw embedded and who out of curiosity desired to remove it: "Accustomed only to nails, they had made one effort to pull out the screw by main force, and now that it had failed they were devising methods of applying more force still, of obtaining more efficient pincers, of using levers and fulcrums so that more men could bring their strength to bear. They could hardly be blamed for not guessing that by rotating the screw it would come out after the exertion of far less effort."⁴

Such images still mark most views of the war, especially among scholars who are not experts on the First World War. But such views are not only distorting and incorrect, they also cloud what was occurring.⁵ As Paul Kennedy has suggested:

> For it seems worth claiming that it was at the tactical level in this war (much more than in the 1939–1945 conflict) that the critical problems occurred. The argument, very crudely, would run as follows: because soldiers simply could not break through a trench system, their generals' plans for campaign success were stalemated on each side; these operational failures in turn

---

[3] Along these lines, a study on some of the war's historiography, edited by one of the leading historians of the British Army, devotes not a single chapter to the tactical issues involved in fighting the war. See Brian Bond, ed., *The First World War and British Military History* (Oxford, 1991).

[4] C. S. Forester, *The General* (Baltimore, MD, 1982), pp. 195–196.

[5] A number of important monographs have appeared over the past twenty-five years and have altered in fundamental ways our understanding of what was actually happening in the First World War. Among others see Timothy Lupfer, *The Dynamics of Doctrines: The Changes in German Tactical Doctrine during the First World War* (Leavenworth, KS, 1981); Shelford Bidwell and Dominick Graham, *Fire-power: British Army Weapons and Theories of War, 1904–1945* (London, 1982); Timothy Travers, *The Killing Ground: The British Army, The Western Front, and the Emergence of Modern War, 1900–1918* (London, 1987); Timothy Travers, *How the War Was Won: Command and Technology in the British Army on the Western Front, 1917–1918* (London, 1992); J. P. Harris, *Men, Ideas, and Tanks, British Military Thought and Armoured Forces, 1903–1939* (Manchester 1995); Robin Prior and Trevor Wilson, *Command on the Western Front: The Military Career of Sir Henry Rawlinson, 1914–1918* (Oxford, 1992), *Passchendaele: The Untold Story* (New Haven, CT, 1996), and *The Somme* (New Haven, 2005); Martin Middlebrook, *The Kaiser's Battle, 21 March 1918: The First Day of the German Spring Offensive* (London, 1978); Holger Herwig, *The First World War: Germany and Austria-Hungry, 1914–1918* (London, 1997); Hull, *Absolute Destruction: Military Culture and the Practices of War in Imperial Germany* (Ithaca, NY, 2005); and David Zabecki, *The German 1918 Offensive: A Case Study in the Operational Level of War* (London, 2006).

impacted on the strategic debate at the highest level, and thus upon the strategic options being considered by national policy makers; and these, *pari passu*, affected the considerations of ends versus means at the political level, the changing nature of civil-military relations, and the allocation of national resources.[6]

Kennedy is quite right; the First World War was a conflict in which armies succeeded or failed on the tactical level. But that arena presented a host of interlocking problems, none of which were open to easy or simple solutions. Nor were any of the solutions, which seem obvious today, necessarily obvious at the time. Moreover, the solution to one particular problem, or set of problems, in World War I rarely opened the door to success, because other factors often negated whatever tactical improvements or advances might be developed on one side of the trench lines. In fact, the tactical battlefield of the Western Front was one of constant and steady innovation and adaptation on both sides.[7]

The great tactical problem in the First World War was that prewar technological and scientific development had fundamentally distorted the balance between firepower and maneuver in a fashion that had never before occurred in history. Regarding the former, automatic weapons and artillery now provided twentieth-century armies unprecedented destructive power on the battlefield. In contrast, maneuver still depended largely on the centuries-old means of movement: the muscle power of men and horses. And while by 1918 the imbalance between the two had decreased, even the last battles demonstrated that the exploitation of battlefield success still depended on men on foot or horse.

In a macro sense, we might best think of the armies that fought on the Western Front during the First World War in biological terms: as complex adaptive systems – changing, adapting, and innovating in response to the actions of their opponents. Indeed the war took on a life of its own, itself becoming a complex adaptive system in which the tactical face of the

---

[6] Paul Kennedy, "Military Effectiveness in the First World War," in Allan R. Millett and Williamson Murray, eds., *Military Effectiveness*, vol. 1, *The First World War* (London, 1988, reprint Cambridge, 2010), p. 330. The *Military Effectiveness* volumes were sponsored by Andrew Marshall's Office of Net Assessment in the mid-1980s – the first of a series of studies attempting to use history to illuminate current problems.

[7] Hubert C. Johnson's *Breakthrough! Tactics, Technology, and the Search for Victory on the Western Front in World War I* (Novato, CA, 1994) represented a step in the right direction but failed to lay out many of the tactical developments that occurred on the Western Front during the course of the war. Johnson is particularly weak in his depiction of artillery developments, which in the end were crucial to finding a solution to the extraordinarily difficult problems posed by the defensive systems.

battlefield radically altered during its course.⁸ The opposing sides changed their approaches to tactics as the battlefield changed. They learned and adapted from their mistakes, and they learned from what their opponents were doing.⁹ All too often, however, the tactical advances their opponents were making at the same time overtook the lessons drawn from current battles and the changes put in place.

A particularly good example of this phenomenon occurred at the beginning of 1917. In this case, the French put in place a set of tactical solutions to the problems raised by the 1916 battlefield. Had these tactical solutions been available at the beginning of 1916, they might well have won a series of major successes. But in spring 1917, those new offensive tactics led to a disastrous offensive that almost resulted in the collapse of the French Army. What had happened was that the Germans had simultaneously devised an entirely new defensive doctrine, in effect creating a truly modern system of defense in depth that minimized much of the Allied advantage in artillery. In spring 1917 there were no solutions to the problem of breaking through an enemy system based on defense in depth, because that tactical problem had not existed before.¹⁰ Moreover, it was to take the British and French armies nearly a year to unravel this new German approach to defense.

One might suggest the magnitude of the 1914–1918 tactical revolution by the following allusion: by 1918, a competent regimental or battalion commander on the Western Front in the British, German, or French armies would have been able to understand the modern high-intensity battlefield, whether one speaks of 1944, Korea, or even the 2003 invasion of Iraq – once, of course, he had become acquainted with the intervening changes in the variety, speed, and ranges of modern weapons. But *no* regimental or battalion commander of 1914, deposited on the 1918 battlefield, would have possessed the experiential tools to understand what was happening in the tactical arena that he was now observing. In fact, the tactical developments between 1914 and 1918 represent the most

---

⁸ I am indebted to Lieutenant General Paul Van Riper, USMC (retired), for this insight. The term *complex adaptive system* comes from John Holland's work on genetic algorithms and biological adaptation.

⁹ In fact, the British and French seem to have learned more from the Germans on the battlefield than they learned from each other.

¹⁰ On the processes through which the Germans developed their system of defense in depth, see Lupfer, *The Dynamics of Doctrine*, pp. 7–29. See also G. C. Wynne, *If Germany Attacks: The Battle of Depth in the West* (London, 1940) for the most thorough examination of the development of German defensive doctrine.

important and complex revolution in military affairs to occur during the course of the twentieth century and perhaps in history.[11]

There are a number of reasons why historians have willingly accepted the notion that the Western Front represented little more than unimaginative slaughter. To begin with, too few historians understand the nuts and bolts of what actually transpires on the tactical battlefield.[12] Consequently, many have accepted simple, facile explanations for the stalemate on the Western Front. There are other explanations as well. From 1914 through spring 1918, virtually no movement forward occurred in the west; instead, battles in the west were concentrated within a few square miles of territory on either side of the front. That lack of maneuver and the resulting concentration of combat along the long thin line reaching from the English Channel to Switzerland have given the appearance of stagnation on the battlefield, when in fact immense, significant adaptations were taking place.

Ironically, too many historians have allowed the horror of the war's "killing grounds" to lead them to believe that somehow the casualty bill of modern war declined with the introduction of movement into the equation. Nothing could be further from the truth. A few figures underline the error. In the Passchendaele Battle (31 July 1917 to mid-November 1917), from a British perspective the worst of the war, the British Expeditionary Force (BEF) suffered 271,000 casualties in three-and-a-half months. Yet, in a like time period in 1918, when the BEF, supported by Dominion armies, won the greatest victories in the war, it suffered 314,000 casualties – a 16-percent higher rate than on the Somme. And in the German Army's great spring offensives of March to

---

[11] Unfortunately, only now over the course of the past several decades have historians begun to unravel the tactical complexities of the First World War battlefield. For a discussion of the nature of revolutions in military affairs and the place that the First World War played in their development, see MacGregor Knox and Williamson Murray, eds., *The Dynamics of Military Revolution* (Cambridge, 2000), chap. 1.

[12] There is a graphic indication of this in a book on the social and intellectual history of the First World War published in the late 1980s. Despite the rave reviews the book received, the author possessed a general lack of knowledge of the tactical realities of the battlefield. He quotes a passage from the German translation of Captain André Laffargue's 1915 pamphlet on trench war – a pamphlet that was to play a crucial role in the development of infantry tactics during the course of the war. He then argues that the passage underlines a serious misunderstanding of trench war – a line of argument that only underlines his own ignorance. Moreover, it is obvious that the author does not know who Laffargue was or the importance of his tactical appreciation. See Modris Ekstein, *Rites of Spring: The Great War and the Birth of the Modern Age* (New York, 1989), p. 188.

June 1918, during which it chalked up impressive territorial gains, the Germans suffered nearly one million casualties.[13] One only has to revisit the great maneuver battles of 1944 and 1945 on the Eastern and Western Fronts to discover that great movement forward does not necessarily equate to light casualty bills.[14]

This chapter describes the general direction that tactical innovation and adaptation took during the course of the First World War on the Western Front. In particular, it aims to underline why it was difficult for the armies on the Western Front to learn and adapt and how mutual adaptation – the fact that the opponents together constituted a complex adaptive system – added immeasurably to the problems that each side confronted. Significantly, the prewar military and political cultures contributed to the problems of adaptation. Confronted by largely unforeseen circumstances, politicians and generals alike persisted in their attempts to mold reality to prewar conceptions and assumptions. We begin our examination with a look at the prewar period and the first clash of arms; discuss the development of the artillery war, 1915–1916; and conclude with the development of modern conceptions of war in the 1917–1918 period.

Tactical Conceptions before the War and the Results in 1914

There are legitimate as well as faulty charges that one can make against the preparations that European armies made for war in the period before 1914. Perhaps the most legitimate is that there was a general unwillingness in the officer corps to take seriously the study of the military profession.[15] It is not that more rigorous study might have avoided the tactical pitfalls of the First World War entirely, but that such study would

---

[13] A thought-provoking analysis of the 1917 and 1918 casualty figures is in Travers, *How the War Was Won*, pp. 179–181.
[14] For the Normandy battle – 6 June to 29 August – Carlo D'Este gives the figure of 225,606 Allied casualties. Carlo D'Este, *Decision in Normandy* (London, 1984), p. 517. Soviet and German casualties in the encirclement and destruction of Army Group Center in the June–July 1944 time period were astronomical, even in comparison to the greatest battles of World War I.
[15] For the intellectual atmosphere in the German Army during the prewar period, see particularly Eric Dorn Brose, *The Kaiser's Army: The Politics of Military Technology in Germany during the Machine Age, 1870–1918* (Oxford, 2001); and Antulio J. Echevarria, II, *After Clausewitz: German Military Thinkers before the Great War* (Lawrence, KS, 2000). For the intellectual environment of the British Army in the prewar period, see particularly Travers, *The Killing Ground*, chaps. 1, 2, and 4.

have prepared military organizations to adapt more quickly to the new and terrible environment in which they found themselves in 1914. Equally important, a greater emphasis on study would have alerted senior officers at home at least to some of the harsh lessons of the Russo-Japanese War. During that conflict, all the major European armies had observers on the scene, and much of their reporting suggested the kinds of tactical problems the European armies would encounter in 1914. All reported on the impact of firepower, both rifled and artillery, on the pernicious impact of barbed wire, and on the nature of the battlefield. Tragically, the evidence suggests that despite the clear warnings encompassed in such reporting, professional incomprehension, cultural arrogance, and the business of keeping peacetime military organizations running, all contributed to the failure to learn significant lessons from a distant conflict.[16]

Nevertheless, perhaps the most unjustified charge against Europe's prewar military organizations is that they failed to recognize the killing potential of modern weapons and threw their infantry, deployed in Napoleonic tactical formations, against machine guns and massed artillery without recognizing the casualties they would incur. In fact, Europe's senior military leaders did recognize that the future battlefields of a European war were going to be lethal places indeed – that much they drew from the experiences of South Africa and Manchuria.[17] But that expectation of heavy casualties led them to emphasize tightly controlled, mass formations that inevitably increased the casualty bills. In effect, they emphasized tactical conceptions that would prevent their troops from going to ground in the killing zone.

The strategic and political wisdom of the time reinforced the tactical inclinations of senior officers. In the period before 1914, much of informed civilian opinion, academic as well as political, believed the next

---

[16] What was undoubtedly occurring in this case was the "not invented here" syndrome. For an incisive, new examination of what was learned or not learned from the fighting in Manchuria, see Major General Jonathan Bailey, "Military History and the Pathology of Lessons Learned: The Russo-Japanese War, A Case Study," paper delivered at the Past Futures Conference at the Royal Military Academy, Sandhurst, 3–4 July 2003, and Quantico, Virginia, 9–10 September 2003. A considerable irony of that period is that one of the most perceptive observers in Manchuria, the future general Sir Ian Hamilton, applied virtually none of those lessons that he had passed along to the War Office during the period 1904–1905 to his own conduct of the Gallipoli campaign in 1915, the one strategic alternative to the battles of attrition on the Western Front. Thus, the campaign failed dismally, leaving no alternative to the Western Front.

[17] Michael Howard, "The Doctrine of the Offensive," in *Makers of Modern Strategy*, ed. by Peter Paret (Princeton, 1986), p. 522.

war had to be short, or European society would collapse under economic and political pressures.[18] Thus, there was a strategic rationale behind political and military demands that the armies win the next war quickly and decisively – however great the cost – before financial and political strains resulted in revolution or economic collapse. In the coming war, many military experts argued that victory would come to the army that threw the last battalion into the fight – much as had occurred in the Japanese victories in Manchuria. In other words, because of the strategic straitjacket within which the general staffs found themselves, they fully expected heavy casualties, but focused not on how to minimize those losses but instead on how to compel the troops to tolerate them.

The tactics recommended by Colonel de Grandmaison – *offensive à outrance,* that the offensive should "be pushed to the end, with no second thoughts, up to the extremes of human endurance" – was perhaps an extreme expression of an approach that made a certain sense within the parameters of European strategic and political conceptions.[19] Such an approach was not obviously wrong unless one believed the next European conflict would be a long war. Few did.[20]

So in August 1914, Europe went to war. Most senior generals and many politicians had foreseen the immediate slaughter. What politicians, generals, and academics had not foreseen was the failure of the armies to achieve decisive results.[21] What they also failed to foresee was the ability

---

[18] This was a misperception that the results of the Russo-Japanese War only served to reinforce. After barely a year of heavy fighting in Manchuria, the czarist regime confronted a revolution that came close to toppling the Romanov dynasty. Only the most desperate measures prevented the revolution's success. Similarly, while the Japanese were not on the brink of revolution, they were on the brink of financial collapse. Thus, the former case seemed to support those who argued that the fragility of the modern state would quickly lead to revolution, while those who argued about the financial fragility of the modern state pointed to Japan's financial difficulties. Both cases, however, seemed to point to the need for a quick victory, whatever the cost on the battlefield might be to the armies slugging it out.

[19] Tuchman, *The Guns of August,* p. 33.

[20] The repetitive references in historical works to Bloch, the elder Moltke, and Kitchener (three individuals who did believe that the next European war would be a long one) suggest how few in Europe actually believed that the next war would be a long struggle.

[21] As was to be the case throughout the twentieth century, military organizations sought to accomplish the same decisive results that the great Napoleon had supposedly achieved in his wars. In fact, the only decisive victory Napoleon achieved was at Austerlitz in 1805. Even his great double victory in 1806 at Jena-Auerstadt failed to end the war against the Prussians – the fighting continued until the following year, when the Peace of Tilsit brought a temporary halt to the fighting. In subsequent campaigns Napoleon was to win a number of stunning victories, but none proved to be decisive against European

of modern industrialized societies to sustain the burden of enormous economic and human sacrifices in a struggle for what they perceived as national survival. Here the triumph of the Industrial Revolution provided the immense resources required to wage a long, drawn-out war, while the principles of the French Revolution provided the political means and the rationale for the complete mobilization of the nation-state's populace.[22]

The tactics of the opposing armies in the opening battles provided heaps of corpses but no decisive victories. The French threw vast numbers of young soldiers into the execution of Plan XVII with only dismal lists of casualties and defeat on their frontiers to show for their efforts. Throughout its execution of the Schlieffen Plan, the German Army was just as profligate with its soldiers. At Langemark in Belgium in early November, the Germans threw in a corps of ill-trained university students called up that August; slaughtered by the thousands by deadly rifle fire from the BEF's "Old Contemptible," only 7,000 German soldiers out of 37,000 remained unwounded when it was over.[23] Ironically, Adolf Hitler was one of the few survivors.

By late fall 1914 the armies had shot their collective bolts. They had nothing more to give. On the Western Front, the German, French, and British armies – or what was left of them – collapsed into ragged, ill-prepared, and ill-sited trench lines. The Germans at least had the advantage in that during their retreat from defeat on the Marne, they could select positions favorable to the defense.[24] In late December 1914, the situation was clear enough for Winston Churchill to write Herbert Asquith, Britain's Prime Minister:

> I think that it is quite possible that neither side will have the strength to penetrate the other's lines in the Western theatre. Belgium particularly... has no doubt been made into a mere succession of fortified lines. I think it probable that the Germans [will] hold back several large mobile reserves of

enemies who had finally begun to adapt to the political and strategic realities of the new form of warfare occasioned by the French Revolution. As Clausewitz observed: "Not until statesmen had at last perceived the nature of the forces that had emerged in France, and had grasped that new political conditions now obtained in Europe, could they foresee the broad effect all this would have on war... in short, we can say that twenty years of revolutionary triumph were mainly due to the mistaken policies of France's enemies." Carl von Clausewitz, *On War*, trans. and ed. by Michael Howard and Peter Paret (Princeton, 1976), p. 209.

[22] For further discussion of these issues, see Knox and Murray, *The Dynamics of Military Revolution*, chap. 1.

[23] Herwig, *The First World War: Germany and Austria*, p. 116.

[24] It was not that they thought they were going to stand on the defensive in these positions for much of the next four years, but rather that they believed such positions offered useful positions from which to resume the offensive in the near future.

their best troops. Without attempting to take a final view, my impression is that the position of both armies is not likely to undergo any decisive change – although no doubt several hundred thousand men will be spent to satisfy the military mind on the point.[25]

By winter 1914, front-line soldiers had learned a number of useful lessons: dig deep and provide dugouts and bunkers where possible; above all provide cover from small-arms and particularly artillery fire, which had proven such a terrible killer in the first months of fighting. During the initial period of trench warfare, the troops devoted their energy to protecting themselves. In addition to building trench systems, the opponents soon strung increasingly complex and dense barbed-wire obstacles in "no-man's land" between the trenches. Such defensive systems were at first simple but became more complex throughout 1915 in reaction to increasing artillery fire. By summer 1915, the Germans were siting new positions behind their front lines to prevent an Allied breakthrough.[26]

A number of structural problems hindered military institutions in dealing with this unexpected situation. The first had to do with the general weaknesses in the professional standards of the officers themselves. As two of the more observant commentators have noted about the Edwardian army: "Anti-intellectualism was the ruling mode of thought."[27] Even one of the more thoughtful British senior officers, Field Marshal Lord Wolseley, remarked in 1897: "I hope that the officers of Her Majesty's Army may never degenerate into bookworms. There is happily at present no tendency in that direction, for I am glad to say that this generation is as fond of danger, adventure, and all manly out-of-door sports as their forefathers were."[28]

While French and German officers may have paid more attention to serious study, they confined such study largely to the general staffs and staff colleges, while regimental soldiering demanded little more than drill and sports. Moreover, not even the most serious professional military institution in Europe, the German general staff, focused on the tactical level of war. The Germans would not do so until Erich Ludendorff assumed control of the general staff in late summer 1916, as Hindenburg's de facto chief of staff. Thus, there was precious little thinking, much less experimentation, on tactical matters, the level of war most profoundly affected by revolutionary changes in technology. The second

---

[25] Martin Gilbert, *Winston S. Churchill*, vol. 3, 1914–1916 (London, 1971), p. 226.
[26] Wynne, *If Germany Attacks*, p. 63.
[27] Bidwell and Graham, *Fire-power*, p. 19.
[28] Quoted in Travers, *The Killing Ground*, p. 39.

obstacle that confronted the European armies in adapting to the conditions of the battlefield had to do with the complex and demanding business of running a massive war, for which none had prepared. The first months of the war raised difficult and intractable problems ranging from the massive expansion of force structures, to the mobilization of national economies to support the war, to the development of numerous new weapons to support the fighting.[29] These problems presented all the powers, but particularly the British, with significant challenges.[30]

Much of the war's first year-and-a-half involved adaptation to the vast *organizational* changes that the war caused *all* the armies to make at the outset. All the innovative tactics in the world would not have made the slightest difference without the support of masses of shells, bullets, uniforms, and sustenance. The first problem was to create efficient organizations to manage the deployment of vast amounts of material to the European battlefields. The second was to make those forces materially effective in a constantly changing environment. These two tasks were, and remain, quite different and are often contrary in nature. The Continental powers with their great conscript armies possessed the organizational structure on which to mobilize and train ever-larger armies.[31] Because the French and Germans possessed the structure to expand their armies, they could focus on the tactical difficulties at an earlier point in the war. In contrast, the British, with a small professional army, had no administrative structure through which to manage a mass conscript army. Then, on the outbreak of the war, they exacerbated their difficulties by shipping everyone, including staffs and training establishments, to the battlefields of France.

A major additional constraint resulted from the bloodletting of the early battles. The horrific casualty bills of 1914 fell disproportionately

---

[29] The technical inventions ranged from tanks, to gas shells, to various specialized forms of aircraft, all involving vast research and development organizations. For the first time, human society marshaled science and technological development to the needs of war, as the conflict was being waged. The result was a spurt in technological development even compared with what had been happening before the war. In regard to technological innovation, see particularly Guy Hartcup, *The War of Invention: Scientific Developments, 1914–18* (London, 1988).

[30] For the extent of the problems that governments and their military organizations confront in mobilizing their economies and manpower for war, see the essay by Allan R. Millett, Williamson Murray, and Kenneth Watman, "The Effectiveness of Military Institutions," in Allan R. Millett and Williamson Murray, eds., *Military Effectiveness*, vol. 1, *The First World War* (London, 1988), chap. 1.

[31] Ibid.

among junior officers and noncommissioned officers (NCOs).[32] In the case of the British, the fighting in Flanders in fall 1914 effectively wrecked the regular army.[33] The desperate need then was for junior officers and NCOs, whatever their level of training – a state of affairs hardly conducive to improving the overall tactical leadership in a force undergoing massive expansion. In addition, the nature of the First World War battlefield with its size, complexity, and confusion, not to mention horror, prevented senior officers, even had they wished to, from gathering much insight into what was occurring. Nor were junior officers, ingrained with the habits of top-down control, easily able or willing to pass on to their superiors realistic appreciations of what was actually transpiring. It would take considerable changes in the primitive processes of absorbing and then learning lessons, as well as in the capacity to filter combat experiences up the chain of command, before coherent and sustained adaptation could take place. In this process, the Germans eventually enjoyed an important advantage with the feedback loops provided by the general staff system but only *when they chose to use them*. And that was not to occur until late summer 1916.

Aggravating these problems was the fact that the generals leading the armies in 1914 brought into the conflict tactical paradigms of how they thought war should be fought. Separated from the battlefield and cocooned with comfortable, sycophantic staffs, which agreed with their every statements, too many generals persisted in imposing their prewar tactical paradigms on the actual conditions of war, conditions that rapidly rendered such conceptions dangerously misleading or even false. In fact, this phenomenon is not confined to the First World War but is to be found in virtually every war in the twentieth century – and earlier.[34]

The final point is that by and large, the senior leaders of the European armies displayed little interest in tactical matters. Field Marshal Sir Douglas Haig, commander of the BEF for the last three years of the war, for example, confused the term "tactics" with what we would today call operations. In all of the voluminous entries in his extensive diaries, there

---

[32] Alistair Horne estimates that the French Army suffered 300,000 casualties in the first two weeks of fighting, while the officer corps lost 10 percent of its strength during that period. Alistair Horne, *The Price of Glory: Verdun, 1916* (London, 1963), p. 26.

[33] In this respect, see particularly the outstanding account in A. H. Farrar-Hockley, *Death of an Army* (London, 1972).

[34] For the British, see Travers, *The Killing Ground*, chap. 2; for the French, see James K. Hogue, "Puissance de Feu: The Struggle for New Artillery Doctrine in the French Army, 1914–1916," MA Thesis, The Ohio State University, 1988, p. 34.

is hardly a reference to the crucial element of military effectiveness in World War I: tactics and tactical innovation.[35] Haig turned the development of tactics over to his army commanders, and they in turn often passed that responsibility down to corps and even division commanders. The result was an enormous disparity in the British Army's performance on a unit-to-unit basis.[36] At times, this was an advantage but in other circumstances – such as when Haig attempted to institute a defense in depth in late winter 1918 – the efforts were spotty, which contributed considerably to the success of the German "Michael" offensive in March 1918.

Again, as Michael Howard has pointed out on a number of occasions, military organizations inevitably get the next war wrong. Their business is then to adapt as quickly as possible and at the least cost in their soldiers' lives to the actual conditions they confront.[37] In the First World War, Napoleonic concepts persisted in Haig's planning and designs of his offensives right through the Passchendaele offensive of late summer 1917, despite every battlefield experience at the tactical and operational levels that underlined how unrealistic such an approach was.

[35] Each night during the war, Haig took the time to enter into his diary those whom he met, what was discussed, his opinions of generals and politicians, his specific thoughts on what was occurring in the war, as well as references to his family affairs. Hardly ever in all the voluminous entries that he made is there a reference to tactics or the tactical problems that confronted his soldiers in the front lines. Haig's general lack of interest in the subject is worth comparing to General Erich Ludendorff's interest in the subject once the latter took over general command of the war effort in the Reich. The originals of Haig's diaries are in the National Library of Scotland. For the recent publication of his diary and letters, see Douglas Haig, *Douglas Haig: War Diaries and Letters, 1914–1918*, ed. by Gary Sheffield and John Bourne (London, 2005).

[36] Travers, *How the War Was Won*, pp. 142–146. Unfortunately, this was also to be true for much of the British Army at the beginning of the Second World War. The larger point in terms of British difficulties lay in the fact that the British failed to invest seriously in the intellectual development of their officers before the war.

[37] Through the first two years of the American Civil War, generals on both sides of the line persisted in following the Napoleonic maxims of the Baron Jomini, despite their general lack of relevance to a war that was being fought with new technologies. The best general military history of the war remains James McPherson, *Battle Cry of Freedom: The American Civil War* (Oxford, 1988). For this phenomenon in wars of the twentieth century, one might particularly note the conduct of the Combined Bomber Offensive during the Second World War by Bomber Command under Air Marshal Sir Arthur Harris and by Eighth Air Force under Lieutenant General Ira Eaker. (For an examination of the former's conduct of the British portion of that campaign, see Chapter 6 in this book.) The performance of the U.S. Army during the Vietnam War is also especially noteworthy in this regard: see Andrew Krepinevich, *The Army in Vietnam* (Baltimore, MD, 1986).

1915–1916: Learning in the Slaughterhouse

From the German point of view, World War I was never a war of stagnation. By strategic choice in 1915, the Germans remained on the defensive in the west, while their forces on the Eastern Front and in the Balkans were smashing the Russian and Serbian armies. In those theaters, the force-to-space ratios were such that the Germans could mass sufficient superiority on certain sectors of the front to achieve breakthroughs without making major tactical changes to prewar doctrine. But because they chose to remain on the defensive in the west, they had only to defend their trench systems. Throughout 1915, they did not have to fight their way through their enemies' firepower and over the killing ground of no-man's land – with the exception, of course, of raiding parties.

In many ways, the Germans minimized the tactical potential of their defensive stance in the west during the first two years of the war by attempting to hold on to every piece of ground they had seized in the opening campaign. Nevertheless, in overall terms, the Western Front was much to their advantage: they could observe the actions, innovations, and adaptations of their opponents and then adopt what was useful and effective to their own forces. Moreover, in the age of modern firepower, the defense stood to gain the most from the increasing lethality of the weapons available – at least at first. However, for political reasons, the Allies, and particularly the French, had no choice but to attack. The large sections of northern France the Germans had occupied in 1914 resulted in considerable pressure from French politicians for the army to regain what it had lost in August and September 1914.[38]

Artillery was the obvious answer to front-line defenses equipped with machine-guns and rifles, but the infantry themselves were soon augmented with mortars, grenades, and other infantry support weapons. Before the war, the French had heavily emphasized artillery's direct fire support role for the infantry with their famous 75-mm gun. But even they were familiar with principles of indirect fire.[39] The fighting in 1914 underlined that

---

[38] Even more important than simply the territory the Germans occupied was the fact that they had occupied the most important industrial regions of France, which not surprisingly put the French at a considerable disadvantage throughout the war. For the conduct of the war by the French at the highest level, see Robert Doughty's *Pyrrhic Victory: French Strategy and Operations in the Great War* (Cambridge, MA, 2005).

[39] Direct artillery fire involves a situation in which the gunners can see the target directly, fire at it, and then make adjustments depending on where the shots fall in relationship to the target. Indirect fire, however, occurs when the target is out of the direct sight of the gunners – blocked by meteorological conditions, terrain, or man-made obstacles. In

direct artillery support was a nonstarter. It got the gunners killed even faster than the infantry because they had to fire their weapons in full view of the enemy and usually within range of his small-arms weapons. The battlefield's harsh judgment put the French at a considerable disadvantage, because their 75-mm gun was primarily a direct-fire weapon. Thus, for most of their attacks in 1915, the French did not possess the medium and heavy howitzers to provide the degree of indirect fires needed to break up the German defensive systems, even though those defenses were quite primitive.

But indirect artillery fire raised a number of intractable problems.[40] It was not necessarily difficult to call in the fire of a single gun or battery against a small number of targets by indirect fire. The problem lay in controlling large numbers of guns against a large number of targets in a consistent and coherent fashion. To make the problem even more difficult, a number of those targets might move at relatively short notice.[41] The solution demanded the development of a host of new techniques: firing off the map, massing of fires, understanding of and calculating to compensate for meteorological conditions, the use of spotter aircraft, the development of effective communication systems with airborne and ground observers, and the ability to fire accurately without the registering of artillery pieces.[42] Indirect artillery fire also required particular types

such a case there are two choices: one can either fire blindly at the target or targets or one can rely on an observer, either in the air or on the ground, who does have direct, visible contact with the target and who is in communications with the artillery. By 1917–1918, more complex means of indirect fire had been introduced. By using accurate air photographs that artillerymen could correlate with survey data to establish the exact geographic location of targets, calibrating the firing characteristics of each individual artillery piece, and factoring in meteorological conditions such as wind, temperature, and humidity, artillery could hit targets with a fair degree of accuracy by using indirect fire, even when there was no observer to direct fires onto the target. But it would take three years and a great deal of work to develop such capabilities. For a discussion of these issues, see David T. Zabecki, *Steel Wind: Colonel Georg Bruchmüller and the Birth of Modern Artillery* (Westport, CT, 1994); Colonel J. B. A. Bailey, *Field Artillery and Fire-Power* (Oxford, 1989); and Shelford Bidwell and Dominic Graham, *Fire-Power: British Army Weapons and Theories of War, 1904–1945* (London, 1982).

[40] One of the most thorough discussions of the problems involved in firepower is in Bidwell and Graham, *Fire-Power*, chap. 1.

[41] There is a particularly useful discussion of the problems involved in developing effective artillery tactics in World War I in Bradley Meyer, "Operational Art and the German Command System in World War I," Ph.D. Dissertation, The Ohio State University, 1988, chap. 5.

[42] In World War I, the use of indirect fire was also intimidating to a number of officers, because unlike direct fire, which depended on a good eye, indirect fire demanded an ability to use complex mathematics, at least to most officers of the time. Registering guns

of guns. Here the Germans enjoyed a significant advantage, because of their procurement choices before the war. Moreover, some artillerymen proved obdurately unreceptive to the possibility that indirect artillery might dominate the next war and so were completely unprepared technologically and intellectually for the adaptations they would have to make. Not surprisingly, this was particularly the mark of the British artillery communities, where a small-war mentality drove much of the thinking. A prewar lecturer, who had the nerve to argue that meteorological data would be essential for artillery within two months of the start of a major war on the Continent, found himself greeted with hoots of laughter by the assembled officers of the Royal Field Artillery.[43]

Because the techniques of indirect fire were still immature, Allied offensives in 1915 and 1916 relied on prolonged bombardments to achieve sufficient levels of area damage to suppress German defenses, so that Allied infantry could break into enemy trenches. By their nature such bombardments depended on massed firepower to wreck the enemy's defensive system. Allied artillery possessed little ability to attack and destroy specific targets or defensive positions. Moreover, the weight of the artillery fire available was rarely sufficient to destroy the whole system. When their first offensives in 1915 failed to break through German defenses, Allied commanders looked to more prolonged bombardments as the best means to break through. But such an approach offered the Germans an immediate counter: the defenders simply dug their front-line dugouts deeper, where even prolonged bombardments could not reach them. The lengthening bombardments also provided defenders with the time to get their reserves moving toward threatened sectors with the result that penetration – even if achieved – could not be exploited.[44]

---

before a bombardment was a relatively easy matter. One fired off a number of rounds under the observation of liaison officers working with the infantry in the front lines and then calculated the ranges to other targets from known shots. But the registration of literally hundreds of guns before a major offensive provided the enemy with advance warning as to what was about to transpire. Thus, by 1918 artillery officers were using topographical data, weather conditions, the individual calibration of each weapon, aerial reconnaissance, and sound and light calculations as to the location of enemy artillery batteries to launch precise bombardments that did not rely on the registration and that attacked the enemy's known positions and strong points with great precision. The most thorough examination of artillery tactics by the Germans during the war is Zabecki, *Steel Wind*.

[43] Bailey, *Field Artillery and Firepower*, p. 120.
[44] The availability of reserves allowed the defender to plug any breakthrough before the attacker could reach open ground.

The Allied tactical approach of massive artillery "preparation fires" also ran up against the fact that their armaments industries were not in position to supply the weight of shells required to support lengthy bombardments. The British were in particularly bad shape: the prewar ammunition establishment for the Royal Artillery provided sufficient ammunition for each gun to fire six maximum periods of fire (44 minutes of fire each), with sufficient reserves for 75 minutes of firing available in the United Kingdom and 60 minutes more of ammunition in the United Kingdom to arrive in the next six months.[45]

The French

In spring 1915, one of a new group of French generals undertook a set of striking innovations. In August 1914, Philippe Pétain had been an obscure regimental commander with few prospects of promotion because of his dour, pessimistic personality, as well as his tendency to disagree with his superiors over the army's emphasis on the offensive. But under the pressures of war, Pétain had shone, while the army's commander in chief, General Joseph Joffre, had replaced large numbers of generals for failures. Of all the French officers, Pétain understood not only firepower and how to use it but the limitations it placed on tactics as well.

At Arras in May 1915, in one of the many grim failures of the French Army that year, Pétain, now a corps commander, integrated his infantry attacks with artillery so that there was no time lag between the lifting of the bombardment and the infantry assault. Moreover, he used heavy naval artillery against selected targets on Vimy Ridge, the main objective of his corps. The naval gunners provided much more accurate fire with their heavy guns than army gunners, who could not provide similar accuracy without resorting to registration, which in turn alerted the Germans as to what was coming. The naval gunners were able to achieve these results because of two factors: they used up-to-date aerial photographs to map out and calculate their targets and then utilized meteorological and gun calibrations to adjust their fire at particular targets. Neither of these methods was in use among the army's artillerymen at the time.[46]

---

[45] Bailey, *Field Artillery and Firepower*, p. 122.
[46] The German novelist and wartime combat leader Ernst Jünger, who fought on the Western Front from 1915 through to the end, relates in his memoir that as late as 1917, some German artillerymen were not taking meteorological conditions into account in their calculations. See Ernst Jünger, *Storm of Steel: From the Diary of a German Storm-Troop Officer on the Western Front* (London, 1929), p. 159.

Pétain's troops captured most of Vimy Ridge. Admittedly, they failed to hold their gains when German counterattacks swept in because the French infantry had advanced beyond the effective range of its artillery. Nevertheless, Pétain's conclusions about his troops' initial success were significant. He argued that the technical and tactical conditions of the 1915 battlefield were such that breakthrough operations were not possible. Enemy defenses were just too powerful. Thus, in his view, the French Army should undertake a siege war against German defensive positions in the west. Such an approach, however, demanded that the French go over to the defensive and retrain their troops in new tactical conceptions while they reequipped their artillery with heavier guns.[47]

The culpable failure of the French high command does not lie in the disasters of 1914 but rather in brushing off Pétain's suggestions, which reflected the *real* conditions of the battlefield. Pétain was promoted to army command. But the high command rejected his proposals and persisted in a series of ill-prepared attacks, culminating in the failure of the Champagne offensive in August 1915. Despite commitment of 1,100 light (75-mm) pieces and 872 heavy and medium artillery pieces and the expenditure of masses of ammunition – 1,387,370 75-mm shells, 265,483 medium shells, and 30,317 heavy shells – the attacks failed almost completely.[48] Moreover, the French had no system through which they could pass Pétain's artillery techniques along to the rest of the army. Over the course of the year, the French Army had 1,500,000 casualties – dead, wounded, or missing.[49]

The bloodletting did cause considerable rethinking throughout the French Army. During summer 1915, Captain André Laffargue, recovering from wounds suffered in the spring, wrote a groundbreaking tactical study: *Etude sur l'attaque*. The young captain argued for echeloned, offensive tactics that would emphasize the identification and isolation – not destruction – of enemy strong points. He also urged allowing junior officers greater initiative on the battlefield as well as major increases in infantry firepower by equipping soldiers with automatic weapons.[50] In some respects, his arguments remained tied to current tactical formations

---

[47] Hogue, "Puissance de Feu," pp. 41–43.
[48] Ibid., p. 50.
[49] Robert Doughty, *Seeds of Disaster: The Development of French Army Doctrine, 1919–1939* (Hamden, CT, 1983), p. 72.
[50] Lupfer provides a useful summation of Laffargue's conceptions in his study, *The Dynamics of Doctrine*, p. 39.

rather than exploring new structures, but in the largest sense they represented a substantial break with the past.[51]

General Ferdinand Foch, one of the leading lights in the French Army, immediately recognized the importance of Laffargue's tactical conceptions.[52] He passed not only Laffargue's ideas up the chain of command but the captain himself along to Joffre. Laffargue arrived at Joffre's general headquarters in late 1915. There he immediately ran into Lieutenant Colonel Maurice Gamelin, a man who would be largely responsible for the catastrophic defeat in 1940. At this time, Gamelin was Joffre's *chef de cabinet,* a position he had achieved by his slavish devotion to those above him in the chain of command; he would display throughout his career the "looking-good mentality" of the worst kind of staff officer. Taking a quick look at Laffargue's dirty, mud-stained horizon-blue uniform, Gamelin ordered that the captain be transferred to the map room to move flags around. It appeared that once again, the French had run into another dead end – this time one driven by the obdurate ignorance of, or interest in, front-line conditions by a senior staff officer.[53]

The Germans

On the defensive, the Germans had not confronted the extensive technical and tactical problems of offensive warfare.[54] Nevertheless, they did attempt some technological innovations that ironically helped their opponents more than the Germans. In April 1915 they used gas against French

---

[51] In 1916, the Germans captured a copy of Laffargue's pamphlet, which the French high command had distributed widely to the troops. The Germans immediately translated it and gave it wide distribution among their troops and staffs. Bruce Gudmundsson argues that Laffargue played little role in influencing the Germans: Bruce I. Gudmundsson, *Stormtroop Tactics: Innovation in the German Army, 1914–1918* (New York, 1989). The fact that the Germans took the trouble to translate Laffargue's pamphlet and then distribute it widely throughout the staffs suggests that he underestimates its importance. See Pascal Lucas, *The Evolution of Tactical Ideas during the War of 1914–1918* (Leavenworth, KS, 1925), p. 41.

[52] It is also worth noting that Laffargue's ideas got through the army's bureaucracy to Foch within a relatively short period of time.

[53] I am indebted to James Hogue for this story. Hogue interviewed Laffargue extensively in the late 1980s when working on his master's thesis at Ohio State. Laffargue's ideas would prove influential in the successful French attack against Verdun in fall 1916, and he would rise to the rank of general in the interwar army.

[54] The best examination of the development of German defensive tactics on the Western Front remains Wynne's *If Germany Attacks,* first published in 1940 and then largely ignored during the course of the Second World War and thereafter.

colonial troops in a local offensive in Flanders. The Germans achieved a stunning local success in taking out the French colonial division, but they had prepared no reserve forces to exploit the success. Thus, the Allies were able to respond, and their quickly arriving reserves dammed up the hole. Moreover, the Germans had no reserves of gas; their strike had been nothing more than a tactical experiment to see whether gas could kill.

How much the sloppy thinking of the German high command came back to haunt them is suggested by the unintended effects of their decision. First, it placed German troops at a considerable disadvantage on the Western Front for the remainder of the war, because prevailing winds blow from west to east, thus providing the Allies a considerable advantage in gas warfare. Second, the perception that the Germans were using barbaric means on the Western Front allowed the British more diplomatic leeway to tighten their blockade. That blockade robbed Germany of its sources of rubber, which in turn made it impossible for them to manufacture decent gas masks.[55] Finally, the use of gas in contravention of the international agreements that the Germans themselves had signed served as one more incident that drove the Americans to join the Allies in 1917. In every sense, the German decision to test gas in April 1915 represented a triumph of what the Germans termed "military necessity" over common sense.[56]

As Allied combat power in the west gradually increased, the German reaction to the growing Allied threat in the west was slow and initially unimaginative. General Erich von Falkenhayn, the younger Moltke's replacement as chief of the general staff, demanded that German forces hold all the territory conquered in 1914, including tactically indefensible positions.[57] As a result, the German Army in the west received little latitude for adaptation during the course of the war's first two years. Nevertheless, the Germans did learn some important lessons from the Allied attacks of 1915. By summer, they were constructing second-line defensive positions. Where possible they sited these lines on reverse-slope positions to mask them from Allied artillery. And they took full

---

[55] See Albert Palazzo, *Seeking Victory on the Western Front: The British Army and Chemical Warfare in World War I* (Lincoln, NE, 2000). Palazzo's work is particularly good on the difficulties both sides confronted in adapting to chemical warfare.

[56] For a thorough discussion of the disastrous impact that the constant refrain of "military necessity" had on the German conduct of the First World War, see the extensive discussions in Hull, *Absolute Destruction*.

[57] Falkenhayn had replaced the younger Moltke as the chief of the general staff after the defeat of German forces in the Battle of the Marne.

advantage of the numerous new forms of barbed wire to hinder Allied offensive operations.

In early 1916 Falkenhayn switched the focus of German military effort from the Eastern and Balkan Fronts to the west. He determined to launch a late-winter assault on the great French fortress city of Verdun. In a memorandum to the kaiser, he argued that Germany was fighting in a prolonged war of attrition with an enemy coalition – led by Britain – that possessed superior resources. The logic of the argument should have been that this was a war Germany could not win.[58] But Falkenhayn went on to argue that while Britain was the linchpin of the enemy coalition, his forces should attack the French in a battle of attrition to bleed the latter white.[59]

To achieve his purpose, Falkenhayn deliberately limited the initial attacks on Verdun to prevent any rupture of French lines. Moreover, he refused to provide reserves to exploit any tactical advantages the initial attacks might gain. Falkenhayn was counting on the superiority of German artillery to dominate the battlefield and inflict disproportionate casualties on the French. But as the Germans advanced into the French defenses, it became difficult for them to move their heavy artillery and ammunition through the churned up mud of the battlefield.

In fact, the Germans soon out ran their artillery support, while they advanced steadily into a lethal killing zone dominated by increasingly powerful French artillery. Moreover, by limiting the advance to the right bank of the Meuse, Falkenhayn permitted the French to mass their artillery on the left bank and massacre German troops advancing on Verdun.[60] German losses steadily mounted, as the advance slowly ground to a halt. Verdun was probably the least imaginative battle of the war. Both attackers and defenders packed the front-line trenches with infantry, where improvements in artillery tactics allowed the opposing gunners to slaughter the huddled masses of soldiers in huge numbers. The result was horrific losses on both sides.

---

[58] In fairness to Falkenhayn, he had suggested in fall 1914 that Germany could not win the war and should therefore seek a compromise peace. He was overruled by Chancellor Theobald von Bethmann Hollweg, who argued that, politically, Germany could not afford to seek a compromise peace.

[59] The best account of the battle remains Alistair Horne, *The Price of Glory: Verdun, 1916* (New York, 1962); see also Reichskriegsministerium, *Der Weltkrieg: 1914 bis 1918*, vol. 10, *Die Operationen des Jahres 1916* (Berlin, 1936).

[60] Looking at the initial situation with the German attack confined to the right bank of the Meuse, Pétain commented, "They [the Germans] don't know their business." It appeared inconceivable to him that the Germans would wage a battle simply to attrit the French Army. Horne, *The Price of Glory*, pp. 156–157.

The British, the Somme, and the Impetus for Change

As German attacks on Verdun died down in June 1916, the British launched their great offensive on the Somme.[61] That offensive began with the terrible bloodletting of 1 July in which the attacking troops suffered nearly 50 percent casualties out of the 120,000 soldiers committed. However, by the end of the battle, the British had managed to hurt the German Army severely. The Somme itself raises a number of interesting questions about British military institutions, their approach to the war, and the culture of the officer corps. The disaster on the first day of the offensive has haunted the British conduct of war ever since, while the opprobrium attached to the commander of the BEF, Sir Douglas Haig, as a result of the disaster, has permanently stained his reputation.

What is clear is that the British high command showed scant disposition to incorporate the battlefield experiences through which its regular and territorial troops had suffered in 1914 and 1915 in the training of its new Kitchener armies. There are a number of reasons for this omission. Some senior officers were afraid that exposing the volunteer soldiers to the weary veterans would rob the new units of their lust for combat. Of equal importance was the stripping of the base to support the troops in the field and the general absence of a lessons-learned process that would have ensured that training in Britain remained in touch with what was happening in France. Nor did Haig's lack of interest in tactical matters help matters.[62] Not surprisingly, since the British had little interest in learning from their own experiences, they displayed even less interest in learning from the French. Yet by summer 1916, the French were far more proficient in both artillery and infantry tactics.[63]

Nevertheless, one should not disregard the fact that the British confronted a formidable set of problems in creating the great mass army that attacked the Germans along the Somme. In the largest sense, as even Haig recognized, the Kitchener divisions were not yet fully trained. But

---

[61] It is worth noting that the cessation of the German offensive against Verdun was largely the result of a highly successful Russian offensive – the so-called Brusilov offensive – against the Austro-Hungarian Army, which for a time threatened the entire stability of the Eastern Front.

[62] See Travers, *The Killing Ground*, chap. 5. For a more favorable, but still nuanced, view of Haig, see Gary Sheffield, *Forgotten Victory, The First World War: Myths and Realities* (London, 2002), p. 135–136. For a favorable view of Haig that is directly contrary to this author's, see John Terrain, *Douglas Haig: The Educated Soldier* (London, 1963). By far and away the best study of Haig's generalship has recently appeared: see J. P. Harris, *Douglas Haig and the First World War* (Cambridge, 2008).

[63] That superiority showed most clearly in the relative success the French enjoyed on the first day of the Somme.

the political and strategic situation, with the Russians in serious difficulty and the French under heavy pressure at Verdun, forced the British to undertake a major offensive to relieve the pressure on their allies. How they arrived at the decisions resulting in the disaster of 1 July, and the rather effective adaptations thereafter, is an interesting story.

As early as March 1915, General Sir Henry Rawlinson had glimpsed that the means did not yet exist to achieve a major breakthrough of German defenses.[64] In 1916 he, as did Lord Kitchener, argued that the British Army should conduct a number of small operations – "bite and hold" attacks – which would maximize British firepower and the enthusiasm of the new armies, provide combat experience and thereby improve tactical effectiveness, and keep casualties down to acceptable levels, while inflicting heavy casualties on the Germans.[65] Unfortunately, Haig had his heart set on a great breakthrough battle that would allow him to unleash his cavalry to achieve victory on the Napoleonic scale.[66] His conception clearly rested on his prewar assumptions about the nature of the coming war, which the experiences of two years on the Western Front had done little to change.[67] In the culture of command among senior officers on the Western Front, Haig refused to listen to his subordinates, while army commanders such as Rawlinson or Allenby displayed little consistency in their vision and rarely, if ever, were willing to disagree with Haig's assumptions and conceptions – no matter how wrong-headed.[68]

The attack on 1 July represented a compromise between Haig's and Rawlinson's divergent views, which further contributed to the disaster. The major cause of the failure was the fact that British artillery generally failed to destroy the enemy's defensive positions and especially his massive wire obstacles. In addition, most British commanders failed to coordinate their infantry attacks with the bombardment. Even the official history admits "that greater success was not gained was as much due to the faulty tactical direction from the General Staff, and the lack of experience in the higher ranks, as to the rawness in the lower ranks."[69] It was a dismal

---

[64] Bidwell and Graham, *Firepower*, p. 75; see also Johnson, *Breakthrough!*, p. 102.
[65] Ibid., p. 80.
[66] Travers, *The Killing Ground*, pp. 130–132.
[67] Here it is worth noting that Haig was a considerable supporter of technology, especially the tank, as a means to break the tactical stalemate on the Western Front. But on the operational and strategic levels, he displayed little understanding of the impact of the tactical stalemate for the conduct of his battles.
[68] Prior and Wilson, *Command on the Western Front*, p. 395.
[69] Quoted in Wynne, *If Germany Attacks*, p. 117. The British official histories were deliberately skewed to give a more favorable view of the BEF's leadership by the official

performance from beginning to end. As a recent historian of the BEF notes:

> Major J. H. Gibbon (460th Battery) remembered that he knew that the 1 July attack in his sector was doomed when the GOC [general officer commanding] of VIII Corps [Lieutenant General Hunter-Weston] ordered the heavy artillery to lift off the enemy front line trenches ten minutes before zero, and the field artillery two minutes before zero hour. Having served in Gallipoli, Gibbon knew that the artillery should keep firing until after the infantry left the trenches. He wrote to Hunter-Weston on the subject, but received no reply, perhaps because he was only of the rank of major.[70]

Nevertheless, acknowledging the tragedy, one of the distorting aspects of British military historiography of the Somme has been an overconcentration on that first day.[71] In fact, throughout the remainder of the Battle of the Somme, the BEF dealt the Germans a series of heavy blows, while casualty exchange ratios were close to one-to-one despite the fact that the British were attacking.[72] There were a number of reasons why this was so. But the central reason was that after the failure of 1 July, the British conducted their attacks more in line with Rawlinson's conceptions than with Haig's search for the elusive breakthrough.[73]

Thus, on 14 July Rawlinson launched a particularly effective night attack that deployed most of the attacking infantry well out into no-man's land, in proximity to the bombardment. Immediately after fires were lifted, the British infantry swarmed into the German trenches and caught most of the German defenders still in their dugouts. The crucial element in Rawlinson's success was the weight and effectiveness of the

---

historian, Brigadier Sir James Edmonds, whose reputation Haig had saved after the former had collapsed in the dark days of September 1914. The two had attended the staff college at the same time.

[70] Travers, *The Killing Ground*, p. 139.

[71] John Keegan's *Face of Battle* (London, 1976), chap. 4, and Martin Middlebrook's *The First Day on the Somme: 1 July 1916* (New York, 1972) are both examples of this understandable overemphasis on what was admittedly the worst day in the history of the British Army but which kicked off what was to be a battle that cost the Germans as heavily as the Allies.

[72] For the German side of the battle, see Christopher Duffy, *Through German Eyes: The British & the Somme 1916* (London, 2006); and Jack Sheldon, *The German Army on the Somme, 1914–1918* (Barnsley, UK, 2005).

[73] Nevertheless, as the best work on Rawlinson has underlined, the general displayed little ability to think through the significant implications of what was occurring on the Somme battlefield. Nor did he possess the strength of character to argue with Haig over major issues dealing with the operational and tactical possibilities. See Prior and Wilson, *Command on the Western Front*, pp. 135–260.

bombardment – the British used two-thirds the weight of artillery used in the 1 July attack against one-eighteenth the length of defenses, or approximately a 1,200 percent greater weight in artillery per kilometer of front.[74] The bombardment obliterated most of the German wire and much of the defensive system. But the slow movement forward of British reserves prevented a breakthrough. Indeed, none of the armies of 1916 possessed the ability to exploit such a success. Even had the attackers reached the open fields behind the German front lines, they would have gained little significant advantage, because German reserves were sure to arrive and plug the hole.

Meanwhile, at the small unit level, exposure to combat over the period of the July battles resulted in a salient educational process, through which British front-line troops acquired the combat experience to develop commonsense tactical adaptations to the problems they confronted. Complicating the processes of adaptation was the fact that new weapons were making their appearance on the Somme battlefield: "The integration of Lewis gun, rifle grenade, and trench mortar fire with the advances carried out by riflemen and bombers, all blended with an increasing confidence on the gunners' ability to lay down effective creeping barrages, transformed the British battle performance."[75]

Learning from mistakes, of course, is part of how all military forces gain the experience to fight effectively. In World War I, however, the peculiar aspects of Edwardian culture and the nature of the British officer corps made that learning on the Somme particularly costly. The fact that Haig would not appoint a director of training in his headquarters until 1918 underlines a failure to recognize the need for a coherent and consistent response to the tactical conditions encountered. In addition, the distance of senior officers from the battlefields limited this commonsense experiential learning largely to those serving in the front lines. It also kept many in leadership positions and on the staffs ignorant of front-line conditions, often, as the example of General Hunter-Weston suggests, willfully so.[76] Yet, the British did learn, primarily, as General Mattis has

---

[74] The above is based on the calculations and figures provided in Prior and Wilson, *Command on the Western Front*, p. 191.

[75] John Lee, "Some Lessons of the Somme: The British Infantry in 1917," in *"Look to Your Front": Studies in First World War*, ed. by Brian Bond (London, 1999), p. 80.

[76] The great German defensive expert Fritz von Lossberg seems not to have been cut in this pattern. Lossberg, chief of staff to First Army on the Somme, spent much of his time in the front lines examining what was actually happening. Wynne, *If Germany Attacks*, p. 127. The Haig diaries underline the remoteness of British commanders and their staffs from the stark realities of the tactical world.

suggested, by filling body bags. A German account, written in the 1920s, notes:

> [I]ndividual machine-gun crews, patrols, bombing parties and the troops who were assigned to seal off trenches were behaving very well. The explanation is that they were trained in independent action.... If it [were] a question of seizing small sectors of trenches, the British pushed forward small groups or simple bombing parties which advanced cautiously, in that they made skillful use of ground, but also in an aggressive spirit. Once they had broken in they lost no time in exploiting to the flanks and planting their light machine guns.[77]

The German Army's discomfiture on the Somme was similarly the result of its own making.[78] From the first, Falkenhayn – most probably for political reasons but that is not entirely clear – had demanded that German forces on the Western Front hold the ground captured in 1914.[79] This led the Germans to follow a path of "*Halten, was zu halten ist.*"[80] In his decision to concentrate on the Eastern Front in 1915, Falkenhayn ordered his commanders in the west to fortify their fronts to the greatest extent possible. However, his demand that they hold every inch of territory robbed his subordinates of the flexibility to site defensive lines on the most suitable terrain or extend their defenses in depth to move the bulk of their troops out of the range of Allied artillery. Nevertheless, there came a point of diminishing returns, in which efforts to fortify front-line positions foundered under the weight of artillery bombardments. The principle on which German defenses rested – that everything must be held – forced German commanders to pack their infantry into the front-line trenches, which only maximized their vulnerability to Allied artillery fire. Moreover, Falkenhayn's guidance forced his commanders to launch immediate counterattacks to regain whatever ground front-line troops had lost, whether or not they had sufficient reserves. During the Somme, the German command reinforced that message by sacking a number of subordinate commanders for failure to hold onto front-line positions.[81]

The result was that the Germans suffered needlessly heavy casualties. British artillery preparations, which tended to be heavier and more narrowly concentrated as the battle progressed, butchered German infantry in front-line dugouts, while increasing British sophistication in

---

[77] Duffy, *Through German Eyes*, pp. 272–273.
[78] For an excellent study of how badly the Battle of the Somme hurt the Germans, see Duffy, *Through German Eyes*.
[79] Wynne, *If Germany Attacks*, p. 118.
[80] Lupfer, *The Dynamics of Doctrine*, p. 3.
[81] Wynne, *If Germany Attacks*, p. 101.

coordinating infantry and artillery attacks added to the German casualty bill. Ernst Jünger, one of the great figures in German literature but also a winner of the Pour le Mérite for heroism, recalled the following about the Somme:

> It was the days at Guillemont [on the Somme] that first made me aware of the overwhelming effects of the war of material. We had to adapt ourselves to an entirely new phase of the war. The communications between troops and the staff, between the artillery and the liaison officers, were utterly crippled by the terrific fire. Dispatch riders failed to get through the hail of metal, and telephone wires were no sooner laid than they were shot to pieces. Even light-signaling was put out of action by the clouds of smoke and dust that hung over the field of battle. There was a zone of a kilometer behind the front line where explosives held absolute sway.... The terrible losses, out of all proportion to the breadth of the front attacked, were principally due to the old Prussian obstinacy with which the tactics of the line were pursued to their logical conclusion.... One battalion after another was crowded up into a front line already over-manned, and in a few hours pounded to bits.[82]

If the Germans were in trouble on the Somme, they had an even worse time in the fall of 1916 at Verdun. A French offensive, directed by General Robert Nivelle and executed by General Charles Mangin, drove the Germans back to their February positions. In only a few days, the French regained the ground that had taken the Germans months and hundreds of thousands of casualties to capture. Their success reflected tactical adaptations the French had made over the previous two years. The sophistication of their artillery and infantry cooperation had already made a difference in the fighting on the Somme, where French troops had made major gains in the fighting on 1 July. Laffargue appears to have played a considerable role in the Verdun offensive, where a combination of superior artillery preparations and close cooperation between combat arms inflicted the defeat on the Germans.[83]

In effect, the French were on the way toward creating the fire-and-maneuver tactics that characterize modern ground warfare.[84] The new tactical French approach aimed at breaking down a defensive system in which the Germans concentrated defensive forces in forward battle areas, where they were most vulnerable to artillery fire. Unfortunately,

---

[82] Jünger, *Storm of Steel*, pp. 107, 108, 110.
[83] Conversation with James Hogue, 4 August 1994, about his interview with General Laffargue in 1988. For the superior French performance on the Somme, especially the first day, see A. H. Farrar-Hockley, *The Somme* (London, 1964), pp. 156–158.
[84] Richard M. Watt, *Dare Call It Treason* (New York, 1963), pp. 148–149.

the French success at Verdun received minimal attention from the British and not much more from historians of the First World War writing in later periods.[85] In fact, the French adaptations represented the development of sophisticated tactical conceptions to the problem at hand – the German defenses as they existed in 1916.

The Revolution in War: 1917, the First Steps

It was during this trying time that major changes occurred in the German leadership. Under considerable political pressure in August 1916, the Kaiser replaced Falkenhayn with Field Marshall Paul von Hindenburg and the latter's chief of staff, General Erich Ludendorff. The team of Hindenburg and Ludendorff had been the driving force behind German successes on the Eastern Front, and so it was natural that given Falkenhayn's failures, they would take over the control of Germany's conduct of the war.

Historians have quite rightly condemned the strategic and political leadership that Germany's new military leaders provided the Reich in 1917 and 1918.[86] What most, however, have missed is Ludendorff's extraordinary contribution to rethinking the tactical problems the Germans confronted at the end of 1916.[87] Almost immediately on assuming his responsibilities, Ludendorff set out to discover what was actually happening on the Western Front. He visited not only senior commanders but front-line tactical commanders down to platoon level as well. What he discovered was not encouraging.

> The loss of ground up to date appeared to me of little importance in itself. We could stand that, but the question how this and the progressive falling off of our fighting power of which it was symptomatic was to be prevented was of immense importance.... on the Somme the enemy's powerful artillery, assisted by excellent aeroplane observation and fed with enormous

---

[85] One of the British liaison officers attached to the French Army for much of the war, Edward Spears, derisively referred to Nivelle's attacks in his memoirs as "the glorified raids on Verdun." Edward L. Spears, *Prelude to Victory* (London, 1939), p. 31.

[86] The most egregious mistake Ludendorff and von Hindenburg would make was to allow the German Navy to resume unrestricted submarine warfare, which brought the United States into the war and sealed Germany's fate. For the nature of that leadership, see particularly Holger Herwig, "Strategic Uncertainties of a Nation State: Prussia-Germany, 1871–1918," in Williamson Murray, MacGregor Knox, and Alvin Bernstein, eds., *The Making of Strategy: Rulers, States and War* (Cambridge, 1994). For the most recent critique of the "German way of war," see Hull, *Absolute Destruction*.

[87] Lupfer's *The Dynamics of Doctrine* represented a major break with the traditional view of Ludendorff by underlining his contribution to the processes of tactical change in the last two years of the war.

supplies of ammunition, had kept down our own fire and destroyed our artillery. The defense of our infantry had become so flabby that the massed attacks of the enemy always succeeded. Not only did our morale suffer, but, in addition to fearful wastage in killed and wounded, we lost a large number of prisoners and much material.... I attached great importance to what I learned about our infantry... about its tactics and preparation. Without doubt it fought too doggedly, clinging too resolutely to the mere holding of ground, with the result that the losses were heavy. The deep dugouts and cellars often became fatal man-traps. The use of the rifle was being forgotten, hand grenades had become the chief weapons, and the equipment of the infantry with machine guns and similar weapons had fallen far behind that of the enemy.[88]

In his survey of the Western Front, Ludendorff demanded thorough and complete briefings from the chiefs of staff of the units he visited. He demanded reporting and not "favorable report[s] made to order."[89] Drawing on the experiences of the previous two years, Ludendorff ordered a fundamental recasting of the German Army's entire defensive philosophy.[90] By late 1916, staff officers, in combination with experienced front-line officers, had developed the first modern doctrine for defensive warfare in the era of machine guns and artillery. The new doctrine rested on the conception of holding front-line positions lightly with machine gunners with successively stronger defensive positions echeloned in depth. The heaviest concentrations of reserves and defensive positions would lie in rear areas – out of range of all but the heaviest artillery and no longer under direct observation and adjustment of direct fires except by air. The reserves were now positioned to counterattack enemy penetrations.

The emphasis in the new approach to defensive tactics was not on trench lines but rather on well-camouflaged strong points to shield the defenders from observation and bombardment. The deeper the enemy worked his way into the new defensive system, the heavier would become the resistance and the farther he would move from his own artillery. The new doctrine also demanded that battalion commanders and their subordinates, junior officers, and NCOs exercise initiative on the battlefield and not wait for directions from above. Finally, the new system moved the bulk of German troops beyond the effective range of Allied artillery.

---

[88] Erich Ludendorff, *Ludendorff's Own Story: August 1914–November 1918*, vol. 1 (New York, 1919), pp. 313, 316, 321.
[89] Ibid., p. 24.
[90] The best examinations of this process are in Lupfer, *The Dynamics of Doctrine*, and Wynne, *If Germany Attacks*.

What is particularly impressive about the processes of tactical change and adaptation through which the German Army passed was this: from the moment that Ludendorff set in motion his efforts to develop a more flexible tactical system, the Germans needed only two months to come up with a workable solution. On 1 December 1916, the German Army promulgated a doctrinal manual encompassing the new tactical conceptions – *The Principles of Command in the Defensive Battle in Position Warfare*. Moreover, Ludendorff and the general staff ensured that this new doctrine was thoroughly inculcated at *all levels* in the army, to the extent that even senior commanders and staff officers attended the schools introducing the new methods.[91]

This ability to execute a radical restructuring of the army's doctrinal conceptions stands in stark contrast to the other armies on the Western Front. Admittedly, there were some problems with the new doctrine in its initial test in the battle of Arras. After a nineteen-day bombardment that fired 2,687,000 shells, the British attacked German positions and achieved a substantial success. But the German commanders on the spot had only half-heartedly applied the new doctrine, and a number of mistakes were made at different levels of command. Luckily for the Germans, the Arras attack was only a diversion for the Nivelle Offensive that came later in the month.[92]

The real test for the new German doctrine came against the massive offensive the French launched on the Chemin des Dames. At the end of 1916, Nivelle had assumed command of the French Army. He immediately announced his discovery at Verdun of *the* method that would lead the French Army to final victory; French forces would now repeat on a wider front what had been a local success at Verdun. Over the winter, Nivelle set about inculcating his new methods throughout the army. It is not entirely clear what occurred in this program, but it appears French commanders applied Nivelle's tactical conceptions more loosely than was the case with how German commanders instituted Ludendorff's defensive doctrine. Too much enthusiasm and too little careful application marked French training.[93] Moreover, the Germans executed a strategic and operational withdrawal from their positions immediately before

---

[91] Lupfer, *The Dynamics of Doctrine*, p. 24.
[92] Ibid., p. 29. For the British side of the battle, see Sheffield, *Forgotten Victory*, pp. 190–199.
[93] Spears is particularly good on the facile optimism that marked French preparations in the new tactics. Spears, *Prelude to Victory*, pp. 90–93.

Nivelle's attack to new positions sited and prepared in accordance with the new tactical doctrine of defense in depth. Ludendorff's retreat thus undermined the operational conceptions of the French offensive.[94]

The real reason for the French defeat was the fact that German defenses rested on entirely new tactical conceptions – conceptions with which the French had no experience.[95] The French artillery barrage only smashed up the screening positions. The Germans held back their artillery until the French offensive began. The increasing strength of the defensive system as the French advanced first entangled and then destroyed the attackers, while well-coordinated German counterattacks smashed what was left. It is worth noting that through 1918, major offensives rarely succeeded against well-sited and well-defended positions echeloned in depth, no matter who was launching them.[96]

Until Arras and Chemin des Dames, no one had ever run into such a defensive system. Thus, the French were in an impossible situation – their experiences and tactical innovations were largely irrelevant to solving the new tactical problems.[97] To make matters worse, German air power drove French aircraft off the battlefield and thus blinded French artillery.[98] Unfortunately, despite the fact the offensive was in trouble, Nivelle persisted in continuing the attacks, and the resulting pointless casualties triggered widespread mutinies throughout the French Army. It was in that persistence in the face of failure that makes Nivelle culpable for the ensuing collapse in discipline, not the lack of imagination or willingness to innovate. In the event it would take Nivelle's successor Pétain the spring and summer to restore the army's morale, offensive operations would now exist only on a limited scale, with artillery carrying the greatest burden and infantry making only limited advances.[99]

---

[94] For a discussion of the offensive, see Watt, *Dare Call It Treason*, chap. 10.
[95] Johnson, *Breakthrough!*, p. 194, underestimates the extent of the French defeat and the contribution that the new German tactics made to it. He does point out, however, that Nivelle's tactical conceptions were forward-thinking.
[96] The German "Friedensturm" (peace offensive) in July 1918, which failed dismally, is a case in point. See Barry Pitt, *1918: The Last Act* (New York, 1962), pp. 178–181.
[97] In general, most histories depict Nivelle as an incompetent who forced the French Army to employ an unworkable concept. They miss the new tactical context within which the French offensive in April had occurred, with the attackers, however, confronting a new German system of defense in depth – a tactical problem that no one on the Western Front had yet faced, much less come to grips with.
[98] Lupfer, *The Dynamics of Doctrine*, p. 66, n. 115.
[99] "Report on Pétain's '3rd Directive issued to Army Group and Army commanders,'" Spears papers, Fall 1917, Liddell Hart Archives, King's College, B 2/7.

By fall 1917, the French had a good idea of the new German defensive system, their understanding largely drawn, interestingly enough, from British experiences in Flanders. Circulars then went out to senior commands underlining the principles of defense in depth and counterattacks that had worked so well for the Germans. How deeply those directions actually affected defensive preparations we examine later in this chapter.[100]

The British assault in Flanders began in summer 1917. It culminated in the fighting around the dismal Belgian village of Passchendaele where troops floundered in the mud and which was to give the battle its name. Passchendaele certainly introduced one of the gloomiest chapters in the history of the war. The British attacks hit a German defensive system that was significantly advanced over the one that had halted Nivelle's spring offensive. Colonel Fritz von Lossberg, the defensive genius of World War I, placed greater emphasis on the holding of front-line positions than had been the case against the French in the spring. But defense in depth remained at the heart of the German approach, as well as the emphasis on timely, well-planned, well-executed counterattacks. As one observer has noted, in Flanders "the front divisions...fought [the battle] in and for the foremost line, and by doing so they...succeeded in breaking up and delaying the waves of the assault; the *Eingreif* [counterattack] divisions...fought [the battle] behind the foremost line."[101]

Nevertheless, the battle was anything but a walkover for the Germans. Ernst Jünger suggests just how painful an experience it was for German troops:

> At six in the morning the Flanders mist lifted and gave us a glimpse of our ghastly surroundings.... Any scattered detachments of infantry that were above ground instantly endeavored to hide themselves in shell holes. Half an hour later a terrific artillery fire set in. It raged round our refuge [one of the concrete strong points] like a typhoon-scourged sea around an island. The hail of shells thickened to a throbbing wall of fire. We crouched together, expecting each second the crashing hit that would sweep us up with our concrete blocks and make our position indistinguishable from the desert craters all around.[102]

---

[100] See particularly "Note pour les Armées," Des Armées du NORD et du NORD-EST, ÉTAT-Major, 2e ET 3e BUREAUX, No 20.650, 18 octobre 1917, Spears papers, Liddell Hart Archives, King's College, B 2/17.
[101] G. C. Wynne, *If Germany Attacks*, p. 302.
[102] Jünger, *Storm of Steel*, p. 167.

Although the Germans held their ground at less cost than had been the case on the Somme, they still suffered grievously. On the British side, there were glimmerings that the troops and at least some commanders were beginning to grasp the complex interactions needed to make combined-arms tactics work. Haig still remained out of the picture as far as the tactical world was concerned, both because of his lack of interest and because his staff continued to shield him, as well as themselves, from the sharp realities of what was happening on the battlefield.[103]

British operations in 1917 kicked off with two substantial successes, both in the "bite and hold" mold. Their aim was to achieve a limited success against an important but vulnerable section of the German defensive line. The first, at Arras, we discussed earlier in this chapter. The second came against German positions at Messines. The attack began with massive artillery preparations that targeted not only German front-line positions but German artillery as well. Over an 11-day period, British artillery fired approximately 3,500,000 shells. A German machine gunner noted its impact on his own artillery. "This is far worse than the Battle of Arras. Our artillery is left sitting and is scarcely able to fire a round ... the sole object of every arm that enters the battle is to play itself out, in order to be withdrawn as quickly as possible."[104] The pièce de résistance came on 7 June with the explosion of 19 mines beneath the main German positions. Immediately after those explosions, infantry from nine divisions attacked. By the end of the day, the attacking British infantry had captured the Messines Ridge, which the Germans had held since October 1914. Haig desired a continuation of the offensive, but General Herbert Plummer, commander of the operation, demurred, stating that he could not get his artillery forward for at least three days.

These two battles suggest that the British were in a position to deal the Germans a series of telling blows, provided they were willing to limit the scope and length of their attacks. That was not the case at Passchendaele.[105] Here the British again enjoyed limited success at first.

---

[103] Haig's chief of staff, Lieutenant General Sir Launcelot Kiggell, visited the battlefield for the first time on 5 November 1917. His comment ("Good God, did we really send men to fight in that?") speaks volumes on the nature of generalship in the British Army at the higher headquarters. Leon Wolff, *In Flanders Fields: The 1917 Campaign* (New York, 1958), p. 383.

[104] Quoted in Sheffield, *Forgotten Victory*, p. 201.

[105] See particularly Prior and Wilson, *Passchendaele*, for a clear examination of Haig's failure to understand what was actually occurring in the front lines. The authors are also most perceptive on Lloyd George's political responsibility for the disaster.

That initial success reflected the ability of British artillery to dominate the landscape and of British infantry to work its way forward with the support of the panoply of weapons it now possessed. But on the Gheluvelt plateau, crucial to the success of further attacks, the British made only insignificant gains. Here, as one of the more perceptive British staff officers noted: "The further we penetrate his line, the stronger and more organised we find him... [while] the weaker and more disorganized we are liable to become."[106] German counterattack formations added to British woes, driving them back from much of their initial gains on the Gheluvelt plateau.

Even so, had Haig stopped after the first or second day, he would have achieved a reasonable success – but he did not. His conception of war still rested on his picture of a great Napoleonic breakthrough that would allow him to unleash the British cavalry on German rear areas. Moreover, he was also preparing an amphibious landing on the German-held portion of the Belgian coast – an operation which luckily for those who would have been involved, he never launched.

The weather now turned. Massive thunderstorms and heavy rains flooded the Flanders plain, an area British artillery had thoroughly plowed up and in the process destroyed the drainage system of what had once been a great primeval swamp. Haig's chief of intelligence, Brigadier John Charteris, continued to manipulate his reports to support his boss's belief that the Germans were on the point of breaking.[107] The Flanders area returned to its former state, except that no vegetation survived – only men and rats. There were some additional British tactical successes in the battle, particularly the attack on the Menin Road Ridge on 20 September. For the most part, the struggle degenerated into a dreadful slogging match, where men quite literally floundered and in some cases even drowned in the mud.

At the end of the year, the British were able to achieve another startling success – largely because of the successful integration of tanks into the combined-arms team. Haig had been a strong supporter of technological developments in general and of the tank in particular.[108] He had first used the tank in the last battles of the Somme, a decision that some historians have criticized. However, as the tank pioneer J. F. C. Fuller admitted

---

[106] Quoted in Sheffield, *Forgotten Victory*, p. 207.
[107] Haig, *Douglas Haig*, pp. 332, 336.
[108] Here Haig had received bad press from postwar pundits such as Liddell Hart. In fact, his diaries indicate that he was a supporter of technological adaptation.

after the war, there was good reason at the time to discover what the tank could and could not do before proceeding on a major construction program.[109] As the Passchendaele battle ended, Haig agreed to a proposal from the tank corps for a major tank raid with heavy artillery and infantry support against the German positions in front of Cambrai. Moreover, unlike battles earlier in the year, British artillery entered the modern era of artillery tactics. There was to be no prolonged bombardment. There would not even be a registration of guns. Instead, building on what the British had learned about German defense-in-depth tactics over the course of the year, there was a careful identification of enemy strong points and artillery positions, close work between the artillery and its spotters on the ground and in the air, careful preparation of infantry and tankers to work together in attacking known enemy strong points, and a massive artillery barrage that would provide the Germans with no advance warning.[110]

The one weakness in the plan was the fact that there were no reserves available to exploit success – Haig had killed or maimed them in Flanders. Nevertheless, the result was a stunning success. The British broke through the entire German system. Combat casualties, mechanical failures of virtually all the tanks – to be expected with a new technology – and the swift arrival of German reserves prevented the British from breaking out into the open.[111]

Within a week, the Germans launched a devastating counterattack that regained the ground lost at Cambrai. That counterattack underlined how much the Germans as well had learned over the course of 1917 with their new defensive tactics.[112] Those tactics had depended on both local and major counterattacks – the latter launched by arriving reserve formations. Exploiting improvements in indirect artillery fire and innovations in infantry tactics that emphasized fire and maneuver, speed in execution, decentralized decision making down to the junior officer and NCO ranks,

---

[109] Harris, *Men, Ideas, and Tanks*, p. 74.
[110] For an excellent analysis of the Cambrai success, see Travers, *How the War Was Won*, pp. 19–31.
[111] Not that the British were in a position to exploit such a breakthrough. Like everyone else on the Western Front, their focus had been on creating a breakthrough. As the Germans would discover the next year, creating one would raise a completely new set of problems associated with exploitation.
[112] Both Lupfer and Gudmundsson are good on this, although the latter tends to be too favorable to German combat innovations. See Lupfer, *The Dynamics of Doctrine*, pp. 27–29; and Gudmundsson, *Stormtroop Tactics*, chap. 9.

and exploitation of weak points in the enemy line, the Germans were in the process of returning tactical movement to the Western Front.[113]

Thus, the German counterattack at Cambrai reflected a fundamentally new offensive approach – one that allowed the attacking forces to break not only into but also through their opponent's defensive trench system. The British official history records the German counterattack at Cambrai in the following terms:

> Preceded by patrols the Germans had advanced by 7 a.m. in small columns bearing many light machineguns, and, in some cases, flamethrowers. From overhead low flying airplanes, in greater numbers than had hitherto been seen, bombed and machine gunned the British defenders, causing further casualties and, especially, distraction at the critical moment. Nevertheless, few posts appear to have been attacked from the front, the assault sweeping in between to envelop them from flanks and rear.[114]

The Revolution in War: 1918

On 1 January 1918, the German high command issued a major doctrinal pronouncement, *Angriff im Stellungskrieg* (the Attack in Position Warfare).[115] Here the Germans brought the tactical pieces of infantry and artillery adaptation together in one coherent and devastating framework. The crucial component was artillery with its increasing ability to hit targets accurately and in mass.[116] Moreover, there was a basic change in the concept of bombardment. As one commentator has noted, "[Armies] had to stop expecting the artillery bombardment to destroy the defensive system – which was impossible – and settle for an artillery bombardment which neutralized the defensive system – which was possible."[117]

---

[113] Johnson, *Breakthrough!*, p. 199. Most historians have pointed to the German attack on Riga as being partly responsible for the development of these new tactical conceptions. There is little evidence of this – especially given that Russia's armies were in a state of complete collapse in fall 1917 and thus represented neither a tactical nor an operational challenge to the attacking Germans. Nevertheless, the commander of German artillery in the offensive, Bruchmüller, did utilize a number of innovative tactics in his artillery preparation of the battlefield.
[114] Quoted in Lupfer, *The Dynamics of Doctrine*, p. 40.
[115] Ibid., p. 41.
[116] For what artillery could do under the control of a first-rate innovator, see Zabecki, *Steel Wind*.
[117] Meyer, "Operational Art and the German Command System in World War I," p. 279.

The purpose of artillery was now to disrupt the enemy's defensive system, infantry as well as guns, sufficiently to create breaks and fractures, which those on the spot could exploit to further disrupt, with the aim of causing systemic failure. With the emphasis on disruption rather than total destruction, there was no need for a prolonged preparatory bombardment, which reintroduced the possibility of tactical surprise. That in turn ruled out preregistration of guns and demanded that those conducting the attack mask the concentration of guns and ammunition dumps as well as the other indicators of the coming attack. The artillery preparation would consist of a sudden and massive bombardment of enemy positions, lasting no more than a matter of hours. The artillery of 1916 could not have executed such an approach; it required the processes of adaptation over the intervening period to create the tactical pieces and then fit them together.

Equally important was the need for infantry to carry its own firepower – mortars, light machine guns, and other weapons to neutralize strong points in their path. But it was in their conception that the infantry must advance quickly and deeply with the aim of driving through the enemy defensive system – in other words, exploiting the seams without regard to the tactical flanks – that the Germans altered the tactical equation in a fundamental way. The crucial emphasis was for the advance to flow around enemy strong points, exploit the weaknesses in the enemy's system, and achieve disruption rather than absolute destruction.[118]

In promulgating this synthesis of tactical adaptations, the Germans demonstrated how quickly they could share lessons learned across their combat forces. By the end of January 1918, the army in the west, under the direction of the general staff, had established a number of schools through which junior officers and NCOs were funneled. Interestingly, a number of senior officers – up to the rank of division commanders – were also sent through the schools, although one doubts whether they were exposed to the full curricula. Significantly, Ludendorff wanted to ensure that senior officers understood the new doctrinal approach fully.

Even more important was the fact that the general staff system provided the intellectual and organizational means to ensure that the lessons-learned process would end up in coherent and consistent learning at the troop level throughout the whole army. By early March 1918, the Germans had worked up 30-plus "attack" divisions, fully trained in the

---

[118] In effect, this completed the adaptation in German doctrine and practice to the modern system of combined-arms tactics.

Complex Adaptation

new exploitation tactics.[119] But to do so, they stripped the rest of the army's divisions of their best junior officers, NCOs, and enlisted men, which in the long run debilitated the army's overall quality and combat strength.[120]

On the other side of the lines, the British were grappling with the fact that they would most probably be standing on the defensive for the first time since 1914.[121] Having experienced firsthand the grim effectiveness of defense in depth over 1917, the BEF made some effort to introduce such a system into their units. But on the British side, there existed no organizational mechanism, similar to the German general staff, that allowed for rapid, consistent adaptation to new tactical methods of combat. With no coherent ability to pass doctrinal changes throughout the BEF, adaptation of the German approach was very much on a higgledy-piggledy basis.[122] The British Third Army, for example, managed to get most of its units to adapt to a system of defense in depth, while Fifth Army at the southern end of the British line almost completely failed to understand, much less implement, the changes. Thus, the divisions of the latter army had their troops packed in the forward trenches, where German artillery fire butchered them in the first hours of the offensive.

In mid-March 1918, the Germans struck the British Fifth and Third Armies. In most of the sectors of the Third Army, defense in depth allowed British units to absorb the shock of the attacks without losing tactically significant terrain. In the south, it was a different story. With its divisions deployed in the forward trenches, Fifth Army lost much of its infantry in the first hours of the German attack. Moreover, few of its corps or division commanders displayed initiative, while the army commander,

---

[119] Reichsarchiv, *Der Weltkrieg: 1914–1918*, vol. 14, *Die Kriegführung an der Westfront im Jahre 1918* (Berlin, 1944), pp. 41–42.

[120] Holger Herwig gives a grim picture of the German Army in spring 1918. See Holger Herwig, "The Dynamics of Necessity, German Military Policy during the First World War," in Millett and Murray, eds., *Military Effectiveness*, vol. 1, *The First World War*, ed. by Allan R. Millett and Williamson Murray (London, 1988), pp. 102–103.

[121] The collapse of Russia led the Western Allies to expect that the Germans, having transferred divisions from the east, would launch an offensive in the west before the Americans arrived. Many historians have repeated that argument. In fact, the Germans, pursuing Ludendorff's dreams of conquest in the east, refused to make such transfers until summer 1918. There was an additional reason. Over the course of 1918, the numbers of deserters in the German Army ranged from 200,000 in January 1918 to 700,000 by November; the troops in the east were already infected by deep problems in morale. Reichsarchiv, *Der Weltkrieg*, vol. 14, p. 760.

[122] For the British difficulties in understanding the defense-in-depth system, see Travers, *How the War Was Won*, p. 31.

General Sir Hugh Gough, could think only of firing squads as a means to restore a collapsing situation. Ernst Jünger best captures the fury of the opening moments of the German attack:

> At once the hurricane broke loose. A curtain of flame was let down, followed by a sudden impetuous tumult such as was never heard, a raging thunder that swallowed up the reports even of the heaviest guns in its tremendous reverberations and made the earth tremble.... The terrific tumult behind us rose higher and higher.... One could scarcely hear the thousands of machine-guns in our rear that swept the blue sky with swarm upon swarm of lead.... The turmoil of our feelings was called forth by rage, alcohol, and the thirst for blood as we stepped out, heavily and yet irresistibly, for the enemy's lines.... We crossed a battered tangle of wire without difficulty and at a jump were over the front line, scarcely recognizable any longer.[123]

After the crushing artillery barrage had wrecked most of the front-line defenses, storm-troop battalions spearheaded the German advances into the British rear areas. With most of their communications in shambles, British commanders had few means to coordinate their counterattacks. The German emphasis on dislocating their opponents' command and control system began with the artillery bombardment. One British officer recalled: "We had in the division area deep cable trenches to a very large degree. These were a snare and a delusion. They had been photographed from the air by the Germans with the result that they fired at the junctions (with armour piercing shell) and everyone was disconnected in a few moments."[124]

One of the foremost historians of the war has rendered a devastating judgment on the tactical state of the British Army in March 1918:

> [One] does not therefore have to look very far to explain the German success in March 1918. This was not primarily due to German superiority in divisions, nor to the mist, nor to the [sections of] French line taken over by the BEF, nor to the lack of manpower, nor to the reduction of infantry battalions in the BEF, nor to the divisions sent to Italy. *Rather it was due to a defensive system that was not understood, did not work, and did not properly exist at all.*" [emphasis in original][125]

Nevertheless, having accumulated so much combat experience by this point in the war, the British proved quick learners. By the end of March,

---

[123] Jünger, *Storm of Steel*, pp. 250–255.
[124] Travers, *How the War Was Won*, p. 55.
[125] Ibid., p. 65.

the survivors of the Fifth Army debacle were doing a creditable job in building defensive positions based on defense in depth – one that brought the German advance to a halt before it reached the crucial railroad center at Amiens.[126]

Meanwhile, the Germans were having their own problems despite having succeeded in doing what no one else had been able to achieve thus far in the war in the west: they had punched an enormous hole in the British lines.[127] But Ludendorff had not a clue about what should follow such a success. Before the offensive was launched, Crown Prince Rupprecht of Bavaria, army group commander for this sector of the Western Front, had queried Ludendorff as to the operational goal for the spring offensive. Ludendorff had acerbically replied, "I object to the word 'operation.' We will punch a hole into [their line]. For the rest we shall see."[128]

With no operational goal in sight, the Germans simply seized territory, none of which threatened the overall strategic position of Allied armies on the Western Front. Like the British at Cambrai, the Germans had no clear idea of what they would do next were they to achieve a clear breakthrough. Moreover, because German infantry was exploiting the breakthrough, the speed with which the infantry could advance entirely dictated the speed of the exploitation. To complicate matters, because the opening bombardment (as well as earlier battles on the Somme) had so wrecked the landscape, German batteries could not displace to new positions fast enough to keep up with the pace of the infantry advance. In the end the Germans managed to grab a substantial amount of worthless real estate – which only made their defensive problems greater – but at such a heavy cost that defeat came that much faster in late 1918.

The next major German attack came on the Chemin des Dames front near the Aisne River.[129] Again, the Germans hit a position that possessed no depth – in fact, its back was to the river. The French Sixth Army defended this sector, reinforced by three badly bashed British divisions that had borne the brunt of the German March offensive. Those three divisions, not surprisingly, were enthusiastic converts to the concept of defense in depth. The experience of the British divisions should have been welcomed by the Sixth Army, which after all had been ordered along with

---

[126] Ibid., p. 90.
[127] For a clear examination of the reasons behind the failure of the Ludendorff offensives on the operational level, see Zabecki, *The German 1918 Offensives*, pp. 311–328.
[128] Crown Prince Rupprecht, *Mein Kriegstagebuch*, vol. 2, ed. by Eugen von Frauenholz (Munich, 1929), p. 372 note.
[129] The best description of the German success in this attack is in Pitt, *1918*, chap. 6.

other French armies by Pétain, now commander-in-chief of the French Army, to prepare defensive positions in depth. However, Sixth Army's commander, General Duchesne, thought he knew better and refused to introduce such a system into his area of command. He ordered the British as well as his own divisions to pack their front-line positions with infantry. Unlike the Germans but like the British, the French military did not possess the command mechanisms to ensure that subordinates paid attention to adaptations that had already proved effective on other sectors of the front.[130]

The result was another tactical disaster. The massive German initial barrage butchered British and French defenders in their front-line positions along the Chemin des Dames. Almost immediately thereafter, German storm-trooper formations infiltrated through the front-line positions and drove deep into Sixth Army's rear. Communications collapsed. But now in the open, the Germans confronted the same operational problem that had brought the "Michael" breakthrough to a halt. Their offensive tactics could break the crust of Allied defenses, but they did not possess the mechanized means to exploit such a success. Ironically, in an operational sense, the Germans were the net losers, because the great salients their infantry created in these offensives were harder to defend and required more troops to hold than the lines from which they had launched their attacks. And there were fewer troops because the Germans took extraordinarily heavy casualties – casualties which they could not afford and which fell largely on the cream of the German Army, the hand-selected officers and men of the attacking storm-troop units.[131]

Over spring 1918, the Allies learned and adapted in a tough school. By late June, they had finally forced commonsense tactical doctrine down through the levels of command. The results showed when the Germans launched their last major offensive of the war against French positions west of Rheims.

> Along a twenty-mile front the [German] infantry raced forward easily at first, their only casualties caused by the widely spaced and isolated French

---

[130] This was to be a consistent aspect of British tactical difficulties in the Second World War. See particularly Williamson Murray, "British Military Effectiveness: The World War II Experience," in Murray and Millett, eds., *Military Effectiveness*, vol. 3, chap. 3.
[131] One of the great myths of maneuver war is that it results in lower casualty rates. That was certainly not the case in 1918, nor was it the case with the initial tactical battles that allowed the Germans to seize the right bank of the Meuse in 1940. In the former case, the Germans suffered nearly a million casualties in a four-month period, while in the latter case, the lead German infantry battalions that crossed the Meuse suffered between 50 and 70 percent casualties in the two-day operation.

machine-gunners, who nevertheless manned their suicidal positions. But as the storm troopers penetrated deeper and deeper into the French positions, machine-gun posts were uncovered more often, and their withering fire cut wide swathes in the advancing ranks.... [the Germans] pressed onwards... past the curiously empty and deserted French lines, onwards through increasing... hostile shell-fire... until at last they reached the area of smoking and cratered ground which marked the limit of their own artillery barrage. And there, just beyond it, they saw the solid line of French defenses, unshelled, unbombed, ungassed, the riflemen and machine-gunners waiting.[132]

The stunning defeat of Ludendorff's *Friedensturm* offensive completed the job of exhausting the German Army. The Allies were now in a position to launch a series of devastatingly heavy counterblows against a beaten opponent. The tactical approach of the French Army, not surprisingly given the terrible bloodletting of 1914–1917, was careful and prudent. In that prudence, one sees the birth of the "methodical" battle that was to characterize French preparations in the interwar period and that, ironically, eventually led to the disaster of 1940.[133]

By summer 1918, the Americans were at last arriving on the battlefield in substantial numbers. Given American bravado, it is not surprising that they felt they had little to learn from their Allies. Thus, they repeated in excruciating detail most of the mistakes the French and British had made early in the war. Only their extraordinary unpreparedness and atrocious staff work prevented them from getting enough soldiers into the line to suffer casualties on the order of those suffered by their allies in 1914 through 1916. Where they did fight, luckily for them, the Germans were less able to deal out heavy punishment than earlier in the war. But the Americans proved faster learners than the Allies had earlier in the war. They also proved far more willing to pass tactical lessons and solutions up the chain of command. By the time they attacked the nightmarish German defenses in the Meuse-Argonne, a number of their divisions were first-rate combat formations.

The British Army is the most interesting case of adaptation in the last half of 1918. Its divisions, ably supported by the Dominion armies of Canada, Australia, and New Zealand, carried the great weight of the Allied offensives that broke the German Army in the last half of 1918. Timothy Travers has argued that the British Army attempted

---

[132] Pitt, *1918*, pp. 179–181. Also see Gudmundsson, *On Artillery*, pp. 95–102.
[133] For the development of French doctrine, see Doughty, *Seeds of Disaster*. Doughty lays out in detail the sad path that led the French Army from the First World War to its disastrous defeat in 1940.

two approaches in its last offensives – the first emphasizing a mechanical approach and the second "manpower-oriented and semi-traditional forms of warfare."[134] Travers is correct in identifying a serious dichotomy between the form that the devastating British offensive of 8 August took – an offensive that Ludendorff rightly characterized as "the blackest day of the German Army in the war" – and the remaining British offensives. The 8 August offensive was an effective combined-arms attack that rested to a great extent on the successful actions of British tanks and even involved limited exploitation by armored vehicles into the German rear areas.[135]

Thereafter, despite the availability of considerable numbers of tanks, British offensives largely emphasized an infantry-artillery combination with a few tanks thrown in for good measure. Part of the explanation for the change had to do with the speed with which tanks broke down or were used up in combat. But part of the British high command's failure to take full advantage of their tanks had to do with the BEF's advance – slow by World War II standards but extraordinarily fast by the standards of the time, especially when one considers that the British Army had remained in virtually static positions for nearly four years. The war of maneuver now presented enormous logistic difficulties, which prevented the concentration of tanks such as had occurred in the 8 August attack in front of Arras.[136]

There is another way to look at these battles. The success on 8 August resulted from effective exploitation that got through the German defenses and into the enemy's rear areas. British armored cars and Whippet tanks did considerable damage throughout the German rear areas – damage as much psychological as physical; in effect, they played the same role that German storm troopers had played in Ludendorff's spring attacks. One should not miss the fact that British artillery tactics and the skillful use of gas, as well as the work of Australian and Canadian infantry in the 8 August attack, possessed considerable similarity to how the German storm troopers had broken through Allied positions earlier in the year.[137] In effect, the British had adapted to the German style of war, but the addition of the tank significantly enhanced their ability to deal with a

---

[134] Travers, *How the War Was Won*, p. 175. The British offensives in the last months of the war have finally begun to attract the interest of historians. In this regard, J. P. Harris's *1918: Amiens to the Armistice* (London, 2002) is particularly worth consulting.
[135] For a discussion of the tactical exploitation by British armored cars, see Pitt, *1918*, pp. 200–204.
[136] Harris, *Men, Ideas, and Tanks*, pp. 180–186.
[137] For the 8 August offensive, see Pitt, *1918*, pp. 195–205.

defensive system that was based on defense in depth at least on 8 August. Tragically, in the coming interwar period, the British Army would look to the other offensive actions of 1918 – when it looked at all – for lessons that suggested how the next war would be fought. In no sense did those subsequent attacks involve exploitation or rapid movement forward to disrupt the enemy's defensive system at either the tactical or the operational levels of war.

To a considerable extent, the performance of the armies that would fight in the next war would depend on the tactical conceptions they developed during the First World War and how they thought about and analyzed those tactical experiences during the interwar period.[138] Tactics based on the rapid exploitation of weaknesses in the enemy's defensive system would translate into exploitation at the operational level. Armies that missed the importance of tactical exploitation and combined-arms tactics – or that lost those lessons in careless lessons-learned analyses – would not be able to adapt themselves to the war of exploitation at the operational level in World War II. Consequently, Haig's failure to repeat the formula of the 8 August attack was to have a significant influence on how the British Army would perform in the next war.

Conclusion

It is easy to dismiss the learning experiences of the European armies in grappling with the tactical and operational problems raised by the First World War. The solutions to the tactical and technological problems raised by the war appear to be simple in retrospect. Our vantage point at the start of the twenty-first century makes those problems almost indiscernible. Nevertheless, what is obvious today was not necessarily obvious to those in the past. As the introduction to this chapter suggested, the problems that the technological and industrial revolutions raised for military organizations, which had not found themselves engaged in major wars for more than four decades, were almost insoluble from the perspective of 1913. Moreover, to add to the difficulties of adaptation in the period between 1914 and 1918, both sides attempted to adapt not only to a rapidly changing battlefield but also to the adaptations that their opponents were developing and utilizing as the conflict unrolled.

---

[138] For a discussion of these issues, see Murray, "Armored Warfare," in Williamson Murray and Allan R. Millett, eds., *Military Innovation in the Interwar Period* (Cambridge, 1996), chap. 1.

If history is a laboratory, then the First World War, as it is now understood, provides almost perfect conditions for examining the phenomenon of complex adaptation in an environment where both sides adapt on a continuous basis to the ever-changing conditions of the battlefield. The result of the four terrible years of slaughter was what we would today consider combined-arms tactics, perhaps in rudimentary form but in a form that is thoroughly recognizable. Part of the explanation as to why it took so long for solutions to emerge was the fact that deriving and applying lessons on the fly is not easy – especially when the enemy is changing under the pressures of combat as well.

Yet, one should not lose sight of the fact that human incompetence – often willful and truculent – played a considerable role in the failures to adapt at anything other than a glacial pace, especially considering the price in blood and treasure that the European nations were paying. The mastery of tactics is the basic and essential skill demanded of all practitioners of the military profession. For the most part, the generals and armies of World War I failed to achieve anything close to mastery of the tactical world. Yet there is a significant lesson here, because the tactics that most failed to master contradicted everything they thought they knew. Thus, the real problem was not simply to establish a competence in tactics but also to balance that competence with the ability and openness to recognize when it ceased to be productive or relevant.

4

Flawed Adaptation: German Adaptation
The Opening Battles of World War II

Perhaps nothing makes clearer the importance of peacetime military culture and its influence over the ability of military institutions to adapt to the actual conditions of war than the case of the German Army and the *Luftwaffe* between 1920 and 1939. This is true both in a positive and a negative sense. Unlike other European military organizations after 1918, the German Army learned the tactical lessons of the First World War, and the innovations and force structure it developed in the interwar period reflected what had actually happened on the battlefields.[1] The reference to actual combat experience provided the *Wehrmacht* with an inestimable advantage over its opponents in the first three years of the Second World War. But in terms of learning from their operational and strategic errors, German performance during the interwar years was not nearly so impressive. Accordingly, those weaknesses would reappear during the Second World War and, in the end, negate the initial advantages with which the Germans launched their second great attempt to gain European hegemony.

It has been accepted as a truism by many historians, including military historians, that military institutions study the last war, and that is why they do badly in the next conflict. Nothing could be further from the truth: for most of history, military institutions have *not* studied the last war, which is precisely why they have so often failed to adapt to the realities of the next war. Moreover, even when they have studied the last

---

[1] This refers to both the ground and air portions of the First World War, because German air power remained a part of the army throughout the war. Thus, this chapter examines both the German Army's and the *Luftwaffe*'s efforts at adapting.

war, they have tended to study what made their political and military leaders feel comfortable and to disregard those areas in which they have been least effective or confronted the greatest difficulties.

One of the most significant problems military institutions have faced over the past century with the increasing pace of technological change has been how to turn the lessons of war into coherent training programs that allow for significant adaptations to the conditions their forces confront. All organizations have a finite ability to absorb change; overload that ability, and they tend to become dysfunctional. Moreover, the frictions, horror, and chaos of combat have inevitably made it difficult to draw clear and unambiguous lessons they can then turn into coherent training programs for those who will be exposed to the sharp end of combat.[2] It is likely that such difficulties will continue into the future.

Yet, modern war is much more than simply performance on the battlefield. It demands vision at the strategic level, as well as support structures that provide not only reasonable pictures of their opponent and his prospects but the logistical systems to provide sustenance as well as fuel, ammunition, and spare parts in reasonable time. This chapter addresses how in the period after the Polish campaign, the Germans succeeded in learning and adapting at the tactical level in a fashion their opponents could not – but failed to learn and adapt to the larger issues raised by the war on which they had embarked. The result was the German Army's great tactical and operational victories in the opening years of World War II – victories, however, that in the end only paved the way for an even more catastrophic national defeat, reflecting a failure to learn and adapt to the larger strategic and political issues that war throughout history has inevitably involved.

The Background: The German Army in the Interwar Period

In the period between the First and Second World Wars, the German Army and its spinoff, the *Luftwaffe,* proved the exception to the normal pattern of behavior for military institutions.[3] The culture of the *Heer* (army) reflected the pattern of learning from battlefield experience that had marked the Imperial Army's performance in the last two years of the

---

[2] This is less true for air forces and navies than it was in the past, but ground forces, no matter how improved their training methodologies, will still confront the uncertainties that have always made ground combat difficult to prepare for.

[3] For the German Army's development of armored warfare during the interwar period, see Williamson Murray, "Armored Warfare," in Williamson Murray and Allan R. Millett, eds., *Military Innovation in the Interwar Period* (Cambridge, 1996).

First World War.[4] By 1917, all the armies on the Western Front had instituted comprehensive "lessons learned" processes, although the Germans were undoubtedly better at actually learning the lessons. What set the Germans apart was the fact that they instituted a rigorous, coherent, and consistent program to review those lessons even after the conflict had ended.[5] The individual primarily responsible for establishing this process was General Hans von Seeckt, chief of the disguised general staff – the so-called *Truppenamt* – and then the commander-in-chief of the army from 1920 to 1926.

Confronted by the harsh demands of the Versailles Treaty that the German Army decrease its officer corps from 20,000 to 4,000, Seeckt took advantage of that downsizing effort to establish a major program to examine the lessons of the last war.[6] As he noted at the time, "it is absolutely necessary to put the experience of the war in a broad light and collect this experience, while the impressions won on the battlefield are still fresh and a major proportion of the experienced officers are still in leading positions."[7]

To accomplish that task, he established no fewer than 57 committees throughout the various branches of the army. His brief to the officers who made up these committees was simple and direct: their guidance was to produce short, concise studies on the newly gained experiences of the war and consider the following points:

1. What new situations arose in the war that had not been considered before the war?
2. How effective were our prewar views in dealing with those situations?

---

[4] For the development of German defensive doctrine over the course of the First World War, see particularly G. C. Wynne, *If Germany Attacks: The Battle in Depth in the West* (London, 1940). For the development of German offensive doctrine during this period, see Timothy T. Lupfer, *The Dynamics of Doctrine: The Changes in German Tactical Doctrine during the First World War* (Leavenworth, KS, 1981).

[5] The British Army failed to create a lessons-learned committee to study the lessons of the last war until 1932; then, when the results upset the Chief of the Imperial General Staff, Field Marshal Sir Archibald Montgomery-Massingberd, he had the report sanitized so that the parts critical of the army's performance were softened to the point of irrelevance. Thus, all too many officers who read the report missed the significant criticisms it had made when it was originally written.

[6] Significantly, in the choices that Seeckt had the army's personnel office make in determining the officers the Reichswehr would retain and those it would send home, he retained the general staff in its entirety. The result was that it came to dominate the postwar army in a fashion that had not been the case before the First World War.

[7] James S. Corum, *The Roots of Blitzkrieg, Hans von Seeckt and German Military Reform* (Lawrence, KS, 1992), p. 37.

3. What new guidelines have been developed from the use of new weaponry in war?
4. Which new problems put forward by the war have not yet found a solution?[8]

It was on the basis of that careful examination of best practices from the last conflict that the *Reichsheer* and the *Wehrmacht* developed a coherent and realistic doctrine – one that emphasized maneuver; decentralized command and control; and rapid, driving exploitation. In late 1932 and early 1933, three of the army's leading generals, Werner von Fritsch, Ludwig Beck, and Otto von Stulpnägle – the first of whom would become the army's commander-in-chief and of whom the second chief of the general staff in 1934 – codified German doctrine into the famous *Truppenführung (Troop Leadership)*. That doctrinal statement provided the intellectual framework that would guide the *Wehrmacht* throughout World War II and form the basis for how it would conduct war at the tactical level both in the air and on the ground.

Moreover, throughout the interwar period the Germans conducted realistic maneuvers that tested doctrinal assumptions and tactical precepts to the breaking point. Seeckt continued to emphasize the importance of lessons learned throughout his tenure as the army's commander. The first experiments on mechanization and mobility in 1921 received Seeckt's full support: he insisted that the lessons from those experiments were widely distributed throughout the army. As he noted regarding an experiment in motorized warfare carried out in the Harz mountains in 1922 at his direction:

> I fully approve of the Harz exercise's conception and leadership, but there is still much that is not clear about the specific tactical use of motor vehicles. I therefore order that the following report be made available by all the staffs and independent commands as a topic for lectures and study. Troop commanders must see to it that experience in this area is widened by practical exercises.[9]

The general staff then followed up on the exercises with a careful examination aimed not only at criticizing performance but also at

---

[8] Ibid., p. 37.
[9] Reichswehrministerium, Chef der Heeresleitung, Betr: "Harzübung," 8.1.22, National Archives and Records Service (NARS), T-79/65/000622.

ensuring that troops as well as commanders learned the proper lessons. The result was slow but steady improvement.[10]

Hitler's arrival in power as the Reich's Chancellor in January 1933 provided the army with the resources to conduct a massive rearmament program. Hitler also allowed the army to disregard the provisions of the Treaty of Versailles and incorporate the tank into its rearmament programs. Fritsch and Beck created the first three panzer divisions in 1935, but teething problems in tank design and production and uncertainty over its role delayed the creation of the next panzer division until late summer 1938.[11] Nevertheless, the concepts and capabilities of armored warfare fit in with the larger combined-arms approach to war that German doctrine had emphasized since 1917. There was nothing in terms of armored exploitation that was not already inherent in German combined-arms doctrine.

In the late 1930s, the Germans conducted a number of peacetime operations that subjected commanders, staffs, and troops to many of the demands they would meet in war. The first, which had the least influence because of its size, was the remilitarization of the Rhineland in March 1936. But in summer of that year, the Germans committed significant numbers of advisors to the Spanish Civil War in support of Franco's Fascists. The tank pioneer Wilhelm Ritter von Thoma later claimed after the Polish campaign that the German Army had learned nothing new in Poland about the tactical employment of tanks that it had not already learned from its experiences in Spain.[12]

In March 1938 Hitler ordered the *Wehrmacht* to occupy Austria (the *Anchluss*) with virtually no notice and with no coherent plans in place.[13] While most Austrians greeted advancing German troops with open arms – the Austrian Jews and socialists the obvious exceptions – the

---

[10] One of the most persistent myths of military history – one substantially perpetrated by the dishonest memoirs of the panzer commander Heinz Guderian – was that the development of German panzer forces was revolutionary in nature; it was not. See particularly Murray, "Armored Warfare," in Murray and Millett, eds., *Military Innovation in the Interwar Period*.

[11] Robert O'Neill, "Doctrine and Training in the German Army," in Michael Howard, ed., *The Theory and Practice of War* (New York, 1966), p. 157.

[12] Panzer Regiment 3., 20.1.40, "Erfahrungsbericht aus dem poln. Feldzug," NARS T-78/379/6344436.

[13] Hitler instigated the international crisis surrounding the *Anschluss* at the same time that he confronted his generals over the firing of Generaloberst Werner Freiherr von Fritsch as the army's commander, the result of trumped-up charges of homosexuality – a charge that Heinrich Himmler and the SS had manufactured and that rested entirely on perjured testimony.

military operation itself was less than a notable success. In fact, after-action reviews conducted by the Eighth Army, its operational headquarters, revealed significant weaknesses at every level.[14] What is particularly interesting about this review was that the supporting reports became more and more critical the higher the level of command.[15]

By the Czech crisis in late summer and early fall 1938, the *Wehrmacht* had cleared up many of these problems, but a host of new ones now appeared. Given that the Germans executed a national mobilization and deployment of their military forces on a scale they had not yet practiced since beginning to rearm in 1933, this was not surprising.[16] One after-action report by the Twelfth Army from the Polish campaign declared that incorporating lessons from the Czech crisis and the occupation of rump Czechoslovakia in March 1939 into its training program for officers and NCOs had played a major role in the combat effectiveness of its units against the Poles.[17] Again, one notes a careful and rigorous effort to identify military deficiencies and a willingness to establish training regimens to correct those deficiencies.

The final peacetime crisis came with the successful employment of military forces in the occupation of the remainder of Czechoslovakia in March 1939. One of the interesting aspects of this operation and its predecessors was the willingness of German commanders and planners to concentrate mechanized and motorized formations in increasingly large units of employment. In March 1938 the Eighth Army had employed only one panzer division and a number of independent panzer brigades in the advance on Vienna. That fall, planning for an invasion of Czechoslovakia detailed three panzer divisions to support separate infantry corps and exploit their breakthrough efforts into Bohemia and Moravia. By the Polish campaign of the following year, the Germans had organized their

---

[14] For the German Army's lessons learned from the *Anschluss*, see particularly Heeresgruppenkommando 3., 18.7.38, "Der Einsatz der 8. Armee in März 1938 zur Wiedervereinigung Österreichs mit dem deutschen Reich," NARS, T-79/14/000447. See also Generalkommando XIII. A.K., "Erfahrungsbericht über den Einsatz Osterreichs März/April 1938," 6.5.38, NARS, T-314/525000319.

[15] This was in stark contrast to the author's own experience with the United States Air Force, in which he served as a junior officer in the mid- to late 1960s.

[16] For the after-action reports dealing with the Czech crisis and the occupation of the Sudetenland, see among others: Gkdo. XIII A.K., Nr. 5800/38, Nürnberg, 15.11.38, "Erfahrungsbericht 'Einsatz Sudetendeutschland,'" NARS, T-314/525/000537; 7. Div. München, 15.11.38, "Erfahrungsbericht über Aufstellung und einsatz der 7. Div. beim Einmarsch in die Tsch.," NARS, T-79/47/000250.

[17] Armeeoberkommando 12, Betr: "Erfahrungsbericht," 25.10.39, NARS, T-315/671/000890.

panzer divisions and motorized infantry divisions into independent mechanized corps to exploit breakthroughs on the operational level. Finally, in the French campaign the Germans established a panzer group – to all intents an independent army. It was the force that broke the back of French defenses along the Meuse and then exploited that advantage all the way to the English Channel to achieve one of the most decisive operational victories of the Second World War.

In this process of preparing for war, after-action reporting and learning lessons at the tactical level played a crucial part in the German successes in the early years of World War II. It had proven to be a difficult matter for most military organizations in the first half of the twentieth century, given their top-down command emphasis. It was one thing for military organizations to discern what had been occurring on the battlefield or in exercises. But it was another for them to translate those lessons into coherent training programs to remedy major deficiencies. The latter happened all too rarely. Unfortunately, after the Polish campaign, the Germans would prove particularly adept at learning from their combat experience.

The German Response to Victory in the Polish Campaign: The Tactical Lessons

On the surface, the Polish campaign of September 1939 was a smashing success for the German Army. In a matter of weeks, its ground forces had completely destroyed an army of 40 divisions and over a million men. By 1 October, Polish resistance had ceased. In the course of military operations, the Germans managed to occupy more than two-thirds of Poland. In every respect, the campaign appeared to be an outstanding operational and tactical success. It certainly caught the world's attention.[18]

Yet, the *Oberkommando des Heeres* (OKH, the German Army's high command) judged that the operational and tactical performance of its units had not come up to the standards set in the prewar period. Its critical stance reflected the after-action reports that began working their way up from the lowest levels of the army in the first weeks of October 1939. Significantly the higher the headquarters, the more demanding

---

[18] Unfortunately, it did not catch the attention of the French high command, which, despite the warnings of French observers on the scene, appears to have dismissed the rapidity of the German victory as being largely the result of Polish incompetence and not German military effectiveness. For the course of the Polish campaign, see, among others, Robert M. Kennedy, *The German Campaign in Poland, 1939* (Washington, DC, 1956); and Nicholas Bethell, *The War Hitler Won* (London, 1972).

and dissatisfied commanders were with the performance of units under their command, a progression earlier reflected in the army's peacetime practices and one that demonstrated the considerable degree to which the German system of after-action reporting involved trust and honesty between different levels of command. Thus, German commanders were not afraid to be critical of the performance of their own units as well as others that served under their command. This willingness to be self-critical was one of the major factors that enabled the *Wehrmacht* to perform at such a high level throughout World War II.[19]

Within a week of the conclusion of military operations, the *OKH* had issued a circular to all army units demanding after-action reports of their experiences at the tactical and operational levels. Much like Seeckt's earlier-described memorandum to the *Reichsheer,* the *OKH* pointed out to its subordinate commanders that it was "in the interest of the whole army to collect as soon as possible the combat experiences in both the tactical and technical spheres" and to disseminate those experiences widely among the troops as the basis for training in preparation for future campaigns.[20] In fact, the army's units were already hard at work developing after-action reports to be forwarded up the chain of command to the *OKH*.[21]

The reports themselves reveal an organization still grappling with the consequences of its massive program of rearmament, through which it had transformed a force of 100,000 men in 1933 into an army of more than two million by 1939. They confirm that the process was not yet complete by the time the Polish campaign had begun. Yet the institutional insistence on critical self-examination enabled the army to examine its performance and, through self-criticism, to upgrade battlefield performance and combat capabilities.

By mid-October, the *OKH* was in a position to issue its preliminary findings on the lessons of Poland. The report reflected on a number of divisional, corps, and army after-action reports. The *OKH* then issued it at least down to the divisional level. The report underlined that, while the

---

[19] It was not, however, the only one. Ideological motivation was also a major factor in German military effectiveness throughout the war. See particularly Omar Bartov, *Hitler's Army: Soldiers, Nazis, and War in the Third Reich* (Oxford, 1991).
[20] OKH, Berlin, Okt 7, 1939, Betr.: "Erfahrungsbericht bei der Operationen im Osten," NARS, T-315/435/000491.
[21] What is apparent in reading the documents is that the army's culture had a deep sense that honest lessons-learned processes must be inherent in its approach to combat and that those processes must be connected to the training establishment.

Polish campaign had "fully confirmed our tactical principles," a number of significant weaknesses had emerged. Accordingly, it emphasized that a number of important principles needed reemphasis by commanders and staffs. Above all, it suggested that the confusion and chaos of combat should not allow leaders and their soldiers to ignore the basics of discipline and training.[22]

From the *OKH*'s perspective, the first and most important lesson was that effective combat leadership, no matter what the level, had to be from the front, rather from the rear. Second, front-line commanders had consistently exaggerated losses, the enemy's strength, and the difficulty of the terrain in combat reporting. Thus, they needed to work on sending more accurate, terse reports as to what was actually happening in the combat actions conducted by their troops. Third, the troops had not received adequate training to carry out reconnaissance or security missions accurately. Fourth, in terms of offensive tactical performance, infantry fire discipline had not been satisfactory, while combined-arms tactics had rarely met standards of performance. Thus, the infantry had not always received the necessary support from their heavy weapons or the artillery. Fifth, the transition from the offensive to the defensive had not worked well, with advancing troops often forming linear defenses rather than a system based on the defense in depth that German doctrine demanded. Finally, the *OKH* paid tribute to the *Luftwaffe*'s contributions to the campaign.[23] Nevertheless, its overall analysis of the campaign closed on a warning note: because ground forces had enjoyed air superiority throughout the campaign, they had become careless in camouflaging their positions and movements. Such carelessness, in the future against the British or the French, the report suggested, might have disastrous results before the *Luftwaffe* managed to win air superiority.[24]

After-action reports on the performance of the panzer and motorized infantry divisions followed a similar pattern. The war diary of General Heinz Guderian's XIX Panzer Corps reported that the performance of his troops had lived up to prewar expectations of what armored and

---

[22] OKH, Gen StdH, O Qu 1/Ausb. Abt. (Ia), 15.10.39, "Taktische Erfahrungen im polnishen Feldzug," NARS, T-315/436/000462. For the same report in the files of the 16th Division, see T-315/671/000909. The latter suggests that the OKH report was issued down to the divisional level.

[23] See later in the chapter for a discussion of the lessons the Germans learned about close air support cooperation between the army and the *Luftwaffe*.

[24] OKH, Gen StdH O Qu 1/Ausb. Abt. (Ia), 15.10.39, "Taktische Erfahrungen im polnischen Feldzug," NARS, T-315/436/000462.

mechanized forces could achieve.[25] Nevertheless, Guderian did admit in his memoirs that at least on one occasion on 9 September, he had to intervene in company-level operations to keep the momentum of his XIX Panzer Corps going:

> In the front line an extraordinary performance was going on; when I asked what was happening I was told that the foremost companies were being relieved. It looked like nothing so much as a guard mounting parade. The troops knew nothing about any order to attack.... No one knew where the enemy was; there was no sort of reconnaissance being carried out. I first put a stop to the remarkable manoevre of company reliefs, and then ordered that the regimental and battalion commanders be brought to me.... I cannot pretend that I was anything but very disappointed by what had happened so far.[26]

While the overall performance of panzer units had lived up to the army's expectations at the operational level, a number of tactical weaknesses had appeared during the campaign. Cooperation between armor and infantry had run into significant difficulties. In some cases, commanders of panzer units had piecemealed their tanks rather than concentrating them to deliver a powerful blow as called for in the *Wehrmacht*'s armor doctrine. The 7th Panzer Division (formerly the 2nd Light Division) reported that units must carefully prepare and execute their attacks, although it emphasized that they must make every attempt to avoid too methodical an approach that would rob subordinate commanders of initiative.[27] A number of after-action reports of the mechanized forces also stressed that march discipline and traffic regulation for both infantry and motorized forces had, for the most part, been unsatisfactory – a situation that repeated the same pattern of bad driving that had marked the *Anschluss*, as well as the occupations of the Sudetenland and rump Czechoslovakia.[28]

---

[25] KTB XIX A.K., "Feldzug in Polen," 1.9.39–25.9.39, p. 211.
[26] Heinz Guderian, *Panzer Leader* (New York, 1996), pp. 76–78.
[27] The future field marshal Erwin Rommel was soon to become the commander of the 7th Panzer Division. 7. Division, 31.10.39, "Auszug aus den Erfahrungsberichten des XVI und XIX Armeekorps sowie A.O.K. 10," NARS, T-315/436/000467.
[28] This recurring deficiency in march discipline and traffic regulation reflected German attitudes toward driving as well as the fact that far fewer Germans had driving experience before coming into the army than was to be the case with the U.S. Army once American mobilization began. See, among others: 16. Div., 31.10.39, "Erfahrungsbericht;"

The light divisions – an amalgamation of motorized, mechanized, and cavalry units, established in 1935 as a sop to the cavalry – did not perform well in the Polish campaign, and after-action reports stressed that the combat conditions in Poland against a weak and disorganized opponent would probably not occur in a campaign in the west.[29] Before the war Guderian had argued that the light divisions would not possess the combat power of the panzer divisions, while the *Luftwaffe* would be able to perform its long-range reconnaissance mission more accurately and economically.[30] The 2nd Light Division's after-action report confirmed Guderian's prewar impression.[31] The end result of such analysis was that the *OKH* authorized the conversion of the light divisions into panzer divisions, which took place over the course of the winter.

Even more useful was the overall impression the mechanized and motorized divisions made on the senior officer corps by their ability to turn tactical breakthroughs into mobile, fast-moving exploitation with operational consequences. Thus, the Polish campaign served not only to substantiate the opinions of tactical innovators, such as Guderian, but to win over a number of skeptics, such as the future field marshals Gerd von Rundstedt and Erwin Rommel, both of whom had harbored considerable doubts about the operational potential of armored forces.[32]

The *Wehrmacht*'s basic units – the infantry and mountain divisions making up nearly 80 percent of German divisions – learned similar lessons. In late November 1939, the *OKH* reported that combat in Poland had largely confirmed the validity of German infantry tactics, organizations, weapons, and doctrine. But it was simply not possible to accommodate requests from certain quarters in the infantry establishment

and "Erfahrungsbericht des XV A.K. über den Polenfeldzug: Anlage 1: Erfahrungen beim Marsch motorisieter Verbände während des Feldzug in Polen," NARS, T-315/37/000256.
[29] Korpskommando XV. A.K., 3.10.39, "Erfahrungsbericht über den Feldzuig in Polen," NARS, T-314/550/000297.
[30] Heinz Guderian, "Schnelle Truppen einst und jetzt," *Militärwissenschaftliche Rundschau*, Heft 2 (1939), p. 241.
[31] 7. Panzer Division (2. Leichte Division), 19.10.39, Betr: "Erfahrungen by den Operationen im Osten," NARS, T-315/436/000480.
[32] Rundstedt had gone so far during one of the army's peacetime maneuvers during the late 1930s to comment to Guderian about the performance of tanks: "Alles Unsinn, mein lieber Guderian, Alles Unsinn" ("All nonsense, my dear Guderian, all nonsense"). M. Plettenberg, *Guderian: Hintergründe des deutschen Schicksals, 1918–1945* (Dusseldorf, 1950), p. 14.

for greater motorization of the regular infantry divisions or for equipping those divisions with tanks and armored artillery. The equipment to do so was not available in sufficient quantities, given production difficulties, and to do so would also violate the principle of concentration (*Schwehrpunktsbildung*).[33]

At the beginning of its after-action report, the 8th Infantry Division emphasized that "infantry tactics and training principles as well as German organization and weapons had completely proven themselves." But it also reported that difficulties had emerged: German infantry had not come up to expectations either in night fighting or in combat in heavily forested or mountainous terrain. Troops in meeting engagements had a tendency to halt and fire instead of maneuvering. They thus forced the enemy to ground. Moreover, infantry units more often than not failed to push home their attacks.[34]

Contrary to many other reporting headquarters, the Twelfth Army indicated that cooperation between infantry and artillery had been outstanding (*ausgezeichnet*). But battalions formed from reservists had not performed well, suffering heavy casualties from exhaustion during extended marches. Moreover, such units had neither the necessary training nor the cohesion to stand up to the demands of German elastic defensive tactics. The Twelfth Army's report then added that the Poles had better prepared their infantry to fight at night than had the units under its command.[35]

Such after-action reports represent only a small sample of the massive effort to capture the experiences of the Polish campaign, particularly of the army's tactical performance, an effort ranging from the highest levels of command down to regiments. There appears to have been little fear on the part of German commanders – whatever the level of their command – that critical comments and honest evaluations of their unit's performance would have a negative effect on their careers. In fact, Colonel General Walter von Brauchitsch, the army's commander-in-chief, underlined to his subordinates his expectation that commanders at all levels could and would pass critical after-action reports up the chain of command. In October 1939 he established a monthly evaluation report for divisional

---

[33] OKH, 28.11.39, "Auswertung der Erfahrungen bei den Inf.-u. Geb. Division in Polen Feldzug," NARS, T-312/372/778373.
[34] 8. Division, 19.10.39, "Erfahrungsbericht," NARS, T-314/372/000189.
[35] Armeeoberkommando 12, "Erfahrungsbericht," 25.10.39, NARS, T-315/671/000890.

and corps commanders to indicate the level of combat effectiveness of their units in order to avoid the mistakes the German high command had made in 1918 in overestimating the fighting capabilities of its front-line units.[36]

The *OKH* then assembled and distilled these after-action reports for the express purpose of establishing a massive retraining program for the army as it confronted the possibility of a campaign in the West. The impression the army's high command gained from this effort was that the Polish campaign had confirmed the army's doctrine and training. Nevertheless, the deficiencies that had occurred were sufficient to make the *OKH* dubious about Hitler's desire to conduct a fall campaign against the West. The result was to be a huge blowup between the Führer and his senior commanders in late fall 1939.[37] In the end, the western campaign had to be postponed because of ferocious winter weather, and the *OKH* thereby gained more than six months to execute an extensive program to retrain the army, regular as well as reserve. How it organized and utilized this additional time would exercise a profound influence over the outcome of the campaign against the Low Countries and France in the campaign of May–June 1940.[38]

The Learning Part of Lessons Learned: Training the Army for the Spring 1940 Campaign

On 13 October 1939, even before all of the unit after-action reports were in, the *OKH* released a preliminary memorandum to its subordinate commands, "The Training of the Field Army."[39] This directive formed the basis for the training program over the coming six months. The directive

---

[36] Der Oberbefehlshaber des Heeres, 24.10.39, "Zustandsberichte," NARS T-315/1025/000357.

[37] For a discussion of the import of these arguments, see particularly Williamson Murray and Allan R. Millett, *A War to Be Won: Fighting the Second World War* (Cambridge, MA, 2000), p. 53.

[38] Historians continue, quite rightly, to emphasize the development of operation plans that would lead to the breakthrough on the Meuse on 13 and 14 May 1940. For a discussion of these issues, see Williamson Murray, "May 1940: Contingency and Fragility of the German RMA," in MacGregor Knox and Williamson Murray, eds., *The Dynamics of Military Revolution, 1300–2050* (Cambridge, 2000); and Karl Heinz Frieser, *Blitzkrieg-Legende: Der Westfeldzug 1940* (Munich, 1995).

[39] "Des Oberbefehlshaber des Heeres, Gen St d H/Ausb. (Ia), Nr. 400/39g, 13.10.39, Betr.: "Ausbildung des Heeres," NARS, T-312/234/7787781.

received wide dissemination throughout the army's entire structure.⁴⁰ The *OKH* pointed out that

> The conclusion of the Polish campaign and the quiet in the west will give the field army the possibility of perfecting its performance, discipline, and coherence.... The exclusive goal of each training exercise is the insertion of troops in battle. Besides weapon and battle training the education of the soldier stands in the foreground. Troops are to be hardened and prepared to meet the highest demands of war, especially against an enemy trained and equipped with modern weapons.⁴¹

In specific terms, the *OKH* ordered that troops of the first, second, fourth, and fifth waves be "prepared to attack fortifications; to exploit success; to defend themselves against enemy attacks and tanks."⁴² It strongly urged that its subordinate units and training establishments tie the experiences of Poland directly to combat preparations: reconnaissance and security; march discipline; infantry fire discipline, especially after long marches; cooperation among the combat-arms branches; offensive and defensive tactics during periods of twilight and at night; and transition from an offensive to a defensive posture were all areas that the *OKH* felt needed considerable improvement over the combat performance of units in Poland.

The second section of the *OKH*'s report emphasized that training must stress leadership and especially the combat leadership of junior officers. Units were to bring their reserve officers up to the standards of the regular army. In addition, reserve NCOs were to be brought up to the standards of the peacetime army, so that "the position of the NCO as leader, trainer, and educator would not decline as it had in the last years of the First World War."⁴³ Finally, for the benefit of those who might denigrate the role of spit and polish in military affairs, the *OKH* underlined for its subordinate organizations that "discipline was the basis of victory" and

---

⁴⁰ For other indications of its wide dissemination throughout the army, see particularly: 16. Division, "Rictlinien für die Erziehung und Ausbildung," 24.10.39, NARS T-315/671/000868; and Brauchitsch's circular from 12.12.39, Gen Std H/Ausb. Abt. (Ia), Nr. 800/39g, Betr.: "Ausbildung des Feldheeres," NARS, T-312/234/7788296 and T-312/752/8396808.
⁴¹ Des Oberbefehlshaber des Heeres, Gen St d H/Ausb. (Ia), Nr. 400/39g, 13.10.39, Betr.: "Ausbildung des Feldheeres," 13.10.39, NARS, T-312/234/7787781.
⁴² Ibid., Each wave represented the calling up of certain categories of men based on age, previous training and service in the military and specialty, and civilian specialty.
⁴³ Ibid.

that all ranks must be clear that their maintenance in obedience as well as in military courtesy would have to be "implacably" maintained.[44]

The scheduling of divisions for intensive workups at military training sites such as Grafenwöhr and Ohrdruf simplified the *OKH*'s control of the training program.[45] Moreover, the *OKH* took control of scheduling officers and NCOs to attend various training schools that it had established. Significantly, most of the staff of the infantry training school at Doberitz were promptly transferred to active units on the Western Front in October, replaced by soldiers experienced in active operations either in Poland or the west.[46]

The training section of the general staff now laid out a detailed set of standards and objectives for the training schedules of the infantry and artillery schools within each army group. A Sixth Army circular stressed that the basic purpose of the training program was to improve the standards for officers and NCOs and train newly established units in offensive tactics.[47] *OKH* interest in the training program extended to the point of actually laying out 12-day schedules for the training of company and platoon commanders.[48] Perhaps most importantly, the *OKH* required lower headquarters to forward up the chain of command after-action reports (*Erfahrungsberichte*) on the school sessions their personnel had attended, so that it could maintain a grasp on the overall quality of the training programs.[49]

The training programs within the divisions aimed at (1) improving the combat skills of the common soldier and (2) then establishing the abilities of platoons and companies to work together. There was nothing new in this approach except for its rigor and how closely it remained tied to experiences gained in Poland. Once small-unit training reached a satisfactory level, then larger-scale battalion and regimental training could

---

[44] Ibid.
[45] Oberkommando des Heeres, Gen St d H/Ausb. Abt. (Ia), Nr. 135/40g, 19.1.40.
[46] Oberkommando des Heeres, Betr.: "Austauch von Ausbildungpersonal der Infanterieschule," 14.12.39, NARS, T-311/47/7057948.
[47] Armee-Oberkommando 6, 14.12.39, Betr.: "Ausbildung des Feldheeres," NARS, T-312/752/8396799.
[48] Ob d H Gen St d H/Ausb. Abt. (Ia) Nr. 900/39g II Ang, 13.12.39, "Stoffplan für einen Kompanieführer- und Zugführerlehrgang der Infanterie und Stoffplan für einen Lehrgang der Unterführer der schweren Infanteriewaffen," NARS, T-312/752/8396772; and OKH Gen. St. d. H.-Gen. d. Art., Ia/Nr. 40/40, 4.1.40, "Lehrplan für Batterieführer-Lehrgänge bei den H. Gr," NARS, T-311/47/7057905.
[49] Heeresgruppenkommando C, An OKH, Gen.St.dH./Ausb. Abt., Nr. 1300/40; A.O.K. 1, Ia/Art, nr. 174/40. An Oberkommando Heeresgruppe C, NARS, T-311/47/7057900–904.

begin. Complicating training programs in the west was the inadequacy of training facilities in western Germany – where most of the army was deployed – for even battalion-level training, and large-unit training often had to be delayed until divisions could move to regular training areas.[50]

Divisional reports on their internal training reveal a careful, detailed, and methodical approach – all aimed at overcoming the weaknesses that had shown up in Poland. Division staffs consistently urged subordinate units to make the best use of training time. The 88th Infantry Division suggested that at the end of every exercise, the instructor should ask himself "whether his soldiers had learned something or not."[51] The Germans believed that realistic training was of prime importance, one training officer suggesting to his superiors that exercises that did not present a realistic impression of the enemy and combat conditions were useless.[52] As directed by the *OKH*, division commanders consistently emphasized that all units must rigidly maintain discipline and appearance as a key element in morale.[53] As the staff of the 44th Division noted, "The sharpest discipline of units and individual soldiers is the basic principle [of military effectiveness]."[54]

This same report captured one of the key elements in the success of the German Army in the coming campaign – and war – with its criticism that lower-ranking officers and NCOs were not sufficiently willing to take initiative. Thus, it suggested that more senior officers needed to encourage subordinates to act as the situation demanded, while not ignoring their stated orders. Over the course of the war, this tension between initiative and obedience would be a major factor in German combat effectiveness. In effect, the training standards demanded that junior officers use their judgment in tactical situations: an officer who failed through an unwillingness to take the initiative was as culpable as one who failed to follow

[50] 211. Division, Abt. Ia, Betr.: "Gelände für Verbandsbildung," 10.12.39, NARS, T-314/238/000029.
[51] 88. Inf. Div., 18.1.40, Abt. Ia, "Bemerkungen für Ausbildung und Erziehung (Nr. 1–Nr. 3)," NARS, T-315/171/706/712.
[52] Today, of course, as a result of the training revolution in the American military that occurred in the 1970s and 1980s, realistic training at the tactical level lies at the heart of U.S. preparations for war. This was not the case with most military organizations in the interwar years.
[53] Among other divisional training reports, see: 87. Inf. Div., Abt. Ia. Nr. 117/40, "Richtlinien für die Ausbildung," NARS, T-315/1139/000389; and 211. Division, Abt. Ia Nr. 344/39, 27.10.39, Betr.: "Ausbildung," NARS, T-314/238/000065.
[54] 44. Division, Abt. Ia. Betr.: "Bemerkungen zu der Übersetzung am 19.4.40," 20.4.40, NARS, T-315/910/000467.

his orders. Success, not rigid obedience to orders, was the standard the *Wehrmacht* prized.

The experience of the 208th Infantry Division in working up to combat-ready status over winter 1939–1940 was typical of the army's divisions. The division itself had formed over summer 1939, shortly before the outbreak of war. Initially, it contained a substantial number of *Landwehr* personnel. In October it moved to Sobotka in the military district of Posen. There it began an arduous program to turn itself into a first-class infantry division. Its entire emphasis in training was to ensure mistakes made in Poland would not recur in its upcoming combat operations.

The 208th Infantry Division's training program aimed at exercising troops to the maximum extent possible, while emphasizing weapons training, the duties of the German soldier, technical training, and the proper use of terrain in combat operations. The division staff gave special emphasis to upgrading the performance of junior officers and NCOs. The initial training schedule called for two weeks of individual training, one week for squad training, one week for platoon training, one-and-a-half weeks for company training, and one-and-a-half weeks for battalion and regimental training.[55] Above all, the division trained hard, in some cases 16 hours a day, six to seven days per week, demanding that officers and soldiers get it right. The division succeeded in weeding out a number of reservists and *Landwehr* personnel who could not meet its standards, while a number of untrained replacements arrived to fill up vacancies. Urged on by its corps commander, the 208th attempted to integrate these replacements into the division as quickly as possible.[56]

In February the division reported to its corps headquarters that it had ceased large-unit training and was devoting all of its training time to an intensive program to bring up the replacements to reasonable standards of tactical performance.[57] One month later, the division reported it had returned to battalion and regimental training that emphasized offensive spirit and movement "schnell vorwärts."[58] The division commander was

---

[55] 208. Infanterie Division, Abt. Ia. Betr.: "Ausbildung während des Einsatzes im Mil. Bezirk Posen," 10.10.39, NARS, T-315/1609/000464.
[56] Korps Kommando XXXIII, Oberbefehlshaber, 10.1.40, 68/40, NARS, T-315/1609/00549.
[57] 208. Infanterie Division, Abt. Ia., 6.2.40, Betr.: "Vorlage von Dienstplänen und Ausbildungrictlinien," NARS, T-315/1609/000608.
[58] 208. I.D., Abt. Ia, Tgb. Nr. 526/40, 8.3.40, "Allgemeine Richtlinien für die Ausbildung," NARS, T-315/1609/000608.

also able to report that the individual and small unit training in February had successfully integrated the replacements into the division. The new troops, he reported, had reached a state of combat readiness after three months sufficient to meet the demands the coming campaign would place on them.[59]

The bare training reports, plans, and schedules in the archives only hint at the rigor with which the German Army executed its program to correct the deficiencies that had shown up in the Polish campaign. That program aimed to bring all its units up to the standard the German Army had set in its examination of the lessons of the First World War.[60] The training aimed at pushing officers and men to the limits of their endurance in terms of physical conditioning and mental stamina. By demanding that the troops exercise to the breaking point, the German Army sought to eliminate those who might break in combat. As the training report for the 10th Panzer Division underlined, the troops must learn that "the removal of weak elements lies in their own interest."[61]

Above all, the training based on the experiences of the Polish campaign aimed at inculcating an offensive spirit into German troops preparing for the coming push in the west. Nevertheless, in a circular to Army Group B at the end of April 1940, *Generaloberst* (Colonel General) Fedor von Bock proclaimed that he was still not satisfied that his troops and commanders had reached the necessary level of offensive spirit:

> In many exercises recently, particularly at the battalion and regimental levels, an inclination to caution and circumspection has appeared. Therein lies the danger that on one side the German leadership will pass up opportunities to seize favorable situations, . . . while on the other hand the enemy will be allowed time to divine our intentions. . . . Once a commander has decided to attack, so must everything that he orders be established that the eyes, heart and senses of the troops be directed to the front.[62]

Bock's fears, of course, proved groundless. Throughout its units, whether regular, reserve, panzer, or line infantry, the German Army had reached a state of combat readiness that was far superior to that of its

---

[59] 208. I.D. Div., Betr.: "Beurteilung des eingetroffenen Ersatzes," März 1940, NARS, T-315/1609/000643.

[60] For a graphic illustration of what German training methods involved, see Guy Sajer, *The Forgotten Soldier* (New York, 1971), and Hermann Teske, *Bewegungskrieg* (Heidelberg, 1955).

[61] 10. Panzer Division, Abt. Ia Nr. 141/39, Betr.: "Ausbildung," 31.10.39, NARS, T-315/558/ 000812.

[62] Heeresgruppe B, Ia Nr. 2211/40, 28.4.1940, "Bemerkungen zu den Truppenübungen in Früjahr, 1940," NARS, T-312/752/8396741.

French and British opponents. The training that established that state of readiness had emerged from a careful and thorough analysis of what had taken place on the plains of Poland. Thus, across the board its divisions were ready to execute an operationally imaginative, but risky, plan for the invasion of France. The brilliant thrust through the Ardennes has justifiably received the most attention of historians. But it was the movement of Bock's Army Group B, consisting largely of infantry divisions, through northern Belgium that created the conditions necessary for the breakout from the Meuse River crossings to succeed. At the start of the offensive, Bock's forces fixed Allied attention on the north. Once the devastating nature of the German breakthrough in the Ardennes became clear, the hammering pressure of Bock's advance made it impossible for Allied forces to disengage to meet the terrible threat from the south.

Adaptation, Maneuver Warfare, and Close Air Support

The adaptation processes between the German Army and the *Luftwaffe* worked almost as well at the tactical level in developing close air support doctrine and procedures, but in this case, the development took place over the two campaigns against Poland and France, before the Germans perfected the capabilities they felt they needed. That reality flies in the face of one of the great myths of the Second World War that the *Luftwaffe* was the "handmaiden of the German Army."[63] Supposedly, it was only prepared for missions in support of the army.[64] In fact, the highly publicized depiction of the tank-Stuka team was nothing more than a result of Goebbels's propaganda machine, which depicted the two as if they were part of a team in the "new" German concept of *blitzkrieg* warfare.[65]

While the *Luftwaffe* prepared for a wide variety of missions and tasks before the Second World War, it placed close air support at a relatively low level in terms of its priorities. Even then it cast its net far more widely

---

[63] See, among others, Dennis Richards, *The Royal Air Force: 1939–1945*, vol. 1 (London, 1953), p. 29.
[64] For a refutation of this view, see particularly Williamson Murray, *Luftwaffe* (Baltimore, 1985), chap. 1. See also Williamson Murray, "A Tale of Two Doctrines: The Luftwaffe's 'Conduct of the Air War' and Air Force Manual 1–1," *Journal of Strategic Studies*, December 1983.
[65] In fact, the three Stukas were deployed to Spain for evaluation as a weapons system to attack point targets such as bridges, rail yards, and other choke points. Rarely used in the role of close air support for Franco's infantry attacks, the Stukas were viewed by the "Condor Legion's" leaders as too valuable an aircraft for use in such a mission. Conversation with Major General Hans Asmus, 23 June 1984, Baden-Baden, Federal Republic of Germany.

in terms of its prewar preparations than did the Royal Air Force or the U.S. Army Air Corps. Unlike those two organizations, the *Luftwaffe* emphasized the air superiority mission, interdiction, airborne operations, reconnaissance, both near and far, and strategic bombing – in other words a wide array of missions.[66] But the Germans also took close air support seriously and devoted significant resources and force structure to preparing for that mission.

Why they did so again emerges from their close examination of the lessons of the First World War as well as the experience of *Luftwaffe* units in the Spanish Civil War. In the first case, several of the 57 committees that Seeckt established to examine the lessons of the First World War had studied the lessons of the air war. Unlike the British, the Germans had not established an independent air force during that conflict; thus, in the immediate postwar period, there was no direct push for evidence to justify an independent air service. Moreover, the Treaty of Versailles' prohibition on Germany's new military forces from possessing aircraft ensured that the Germans created a more integrated, joint approach to lessons learned because officers with experience in the air and ground war formed combined lessons-learned teams.

The upshot was that the lessons dealing with air power that the Germans drew from the war were more accurate than those learned by the Allies: the German lessons emphasized the importance of air superiority and the difficulties involved in hitting and destroying targets – lessons the Condor Legion's experiences in Spain reconfirmed. As with the British, the Germans had integrated close air support with their major ground offensives in 1918. That support had played a major role in helping German storm troopers break through Allied positions, particularly in the March "Michael" offensive and the May offensive along the Chemin des Dames. But the employment of aircraft in the close air support role had also involved heavy casualties for the aircraft and pilots involved. Not surprisingly, the lesson the Germans drew from World War I was that close air support could prove useful but would invariably be costly in

---

[66] The idea that the *Luftwaffe* had no interest in strategic bombing represents one of the great canards to emerge out of the Second World War. That the Germans had prepared a portion of their bomber force to act as pathfinders and had developed blind bombing technologies (the so-called beams) underline that German airmen had a healthy but more nuanced approach to strategic bombing than their British and American counterparts did in the period before the war. For further discussion of the *Luftwaffe*'s interest in strategic bombing in the interwar period, see Murray, *Luftwaffe*, chap. 1.

terms of men and machines. Thus, it represented a mission best saved for special circumstances, such as the breakthrough battle. But that did not mean that the Germans did not devote serious attention to the preparation of some of their assets for that mission.

When the "Condor Legion" arrived in Spain in summer 1936 to support Franco's rebellion, German airmen discovered that most of the air capabilities they had possessed at the end of 1918 had atrophied during the 13 years when the Reich had neither an air force nor military aircraft.[67] This proved as true for close air support as for air superiority missions. Thus, Spain was as important in sharpening old skills as in developing new ones. But the ground fighting in the Spanish Civil War more closely resembled the infantry battles of the First World War. "Condor Legion" close air support operations involved supporting Franco's troops in offensive actions that resembled the battles of 1916 and 1917.

In effect, the close air support system the Germans developed represented a regression rather than an advance. In some cases, German pilots identified Spanish infantry by the flags they carried.[68] In others, Nationalist infantry wore large pieces of white cloth on their backs, thus making advancing troops easy to spot from the air and at the same time discouraging any thought of retreat on their part.[69] Rarely was there an actual breakthrough of Republican lines, and there were certainly no cases of mobile exploitation throughout the bitter conflict.[70]

By September 1939, the Spanish experiences and exercises in Germany with the army had enabled the *Luftwaffe* to develop the tactics, techniques, and procedures to support the *Wehrmacht*'s ground forces in rupturing a static defensive position. But the Germans had done little work in extending that framework to the mobile exploitation that might take place after a breakthrough. There were a number of weak procedures for cooperation in the mobile environment, few of which the Germans

---

[67] Admittedly, the Germans were able to establish a pilot training school and experimentation base in the Soviet Union during the late 1920s, but in the end, the results were pretty small potatoes, especially when considering the megalomaniacal aims of the new *Luftwaffe*.
[68] Conversation with General Asmus, Baden-Baden, 23 June 1984.
[69] Bundesarchiv/Militärarchiv (BA/MA), RL/57, Auswertung "Rügen," Anlage 2 zu Lw.Gr.Kdo.3, Nr. 7179/38g.Kdos, Heft 2, a) Führung IV bis VI, p. 50.
[70] How bitter is suggested by Paul Preston's outstanding biography *Franco: A Biography* (London, 1993).

practiced on a consistent basis. Thus, during the course of ground war against the Poles the *Luftwaffe* and army employed these procedures with varying degrees of success. Bomb lines, smoke, ground panels, Nazi flags on the top of German vehicles were all used, but radio communications between ground and air simply did not exist.[71]

Moreover, there were two systems of coordination between the army and the *Luftwaffe*. On one hand, a number of close reconnaissance squadrons worked directly with army artillery. *Luftwaffe* liaison staffs (*Kommandeure der Luftwaffe*, or *Kolufts*), which ran down to corps level, coordinated that work. Second, an independent liaison staff (*Fliegerverbindungsoffiziere or Flivos*) also worked down to corps level. Their task was to coordinate *Luftwaffe* direct support strikes, particularly in enabling breakthrough ground attacks on enemy static positions, but they had no capability to work in a mobile environment.

Neither of these liaison staffs coordinated with the other, while requests for close air support under this system provided little of the flexibility and quick reaction time that mobile operations would demand. The army did display some interest in further developing cooperation with the *Luftwaffe*, but that service's chief of staff, General Hans Jeschonnek, suggested at the end of a spring 1939 exercise that he believed close air support was like a cavalry charge: "It could bring great success when it achieved surprise, but only then. When it did not possess surprise and met an enemy who was prepared, then such attacks had little success and then at a disproportionately high cost."[72]

Poland and France: Lessons Learned in Close Air Support

The *Luftwaffe*'s contributions to the defeat of the Polish ground forces had been almost as impressive as those of the *Wehrmacht*. In the first several days of the campaign, close air support for the breakthrough of Polish frontier defenses was crucial in clearing the way for the advance of the panzer corps. Thereafter, *Luftwaffe* interdiction strikes and raids aimed at breaking up Polish reserves as they massed – particularly along the Bzura – all helped to speed the rapid collapse of Poland's military forces.

---

[71] Even as late as Operation Barbarossa, German vehicles were displaying Nazi flags on their tops as a method to keep the *Luftwaffe* from attacking them.
[72] BA/MA, RL7/159 Verlauf der Generalstabsreise Luftwaffe 1939, Lft. Kdo 3, Fhr.Abt. Nr. 2778/39, pp. 6–17.

As with the army, the *Luftwaffe* almost immediately embarked on a thorough lessons-learned analysis of what had gone right and what had gone wrong in Poland. *Luftflotte 1* (First Air Force) reported that communications between ground forces and supporting air force units needed considerable improvement. The high-speed mobile war that the army's mechanized and motorized units waged after breaking through the thin crust of Polish defenses had made it difficult for air elements to keep track of what was happening in the ground campaign and to provide needed support.[73] In the case of breakthrough operations (through prepared fortification systems and defensive lines), *Luftflotte 1* found it relatively easy to coordinate with the army as to time, place, and target selection to provide close air support. Interestingly, after-action reports indicated that the material effects of such attacks were not particularly impressive; instead, it was the impact on the enemy's morale where close air support made the greatest contribution.[74]

That evidence drove *Luftflotte 1*'s after-action report to conclusions fundamentally different from those of the army. At this point in the war, the crucial links between the army and the *Luftwaffe* were the *Kolufts*. Assigned down to corps level, the *Kolufts* also commanded the *Luftwaffe*'s close reconnaissance aircraft. Beyond that mission, they commanded no other aircraft and merely passed along requests for close air support to their *Luftwaffe* colleagues. While the *OKH* had suggested that the *Kolufts* be given the ability to control close air support missions, *Luftflotte 1*'s examination argued the exact opposite, because the *Kolufts* did not possess the necessary command and control links to function successfully.[75] Its report added that the critical element in army–*Luftwaffe* cooperation would have to be the assignment of liaison officers

---

[73] BA/MA, R17/2, Abschrift, "Erfahrungsbericht der Luftflotte 1 über den polnischen Feldzug," p. 1. In the last days of the Second World War, nearly all the *Luftwaffe*'s records were destroyed by that organization's chief historian. As a result, it is more difficult to build a coherent picture of the overall *Luftwaffe* lessons-learned processes. In piecing together the framework of close air support developments, the more robust army records aid considerably in establishing a coherent picture.

[74] BA/MA R17/2, Abschrift, "Erfahrungsbericht der Luftflotte 1 über den polnischen Feldzug," pp. 9–10. This would be the *Luftwaffe*'s greatest contribution to the breakthrough on the Meuse on 13 May 1940. As a result of its attacks immediately before XIX Panzer Corps' crossing operation at Sedan, virtually all the soldiers manning French artillery panicked and ran away, leaving the infantry defenders without artillery support for the ensuing battle.

[75] BA/MA, H35/88, Oberkommando des Heeres, GenStdH/Ausb.Abt. (Ia) Nr. 750/39, "Richtlinien für die Zussamenarbeit Heer-Luftwaffe auf Grund der Erfahrungen im polnischen Feldzug."

to lower levels to improve coordination. The officers would have to possess good radio communications up the chain of command as well as their own aircraft to keep abreast of what was happening on the ground.

In mobile warfare the report indicated, the major problem was that the ground force commanders – not to mention those of the *Luftwaffe* – possessed only the sketchiest information about the front-line situation. At the time, the troops could communicate their positions and those of the enemy only through the use of smoke and recognition panels, neither of which had proven reliable in the past. Because of this, the fluidity of ground operations demanded security zones within which the *Luftwaffe* could attack only those ground formations that it could identify with certainty as belonging to the enemy.[76]

Reports from *Luftflotte 1*'s subordinate commands supported its conclusions about the Polish campaign. *Fliegerdivision 1* (1st Air Division) indicated that the small number of communicators within its force structure represented a major weakness in coordinating with the army's motorized and mechanized units. It suggested major additions to its TO&E (tables of organization and equipment) to bolster its ability to support ground forces that were advancing rapidly. The failure of communications had resulted in requests for close air support arriving so late in the flying squadrons that they had already been overtaken by events. Finally, *Fliegerdivision 1* warned that whatever improvements were made, it was going to prove difficult to keep air commanders informed of the rapidly changing situation on the ground.[77]

Army after-action reports that addressed *Luftwaffe* operations in support of ground operations present a mixed picture. Many units had nothing to say about *Luftwaffe* support, suggesting that there had been little air-ground cooperation, at least within their area of responsibility.[78] Some units reported incidents of fratricide, but concluded that air support generally had done more damage to the Poles than to German units and hence was of some use. However, the 10th Panzer Division, which had played an important role in Guderian's advance, was not at all happy with its *Luftwaffe* close air support. It reported that aerial reconnaissance

---

[76] BA/MA, RL17/2, Abschrift, "Erfahrungsbericht der Luftflotte 1 über den polnischen Feldzug," p. 1.

[77] BA/MA, RL 7/2, Anlage zu Fliegerdivision 1, Br. Nr. 3185/39, "Vorläufiger Erfahrungsbericht über den Einsatz während des poln. Feldzuges."

[78] In most of the after-action formats, there was a specific block in which units could comment on *Luftwaffe* support.

had been either late or inaccurate. In one case in which *Luftwaffe* reconnaissance had reported that Polish fortifications and defensive positions near the town of Lomza were free of defending troops, reconnaissance troops of the 10th Panzer division had discovered those positions strongly held. More distressing to the division was the fact that *Luftwaffe* aircraft had regularly bombed and machine-gunned its units throughout the campaign. But what really outraged those writing the 10th Panzer Division's after-action report was the fact that despite the use of agreed-on recognition devices, one of its battalions had been bombed and machine-gunned for several hours in a graphic demonstration of the *Luftwaffe*'s power that left 13 German soldiers dead and 25 badly wounded.[79]

Not until the immediate period before the offensive in the west did the *Luftwaffe* and the army actually get around to addressing jointly the problems associated with providing close air support to ground forces engaged in mechanized exploitation. In late April 1940, the two services conducted several experiments to see whether panzer units on the move could communicate directly with supporting aircraft.[80] While the experiments suggested that such coordination was possible, provided *Luftwaffe* liaison teams were available with sophisticated communications gear and armored vehicles, there was not sufficient time to establish such teams and incorporate them within the panzer divisions before the offensive in the west began. Still it is worthy of note that the Germans left joint lessons learned as the last to be addressed in their corrective actions. It would take another major campaign before they succeeded in hammering out a solution to the problem of close air support in the mobile environment.

After-action reports on the French campaign showed much the same pattern for close air support in the mobile environment as did those from Poland. The support given to XIX Panzer Corps in its breakthrough on the Meuse represented a major contribution to German victory. Significantly, however, none of the other panzer corps received close air support in their breakthrough efforts. The most successful of these – the crucial breakthrough at Dinant by Erwin Rommel's 7th Panzer Division – received no *Luftwaffe* support until two days after the division had made its difficult

---

[79] 10. Panzer Division, Abt.Ia Nr. 26/39, "Erfahrungsbericht," 3.10.1939, NARS T-314/614/000632.
[80] 1. Panzer Division, Ia Nr. 232/40, 24 April 1940, "Zusammenarbeit Panzer/Stuka," NARS T-314/615/000393.

crossing of the Meuse – one that might well have failed without Rommel's intervention. The future field marshal's account indicates that he was not provided with *Luftwaffe* support until 15 May.[81]

Lessons learned at the conclusion of the French campaign repeated and reinforced what the Germans had learned in Poland. Again the same problems involved in close air support cropped up. *Luftwaffe* units again did great damage to the enemy through their interdiction strikes, while close air support in the breakthrough battle proved enormously helpful to Guderian's units. In the subsequent exploitation phase, however, the *Luftwaffe* continued to bomb fast-moving German mechanized units, including, in one case, Guderian's own headquarters near Amiens as the Germans closed on the Channel coast.[82]

But at this point in the war, the consistent reports of *Luftwaffe* aircraft being unable to identify the *Wehrmacht*'s mobile units on the ground finally forced the Germans to undertake substantive changes in the tactics, techniques, and procedures of close air support. First, they detailed close air reconnaissance squadrons directly to the panzer divisions.[83] A second and more important change was that the *Luftwaffe* now assigned air liaison officers down to the panzer divisions, in some cases supported by an air signal liaison detachment with a driver and four radio operators.[84] The *Luftwaffe* could assign these detachments to critical areas of the front where mobile operations were taking place. With their armored vehicles, they were able to operate directly with the panzer divisions' lead units.[85]

A third significant improvement was the assignment of the control of close air support missions to a specific organization, the *Nahkampführer*

---

[81] Erwin Rommel, *The Rommel Papers*, ed. by B. H. Liddell Hart (London, 1953), p. 15. He was informed of this support by a *Luftwaffe* major who was clearly not familiar, which suggests that the 7th Panzer Division still had no liaison officer directly assigned to it.

[82] Guderian was furious, as he makes clear in his memoirs: his headquarters staff shot down one of the offending Bf 110s, and when the crew, who had parachuted to safety in the neighborhood, were brought to him, he chewed them out unmercifully. Heinz Guderian, *Panzer Leader* (New York, 1953).

[83] General der Flieger Paul Deichman, *German Air Force Operations in Support of the Army: USAF Historical Study No. 163* (Montgomery, AL, 1962), p. 70.

[84] There is some irony in this improvement because the British had broken the *Luftwaffe* "Enigma" codes and were therefore able to gain insight into exactly what the German Army was doing from the reports of the *Luftwaffe* liaison officers at various levels. Among others, see Ralph Bennett, *Ultra in the West* (New York, 1980).

[85] Deichman, *German Air Force Operations in Support of the Army*, p. 132.

(close air support leader), to control close air support missions within the two air corps, II and VIII *Fliegerkorps*, which had thus far in the war carried the bulk of these missions. The *Nahkampfführer* was responsible for the forward displacement of close air support units, for coordination with the army in the ground battle, and for the communications between the air corps and the panzer groups (soon to be renamed "panzer armies").[86] The result of these changes was a considerable increase in the *Luftwaffe*'s ability to provide close air support in the mobile environment, which was to have a significant impact on German tactical effectiveness throughout the first two years of operations on the Eastern Front.[87]

The Larger Framework of Adaptation

As with the analysis of lessons learned after the Polish campaign, careful adaptation and improvement in the procedures of close air support brought the Germans significant advantages in succeeding battles. Through the end of the war, the same deliberate, thorough analyses marked German after-action reviews on the Eastern Front and in North Africa, Italy, France, and the Low Countries from 1942 to 1945. These efforts explain much about the combat effectiveness, and at times the superiority, of German military forces on the battlefields of World War II.[88]

How in addition to explain this excellence? A partial answer lies in the German Army's peacetime culture that regarded professional military education as an essential element in the preparation for the conduct of war. The painstaking selection and education of general staff officers brought the brightest of officers in the army together to receive a thorough grounding in the tactical and to some extent operational conduct of war. The *Kriegsakademie* ensured that the future leaders of the

---

[86] BA/MA, RH 27-18/14, Oberkommando des Heeres, GenStdH/Ausb.Abt. (Ia), H.Qu.OKH, 26.5.41, Nr. 1161/41, "Taktisches Merkblatt für dir Führung von Nahkampf-Verbänden."

[87] The last major impact that German close air support was to have on a battle was at the Second Battle of Kharkov in February–March 1943 when Field Marshal Eric von Manstein's panzers caught the lead armored elements of the Red Army's Don offensive after they had reached their culminating point and destroyed them.

[88] A number of historians have commented on German military effectiveness throughout the war. See among others Martin van Creveld, *Fighting Power: German and U.S. Army Performance, 1939–1945* (New York, 1982); and Max Hastings, *Overlord* (London, 1986).

German Army possessed a rigorous, analytic framework for conducting the self-examinations described throughout this chapter.

The selection processes to attend the *Kriegsakademie* also suggests a great deal about the German Army's culture. Fewer than 5 percent of the captains who took the admission examination managed to gain entrance to the two-year course. Testifying to the importance of academic performance, barely half of those admitted graduated. Those who did gain entrance to the general staff as provisional members then alternated between staff and command positions and were protected for the rest of their careers by the crimson stripe that denoted their membership in the general staff – an elite band of intellectually as well as operationally prepared officers.[89] That educational emphasis of the general staff produced an institutional culture in which even the "muddy-boots" soldiers read – and in some cases wrote – books.[90] The effect throughout the officer corps was to enhance serious thinking; study was a major component in an officer's career – especially in comparison to Europe's other military establishments.

Before the First World War, the general staff was by no means dominant over the German Army. On the contrary, its size and purview were strictly limited. Yet, when engaged to develop tactical answers to problems posed by the Somme battlefield of 1916, where the German Army was taking such a terrible beating, the German general staff played a major role in developing the concepts of defense in depth, combined arms, and exploitation tactics, the last of which contributed so much to breaking the logjam on the Western Front in the spring battles of 1918.

The role of the general staff expanded when Seeckt transformed the downsizing of the German Army in response to the demands of the victors in 1920 into a cultural revolution. The general staff now dominated the culture of the new German Army, and its requirement for rigorous, honest analysis of not only the experiences of the First World War but also its peacetime exercises and maneuvers ensured three things. First, unlike the

---

[89] The best book on the general staff system during the interwar period remains David Spires, *Image and Reality: The Making of the German Officer, 1921–1933* (Westport, CT, 1984). General staff officers were protected by the fact that their efficiency reports were written only by other general staff officers.

[90] The foremost of such officers was Erwin Rommel, who never made the cut to get into the general staff but who read military voraciously and who wrote the classic, *Infantry Attack*, on his experiences as a combat officer in the First World War. The best biography of Rommel remains David Fraser, *Knight's Cross: A Life of Field Marshal Erwin Rommel* (New York, 1993).

French and British armies during the interwar period, the *Wehrmacht* would not forget the lessons of the last war. Second, it would apply the same honest, realistic willingness to challenge assumptions to the incorporation of new technological and weapons developments.[91] Finally, and perhaps most important, that same cultural framework in peacetime carried over into wartime. Thus, the processes of effective adaptation that the Germans exhibited in the aftermath of the Polish campaign reflected habits of mind that they had acquired in peacetime, when the *Reichswehr* and *Wehrmacht* had innovated so successfully.

Yet, military effectiveness is multidimensional: it is much more than simply tactical performance in battle.[92] Good tactics do not necessarily lead to effectiveness at the operational or strategic levels, as the German performance in the 1918 campaign underlines.[93] In other words, brilliant success at the tactical and operational levels does not invariably translate into strategic and political victory.[94] The German Army was extraordinarily good at inculcating the tactical lessons of the battlefield into the preparations of its officers and troops in both world wars. It was not so effective, however, at gleaning operational and strategic lessons. In the largest sense, German tactics – and the operational concepts they derived from those tactics – were sufficient to handle the battles in Central Europe. But away from Central Europe, "the German way of war" fell apart.

The conduct of Operation Barbarossa – the invasion of the Soviet Union in June 1941 – underlines this fact most clearly. In the immediate conduct of the tactical and operational battle, German forces displayed breathtaking combat effectiveness. The advance into and through the Baltic states and the battles of Minsk, Smolensk, Kiev, and Briansk/Viazma ripped the Red Army to pieces and brought the Germans to the

---

[91] See particularly Murray, "Armored Warfare," in Murray and Millett, eds., *Military Innovation in the Interwar Period*. The development of armored warfare by the Germans was not a revolutionary development, but rather the Germans fit the technology of the tank within the paradigm of combined-arms exploitation tactics developed in World War I and then refined in the interwar period.

[92] For a wide-ranging examination of military effectiveness at every level in war and peace, see Allan R. Millett and Williamson Murray, eds., *Military Effectiveness*, 3 vols. (London, 1988), particularly the introductory essay.

[93] In this regard, see David T. Zabecki, *The German 1918 Offensives; A Case Study in the Operational Level of War* (London, 2006).

[94] The recent American military success in defeating Saddam Hussein's military in 2003 suggests a great deal about the difficulties inherent in translating military victory into political success, which, as Clausewitz underlines, is the only reason Western states conduct wars.

gates of Moscow by early December 1941.⁹⁵ Despite these impressive initial victories, two giant miscalculations led to military defeat and national catastrophe: a general collapse of logistics and an abysmal failure in intelligence.

In terms of logistics, there had been clear warnings during the French campaign that there might be troubles ahead – especially were the German Army to confront the problems of supply in the vast distances of the Soviet Union.⁹⁶ On several occasions, lead units advancing to the English Channel had almost run out of fuel. Only the use of French gas stations in undamaged condition allowed German armor to maintain the pace of the advance. Guderian makes light of these incidents in his memoirs, but such reliance on captured stocks in the French campaign would have raised red flags in an army that paid attention to its logistics, especially for an army planning for the invasion of the Soviet Union where there were few stocks to capture. So careless regarding logistics were the German planners that the initial warnings during early war games indicating that the German logistical structure could support military operations only to Kiev, Smolensk, and Estonia raised not the slightest worries during the operational planning for Barbarossa.

The intelligence failure was even more profound. To a considerable extent, the *Wehrmacht* accepted Hitler's belief that the Soviet Union would collapse like a house of cards once BARBAROSSA began. Thus, *OKH* planners, including the chief of staff, Franz Halder, gravitated to a belief that the defeat of the Red Army in the border areas would be sufficient to encompass the Soviet Union's destruction. Two quotes from Halder's diary make clear the extent of the intelligence failure. The first comes from the early days of the campaign – less than two weeks into the campaign to defeat a state the size of the Soviet Union:

> On the whole, then, it may be said even now that the objective to shatter the bulk of the Russian army this side of the Dvina and Dneiper has been accomplished. I do not doubt the statement of the captured Russian corps

---

⁹⁵ The most thoroughly researched account of BARBAROSSA is that produced by a team of eminent historians at the Militärgeschichtliches Forschungsamt. See Horst Boog, Jürgen Förster, Joachim Hoffmann, Ernst Klink, Rold-Dieter Müller, and Gerd R. Ueberschär, *Das Deutsche Reich und der Zweite Weltkrieg*, vol. 4, *Der Angriff auf die Sowjetunion* (Stuttgart, 1983).

⁹⁶ Early in July 1940, the German Army began examining the possibility of invading the Soviet Union barely after the lessons-learned process for the campaign against France and the Low Countries had begun and before Hitler had even raised the possibility with the army's senior leaders.

CG [commanding general] that east of the Dvina and Dneiper we would encounter nothing more than partial forces, not strong enough to hinder realization of German operational plans. It is thus probably no overstatement to say that the Russian campaign has been won in the space of two weeks. Of course, this does not mean that it is closed. The sheer geographical vastness of the country and the stubbornness of the resistance, which is carried on with all means, will claim our efforts for many more weeks to come.[97]

The second quote came little more than a month later – 38 days to be exact – at a point when the *Wehrmacht* had discovered that the Red Army possessed reserve divisions in far greater numbers than German intelligence had calculated the Soviets could possibly possess. Halder now sang a different tune – one that underlines the extent of German miscalculations:

> The whole situation makes it increasingly plain that we have underestimated the Russian colossus, which consistently prepared for war with that utterly ruthless determination so characteristic of totalitarian states. This applies to organizational and economic resources, as well as the communication system and, most of all, to the strictly military potential. At the outset of war, we reckoned with about 200 enemy divisions. Now we have counted 360. These divisions are indeed not armed and equipped according to our standards, and their tactical leadership is often poor. But there they are, and if we smash a dozen of them, the Russians simply put up another dozen.[98]

Yet, the most astonishing aspect to the intelligence failure of 1941 is that over the course of the remainder of the war, the Germans seemed to learn nothing from their mistakes in calculating Soviet strength and resolve. The stock response to the Soviet recovery and then steadily improving combat performance was a combination of the canard that the *Wehrmacht* had been done in by "winter weather" in December 1941 – an explanation that lasted until the disastrous defeat at Kursk – and the massive numbers of men and materiel the Red Army possessed.[99] In other

---

[97] Franz Halder, *The Halder War Diary, 1939–1941*, ed. by Charles Burdick and Hans-Adolph Jacobsen (Novato, CA, 1988), pp. 446–447.
[98] Ibid., p. 506.
[99] A corollary to the canard about winter weather was the argument that the coldness of the Russian winter caught the Germans by complete surprise. To believe that, one would have to ignore the fact that the Germans had been deep in Russia during the First World War where they had experienced the severity of Russian winters for four years. Moreover, weather data from the winter of 1941–1942, just as with the data for Napoleon's retreat from Moscow, indicate nothing abnormally cold about the weather conditions that the Germans confronted during this period.

words, the German intelligence system proved incapable of adaptation to the challenge that Soviet military power presented.

Matters became worse rather than better as the war proceeded. By summer 1943 the Soviets were engaging in wide-scale *maskirovka*, which disguised the location of every major offensive they would launch, from Kursk through the end of the war.[100] Yet throughout this period, German intelligence picked up neither the extent of those deception efforts nor the extent to which the successes of the Red Army reflected the ability of its intelligence organizations – and staff planning processes – to deceive *Wehrmacht* intelligence. (In this case, Foreign Armies East was headed by Major General Reinhard Gehlen, who would ironically play a major role in establishing the postwar intelligence organizations that monitored Soviet military developments during the Cold War.)

In the west, the Germans managed to repeat the pattern. Confident that their communication technology remained unbreakable (despite the fact that the British had managed to break the *Kriegsmarine* codes throughout World War I), the Germans consistently refused to believe the British could have broken into their Enigma codes.[101] Not only did that compromise substantially diminish the effectiveness of German military operations from summer 1941 on, but it also allowed the British and Americans to monitor closely how well their efforts at deception were actually affecting German dispositions and actions.[102] Ironically, misattributing their difficulties to human intelligence leaks, the Germans continuously decreased the size of their staffs, which made it increasingly unlikely that those staffs, especially the intelligence staffs, would possess sufficient robustness to figure out what the Allies were getting away with.[103]

---

[100] Beginning in the 1980s, the groundbreaking work of Colonel David Glantz, U.S. Army (retired), underlined the extent to which patterns of Soviet deception managed to fool German commanders repeatedly in the great battles on the Eastern Front. For a general discussion of the role of deception in the conduct of Soviet offensive operations, see David Glantz and Jonathan M. House, *When Titans Clashed: How the Red Army Stopped Hitler* (Lawrence, KS, 1998). For Glantz's scholarly examination of *maskirovka*, see particularly *Soviet Military Deception in the Second World War* (London, 1989).

[101] A large number of works now deal with "Ultra," but perhaps the most important one is Gordon Welchman's *Hut Six Story*, which underlines that the most important component in the British success in breaking the Enigma codes had to do with German arrogance and carelessness – a lack of signal discipline that was at times breathtaking. See Gordon Welchman, *The Hut Six Story* (London, 1997).

[102] See particularly Michael Howard, *Strategic Deception in the Second World War* (New York, 1995).

[103] Lest American readers become contemptuous of the German mistakes with regard to their codes in World War II, it is worth noting the Walker family managed to

Finally, it is worth noting that during the course of World War II, the Germans managed to repeat every strategic mistake they had made in the previous world war. Obviously, Hitler had a great deal to do with repeating the pattern, but the army's leadership delightedly welcomed their Führer's decision, made in late July 1940, to embark on a racial and ideological crusade against the Soviet Union in summer 1941. At the same time as the initial stages of BARBAROSSA were unfolding in the east, the naval leadership – in particular Admirals Eric Raeder and Karl Dönitz – attempted to persuade Hitler to declare war on the United States.[104] When the Führer decided to declare war on the United States in response to the Japanese attack on Pearl Harbor in December 1941, no one among the senior leaders in the German high command or of the services saw fit to suggest that such a declaration of war might not represent a good idea.[105]

Conclusion

Whatever the difficulties the Germans eventually confronted in the larger framework of World War II, their ability to learn from their tactical experiences in the period immediately after the First World War, and then to institutionalize the culture and methods that made that learning possible, enabled them to dominate the tactical battlefield for most of the early periods of World War II and much of the rest of the conflict. The irony is that despite their outstanding tactical performance, the Germans possessed neither the cultural understanding nor the intellectual vision to turn their temporary advantage into strategic or political success.

At a time when the U.S. military is vigorously exercising and training its forces at the tactical level to participate in counterinsurgency operations in Iraq and Afghanistan, the success the Germans enjoyed in translating the lessons of combat into lessons *learned* should not be minimized. Admittedly, the failure to adapt in other areas suggests considerable limitations in the "German way of war." Yet the larger point is that German

---

compromise the U.S. Navy's most complex codes for nearly two decades before a family dispute exposed what was going on.
[104] For the German Navy's efforts to persuade Hitler to declare war on the United States in summer 1941, see Holger H. Herwig, *The Politics of Frustration: The United States in German Naval Planning, 1889–1941* (Boston, 1976), pp. 228–229.
[105] Gerhard Weinberg has noted that the best explanation for this shortsightedness undoubtedly lies in the fact that the German military's explanation for their defeat in World War I was that their supposedly "unbeaten army" had been stabbed in the back by the Jews and the communists. In such an explanation, there was little room for the role that the arrival of several million Americans on the Western Front in the last half of 1918 had played in the Reich's defeat.

military culture – with its emphasis on learning, intellectual preparation for war, and rigorous honesty between the different levels of command – presents an example that deserves attention.

It is this military culture, with its emphasis on the intellectual as well as the "muddy-boots" aspects of soldiering, that might well serve as an example for the kind of officer corps the United States will need in the twenty-first century. At a far earlier point in an officer's career (the captain level), the Germans were willing to decide those few officers who possessed not only the physical but also the intellectual attributes for senior command. That judgment rested first on how well those officers had performed in the field. But entrance through the narrow gate to senior command – the *Kriegsakademie* – came only through the passing of an intensive examination and schooling process. How those officers then performed in an academic environment was as important for their future careers as their record in the field.

That educational preparation – that inculcation of rigorous intellectual habits of mind – provided the mind-set that allowed the Germans to execute realistic and rapid adaptation to the actual conditions of war. If the United States requires senior officers who are flexible and adaptable to meet the challenges of a complex and ambiguous world, as so many commissions of the federal government have suggested, then the German model with its emphasis on intense education of the best and brightest officers would seem worthy of emulation.[106] But the German example carries with it a warning: too narrow a focus on the purely military attributes of the profession of arms will inevitably carry with it misunderstandings of the broader political and strategic issues involved in war – a sure recipe for disaster.

[106] For the commissions making such recommendations, one might particularly consult the reports of the National Defense Panel and Hart-Rudman Report.

5

The Battle for the British Isles

June 1940–May 1941

Historians usually characterize the Battle of Britain as a great contest between the *Luftwaffe* and RAF Fighter Command that lasted from early July 1940 through to the massive daylight bombing of London during the first two weeks of September. The RAF is slightly more generous in placing the dates for the battle as occurring between 10 July and 31 October 1940.[1] But the long and short of it is that the historical focus has emphasized the daylight, air-to-air struggle that took place over the course of three months – July, August, and September of 1940 – and not the fact that German efforts to knock Britain out of the war persisted through to spring 1941. The Battle of Britain from the perspective of those who fought it did not end until the Germans invaded the Soviet Union in late June 1941.

This chapter aims at examining adaptation over a wider space of time from early June 1940 through to the end of May 1941, when the *Wehrmacht* turned to conduct Operation Barbarossa, the invasion of the Soviet Union, and what *Luftwaffe*'s chief of staff termed "a proper war." It also aims at examining adaptation on both sides in the areas of technology, intelligence, operations, and tactics, rather than simply the contest between British fighters and German bombers and fighters – although the latter is obviously of considerable importance. Moreover, it also examines the questions surrounding the larger strategic issues of German efforts to besiege the British Isles over the course of 1940 and the first half of 1941.

---

[1] Francis K. Mason, *Battle over Britain: A History of German Air Assaults on Great Britain, 1917–1918 and July–December 1940 and of the Development of Britain's Air Defences between the World Wars* (Garden City, NY, 1969), pp. 152, 466.

The period of the Anglo-German war between the fall of France (June 1940) and the German invasion of the Soviet Union (June 1941) is of particular interest because it involved the integration of a whole set of new technologies and concepts into conflict as well as adaptation on both sides to a complex set of problems, which those new technologies raised, the answers to which were largely uncertain and ambiguous. In the largest sense, despite their technological and scientific advantages, the Germans proved less capable than the British in adapting to the strategic and operational challenges that the Battle of Britain raised. Finally, this case study should be of interest because the indefinable qualities of leadership and imagination played crucial roles in determining not only the immediate outcome but the course of the war as well.[2]

This chapter begins by presenting the background to the German siege of the British Isles, moves to an examination of the strategic and operational framework of the initial battle for air supremacy waged by the *Luftwaffe*, and then discusses the course of the prolonged air and naval effort by the Germans over fall and winter 1940–1941 to bring Britain to its knees.[3] The aim is not so much to present a chronology of the battle, with which many readers possess considerable familiarity, but rather to evaluate the decisions and adaptations that the opposing sides made in the hope of gaining insights into the influences that led to successful – or, as the case may be, flawed – adaptation and decision making.

The Technological and Conceptual Background

By the end of the First World War, the rapid improvement of aircraft technology had underlined that aircraft were going to play an essential role in future wars. Nevertheless, what that role might be remained unclear as the war drew to a close.[4] It would soon become a matter of considerable

---

[2] I am indebted to the authors of *The 9/11 Commission Report* for their emphasis on the importance of imagination – or lack of imagination, as the case may be – in determining the failure of the bureaucratic organs of the U.S. government to uncover the al Qaeda plot that resulted in the destruction of the Twin Towers, considerable damage to the Pentagon, and the downing of United Airlines Flight 93. See "Foresight – and Hindsight," in *The 9/11 Commission Report*, specifically pp. 339–348, National Commission on Terrorist Attacks upon the United States, http://www.9-11commission.gov/ (accessed May 1, 2009).

[3] For the most thorough depiction of the day-to-day events of what is officially termed the Battle of Britain, the reader is urged to consult Mason, *Battle over Britain*. Also worth consulting for the larger framework of the strategic and operational context is Basil Collier's *Defence of the United Kingdom* (London, 1995); and Telford Taylor, *The Breaking Wave: The Second World War in the Summer of 1940* (New York, 1967).

[4] For the development of the aircraft as a weapons platform during the First World War, see Williamson Murray, *The Air War: 1914–1945* (London, 2000), chap. 1.

debate.⁵ Only the British had created an independent air force as a result of their experiences in the war. That independence had resulted from a series of German Zeppelin and bomber raids, which had begun in 1914 and continued through to spring 1918. These German attacks engendered enormous publicity in Britain but in fact did relatively little damage, although they had caused considerable excitement among the British media and public. If the RAF's origins were largely defensive in response, almost immediately after the war, the new service sketched out an aggressive role for itself – massive bombing attacks that its senior officers argued would destroy the enemy's morale and bring him to heel without the bloodshed of attrition warfare that had marked so much of the Great War.⁶

Within the RAF's conception of air war, there was little role for air defense. In a 1924 memorandum, the air staff explicitly stated "as a principle that the bombing squadrons should be as numerous as possible and the fighters as few as popular opinion and the necessity for defending vital objects will permit."⁷ There was some justification for that attitude in 1924: while the British had created an air defense system in 1917 and 1918, their efforts had not proven particularly effective in bringing down the attacking German bombers. Nevertheless, whatever the doctrinal attitudes in the RAF, through to the mid-1930s, the British government allowed the infamous "ten-year rule" – invented by Winston Churchill, of all people – to dominate British defense policy.⁸ Simply stated, the rule posited that Britain would not confront a major war for ten years, and as a rolling principle, the ten-year rule moved forward with the beginning of each new year. Thus, successive British governments found a simple excuse to put off serious expenditures on national defense through to the mid-1930s.

But even had Britain's political leadership possessed more foresight, the national mood, particularly among the ruling class, was that anything was better than war – an attitude eloquently expressed in the Oxford Political Union's resolution of 1934: "Resolved that this house refuses to

---

⁵ For the nature of the debate, see, among others, Montgomery Hyde, *Air Policy between the Wars: 1918–1939* (London, 1976).
⁶ Their attitudes were partially influenced by the uproar that broke out in the United Kingdom, driven by the British newspapers, about the German attacks. There was, however, no evidence that the bombing caused any drop in British morale.
⁷ Public Records Office (PRO), United Kingdom, Air 20/40, Air Staff Memorandum No. 11 A, March 1924.
⁸ For its impact, see Williamson Murray, *The Change in the European Balance of Power, 1938–1939: The Path to Ruin* (Princeton, 1984), chap. 2.

fight for King and country."[9] Statements by politicians such as Stanley Baldwin – for example, his comments in November 1932 before the House of Commons that "the bomber will always get through" – further reinforced pacifistic inclinations throughout Britain. Echoing what passed for wisdom in the RAF, Baldwin further declaimed that "[t]he only defence is offence, which means that you have to kill more women and children more quickly than the enemy if you want to save yourself."[10]

The result of a profound national pacifism and the refusal to fund even defensive capabilities at reasonable levels was a policy of appeasement that posited that the dictators were reasonable men and Britain should avoid war at almost any cost. Furthermore, the British service assessments reinforced the government's inclination to appease the Germans and Italians by worst-casing British capabilities in the forlorn hope (at least until March 1939) that the government would finally recognize the need to begin a program that would seriously address the services' minimum needs to defend the national polity.[11]

Nevertheless, even within the extraordinary resource limitations imposed by the government, the British were able to make advances in the area of future air capabilities, particularly with regard to air defense. In 1931 Hugh Dowding was appointed head of the RAF's research and development establishment, perhaps the most important appointment the RAF was to make during the 1930s. In that position, he set the specifications for what would eventually turn into the Hurricane and Spitfire fighter aircraft.[12] He then provided the resources and encouragement that led to the development of functioning radar capabilities.

An eminent historian of science and technology, Alan Beyerchen, has noted the following about Dowding's role in the development of radar:

> Dowding was indisputably the pivotal military figure, providing the pull toward new operational developments and innovation. He took a strong personal interest in radar research and development and even flew in research aircraft to see the project's progress for himself. He also insisted that military personnel be posted right with the 'boffins,' as civilian researchers became known. This insured that RAF personnel actually understood what was happening and that the civilians could be kept

---

[9] Winston S. Churchill, *The Second World War*, vol. 1, *The Gathering Storm* (Boston, 1948), p. 85.
[10] Quoted in John Terraine, *The Right of the Line, The Royal Air Force in the European War, 1939–1945* (London, 1985), p. 13.
[11] For an examination of these complex issues, see Murray, *The Change in the European Balance of Power*, chap. 2.
[12] For the technological side of the equation, see Derek Wood and Derek Dempster, *The Narrow Margin* (London, 1969).

aware of military constraints and needs. Furthermore, the basic tactics and requirements for night airborne interception were his own ideas. Dowding was no orthodox thinker, and perhaps understood the technological implications of radio better than any other figure in the RAF.[13]

In 1936 Dowding lost out in the competition for the post of chief of the air staff, the senior post in the RAF. As a sop, he received the newly created position as the head of Fighter Command, now responsible for defending Britain from air attack. Again, it was a fortuitous appointment, because no one in Britain was more knowledgeable and inclined to understand how Fighter Command might best integrate new technologies and aircraft capabilities into the creation of an effective air defense system. Dowding, indeed, was an exception among the RAF's senior officers, most of whom were ignorant of technology and the implications of technological change – in some cases willfully so. Sir Arthur Harris, the future leader of Bomber Command, would proclaim in early 1941 that the *Luftwaffe* pilots' use of blind-bombing systems only underlined what bad airmen they were, because RAF bomber pilots did not need technological assistance to hit targets accurately in their bombing raids at night – a claim that an independent examination of bomb photos, the Butt report in the summer of 1941, indicated was completely fallacious.[14]

Dowding's efforts were helped considerably by the fact that the British had established an air defense system in the last year of World War I.[15] The technological weaknesses of that system in the 1916–1918 period may well have strengthened a systemic approach. As the head of Britain's air defenses during World War I noted after the war: "The great principle of air defence is that although aeroplanes are the first means of defence, they are ineffective unless supported by a control system on the

---

[13] Alan Beyerchen, "From Radio to Radar, Interwar Military Adaptation to Technological Change in Germany, the United Kingdom, and the United States," in Williamson Murray and Allan R. Millett, eds., *Military Innovation in the Interwar Period*, (Cambridge, 1996), p. 282.

[14] Harris noted in February 1941, "Are we not tending to lose our sense of proportion over these German beams?... We use no beams ourselves but we bomb just as successfully as the Germans bomb deep into Germany." That summer the Butt report indicated that most crews in Bomber Command were not even able to hit cities accurately. Harris quoted in R. V. Jones, *The Wizard War: British Scientific Intelligence, 1939–1945* (New York, 1978), p. 169. For the Butt report, which indicated how futile Bomber Command's efforts were in summer 1941, see Sir Charles Webster and Noble Frankland, *The Strategic Air Offensive against Germany*, vol. 4, *Appendices* (London, 1962), appendix 13, pp. 205–213.

[15] I am indebted to Professor John Ferris of the University of Calgary for this point.

ground."[16] Between 1937 and 1939, Dowding established an integrated air defense system, in which radar provided the warning; and then a command and control network alerted the central headquarters at Bentley Priory, the fighter group headquarters, the army's anti-aircraft guns, and the civil defense system. There were a number of other complexities, but the crucial point is that by the outbreak of the war, the British had a functioning air defense *system* from which experience and adaptations would eliminate the bugs.

Tragically for the defense of the West, the British could have pushed their technological and combat capabilities further and mitigated the advantages the *Luftwaffe* had gained by its sustained six-year preparation for war, but they failed to do so. The Chamberlain government's role in the RAF's preparation for war was somewhat less disastrous than in the other areas of Britain's defense efforts but not necessarily for the right reasons. In 1937, a governmental review of defense expenditures decided that the RAF should emphasize the production of fighters rather than bombers to the horror of many senior officers on the air staff.[17] The rationale for that decision had little to do with a belief in the efficacy of air defense but rather with the fact that fighters cost less than bombers.[18] Nevertheless, the government continued to maintain severe constraints on aircraft production, including production for Fighter Command, which considerably limited production over the course of the late 1930s.

In November 1938, shortly after the Munich Conference, Chamberlain agreed to increase the number of fighters on order by 50 percent. The prime minister was reacting to the heavy pressure the government was under to increase defense spending. A number of historians have argued that that decision represented an indication of the government's seriousness in attempting to repair deficiencies in Britain's defenses. It was nothing of the kind. In fact, the government simply extended the two-year contract for Hurricanes and Spitfires for an additional year and then claimed an increase of 50 percent in fighter procurement.[19] But British

---

[16] Quoted in Richard Hough and Denis Richards, *The Battle of Britain: The Greatest Air Battle of World War II* (London, 1989), p. 11.

[17] Terraine, *The Right of the Line*, p. 51. The Minister for the Coordination of Defense, Sir Thomas Inskip, noted that the RAF's role was not to launch an early knockout blow against Germany, but rather "to prevent the Germans from knocking us out."

[18] For a general discussion of the disastrous defense policies followed by the Chamberlain government and their impact on the ability of Britain to defend itself, see Murray, *The Change in the European Balance of Power*, chap. 2.

[19] For the production plans for fighters and the actual numbers produced, see particularly PRO CAB 23/143, DPR 285, 14.10.38, CID, 24th Progress Report: "Week Ending

aircraft factories would produce no additional fighters in 1939 beyond those called for in the original contracts, despite their capability to ramp up production by a considerable amount, given the latent industrial capacity, a factor that would play a major role in the Battle of Britain. Had the British actually increased fighter production by 50 percent over the next six to nine months, they would have been in a far better position to meet the German air threat in spring and summer 1940. There is a larger point here: with additional resources, Fighter Command might also have possessed night fighters equipped with airborne radars in summer 1940 to make night interceptions, a capability Dowding had strongly urged on the government in 1938 but which he lacked the resources to pursue throughout 1938 and 1939.[20]

On the other side of the hill, the Germans lacked anything close to Dowding's perceptive willingness to include scientists and technologists as partners with his officers in developing the technologies that Fighter Command needed to defend the British Isles. For German military leaders, scientists were the servants of the war machine, not partners. The *Luftwaffe*'s titular head, Hermann Göring, was more interested in acquiring power within the tangled bureaucratic nightmare of Nazi Germany than in dealing realistically with the problems confronting the *Luftwaffe*. Unfortunately for the Germans, Göring's attitude was all too typical of the *Luftwaffe*'s senior officers. The kind of partnership Dowding established with British scientists was just not possible in the world of Nazi Germany. While German technology more often than not was superior to British and American technology, how the Germans used it often minimized its capabilities. This was largely the result of the unwillingness of Germany's leaders, including military leaders, to regard scientists and technologists as their equals. Thus, they rarely listened to, much less paid attention to, expert scientific advice.[21]

1.10.38"; DPR 291, 14.12.38, 25th Progress Report; DPR 297, 26th Progress Report; PRO CAB 16/144, DPR 305, 27th Progress Report, 18.4.39, and DPR 312, 28th Progress Report, 14.6.39. In effect, the Chamberlain government lost the six months after Munich before the German occupation of Prague, while the German economy, fully mobilized, built an ever-greater advantage over the Allies. For an examination of German economic mobilization before World War II, see Murray, *The Change in the European Balance of Power*, chap. 1.

[20] Collier, *The Defence of the United Kingdom*, p. 40.
[21] The most outstanding work on that partnership is the memoir of R. V. Jones, *The Wizard War*, but also well worth consulting are the memoirs of the scientist Solly Zuckerman, who served as Air Chief Marshal Arthur Tedder's chief scientific adviser for much of the war; see Solly Zuckerman, *From Apes to Warlords: The Autobiography (1904–1946)* (London, 1978).

On the military side of the ledger, the Germans possessed the most formidable air force in the world – in terms not only of its broad spectrum of capabilities but of its preparations to execute long-range strategic attacks. Nevertheless, the German conception of the coming war was almost entirely continental in focus.[22] While the *Luftwaffe* emphasized air superiority in its doctrine, it planned to gain air superiority by pushing its Bf 109 squadrons forward behind the army's advance, while interdiction attacks paralyzed the enemy's military structure behind the battlefront and longer-range strategic raids on his industry impaired his war production.[23]

The problem with the United Kingdom for the Germans lay in the fact that the English Channel, the North Sea, and the Atlantic Ocean surrounded and thus protected the island kingdom. Until summer 1938 when the Czech crisis raised the possibility of war with the British, the German military, including the *Luftwaffe*, appears to have believed the *Führer*'s promise that the Reich would not have to fight Britain. Only in high summer 1938 did *Luftflotte* 2 (Second Air Force) examine the problems associated with a conflict against Britain in a series of war games.[24] Its planners came to the conclusion that Germany was in no position to wage such a conflict.

If the *Luftwaffe* began thinking about the problem of attacking Britain late in the game, the army never thought about it at all. It focused entirely on fighting Germany's continental opponents. Only the *Kriegsmarine* gave some thought to a war with Britain, but its preparations focused

---

[22] For the weaknesses in German strategy and understanding of the coming war, see particularly William Deist, "The Road to Ideological War: Germany 1918–1945," in Williamson Murray, MacGregor Knox, and Alvin Bernstein, eds., *The Making of Strategy: Rulers, States, and War* (Cambridge, 1992). See also Williamson Murray, "Net Assessment in Nazi Germany in the 1930s," in Williamson Murray and Allan R. Millett, eds., *Calculations: Net Assessment and the Coming of World War II* (New York, 1992).

[23] For the development of German air doctrine and strategic concepts of operations before the Second World War, see Williamson Murray, *Luftwaffe* (Baltimore, 1985), chap. 1.

[24] Its commander and his staff concluded that the *Luftwaffe* was completely unprepared to execute an air war against the United Kingdom in 1938 and 1939 – a fact that those historians who have supported Chamberlain's surrender at Munich on the basis of the RAF's unpreparedness in 1938 have entirely missed. Among other documents, see L.W. Gr.Kdo. 2, Führungsabteilung, Nr. 210/38, g.Kdos, Chefs., 22.9.39, Betr: "Planstudie 'Fall Blau'"; Vortragsnotiz über Besprechung mit Ia des Befehlshabers der Luftwaffengruppe Braunschweig, 25.8.38, National Archives and Records Service (NARS), T-1022/2307/34562; Bundesarchiv/Militärarchiv (BA/MA), RL 2 II/24, OKL Chef. 1, Abt., 22.11.39, "Luftkriegführung gegen England."

on building an obsolete fleet of battleships, while largely ignoring the submarine and aircraft carriers.[25] Moreover, those who advocated U-boat warfare focused almost entirely on waging a close-in blockade of the British Isles, while ignoring the intelligence and logistical problems of waging a submarine campaign in the central Atlantic or even off the far shores of North America. In effect, the Germans were so focused on continental war against their European neighbors that the larger strategic and logistical issues raised by a potential world war were simply beyond their comprehension.[26]

Setting the Framework for the Battle of Britain: The Initial Lessons of the War

Much to Hitler's surprise, the British and French declared war on the Third Reich two days after the German invasion of Poland. After the destruction of the Polish state, the Germans immediately turned to the problem of the Western Powers. Within the first week of October, Hitler had set out his strategic goals for the German military. The *Führer* directed that the *Wehrmacht* was to attack the Low Countries and northwestern France before the end of the fall. The explicit goal – which most historians have ignored – was not only "to defeat as much as possible of the French Army and of the forces of the allies fighting on their side" but "at the same time to win as much territory as possible in Holland, Belgium, and Northern France, *to serve as a base for the successful prosecution of the air and sea war against England*" (my italics).[27]

Underlying Hitler's response to the strategic difficulties confronting the Reich in fall 1939 was his belief the British would collapse. As he had announced shortly before the invasion of Poland in September 1939, "The men I met at Munich are not the kind to start a new world

---

[25] After the war, the German Navy's surviving senior officers argued that the *Luftwaffe* had prevented them from acquiring aircraft. The documents, however, make it clear that in the prewar period, the navy's leadership had little interest in obtaining aircraft carriers or long-range aircraft.

[26] When Hitler found out about the Japanese attack on Pearl Harbor, he gathered his staff together in celebration of the event. During the toast to Germany's valiant ally, the Führer asked where the great American naval base was located. Not a single officer present – some forty-odd senior military leaders of the Reich – could identify the base's location. I am indebted to Dr. Horst Boog, formerly the chief air-power historian at the Federal Republic's Military History Institute, for the story.

[27] H. R. Trevor-Roper, ed., *Blitzkrieg to Defeat: Hitler's War Directives* (New York, 1965), Directive, No. 6, 9.10.39, p. 13.

war."[28] And if the British had made the mistake of declaring war on the Reich in September 1939, they were certainly not capable of standing against the Reich in their present circumstances. What Hitler and the other senior German leaders failed to understand was the fact that the British leadership had, for the most part, undergone a considerable rethinking of the German danger, a rethinking that Winston Churchill's ascension to power on 10 May 1940 only strengthened. Thus, at the most important level of adaptation – namely, the strategic level – not only Hitler but his military leaders as well failed to recognize a major and crucial alteration in the strategic landscape.[29]

Chance and Allied incompetence allowed the Germans to escape their strategic and economic predicament and launch a far better prepared campaign against the West in May 1940.[30] Throughout the so-called Phoney War, there was minimal fighting on the ground and in the air. The Germans did launch a number of mine-laying and reconnaissance raids against targets in Britain, while in France there were a few air-to-air skirmishes along the Franco-German border. Nevertheless, these small initial contacts provided the British with a number of insights into German capabilities. The use of magnetic mines in small numbers by the *Luftwaffe* led the British to degauss their ships, which removed a substantial long-term danger.[31] Moreover, the first aerial combats with the Bf 110 indicated that the *Luftwaffe*'s long-range fighter was inferior not only to the Spitfire but the Hurricane as well – a lesson the Germans failed to learn until July 1940. Equally important was the lesson that the armorers should harmonize the eight machine guns on the Hurricane to intersect at 250 yards instead of the recommended 450. Finally, the British soon recognized that painting the underside of their fighters light blue, as the Germans did, helped to hinder detection from below.[32]

[28] Franz Halder, *The Halder War Diary, 1939–1942*, ed. by Charles Burdick and Hans-Adolf Jacobsen (Novato, CA, 1988), p. 23.

[29] Interestingly, the Italian foreign minister, Count Galeazzo Ciano, picked up the change in attitude and in the nature of British leadership in London – something his German counterparts failed to do. See Galeazzo Ciano, *The Ciano Diaries, 1939–1943: The Complete Unabridged Diaries of Count Galeazzo Ciano, Italian Minister for Foreign Affairs, 1936–1943* (New York, 1946), p. 286.

[30] For further discussion of the German difficulties at the beginning of the war, see Murray, *The Change in the European Balance of Power*, chaps. 9 and 10.

[31] Steven S. Roskill, *The War at Sea, 1939–1945*, vol. 1, *The Defensive* (London, 1954), pp. 88, 99–102. The Germans inflicted only minimal damage on British shipping but allowed the British a considerable period of time to make their defensive preparations. This was a consistent trait of the German military through both world wars.

[32] Hough and Richards, *The Battle of Britain*, p. 83.

Before the onset of *Fall Gelb* ("Case Yellow"),[33] the Germans launched a major campaign against Denmark and Norway in April 1940. Denmark fell without serious fighting, but the invasion of Norway ran into serious opposition that stressed the *Kriegsmarine* to the breaking point. Much of the German destroyer force was lost at Narvik, Norway, in the campaign's first days, while the cruiser force also suffered heavy losses. Nevertheless, through to the end of May, the *Kriegsmarine*'s two new battle cruisers, the *Gneisenau* and the *Scharnhorst*, remained undamaged.

On 20 May as the German success against Allied forces in France and the Low Countries swelled, Grand Admiral Eric Raeder broached the possibility of an amphibious landing on the British Isles with Hitler, who responded that such an effort might be necessary.[34] Nevertheless, a week later the *Kriegsmarine* launched its two battle cruisers in an operation off Norway's North Cape with the explicit aim, according to that organization's war diary, of influencing the Reich's postwar budget debates.[35] The operation netted the British aircraft carrier *Glorious* but only through the egregious incompetence of its commanding officer. Along with the *Glorious*, the Germans sank a squadron full of Hurricanes on its deck and, what was more important, killed almost all the pilots. But in the operation, both battle cruisers were seriously damaged and would remain in German dockyards until December.[36] By the end of the campaign, the German Navy had lost virtually all of its front-line strength, the fighting having reduced it to a single heavy cruiser and four destroyers.

The German campaign against Allied military power in the west seemingly went more smoothly, at least on the ground.[37] The devastating defeat of the French Army, occasioned by the German breakthrough on the Meuse between Dinant and Sedan, has obscured a number of significant factors and created a number of legends. The most persistent is the myth that the French soldier did not fight. In fact, by the end of the

---

[33] The code name for the invasion of France and the Low Countries.
[34] Erich Raeder, *Struggle for the Sea* (London, 1952), p. 331.
[35] Klaus Maier, Horst Rohde, Bernd Stegmann, and Hans Umbreit, *Das Deutsche Reich und der Zweite Weltkrieg*, vol. 2, *Die Errichtung der Hegemenoie auf den Europäischen Kontinent* (Stuttgart, 1979), p. 224.
[36] Roskill, *The War at Sea*, vol. 1, pp. 194–196.
[37] The best operational history of the overall campaign in the west remains Telford Taylor's *The March of Conquest, The German Campaign in the West* (Baltimore, MD, 1991). The most recent important contribution to the literature on the defeat of the French Army and the fall of France is Karl-Heinz Frieser, *Blitzkrieg Legende, Der Westfeldzog 1940* (München, 1995).

campaign, 123,000 French soldiers had died in the fighting.[38] Similarly, the battles in the air cost the Germans significant losses in pilots and aircraft. Unfortunately for the French, they had begun air rearmament too late: while they were introducing some outstanding new aircraft such as the Dewoitine 520, they were having significant maintenance problems keeping those aircraft in flyable condition. Operational-ready rates were running at approximately 40 percent, while a lack of training in the new aircraft had a significant impact on combat performance.[39]

Nevertheless, the French Air Force, with considerable help from the RAF, inflicted serious casualties on the *Luftwaffe* in the Battle of France. From the campaign's opening moments, German losses were heavy. On 10 May, the *Luftwaffe* lost 83 aircraft, the heaviest loss in any one day during all of 1940, and that number did not include the nearly 100 Ju 52 transports destroyed or written off as a result of the airborne assault on fortress Holland. On the following day, the Germans lost a further 42 aircraft.[40] The *Luftwaffe* continued to suffer heavy losses through to and during the air battles over Dunkirk. During the nine days of the battle, the RAF lost 177 aircraft; the Germans 240.[41]

By the time the campaign in the west was barely six weeks old, the *Luftwaffe* had lost 30 percent of its bomber force, 30 percent of its dive bombers, 40 percent of its transport aircraft, and nearly 20 percent of its Bf 109s.[42] Nearly 50 percent of its surviving aircraft had been damaged on active operations.[43] Even more seriously, the *Luftwaffe*'s single-engine fighter force suffered a loss of more than 15 percent of its Bf 109 pilots.[44] These losses help explain why it took the Germans nearly a month and a half after the French campaign to recover their aerial strength and redeploy to forward bases in Normandy and the Pas de Calais, from whence they would launch air operations against the British Isles.

---

[38] Eugenia Kiesling, *Arming against Hitler: France and the Limits of Military Planning* (Lawrence, KS, 1996).

[39] See particularly Patrice Buffetot and Jacquer Ogier, "L'armé de l'air française dans la campagne de France (10 mai–25 juin 1940)," *Revue historique des Armées*, vol. 2, no. 3, pp. 88–117.

[40] "Der Einsatz der deutschen Luftwaffe während der ersten 11 Tage des Frankreichfeldzuges," Auszüge aus den täglichen Lagemeldungen des Oberbefehlshabers der Luftwaffe, Abt. Ic., Albert F. Simpson Historical Research Center, K 113.306-3, vol. 2.

[41] Major L. F. Ellis, *The War in France and Flanders, 1939–1940* (London, 1953), p. 246.

[42] BA/MA RL 2 III/1025, gen. Qu. 6 Abt. (III A), "Front-Flugzeuge Verluste," 1940.

[43] BA/MA RL 2 III/1025, gen. Qu. 6. Abt. (IIIA), "Front-Flugzeuge Verluste," 1940.

[44] BA/MA, RL 2 III/707, Gen. Qu.6.Abt. (I), Übersicht über Soll, Istbestand, Einsatzbereitschaft, Verluste und Reserven der fliegende Verbände.

The RAF losses were equally high. The Hurricane squadrons in France in early May 1940 were virtually wiped out in the fighting in May and June, along with many of their ground crew and all of their supplies. The Hurricane reinforcements the British rushed across the English Channel early in the campaign also suffered heavy losses, while Fighter Command itself suffered heavy losses among its squadrons in southern England in attempting to drive *Luftwaffe* bombers away from the Dunkirk beaches. Dowding, worried by the swift drain of his forces, warned the air staff, and the British government, that

> if an adequate fighter force is kept in this country, if the Fleet remains in being, and if the Home Forces are suitably organised to resist invasion, we should be able to carry on the war single-handed for some time, if not indefinitely. But if the Home Defence force [i.e., Fighter Command] is drained away in desperate attempts to remedy the situation in France, defeat in France will involve the final, complete and irremediable defeat of this country.[45]

Overall, the RAF lost 950 aircraft during the Battle of France, approximately 50 percent of its front-line strength on 10 May. Among the aircraft lost were 386 Hurricanes and 67 Spitfires.[46] The bottom line was that the attrition on both sides of a battle that had lasted less than four weeks had been extraordinarily high in both aircraft and aircrew.

What is particularly noteworthy is a comparison of how the opposing sides evaluated the larger lessons of the air battles in France. For the British, the battle represented a wakeup call in terms of the production needed to support Fighter Command's front-line strength. In recognition of the critical nature of fighter production, one of the first actions Churchill took as prime minister was to appoint his friend, the Canadian newspaper magnate Lord Beaverbrook, as the minister for aircraft production. While one can overestimate Beaverbrook's contribution, there is no doubt that he gave the air ministry's bureaucracy the severe shaking that it needed and for the short term helped to increase production drastically. The RAF had set the target for production of Spitfires and Hurricanes for May 1940 at 261 new aircraft. The Spitfire and Hurricane factories produced 325. The plan for June called for 292; actual output reached 446. For the critical summer months of July and August, the target had been 611; actual production reached 972, well over 50 percent above what plans had called for. The nearly 600 additional fighters

---

[45] Quoted in Hough and Richards, *The Battle of Britain*, p. 89.
[46] Ibid., p. 100.

produced proved to be a significant factor in the summer battles. Between May and October, the factories producing fighters in the United Kingdom built an additional 692 Hurricanes and Spitfires beyond projected production targets.[47] Moreover, the emphasis on maintaining front-line strength helped to decrease the time required to repair damaged aircraft.

There were, of course, other contributing factors besides Beaverbrook's bullying and cajoling, but the Canadian represented a significant symbol among many that things had changed in Britain. Admittedly, on the tactical side of air-to-air tactics, the RAF failed to see how flawed its approach to aerial combat between fighters had proven in France. But tactical weaknesses paled in comparison to the importance of recognizing that a crucial factor in the upcoming struggle for air supremacy was going to be the number of front-line aircraft and the ability to replace them.

Matters were different on the European Continent. There, the mood was euphoric. The French enemy, who had thwarted the Germans for four long, terrible years in the First World War, had collapsed in a matter of weeks. Quite simply, the Germans believed they had won the war. General Alfred Jodl, the OKW's (*Oberkommando der Wehrmacht*, the Armed Forces High Command) chief of staff, suggested in a memorandum on the overall strategic situation after the fall of France: "The final victory of Germany over England is only a question of time."[48] Jodl's comment reflected the attitude of most of the senior German military leaders.

Field Marshal Wilhelm Keitel, not exactly the brightest lightbulb in the German high command, suggested in a memorandum in mid-July that an assault across the Channel was the equivalent of "a powerful river crossing."[49] Not surprisingly then, the Army's commander-in-chief, Walter von Brauchitsch, and chief of staff, Franz Halder, set in motion initial planning efforts for an invasion of the Soviet Union, among other reasons because neither regarded Britain as a serious long-term problem and because the army would receive a greater role in a war against the Soviets.[50] The army would prove no more interested in defeating Britain than Hitler.

[47] Collier, *The Defence of the United Kingdom*, p. 121. See also Hough and Richards, *The Battle of Britain*, p. 102.
[48] Chef WFA, 30.6.40, "Die Weiterführung des Krieges gegen England," *International Military Tribune: Trial of Major War Criminals*, vol. 28 (Washington, DC, 1948), pp. 301–303.
[49] Quoted in Air Ministry, *The Rise and Fall of the German Air Force, 1933–1945* (New York, 1983), p. 75.
[50] Horst Boog, Jürgen Förster, Joachim Hoffman, Ernst Klink, Rolf-Dieter Muller, and Gerd R. Ueberschär, *Das Deutsche Reich und der Zweite Weltkrieg*, vol. 4, *Der Angriff auf die Sowiet Union* (Stuttgart, 1984).

Immediately after the French surrender at Compiegne, Hitler went on vacation. He and a number of his World War I comrades picnicked across the First World War battlefields, where he had served. The *Führer* then made a whirlwind visit to Paris with Albert Speer as his artistic guide. During these various travels, the last thing on Hitler's mind was grand strategy or the problems Britain raised.[51] While the *Führer* was gone, no one else was capable of making significant decisions.[52] Nevertheless, the fundamental assumption that virtually all the Germans were working under was that Britain was through, and all they needed to do was persuade the recalcitrant British to see the realities of the situation.[53] There was certainly no one in Göring's *Luftwaffe* bureaucracies who recognized that major increases in the production of fighters and bombers were in order, particularly given the ferocious losses German front-line squadrons had suffered in the Battle of France. Thus, the German high command's conception of the war and the *Reich*'s strategic situation in summer 1940 remained befuddled by success and a belief the British remained the same opponent who had so cravenly surrendered at Munich.

Intelligence and Planning: Preparing for the Battle of Britain

On 6 June 1940, a young, 28-year-old physicist named R. V. Jones, at the time serving as the scientific adviser to the air ministry and staff, appeared before Churchill and his war cabinet to argue that the *Luftwaffe* was preparing to use radio-beam technology to improve significantly the accuracy of its bombers at night and in bad weather.[54] Virtually all of Britain's scientific establishment and senior officers on the air staff argued that the Germans not only did not possess such technology but that it was not even worth the effort to test Jones's hypothesis, which admittedly rested on relatively scanty evidence. Nothing underlines more the key role that individuals play in history than Jones's effort to bring this matter to the attention of those comfortable in their illusions, or Churchill's recognition that, whatever the odds, the possession of such a capability

---

[51] For Hitler's mood after the victory over the French, see particularly Telford Taylor, *The Breaking Wave* (New York, 1967), pp. 53–54.

[52] A fact that was inherent in the German system and entirely within Hitler's view on how things should be run at the top. For how the German command system worked, see Geoffrey P. Megargee, *Inside Hitler's High Command* (Lawrence, KS, 2000).

[53] The next section of this chapter examines the German assessment of the strategic and operational framework within which their war on Britain over the next 11 months would take place.

[54] For a discussion of the background of how Jones came to his conclusions on the basis of scanty evidence, see Jones, *The Wizard War*, pp. 92–100.

could have a disastrous impact in the case of a German strategic bombing campaign against the United Kingdom.[55]

The prime minister asked what was to be done. Jones replied that first, the existence of the beams must be confirmed and then a number of countermeasures could be taken. "Churchill added his weight to [my] suggestions... adding as he angrily banged the table, 'All I get from the Air Ministry is files, files, files!'"[56] He, therefore, ordered the RAF to fly the necessary test flights at night to see whether such beams existed. That evening, a British aircraft flying a route that Jones had plotted, a flight that was almost cancelled at the last moment by the obfuscation of an RAF signals officer, established the existence of *Knickebein*. One month later to the day, Göring was to suggest that the *Luftwaffe* should make RAF aircraft factories the immediate target of nighttime harassment raids by German bombers using *Knickebein*. By that time, emergency measures to distort or jam the German blind-bombing radio beams were already in hand.[57]

Not surprisingly, Jones had a spectacular career as one of the most important intelligence analysts of the Second World War. But he was not alone. Forced by the woeful state of their intelligence services in 1939, the British had gone all out in recruiting talented individuals to work in their steadily expanding intelligence organizations. Thus, Jones was only one of a considerable number of individuals recruited from civilian life directly into British intelligence and then, if they were exceptional, given extraordinary responsibilities in analyzing the raw and ambiguous data and materials, on which good intelligence depends.

Another example of how the British used individual talent to repair their weaknesses in intelligence was the case of young Harry Hinsley, recruited directly from Cambridge before he had even earned an undergraduate degree and given the task in September 1939 of analyzing the *Kriegsmarine*'s radio traffic.[58] Two days before the German invasion of Scandinavia, Hinsley warned his superiors that something was afoot in the Baltic; they paid no attention. In late May he again warned his superiors that message traffic suggested that major units of the German fleet

---

[55] For Churchill's side of the discussions, see Winston S. Churchill, *The Second World War*, vol. 2, *Their Finest Hour* (Boston, 1949), p. 384.
[56] Jones, *The Wizard War*, p. 102.
[57] Ibid., pp. 102–105.
[58] David Kahn, *Seizing the Enigma: The Race to Break the U-Boat Codes, 1939–1945* (New York, 1991), p. 121.

were again on the move. Despite the fact that the Royal Navy was making a major withdrawal from northern Norway, no one paid attention.[59]

However, after the sinking of the *Glorious* by the *Gneisenau* and *Scharnhorst*, everyone listened.[60] As a result, in his early 20s, Hinsley was to play a major role in analyzing German naval moves over the course of the remainder of the war and was to set in motion the most important intelligence coup of the war.[61] It was this ability to utilize exceptional people in intelligence and fold them directly into the processes of operational decision making that was to provide the Western Allies an increasingly significant advantage against their German opponents. Beginning in mid-April 1940, Bletchley Park broke into the *Luftwaffe*'s Enigma ciphers on a wholesale basis, unknown and unrecognized by the Germans. The intelligence game had now begun to tip heavily against German military forces.

The testimony of one of the foremost women analysts serving with "Y" Service, the British intelligence organization monitoring German radio transmissions, suggests the extent of the advantage that the British were already enjoying in summer 1940:

> By the end of the summer of 1940 the Air Ministry Intelligence had an almost complete picture of the *Luftwaffe*'s Order of Battle, particularly in Western Europe. With all of this knowledge we were amassing... about the callsigns and frequencies used by the various German squadrons to which we were listening, we were able, for instance to advise No. 11 Group that the enemy raid approaching Beachy Head was probably made up of Me 109s of II/JG 51 based at St. Omer. This would be most helpful for the controllers, who would then be able to anticipate the probable return route of the enemy aircraft.... [E]ven in the summer of 1940, we could almost certainly confirm the height at which the [enemy] formations were approaching, and we also might be able to give some indication, from what we were hearing, of their intended action.[62]

The *Luftwaffe*'s intelligence picture of early July 1940 that estimated RAF capabilities suggests the extent of the gap between British and

---

[59] Ibid., p. 122.
[60] For the sorry story involved in the loss of the *Glorious*, see Williamson Murray and Allan R. Millett, *A War to Be Won: Fighting the Second World War* (Cambridge, MA, 2000), p. 65.
[61] This chapter discusses Hinsley's role in the breaking of the U-boat Enigma code at its end.
[62] Aileen Clayton, *The Enemy Is Listening* (London, 1980), p. 49. Clayton's claims are confirmed by the official history of British intelligence: *British Intelligence in the Second World War: Its Influence on Strategy and Operations*, vol. 1 (London, 1979), p. 180.

German intelligence. On 16 July, General "Beppo" Schmidt, the chief of *Luftwaffe* intelligence, signed out his assessment of the correlation of forces. He estimated that both the Spitfire and the Hurricane were inferior to the *Luftwaffe*'s twin-engine, long-range fighter, the Bf 110; failed to mention Britain's radar capabilities; entirely missed the nature of the air defense system; miscalculated the rate of British fighter production; and ended up on the optimistic note that "the *Luftwaffe*, unlike the RAF, will be in a position in every respect to achieve a decisive effect this year."[63] About the only thing that Schmidt and his intelligence analysts got right in their assessment was the number of Spitfires and Hurricanes that Fighter Command possessed.

Two weeks earlier, *Reichsmarschall* Hermann Göring had signed out an operational directive that underlined the *Luftwaffe*'s operational focus as well as its doctrinal understanding of air war. In it, the *Reichsmarschall* had emphasized that "As long as the enemy air force is not destroyed, it is the basic principle of the conduct of air war to attack the enemy air units at every possible favorable opportunity – by day and night, in the air, and on the ground – without regard for other missions."[64] The destruction of the RAF would then enable wider-scale attacks on British imports and supplies, as well as set the conditions for a successful invasion of the British Isles. Thus, the *Luftwaffe*'s target was not just Fighter Command but the RAF's other commands as well. As a last possibility, "terror" attacks on British cities represented an option, should the British fail to recognize their hopeless position. As Jodl suggested, the army could then launch the invasion of Britain – the final blow (*Todesstoss*) against an already defeated country.[65]

Nevertheless, if there were a certain realism in the first directive, realism was certainly not the mark of the rest of German planning. Nowhere do German documents suggest that the limited range of the Bf 109 – it could barely reach London and return – represented a limiting factor in the coming campaign, perhaps not surprising given the high rating given to the Bf 110. Overall assessments were that it would take the *Luftwaffe* only a few weeks to destroy Fighter Command, the front-line strength of which the Germans believed the British had deployed on forward air bases in southern England. Here *Luftwaffe* planners missed the fact

---

[63] Mason, *Battle over Britain*, Appendix K, OKL, 16.7.40, Operations Staff Ic.
[64] BA/MA RL 2II/27, "Allgemeine Weisung für den Kampf der Luftwaffe gegen England," ObdL, Führungsstab Ia Nr. 5835/40, 30.6.40.
[65] Chef WFA, 30.6.40, "Die Weiterführung des Krieges England."

that Dowding had only a portion of the command forward deployed, while backup squadrons covered the east coast and north of the British Isles, a force that represented a major reserve to be fed into the battle to replace burned-out fighter squadrons or to reinforce the front line should a landing occur.

The initial *Luftwaffe* estimates on the duration of the coming campaign were that it would take four days to defeat Fighter Command. Thereafter, four weeks would be sufficient for German bombers and long-range fighters to police up the remainder of the RAF and destroy Britain's aircraft industry.[66] On 21 July, Göring further explicated his conception for the campaign. Besides the RAF, he emphasized destruction of the aircraft industry as crucial to gaining air superiority. On the tactical level, he underlined that the fighter force should not remain tethered to protecting the bombers but should utilize its speed and maneuverability to attack the RAF wherever possible.[67] Three days later, *Fliegerkorps* I was emphasizing four critical missions in the coming air campaign against the British Isles: the gaining of air superiority; support for the army and the navy, when landings on the British coast eventually took place; attacks on British supplies, ports, and imports; and, finally, ruthless "retaliatory" attacks on major British cities.[68]

All of this made considerable sense. The problem was that the picture provided by German intelligence was and remained so skewed that *Luftwaffe* commanders never gained a clear idea of the nature of their enemy or of the targets that might achieve their goals. And without a clear picture of their opponent or a realistic assessment of the correlation of forces, they were not going to be able to understand the conditions they actually confronted. The problem was that German planning and conceptualization at the strategic and joint operational levels were deeply flawed. Neither Hitler nor his senior military leaders were able to put together a coherent conception or strategic plan about how they might defeat the British. The *Kriegsmarine* was waging an independent war, in which the submarine force was simply trying to sink ships – where it did so and how it might maximize British weaknesses never

---

[66] Collier, *Defence of the United Kingdom*, p. 160. The optimistic estimates by German intelligence in 1940 would find a solid echo in 1941 when its intelligence estimates on the military capabilities of the Red Army, not to mention the productive capacity of Soviet industry, would be even more optimistic – and wrong.
[67] BA/MA RL 2 II/30, "Besprechung Reichsmarschall am 21.7.40."
[68] BA/MA RL 8/1 Generalkommando 1. Fliegerkorps Abt. 1a Nr. 10260/40, 24.7.40, "Gedanken über die Führung des Luftkrieges gegen England."

emerged in Admiral Karl Dönitz's (commander of the U-boats) mind or his headquarters.[69] Thus, while the small U-boat force had sunk a considerable number of British ships over the war's first ten months, the Germans had lost as many boats as their industry and the U-boat training command had managed to produce and train up for combat operations.[70] While the assault on Britain's SLOCs (sea lines of communication) caused serious difficulties, it never really came close to breaking those lines.[71]

The planning for the proposed invasion of the British Isles underlines the general lack of joint cooperation among the German services, as well as the absence of clear guidance from above.[72] In the planning over the course of July, the army argued for a landing over a 90-mile front, a distance far greater than what the Allies would use in Operation Overlord four years later.[73] The navy, given its force structure, planned for a tiny invasion area that would have allowed the British to concentrate easily against the threat. Finally, the *Luftwaffe* talked about supporting the invasion and the joint campaign, but with the exception of bombing raids on Britain's west coast ports, it refused to support the *Kriegsmarine*'s wider efforts to cut the British SLOCs.[74] While joint cooperation in Britain and the United States in 1940 and 1941 was hardly at a more impressive level, the British and the Americans would steadily adapt and

---

[69] For an assessment of the weaknesses inherent in Dönitz's conceptions for the U-boat campaign, see particularly Holger Herwig, "Innovation Ignored: The Submarine Problem – Germany, Britain, and the United States, 1919–1939," in Murray and Millett, eds., *Military Innovation in the Interwar Period*, pp. 236–241.

[70] For the obdurate and largely unimaginative development of the U-boat force in the interwar period, see ibid.

[71] This author is in complete agreement with Gerhard Weinberg's position that the German conduct of the U-boat offensive represented a waste of resources that would have been far better spent on other theaters and capabilities in the German war effort. In March 1943, it placed sufficient pressure on the SLOCs so that some officers on the Admiralty Staff suggested that the convoy system might have to be abandoned. The suggestion, however, was never seriously considered. For Professor Weinberg's analysis of the U-boat campaign, see Gerhard Weinberg, *A World at Arms: A Global History of World War II* (Cambridge, 1994), pp. 386–387.

[72] Of all the campaigns in the Second World War in which German forces were involved, only the Battle of Britain and Operation Sea Lion, the plan to invade Great Britain, drew little interest from Hitler in the planning and execution stages.

[73] The most imaginative discussion of Operation Sea Lion's prospects is in Taylor, *The Breaking Wave*; see also Maier, et al., *Das Deutsche Reich und der Zweite Weltkrieg*, vol. 2, pp. 378–379.

[74] The *Luftwaffe* did provide its Condor aircraft to the Battle of the Atlantic, but throughout that long-term campaign, its interest and support remained at minimal levels.

improve. Matters in Germany, however, only worsened in terms of inter-service cooperation as the war progressed.[75]

With virtually no support from the *Kriegsmarine* available for the invasion, it is difficult to see what options the Germans had, even if their air attacks had imposed a heavier loss rate on Fighter Command. Dowding always had the possibility of pulling his squadrons back from southeastern England, if the pressure on them became too great, and then redeploying them forward again, if the Germans were to attempt an invasion. And once back behind London, the Spitfire and Hurricane squadrons would have been beyond the reach of the *Luftwaffe's* Bf-109s, the only aircraft that could attack Fighter Command's combat strength. Moreover, both Bomber Command and Coastal Command possessed significant resources that would have been thrown into the battle over the English Channel, as their raids on the ports in France and the Low Countries in September underlined.[76]

But the greatest threat to an invading German amphibious force would have come from the large number of destroyers the Royal Navy deployed in the Channel – approximately 35 in the Harwich area and 35 in the Portsmouth area. In May 1941, off Crete where the Germans enjoyed perfect weather and complete air superiority, British light cruisers and destroyers were still able to completely destroy the invading German amphibious force. In the English Channel in September 1940, with the normal weather conditions in that body of water, with the fact that RAF aircraft would be attacking in large numbers, with the German mode of transportation (Rhine River barges), and with more than 70 British destroyers on the loose, it is hard to see a result other than disaster for an invading German amphibious force.[77]

The Opening Moves

At 1100 hours on 3 September 1939, Neville Chamberlain, Prime Minister of the United Kingdom, declared war on Nazi Germany. Later that afternoon, the French air attaché, flying back to London from Paris, set off the air raid sirens throughout southern England. Three days later, the fact

---

[75] A trend that defeats on the battlefield served to exacerbate.
[76] In approximately a ten-day period, RAF attacks destroyed more than 10 percent of the barges the Germans had gathered for the invasion, while their attacks on German airfields damaged or destroyed a significant number of aircraft.
[77] For an excellent discussion of German planning for Operation Sea Lion and the invasion's prospects, see Taylor, *The Breaking Wave*.

that the radar receivers in England were inadequately screened to block the echoes that aircraft flying over Britain caused was to result in controllers launching an increasing number of aircraft against an "enemy" air raid that did not exist but that appeared to be gathering strength by the minute as more and more British aircraft arrived in the area. Before reality set in, the controllers had scrambled three squadrons of Hurricanes and a squadron and two flights of Spitfires. By the end of the Battle of Barking Creek, the British had shot down two of their own Hurricanes and killed one of the pilots.[78]

Over the months of the Phoney War (September 1939 to May 1940), the Germans flew a number of sorties across the Channel, partially to test the defenses, partially to begin mining operations against British ports, and partially to check out *Knickebein* signals. By so doing they gave away a great deal: the loss of one of the special mission He 111 provided R. V. Jones with some of the crucial evidence on which he built his case for *Knickebein*'s existence.[79] These small raids also alerted the British to the fact that the Germans possessed magnetic mines, while an He 111, which had crash-landed in relatively undamaged condition, provided the RAF with an opportunity to examine that aircraft's weaknesses in minute detail.[80]

The opening of the campaign against France and the Low Countries saw a considerable increase in the number of *Luftwaffe* forays into British airspace. The German rationale appears to have been a desire to gather tactical and electronic intelligence. But again the British gained the most by having their vulnerability to night air attack underlined, while providing their air controllers with opportunities to build their skills and evaluate how the Germans would operate in the future at night.

Although the air campaign against Britain was not scheduled to begin until early to mid-August, redeployment of the *Luftwaffe*'s bombers and fighters to bases along the Pas de Calais and Norman coast began immediately after the French had signed the armistice at Compiegne. Two of Göring's *Luftflotten* – the Second under Field Marshal Albert Kesselring and the Third under Field Marshal Hugo Sperrle – were to control the air units in France, while *Luftflotte* 5 under General Hans-Jürgen Stumpff would control a smaller force of bombers and long-range fighters from Norway and Denmark. In stark numbers, Fighter Command confronted an overwhelming force. By mid-July, Stumpff deployed 129 He 111s and

---

[78] For the Battle of Barking Creek, see Hough and Richards, *Battle of Britain*, pp. 66–67.
[79] Jones, *The Wizard War*, p. 85.
[80] Ibid., p. 69.

Ju 88s (95 in commission), supported by 34 Bf 110s (32 in commission).[81] The main forces of *Luftflotten* 2 and 3 in France massed 150 reconnaissance aircraft; 1,131 bombers (Ju 88s, He 111s, and Do 17s; 769 in commission); 316 Ju 87 Stukas (248 in commission); 246 Bf 110s (168 in commission); and 809 Bf 109s (656 in commission).

Opposite the Germans, Fighter Command possessed approximately 800 fighters with a significant reserve of replacement aircraft in the depots.[82] Approximately one-third of Dowding's force consisted of Spitfires, while two-thirds were Hurricanes. Fighter Command also possessed a squadron of useless Defiants and a number of Blenheims, which were the test beds for experiments with airborne radar. At the time, Fighter Command's squadrons were running operationally ready rates of approximately 70 percent. In addition to Fighter Command, the RAF possessed more than 1,000 medium and light bombers, which would not play a direct role in the air-to-air battle but which were in a position to interfere with any German attempts at landing, as their attacks on the invasion barges the Germans were gathering in the Channel ports in early September underlined.[83]

Approximately, 40 percent of Dowding's force was under No. 11 Group, commanded by Air Vice Marshal Keith Park, a feisty New Zealander, its mission to protect the most vulnerable areas of southeast Britain. Directly to the north, defending the east coast and the Midlands of England was No. 12 Group under Air Vice Marshal Trafford Leigh-Mallory, an ambitious and duplicitous officer. Finally, No. 10 Group defended the southwest, while No. 13 Group defended the north of Britain up to Scapa Flow. One of the new factors that significantly improved RAF fight capabilities over those of May was the availability of 100 octane fuel from the United States – a distinct improvement over the 87 octane fuel that the Hurricanes and Spitfires had used during the air battles over France and Dunkirk.[84]

The first phase of the Battle of Britain lasted from early July through mid-August. The Germans launched a series of exploratory raids over the Channel, attacking convoys plying up and down the Channel with smaller

---

[81] Collier, *The Defence of the United Kingdom*, p. 161. See also Hough and Richards, *The Battle of Britain*, p. 111.
[82] For a listing of Fighter Command's squadrons, the strength of each squadron, and the numbers of aircraft in and out of commission on 1 July, 1 August, and 1 September 1940, see Mason, *Battle over Britain*, pp. 130, 203, 333.
[83] This fact underlines why the Germans placed a significant effort in attacking British air bases that belonged to commands other than Dowding's.
[84] Hough and Richards, *The Battle of Britain*, p. 35.

attacks on the ports on England's southern coast. The aim seems to have been to wear Fighter Command's front-line strength down, to feel out how the British would fight the coming battle and, if possible, shut down the Channel convoys. Yet, the payback for the Germans for these initial skirmishes was minimal. Over a five-week period, they managed to sink 30,000 tons of shipping, a minuscule amount given the scale of effort, and inflict minor damage on the ports along Britain's southern coast. Moreover, they lost 286 aircraft of all types (105 of which were Bf 109s), nearly double Fighter Command's loss of 148 aircraft.[85] Nevertheless, the loss in RAF fighter pilots was serious: 84 or 10 percent of those pilots on active duty.[86]

However, the aerial skirmishing had improved the British position considerably. Fighter Command had a month-and-a-half to restore and refresh its front-line squadrons, especially those burned out by the fighting in France. Moreover, the increasingly heavy air-to-air combat provided the British, especially the controllers, considerable experience and thus the ability to adapt to German tactics and procedures. Early mistakes – such as that of 11 July when controllers scrambled six Hurricanes to meet one "lone" raider, which then turned into a raid of 15 dive-bombers escorted by upward of 40 Bf 110s – occurred with decreasing frequency in July.[87]

The ability of radar operators to estimate the size of assembling or incoming raids depended almost entirely on their experience, which the Germans were now providing the British in ample measure. This was particularly important for the defenders because there were so many inexperienced and neophyte operators, given the rapid buildup of the chain home system over the course of the late 1930s.[88] Even more important, as the official historian argues: "The Germans overlooked recent improvements in radio equipment and the ability of radar operators and others to profit from experience. Hence the attackers were ill-served by a policy which gave the defenders every chance of learning from their mistakes, instead of overwhelming them by a series of well-concerted blows delivered without prolonged rehearsal."[89]

For their part, the Germans seem to have learned little about how Fighter Command was using its radar as a key piece of a systematic

---

[85] Collier, *The Defence of the United Kingdom*, p. 171.
[86] Based on the loss tables in Mason, *Battle over Britain*.
[87] Collier, *The Defence of the United Kingdom*, p. 167.
[88] Ibid., p. 168.
[89] Ibid, p. 170.

approach to the air defense of the United Kingdom. Here the Germans failed to use their sites' radar in France to examine how the British were reacting or failing to react to German raids. Nor did they pick up the fact that the performance of British fighters had significantly improved over their performance during the Battle of France. A *Luftwaffe* intelligence report from the beginning of August again underlines how little the Germans had learned from the air-to-air battles over the Channel:

> As the British fighters are controlled from the ground by R/T their forces are tied to their respective ground stations and are thereby restricted in mobility, even taking into consideration the probability that the ground stations are partly mobile. Consequently, the assembly of strong fighter forces at determined points and at short notice is not to be expected. A massed German attack on a target area can therefore count on the same conditions of light fighter opposition as in the attacks on widely scattered targets. It can, indeed, be assumed that considerable confusion in the defensive networks will be unavoidable during mass attacks, and that the defenses may thereby be reduced.[90]

Still, the Channel fighting was a nasty piece of business. Even in high summer, the English Channel is a cold and choppy environment for those unlucky enough to find themselves encompassed in its embrace. Pilots who bailed out over the water had approximately four hours before they succumbed to hypothermia, if they were not already dead from drowning in the Channel's swirling waters.[91]

By the end of this period, despite its losses, Fighter Command was in a far stronger position than at the beginning of July, both in terms of new production from British aircraft factories as well as the experience level of the whole air defense system. Dowding could now view the future with some optimism. On 8 August, British listening posts picked up, and Bletchley Park soon decrypted, a message from *Reichsmarschall* Göring to the *Luftwaffe* forces on the French coast; it was soon in the hands of Britain's political and military leaders: "Operation Adler [Eagle]. Within a short period you will wipe out the British air force from the sky."[92]

---

[90] Quoted in Air Ministry, *The Rise and Fall of the Luftwaffe* (London, 1948), p. 80.
[91] The Germans had rescue amphibian aircraft, but the British regarded such aircraft as combatants and shot them down when they ran across them. The British had no rescue service of their own but soon developed one based on high-speed small aircraft. Hough and Richards, *The Battle of Britain*, p. 135.
[92] Quoted in Terraine, *The Right of the Line*, p. 186.

"Eagle Day" and the Assault on Fighter Command: 11 August–15 September

Eagle Day got off to a bad start. Göring scheduled the start for 13 August, but even before that day, the *Luftflotten* were ratcheting up the pressure. Heavy fighting on 11 August over ports in southern England, for example, cost No. 11 Group 27 fighter pilots, 7 percent of available pilots. *Luftwaffe* losses were high as well: 39 aircraft, 12 of which were Bf 109s.[93]

On 12 August, the Germans with Ju 87s carried out a particularly effective attack on the Ventnor CHL site, which completely wrecked this crucial radar site on the Isle of Wight. It would not be back in operation for three days, as the British struggled to erect a mobile station nearby; the full gap was not covered until 23 August.[94] However, the British radars had overlapping coverage so that other sites picked up a substantial portion of the area that Ventnor had covered.[95] The cost for the Germans was high, with the British shooting down more than 10 percent of the attacking force, including two of the most experienced German dive-bomber pilots. Nevertheless, the attack on Ventnor was exceedingly worrisome to Fighter Command's senior leaders because radar represented the eyes of the whole defensive system, and the Germans appeared ready to poke the eyes out. Ventnor was only one of a number of RAF targets struck that day.

It was clear that the *Luftwaffe* was coming with a vengeance after the RAF. The Germans struck airfields at Manston, Lympne, and Hawkinge, as well as five other radar stations in addition to Ventnor, all of which were operating in a relatively short time. The attacks failed to do significant damage to the other radar stations, and while that failure may have frustrated the Germans to a certain extent, their real failure was to determine how the British were using radar. In retrospect, the attacks on 12 August were meant to set up "Eagle Day" for success; they did not.

German meteorologists predicted that the weather on 13 August would be clear, but as was to be the case throughout the battle, nature refused to cooperate. At the last moment, the *Luftwaffe*'s high command postponed the opening of the offensive, but not all attacking squadrons received the

---

[93] Based on tables in Mason, *Battle over Britain*, pp. 227–230.
[94] Hough and Richards, *Battle of Britain*, pp. 146–148.
[95] On 13 August, for example, the British were able to track a major raid on Portland all the way to the target despite the fact that Ventnor was still off the air by using other radar stations in the system. Collier, *The Defence of the United Kingdom*, p. 186.

word. A number of bomber units executed raids without fighter support and paid a heavy price for the postponement. Their targets were Bomber Command and Coastal Command airfields, not just those of Fighter Command. This fact did not reflect bad intelligence but rather the larger strategy of eliminating the RAF's air capabilities. Returning *Luftwaffe* aircraft claimed 88 British aircraft shot down – for the loss of 39 of their own. In fact, the Germans had considerably overestimated their air-to-air success, which they were to do throughout the battle: the British only lost 15 fighters, with many of the pilots surviving.[96]

Not until 15 August did the Germans get good weather, and air operations on that day reflected a maximum effort. In the north, *Luftflotte 5* executed its only major raid of the battle. Beppo Schmidt's intelligence organization had estimated that Dowding had deployed the whole of Fighter Command in southern England and that attacks from Scandinavia would outflank British defenses. In fact, the Germans ran into seven fighter squadrons of British fighters (three Spitfires, two Hurricanes, and two Defiants). The gleeful Spitfire and Hurricane pilots of No. 12 and No. 13 Groups pounced on the attacking German formations.[97]

The 65 He 111s from Norway were escorted by 35 Bf 110s, with 50 Ju 88s sallying forth from Denmark to attack targets farther south. Altogether, Stumpff's force lost 16 bombers and 7 Bf 110s. Overall, *Luftflotte 5* lost more than 15 percent of the attacking force, a loss level that ensured it would not appear in the battle again. The attacking Germans claimed 11 Spitfires shot down; in fact, only one Hurricane had to return to base slightly damaged.[98] The fact that this was to be the only daytime attack from Scandinavia was the obvious lesson learned from the smoking wreckage littering the east coast of England. The larger lesson the Germans ignored: Fighter Command's devastating riposte to Stumpff's raid should have suggested to the Germans that there were fundamental weaknesses in the other assessments of *Luftwaffe* intelligence. It did not.

In the south on 15 August, a series of massive raids ran into fierce opposition from Fighter Command. *Luftflotten* 2 and 3 launched everything they had in an effort to break Dowding's command. An almost continuous series of raids targeted RAF airfields, radar stations, command and control sites, and a number of other sites. The raids had mixed

---

[96] Terraine, *The Right of the Line*, p. 186.
[97] Hough and Richards, *Battle of Britain*, pp. 171–174.
[98] Collier, *The Defence of the United Kingdom*, pp. 192–194.

success, but when it was all over, the *Luftwaffe* had suffered in one day the heaviest casualties it would suffer during the entire battle. The Stukas suffered particularly heavily. A number of British airfields were badly battered, some to the extent that they had to be closed down for short periods of time. The Germans also attacked a number of radar sites but all were back up and running almost immediately. Unbeknownst to the British, that same day, Göring raised serious doubts as to the wisdom of the raids attacking the radar sites because of the difficulty in damaging them, as well as the heavy losses attacking German aircraft suffered.[99]

The air battles that now ensued placed enormous pressure on both sides. Between 13 and 19 August (a one-week period), the Germans wrote off 284 aircraft, approximately 10 percent of the aircraft deployed against Britain.[100] A sustained battle of attrition was now taking place, beginning in mid-August and lasting through the first week of September. The *Luftwaffe* put extraordinary pressure on Fighter Command and its support structure – with the exception of the radar sites. Both sides suffered a terrible attrition of pilots. In the last ten days of August, Dowding lost no less than 126 fighter pilots, or 14 percent of his force.[101]

The losses were substantial enough to force both sides to make significant adaptations in their approaches. The Germans stopped using their Stukas and limited the use of unescorted bomber attacks. Moreover, much to the disgust of his fighter pilots, Göring placed the Bf 109 fighters on a tighter leash by forcing them to mount close escort of the bombers while decreasing the size of the bomber force to lessen losses. This considerably cut into the effectiveness of the *Luftwaffe*'s single-engine fighter force by robbing its fighter pilots of their height and positional advantages.[102] Moreover, the Bf 109s now had to fly cover for the Bf 110s, which had proven easy meat for the British fighters.[103]

Yet, the Germans still had no clear idea of the nature of the system they confronted. Their intelligence officers continued to provide optimistic assessments as to how well the campaign was proceeding. Here, German

---

[99] BA/MA Besprechung am 15.8.40.
[100] The figures for German aircraft written off come from the tables in Mason, *Battle over Britain*, pp. 241–243, 247, 263–264, 272–272, 274, 281–284, 286–287.
[101] Based on the tables in Mason, *Battle over Britain*.
[102] Much the same situation would obtain in 1944 on the other side of the hill when American bomber commanders would demand that the fighter escorts remain tied closely to the bombers. Lieutenant General James Doolittle, commander of Eighth Air Force, resisted those efforts successfully.
[103] Mason, *Battle over Britain*, pp. 284–285, 289.

estimates of the number of RAF fighters shot down were approximately three times greater than Fighter Command's actual losses. These overestimates skewed the overall picture German intelligence analysts were providing. *Luftflotte 5*'s estimate that its bombers had shot down 11 Spitfires, when in fact the RAF had lost none, suggests that the main culprits in overestimating enemy losses were the *Luftwaffe*'s bomber crews.[104] The British also overestimated the number of German aircraft they had shot down but not by nearly as great a margin. However, based on the number of German aircraft that crashed in the British Isles, Fighter Command's leaders were already having doubts as to the reliability of the claims of their own pilots.[105]

The British also had considerable adaptations to make in the face of the German aerial assault. The rising loss rate forced Air Vice Marshal Park to order his pilots not to pursue damaged German aircraft out over the Channel. More important was his instruction for his fighters to ignore the Bf 109s and go immediately after the German bombers. British fighter squadrons themselves were already loosening up the tight inverted V formations of three aircraft – called "vics" – that had been the basis of prewar RAF fighter doctrine. Nevertheless, by the end of the battle, only a few British squadrons, most notably 605th and 501st, had fully adopted the German finger-four formation, which dominated the remainder of air-to-air combat in the Second World War.[106]

Meanwhile, the losses forced the RAF to cut the time new pilots spent in operational training units in half. It also forced the air staff to take the extraordinary step of transferring pilots from Bomber Command and the Royal Navy directly to Fighter Command after only a few hours transition time in fighters.[107] Perhaps the full measure of the pressure on Fighter Command was Dowding's decision in early September to allow the transfer of a number of the most experienced pilots from the

---

[104] The same pattern of overreporting also appeared in the claims of Eighth Air Force bomber crews as to the number of German fighter aircraft they had shot down during the great air battles of 1943.

[105] Hough and Richards, *Battle of Britain*, p. 311.

[106] Hough and Richards, *Battle of Britain*, pp. 312–313. Werner Moelders, the great German ace in the early years of the war, had invented the "finger-four" formation for fighter aircraft, while participating with the Condor Legion on the Nationalist side during the Spanish Civil War. The finger-four formation replicates the fingers on a human hand. The lead fighter is the tip of the middle finger, covered by a fighter represented by the index finger; the fighter at the tip of third finger is then covered by the fighter at the tip of the little finger.

[107] Collier, *Defence of the United Kingdom*, p. 200.

squadrons in the north to squadrons fighting the battle in the south. This would inevitably lower the capabilities and integrity of the fighter squadrons affected and undermine his strategy of having fully combat-ready replacement squadrons available.[108]

By the first week in September, the opposing sides were exhausted. Thus far, Fighter Command had shown no signs of weakening, although its losses in fighter pilots over the previous two months had been extraordinarily heavy. In July, it had lost 10 percent of its pilots on duty at the month's beginning; in August that number swelled to 26 percent. The *Luftwaffe*'s pilot losses in the Bf 109 force were 11 percent and 15 percent for those two months, a figure that does not include the heavy losses being suffered by German Bf 110 and bomber crews. In September, the British would lose 28 percent of their fighter pilots on active duty at the beginning of the month. German fighter pilot losses would swell to more than 23 percent.[109] Equally indicative for the pressures on the *Luftwaffe*'s combat squadrons was the decline in the percentage of fully qualified aircrew in the bomber squadrons. At the beginning of July, 75 percent of bomber crews were fully mission qualified; by the end of September that number had fallen to below 60 percent.[110]

The Germans now decided on a fundamental shift in their operational approach. At a meeting at The Hague on 3 September between Göring and his *Luftflotten* chiefs Kesselring and Sperrle, the *Luftwaffe*'s leaders recast their strategy. Kesselring, nicknamed "Smiling Albert" by many of his subordinates for his facile optimism, argued that given the heavy losses that Fighter Command had suffered, the British had reached the end of their tether.[111] He noted that Beppo Schmidt's intelligence estimate was that the British were down to between 150 and 300 Hurricanes and Spitfires.[112] What was needed now, the field marshal continued, was a major attack on a crucial objective that would bring the remainder of Fighter Command up so that the Bf 109s could destroy it. Sperrle strongly

---

[108] Hough and Richards, *Battle of Britain*, p. 251.
[109] Based on the loss tables for each day of the Battle of Britain in Mason, *Battle over Britain*; and on BA/MA, RL 2 III/707, Gen. Qu.6.Abt. (I), Übersicht über, Soll, Istbestand, Einsatzbereitschaft, Verluste und Reserven der fliegende Verbände.
[110] Williamson Murray, *Strategy for Defeat: The Luftwaffe, 1933–1945* (Washington, DC 1983), p. 51.
[111] Kesselring's reputation seems largely to have rested on his success in defending the Italian Peninsula against an unimaginative and incompetent Allied offensive. The fact that he was the only field marshal still on active duty in May 1945, who had been promoted to that rank in July 1940, says a great deal about his integrity.
[112] Hough and Richards, *Battle of Britain*, p. 244.

disagreed. He did not believe that the *Luftwaffe* had been as successful as Kesselring argued but felt instead that it needed to continue its attacks on Fighter Command's infrastructure in southern England.[113]

Hitler had already signed on to the idea of "retaliatory" raids because of small British raids on Berlin. The decision to mount an all-out attack on London had been inherent in German conceptions of a war against the British Isles from the beginning. Jodl's memorandum of 30 June 1940 had suggested the possibility of "terror" attacks against the British Isles to break the morale of the population.[114] A British raid on Berlin by Bomber Command, which had not done much damage, aroused the *Führer*'s ire. In a speech on 4 September, Hitler launched into one of his furious tirades against the British: "When they declare they will attack our cities in great measure, we will eradicate their cities.... The hour will come when one of us will break, and it will not be National Socialist Germany!"[115]

On 7 September 1940, the great German assault on London began. The fact that *Reichsmarschall* Göring arrived on the shores of the Channel suggests how important the effort was from the German perspective. As one of the historians of the battle has noted, "The arrival of the porcine warlord in the Pas de Calais, complete with his retinue of personal Staff Officers and his Ruritanian uniforms and impedimenta, was accomplished by all the pomp and flamboyance of a State Visit. The feelings of the grimy and exhausted squadron officers may readily be imagined."[116] Shortly before 1600 hours, the first report of a buildup for a coming German raid came into Bentley Priory, Fighter Command's central command post: 20 plus German aircraft. That number soon multiplied by the moment until it was clear that Fighter Command was confronting the largest raid of the war. Altogether 348 bombers, accompanied by 617 fighters, nearly 1,000 German aircraft, covered 800 square miles. The target was London.

Since Dowding and Park were expecting a continuation of *Luftwaffe* attacks on Fighter Command's airfields and infrastructure, the switch to London caught them by surprise. Nevertheless, the day resulted in ferocious dogfights taking place all over southeast England. When the day's fighting was over, Fighter Command had lost 16 Spitfires – ten

---

[113] Ibid., p. 244.
[114] Chef WFA, 30.6.40, "Die Weiterführung des krieges gegen England," *International Military Tribunal, Trial of Major War Criminals*, vol. XXVIII, pp. 301–303.
[115] Quoted in Maier, et al., *Das Deutsche Reich und der Zweite Weltkrieg*, vol. 2, p. 386.
[116] Mason, *Battle over Britain*, p. 358.

pilots uninjured – and 20 Hurricanes – ten pilots uninjured.[117] Giving some credence to Beppo Schmidt's claims that the RAF was on its last legs at least in the minds of Göring and Kesselring, German losses were relatively light: 12 bombers, 8 Bf 110s, and 17 Bf 109s.[118] The damage done to London, particularly the docks and housing in the East End, was massive.

Moreover, the fires the daylight attack started allowed the night raiders to find London without difficulty. Massive fires broke out because of the afternoon and evening raids:

> It was the practice among the fire services to measure the size of the fires by the number of appliances required to control the blaze; and one demanding thirty pumps is generally regarded as a very large fire. By midnight on 7th/8th September London firemen were fighting nine fires rated at over one hundred pumps each; and in the Quebec Yards of the Surrey Docks raged the fiercest single fire ever recorded in Britain; rated arbitrarily at a three-hundred-pump conflagration.[119]

But the one consolation for the British that came from the German switch in targeting to London was the fact that Fighter Command received a respite from the grueling weeks of attacks that had savaged its bases and force structure. That period sufficed to allow Fighter Command's infrastructure to recover, although its fighter squadrons, as the losses suffered on 7 September underlined, continued to take heavy losses.

Over the next several days, the weather limited the *Luftwaffe*'s daylight attacks. The climax came on 15 September, as Kesselring and Sperrle mounted their second massive raid on the capital. This time the British were ready. They also had the advantage of knowing how hard they were pressing the Germans, while the *Luftwaffe*'s leadership, again misled by its intelligence, believed Dowding was down to his last fighter pilots. Moreover, the planning for the raid, perhaps a reflection of German overconfidence, provided virtually no feints and false alarms to divert and dilute No. 11 Group's response.[120]

What happened on 15 September finally ended the German illusion that Fighter Command was on the brink of defeat. The pause between September 7th and the 15th had allowed Dowding to remove the squadrons that had suffered the heaviest losses in the fighting, so that

---

[117] Ibid., tables, pp. 365–366.
[118] Ibid., pp. 367–369.
[119] Ibid., p. 363.
[120] Collier, *The Defence of the United Kingdom*, p. 242.

Park's No. 11 Group had a relatively fresh force. Moreover, sure that London would again be the target, British controllers scrambled No. 11 Group's fighters quickly, so they could concentrate as well as gain height. Meanwhile, No. 12 Group finally put together its big wing formation, which the fighter ace Douglas Bader had been so strongly advocating.

From the moment they crossed the English coast, German bombers ran into a buzz saw of opposition. Park's fighters, upward of 170 Spitfires and Hurricanes, began breaking up the bomber formations before they reached London.[121] Bomber crews began dropping their loads over Kent and Surrey and then turned desperately for the coast, a sure sign that their morale had cracked. For those brave or lucky enough to reach London, Fighter Command had an even nastier surprise. A mass formation of Spitfires and Hurricanes from Leigh-Mallory's No. 12 Group, more than eight fighter squadrons, tore into the bomber formations.

For the German bomber crews, the appalling shock of meeting upward of 300 fighters in 20 minutes can scarcely be imagined:

> For too long they had been told that the RAF had been swept from the sky, that they faced only the 'last fifty Spitfires.' It [was] too much to ask a young man to feel confidence in his leaders when he [was] limping south again on a summer afternoon, wrists aching from the drag of distorted controls, watching for the first signs of fire with the stink of a ruptured fuel tank filling the cockpit, perhaps a dead friend lolling hideously in his harness inches away – and knowing that tomorrow there [would] still be three hundred fighters waiting for him.[122]

The RAF would claim 185 enemy aircraft destroyed; in fact, the Germans lost approximately 60 aircraft, in comparison to Fighter Command's 30 fighters lost, but the British recovered a substantial number of their pilots unhurt for use in subsequent operations.[123] The crucial point was that the morale of the *Luftwaffe* bomber crews had broken.[124] The Germans would not launch another massive daylight attack, like those that had marked the previous ten days. They would now turn to new avenues of approach, which depended on how willing they were to analyze the larger strategic and operational situation.

---

[121] Mason, *Battle over Britain*, p. 389.
[122] Ibid., pp. 389–390.
[123] Mason, *Battle over Britain*, pp. 391–392.
[124] Just as would occur after months of devastating losses in October 1943 after the second attack on Schweinfurt and in March 1944 with Bomber Command after the Nuremburg raid.

The Night and Sea Offensive against the British Isles

In fact, the German offensive against the British Isles continued over the next eight months, but Nazi political and military leaders consistently failed to address the larger issues confronting them. Instead, each of the services chartered its own independent course without reference to its sister services or to a larger strategic framework. In July 1940, Hitler had already decided that what was keeping the British in the war was the hope that the Americans and the Soviets would intervene on their side.[125] His solution was to launch an invasion of the Soviet Union – an entity that was supplying the Third Reich with a substantial portion of its raw material and foodstuff needs. The invasion was to begin in May 1941, a choice that the army's senior leaders delightedly endorsed.[126]

The *Luftwaffe* began its night campaign against Britain with bomber forces that had already suffered heavy losses in both aircraft and aircrews over the course of the previous five months. With the emphasis already swinging toward efforts to prepare the German Army for the invasion of the Soviet Union – including the doubling of the number of panzer divisions – the Germans failed to increase the production of fighters or bombers to any significant extent.[127] The night offensive against the British reflected a number of factors. On the British side, Fighter Command, despite desperate efforts, would not possess night fighters with airborne radar capabilities until March 1941. Thus, the only factor cloaking Britain would be darkness and bad weather.[128]

On the German side, the *Luftwaffe* had blind bombing capabilities far in advance of what other air forces in the world possessed. But the Germans had already lost much of that advantage, since British intelligence had already uncovered *Knickebein*'s existence. That piece of brilliant intelligence work, coupled with dogged combat against the bureaucracy

---

[125] Halder, *Halder War Diary*, p. 244.
[126] In the fall of 1940, Hitler would approach the Spanish and the French in an attempt to persuade them to join the war, but that effort was at best and seems to have been as much aimed at keeping the British occupied until Barbarossa had halfheartedly disposed of the Soviets as waging a serious effort against them. For a persuasive argument that Hitler had decided to invade the Soviet Union in July 1940 and for the most thorough examination of German planning, see Boog et al., *Das Deutsche Reich und der Zweite Weltkrieg*, vol. 4.
[127] The result would be that the *Luftwaffe* would enter the campaign against the Soviet Union with fewer bombers and fighters than it had possessed the year before.
[128] As the official history notes, the weather during December was such that on 15 nights, no major raids were possible. Collier, *Defence of the United Kingdom*, p. 272.

by R. V. Jones, had set in motion the development of countermeasures, which were already in working order by September 1940.

There were some things British jamming could not do. London was such an enormous target that *Luftwaffe* raids could not miss hitting substantial portions of the city and inflicting considerable damage; nor, as would occur in the raid on Coventry over the night of 14–15 November 1940, could the British do much on a clear, moonlit night. But even in terms of the raids on London by distorting *Knickebein*'s beams, the British impeded German efforts to achieve concentrated bombing – a factor that had an even greater impact on German bombing efforts further inland against smaller, more precise targets. As Jones recounts: "The knowledge that *Knickebein* was jammed spread through the *Luftwaffe* and there was a story current at the time that although the pilots were well aware of it, no one wanted to take responsibility of telling Göring, with the result that *Knickebein* was persisted in for the next two months although it was substantially useless."[129] A raid on 8 May 1941 suggests how effective British jamming efforts could be: *Luftwaffe* bomber crews, who were supposed to bomb Derby, attacked Nottingham, while other crews, assigned to bomb Nottingham, dropped their loads in the open countryside.[130]

Exacerbating the *Luftwaffe*'s difficulties was a considerable dispersion of effort into three distinct areas, each of which reflected different operational objectives and differing conceptions of what the campaign should involve. The bombing of London represented a Douhetan belief that the British morale would collapse under heavy air attacks. Adding to such beliefs was German overconfidence that had marked their approach throughout. The second target set was manufacturing cities: Manchester, Birmingham, Coventry, Sheffield, and Nottingham. Here the Germans inflicted serious damage, but British countermeasures against the blind-bombing beams considerably mitigated the results achieved. The third target set involved raids on major British ports, particularly Liverpool and Glasgow, but Bristol, Portsmouth, Southampton, Belfast, and Plymouth received attention as well.[131] Here again the Germans inflicted painful damage but never on a sufficient level to affect Britain's overall strategic situation.

[129] Jones, *The Wizard War*, p. 129.
[130] Collier, *Defence of the United Kingdom*, p. 280.
[131] Map 26, "The German Night Offensive, September 1940–May 1941," provides a clear representation of German efforts. Collier, *The Defence of the United Kingdom*, pp. 278 and 279.

Moreover, with the exception of London, the Germans rarely followed up major raids with attacks on following nights. Thus, while Coventry lay vulnerable after the devastating raid over the night of 14–15 November, German bombers attacked targets elsewhere, providing the British with the time to recover essential services in that important manufacturing center. The dispersion of German efforts ensured that none of the targets received sufficient attention to cause irreparable harm. Because Hitler had declared a total blockade of the British Isles, a clear emphasis on the major ports might have seemed in order (especially considering the success that the U-boats were enjoying in fall 1940), but as had been the case in the war against Britain thus far, there was no operational, much less strategic, focus to German military actions.

But neither the *Kriegsmarine* nor the *Luftwaffe* was willing to cooperate. In March 1941, British efforts to get radar-equipped fighters up and running finally began to achieve success. Over the course of the first three months of 1941, the Germans lost 90 bombers to the defenses. In April, that total rose to 75 bombers, the majority shot down by the increasingly effective night-fighter force that the RAF now possessed. Losses in May would have been even heavier, but the *Luftwaffe*'s bomber squadrons began to move east during the last half of the month in preparation for the campaign in the east.[132]

While German bombers were dealing out heavy punishment to British cities, the U-boat offensive was posing an increasing threat to Britain's sea lines of communications. The victories of spring 1940 in Scandinavia and Western Europe had significantly improved the geographic position of Dönitz's U-boats by providing bases in Normandy and Brittany, but they were hardly sufficient to overcome the lack of submarines. As with their surface fleet, the Germans had frittered away much of their strength in the Norwegian operation.[133] With Dönitz barely able to keep 17 U-boats on station at any one time, the task of breaking Britain's lifelines by unrestricted submarine warfare was simply not in the cards.[134] Yet,

---

[132] Ironically, the Germans would begin Operation Barbarossa with approximately 200 fewer bombers than they had begun the 1940 campaign against France.

[133] An operation that made little strategic sense because the campaign in the west, if it succeeded, was going to place the German Navy in a far more favorable strategic position than naval bases in Norway, while the Brey-Logway ore fields in France made the imports of iron ore from Sweden that moved along the Norwegian coasts in winter far less important. If the campaign in the west failed, then whatever success the Germans enjoyed in Norway was hardly going to be of much use.

[134] For each submarine on station, another would be transiting to or from shore station, while another was in port refitting for its next patrol.

the German effort over the fall and winter of 1940–1941 was to have a profound impact on the Battle of the Atlantic – and in this case, much in favor of the British, at least over the long run.

It did not seem so at the time. The great difficulty the British confronted in late summer and early fall 1940 was the fact that the concentration of destroyers and a considerable number of other antisubmarine craft in the eastern and southern ports to meet a potential invasion had stripped the convoys of protection.[135] At this time protection for convoys barely reached out to the central Atlantic. With little protection, inbound and outbound convoys were easy target for the U-boats. The result was a slaughter of British and Allied merchant shipping, a period that the Germans termed as the "first happy time." Adding to British woes was the fact that a number of merchant vessels were still sailing without escorts. In the period between July and November 1940, the British lost 144 unescorted vessels to U-boats and only 73 in convoys.[136]

Yet, in the long term, the Germans were the losers. The terrifying losses, which Churchill termed as the only threat that worried him to the bottom of his soul during the course of the war, forced the British to set in motion a set of adaptations in both the immediate and long term that were to have a profound impact on the course of the Battle of the Atlantic.[137] Obviously, the return of the escort vessels as the invasion threat died down improved the situation in the Atlantic. It soon became apparent that the special hunter-killer groups were failing to pay dividends, while concentrating escorts to protect convoys provided greater opportunities to attack the U-boats. It was also clear that air protection would be an important element in convoy protection. In December, a new threat arose as convoy HX 90 was attacked by a wolf pack of four boats, two of which were under the command of two of the most formidable U-boat aces. The attacking U-boats sank 11 merchant vessels.[138]

In the long term, the painful tactical success of the U-boats led the British to develop and push for a whole host of adaptations and changes in their approach to antisubmarine warfare. The most obvious was to

---

[135] This situation had also stripped the Iceland-Faroe Channel and the Iceland-Greenland Channels of their air and sea patrol craft, which enabled German commerce raiders and fleet units to break out into the Atlantic, which exacerbated the British difficulties in protecting their commerce.
[136] Roskill, *The War at Sea*, vol. 1, p. 349.
[137] Winston S. Churchill, *The Second World War*, vol. 3, *The Grand Alliance* (Boston, 1950), p. 122.
[138] Roskill, *The War at Sea*, vol. 1, p. 353.

focus on increasing the number of escort vessels – the deal with the Americans exchanging 50 World War I destroyers for bases in Bermuda and the Caribbean representing the first move to increase the number of escorts. Technologically, the British set in motion a whole set of adaptations from developing and then equipping escorts with radar, improving ASDIC,[139] developing and equipping Coastal Command's aircraft with airborne radar, developing direction-finding gear to allow escorts to identify the immediate position of U-boats shadowing convoys, improving the power of depth charges and developing new weapons such as the "hedgehog" to improve the lethality of escorts, and reintroducing high-powered searchlights on aircraft (the Leigh light).

All of these adaptations would serve to make the environment in which German U-boats operated far more dangerous. On the tactical side, the British moved to the idea of training escort groups of antisubmarine vessels that would work and fight together over the long haul, thus maximizing their potential by developing common understanding and tactics. Finally, the command of Britain's Western Approaches moved in February 1941 from Plymouth to Liverpool; here, along with the colocated headquarters of the RAF's No. 15 Group of Coastal Command, it would be in closer contact with the battle in the North Atlantic.[140]

Many of these factors soon had an influence on the battles occurring in the eastern Atlantic. In March 1941, British escort vessels sank five U-boats, eliminating three of the most successful U-boat "aces" the Germans possessed during the war: Gunther Prien and Joachim Schepke carried to their deaths on U-47 and U-100, respectively, and Otto Kretschmer captured with his U-99. (These five U-boats represented approximately one-fifth of the fleet the Germans had operating at sea.[141]) Already Dönitz was having to move his U-boats out into the central Atlantic where the British would possess the room to maneuver their convoys and where intelligence would become more and more of a crucial player in the battle.

But the greatest adaptation that the British were to make in the battle occurred at the end of our period in the ethereal world of code-breaking

[139] Anti-Submarine Detection Investigation Committee detection device.
[140] And across the North Atlantic, the Americans, who were watching closely and confronting the possibility of a great two-front war, took the losses to heart at least in the sense that they were going to have to set in motion a massive program of merchant-ship production. Unfortunately, they did not pay much attention to what was happening on the tactical side of fighting the U-boats. For the disaster that was soon to befall the Americans, see Eliot Cohen and John Gooch, *Military Misfortunes: The Anatomy of Failure in War* (New York, 1990).
[141] Roskill, *The War at Sea*, p. 365.

and intelligence. So far, the solving of the *Luftwaffe*'s Enigma code had only had an impact on the air battle. Bletchley Park had failed to break the U-boat Enigma ciphers that Dönitz utilized to control his U-boats, particularly the patrol lines he used to find the convoys and then to concentrate them in wolf packs. However, in May 1941, Bletchley Park was able to intervene in this contest in a crucial fashion.

The story begins with Harry Hinsley, the Cambridge undergraduate discussed earlier. By May 1941, the U-boat offensive, despite the loss of three of its greatest aces in March, was swinging into high gear. Monthly losses of merchant vessels in the North Atlantic had reached well over 300,000 tons. Meanwhile, Bletchley Park appeared no closer to breaking into the U-boat Enigma traffic. Hinsley recognized that if British cryptanalysts could get the settings for a sustained period of time, they would have a shot at breaking the U-boat traffic over the long haul.[142]

One day, Hinsley suddenly had "a passing thought" and remembered that the German weather ships off the north coast of Iceland had been transmitting their reports on weather conditions in the same Enigma code as the U-boats were using.[143] And since they were on station for sustained periods of time, he surmised that it was likely that they carried the Enigma settings for the whole period they were at sea. Because of the strain on the Royal Navy in the Battle of the Atlantic, no one had thus far thought it necessary to take the *Kriegsmarine*'s weather ships out. Now on the recommendation of a 21-year-old Cambridge undergraduate, the Royal Navy executed a major cutting-out operation to seize the weather ships. So highly did its leaders think of Hinsley and his advice that the operation was mounted on short notice and counted three cruisers and four destroyers from the home fleet under a vice admiral.[144] The resulting capture of the German weather ship *München* provided the first significant Enigma materials, including settings for the next two months. Almost immediately

---

[142] What such a period would give the British cryptanalysts was a sense of the cribs in the German system, which they had not been able to gain thus far in their efforts. And it was this developed sense of the weaknesses in the German efforts to protect the Enigma that allowed the British to break into the U-boat message traffic even when they no longer possessed the settings. The addition of a fourth rotor to the Enigma machines on U-boats closed off Bletchley Park from reading the U-boat traffic for most of 1942. Nevertheless, that six months' experience of reading the traffic played a major role in creating the second break into the U-boat traffic in January 1943, a success that was one of several contributing factors to victory in the Battle of the Atlantic, a period that lasted the remainder of the war.
[143] Kahn, *Seizing the Enigma*, p. 154.
[144] Ibid., p. 156.

thereafter, the British captured U-110, captained by Julius Lemp, one of the greatest U-boat aces, with more Enigma material. Neither was sufficient, and the British mounted a further cutting-out operation that netted a second weather ship, the *Lauenberg* in late June, which yielded more cipher material, according to the Admiralty, of "inestimable value."[145]

As a result of these seizures, Bletchley Park was able to break into the U-boat Enigma on a regular basis for the next six months. Armed with key decrypts indicating where Dönitz was positioning his U-boat patrol lines, the British could maneuver their convoys around the U-boats for the next six months. British losses of merchant shipping dropped by two-thirds, a dramatic reduction that removed much of the growing tension on Allied shipping for a key period when the British were still fighting alone. By no means was the Battle of the Atlantic over, but the British had gained a key breathing space during which their adaptations, technological and other, would begin to come into full force.

And what were the Germans doing in terms of adaptation during this critical period of the Battle of the Atlantic? Virtually nothing beyond their cloying focus on numbers of ships sunk and the tactical framework of the wolf pack that they began introducing into the increasingly complex battle in the Atlantic. The *Luftwaffe* and the *Kriegsmarine* obdurately refused to cooperate. The naval high command remained entranced by the concept of big-ship cruiser warfare, which the sinking of the *Bismarck* underlined was a dead end. Dönitz screamed for more submarines, but the focus of the U-boat war remained on looking for weak areas where the U-boats could find the kind of success they had enjoyed in the fall of 1940. Quite simply, the Germans sought none of the kinds of innovations that the British were developing in response to the threat. And the U-boat war was now to become the sole means the Third Reich had to strike at the growing threat from the West – a threat that German

---

[145] Beesly, *Very Special Intelligence*, p. 74. Beesly rates the success of these operations in the following terms: "Nor was the German confidence that, once the validity of the current settings had expired our cryptanalysts would be again defeated, justified; we continued to read Hydra, albeit with varying time lags when periodically new settings had to be cracked, throughout the war. The penetration of this cipher, just when our other sources of information were also beginning to produce greatly improved results, at last enabled O.I.C. to function as it had always been hoped that it would. It was equivalent to a major victory in itself, but in addition led [Bletchley Park] on to successes with other ciphers, such as Neptune, the operational cipher for the heavy ships, and Sud and Mesdusa in the Mediterranean. The intelligence scales, which had hitherto been heavily weighted in favor of the Germans, were beginning to swing to our side." Beesly, *Very Special Intelligence*, pp. 74–75.

strategic bungling in December 1941 would catastrophically exacerbate with Hitler's declaration of war on the United States, a decision that his senior military leaders enthusiastically endorsed.

Conclusion

The year 1940 was undoubtedly one of the great watershed years in the history of the twentieth century. The *Wehrmacht*'s victories in the west in spring 1940 allowed the Germans to break out from their scarce resource base. In effect, those victories set the stage for the Third Reich to wage a global conflict. Yet confronting the enormously changed world of summer 1940, the German military proved incapable of making the kinds of adaptations required to fight the war of their *Führer*'s dreams. Instead, like Hitler, they became enveloped in beliefs about their own genius and the racial inferiority of those whom they opposed.[146] In effect, the Germans adapted at best at the tactical level but then only marginally.

At the strategic and operational levels, the German military leadership never seemed to have grasped or understood the extent of the challenges they confronted. In some areas such as intelligence, the general failure of the system should have suggested that a fundamental reevaluation was in order. To a certain extent, one could ascribe the failure to execute such a reassessment to the nature of the *Führer* state itself. But that is too glib an explanation. Within months of the failure of intelligence in the Battle of Britain, German intelligence was proving as overly optimistic as ever about the *Wehrmacht*'s prospects in the upcoming campaign against the Soviet Union. Even in the sphere of technology, the Germans appeared willing to rest on their early-war laurels. The U-boat of 1943 would look virtually the same as the U-boat of 1940; nor would its capabilities change during the course of the three years. The contrast between the technological changes that American fleet boats would undergo in the same period underlines how few technical adaptations the Germans made. In every respect, they seem to have considered virtually no serious changes despite the failure of their campaign.

On the other side of the Channel, British adaptiveness at every level suggests how impressively they were able to adapt to the grim conditions

---

[146] While the Germans did on occasion refer to the British as their racial cousins, they consistently proved incapable of recognizing the full nature of their opponent's skill and cunning. The breaking of the Enigma codes for substantial portions of the war, with the serious consequences that resulted for German military operations, is only one case in point among many.

that confronted them. The air defense system steadily adapted to the threat that the *Luftwaffe* posed. In the long term, the British recognized that the coming struggle with the Germans in the air over the European continent was going to rest on numbers. Thus, the long-term response to the experiences of the Battle of Britain was to emphasize massive programs of crew training and the production of fighters and bombers in numbers that only the Americans would exceed. But the area where the British showed the most stunning set of adaptations occurred in the Royal Navy's antisubmarine forces. Here, in every area from "Huff Duff," to radar, to the weaponry of anti-U-boat warfare, to the training up of escort groups, to the business of intelligence, the British achieved a dominance that was to bring the U-boat to a dramatic end in May 1943 and seal the fate of the Third Reich. In every respect, the Battle for Britain reflected the widest sort of adaptations, encouraged and pushed by a senior leader who demanded "action this day."

It might be useful also to say a few words about the influence of the prewar period on those who conducted the air portions of the Battle of Britain in Fighter Command and in the *Luftwaffe*. Again, the British appear significantly superior. Admittedly, British prewar doctrine with its heavy emphasis on the belief that the bomber would always get through and do substantial damage to the enemy's morale would hardly seem of much use or influence in how Fighter Command fought the Battle of Britain.

But the appointment of Dowding to head up the new command short-circuited the prewar belief system and brought into a position of power (where it counted) an individual with a keen sense of reality and the ability to adapt swiftly to that reality.[147] Dowding was not a scientist; however, he understood not only how to work with scientists but also how to ask them the questions that mattered. And then he was willing to support them wholeheartedly in their work. Moreover, he saw the potential application of their work to the actual needs of Fighter Command: thus, his drive to create a night-fighter capability, which the government refused to support with the necessary resources until almost too late.

---

[147] It is one of the astonishing quirks of academic history that most historians believe that great social trends, and not individuals, exercise the most powerful influence on the course of history. In this case, it is difficult to see how Britain could have won the Battle of Britain without the combination of Dowding's quiet competence and Churchill's inspiring leadership. But then most academic historians have spent their entire lives in universities and colleges where leadership rarely, if ever, exists.

In almost every respect, the German senior leadership – military as well as Hitler and Göring – stood in stark contrast to Dowding and Churchill in its approach to the war. Ironically, the *Luftwaffe*'s prewar doctrine enunciated a far clearer view of the contribution that air power would make to the conflict the Germans had started so enthusiastically.[148] Nevertheless, that doctrine reflected the Continental *Weltanschauung* that had characterized the German military in the First World War and was to dominate the conduct of the second. Thus, while the *Luftwaffe*'s leaders understood that the RAF as a whole must be their target, they never thought through the implications of the fact that they now confronted a pure air war, in which operations on the ground would contribute nothing. Moreover, the German conduct of the campaign against Britain reflected an arrogant assumption of superiority that fed both the intelligence and the operational approaches to the air war. Significantly, that arrogance – the belief in the inherent superiority of German military prowess – would dominate the German conduct of war through to the final smashup in 1945. In effect, the Germans learned nothing and forgot all in their adaptations to the defeat of their campaign against Britain in 1940–1941.

[148] For the *Luftwaffe*'s basic doctrine, see particularly *Die Luftkriegführung* (Berlin, 1936).

6

Adaptation in the Air War

RAF Bomber Command and the Luftwaffe's Air Defenses (15 May 1940–7 May 1945)

In many ways, the British bomber offensive reflected problems of adaption similar to those raised by the rapidly changing tactical and technological arena that had faced Fighter Command and the *Luftwaffe* during the Battle of Britain. Yet even more than was the case in 1940, the RAF's bomber offensive involved a clash between prewar visions and attitudes, intellectual as well as conceptual, and the realities the RAF's Bomber Command and the *Luftwaffe* confronted in the nighttime skies over the Third Reich.

As did its predecessors on the Western Front during the First World War, Bomber Command had to deal with an opponent who was simultaneously adapting his own technology and tactics to the changing conditions of the battle. This case study focuses on the adaptation, or lack of adaptation, that marked both Bomber Command's offensive and the German responses to it – particularly in the years of 1943 and 1944 – as well as the path that led to those difficult years.[1]

The night bombing campaign revolved around technology. Yet, although technology was an enabler, important to developing the capabilities on which the battle revolved, the abilities of leaders at every level to turn technological advances into significant tactical and operational effects were even more important. At the highest levels, senior

---

[1] Three outstanding works delineate the history of Bomber Command's efforts in the Second World War. The first is the extraordinary official history, which represents one of the finest pieces of official history, thoroughly grounded in the facts: Sir Charles Webster and Noble Frankland, *The Strategic Air Offensive against Germany*, 4 vols. (London, 1961). The others are Max Hastings, *Bomber Command* (London, 1979); and Anthony Verrier, *The Bomber Offensive* (London, 1968).

commanders, and even political leaders, played major roles in determining how the equations of technological change and tactical and operational adaptation actually worked out in an environment of ambiguity and uncertainty. And finally, one must not forget that prewar preconceptions and assumptions continued to exercise their influences over those exercising command, and thus over the processes of adaptation to the actual conditions of war.

In discussing something as complex and intertwined with technology as the massive air battles between British night bombers and German night air defenses, one must not lose sight of how unclear matters looked to those charged with waging the battle. Even in the aftermath of war, it has proven difficult for historians to unravel the effectiveness or ineffectiveness of military institutions and their actions, such as the Combined Bomber Offensive or the dropping of the atomic bombs on Japan.[2] For those who actually conducted the air offensive against Germany, it was even more difficult to obtain reliable evidence on how their attacks were affecting the enemy's war economy and ability to continue the war. Those commanding armies could calculate their success or failure in terms of ground gained or enemy formations defeated. Admirals in charge of the antisubmarine war could at least calculate their effectiveness in terms of the number of ships that reached harbor successfully. Airmen directing the strategic bombing campaign had no equally accessible criteria by which to judge the effectiveness of their operations.[3]

For the bomber barons, much of the time there was little to go on beyond the percentage of bombers lost on each operation. Yet, as one of the leading historians of the strategic bombing effort during the Second World War, Anthony Verrier, has noted:

> Thus we are left with one clear reminder of a painful truth: The laws of war applied as much to the strategic air offensive waged over Europe's skies through five-and-a-half bitter years as they did to the sailors and soldiers

---

[2] In this sense, the reader's attention is drawn to Richard Overy's and the author's work, which both make it clear (admittedly 50 years after the ending of the Second World War) that the Combined Bomber Offensive played a major role in the winning of the war. In this regard, see Williamson Murray, "The Combined Bomber Offensive, 1941–1945," in *A War to Be Won: Fighting the Second World War*, Williamson Murray and Allan R. Millett (Cambridge, 2000), chap. 12; Williamson Murray, "Reflections on the Combined Bomber Offensive," *Militärgeschichtliche Mitteilungen*, Heft 51 (1992); Richard Overy, *The Air War: 1939–1945* (London, 1980), and *How the Allies Won the Second World War* (London, 1996).

[3] The results would not begin to emerge until after the war; even then it would take historians decades to figure out what the effects had actually been.

on the distant seas or in the mud and sand below. Occasionally, the airman may have found himself living and fighting in a new dimension, just as the air force commander may have felt he enjoyed a freedom of maneoeuvre denied to admirals and generals. But the airman died, and the air force commander was defeated unless the laws were kept. When they were kept, success came; until they could be kept, hope was kept alive by courage alone.[4]

The British Background

As suggested in the discussion on the background to the Battle of Britain (Chapter 5), airmen in the RAF found little of interest in the study of the first war in the air, much less in military history in general. An Air Staff memorandum, written in 1924, went so far as to claim that, in thinking about a future air war, military history would suggest that the enemy air force should be the first target and that only after its defeat should an attacking air force turn to the enemy's industrial and population centers. Insisting on the contrary – that the past has little relevance for thinking about the future of air war – the authors declared that such an approach was wrong and that the target from the first must be the enemy's population and industry.[5]

In fact, the experience of aerial combat in the First World War essentially confirmed what the history of war had suggested over the centuries about more traditional warfare: without the defeat of the enemy's air forces, air operations (whatever the mission, be it interdiction, artillery observation, reconnaissance, close air support, or strategic bombing) inevitably suffered unacceptably high casualty rates.[6] In other words, the defeat of military forces had been and would continue to be a precondition of victory in battle. However, throughout the interwar period, the RAF made virtually no effort to examine honestly even its own experiences in the First World War, much less those of its German

---

[4] Verrier, *The Bomber Offensive*, p. 327.
[5] Public Records Office (PRO; UK), Air 20/40, Air Staff Memorandum No. 11 A, March 1924.
[6] For a discussion of these issues and the employment of air power in the First World War, see Williamson Murray, *The Air War, 1914–1945* (London, 1998). Webster and Frankland argue that the lesson of the strategic bombing of London in World War I suggested that the bomber would always get through. What that argument misses is the fact that losses in the daylight attacks in 1918 were so heavy that the Germans were eventually forced to move to night attacks; when those proved too costly, the Germans then desisted. Webster and Frankland, *The Strategic Air Offensive against Germany*, vol. 1, *Preparations*, p. 44.

opponent.⁷ Instead, its focus was almost entirely on ensuring that its doctrine and the assumptions underlying it would justify the RAF's continued existence as an independent service.⁸

The one conclusion that the RAF's senior leadership drew from the previous war reflected a claim that its leaders in France had begun to make as the war drew to a close in the fall of 1918. An official memorandum from the Western Front in October 1918 went so far as to suggest that

> In the period August–October [1918] evidence has accumulated as to the immense moral[e] effect of our raids on Germany. Though material damage is as yet slight when compared to the moral[e] effect, it is certain that the destruction of moral[e] will start before the destruction of the factories, and consequently loss of production will precede material damage.⁹

By the early 1920s, RAF leaders were making claims that the morale effect of bombing was three to one compared with the actual physical damage that it managed to achieve.¹⁰

In fact, there was no evidence justifying the RAF's arguments about the psychological impact of its bombing, other than the collapse of the German nation into revolution in October and November 1918, which we now know to have resulted from other factors: the terrible casualties the German Army had suffered over the four years of war; the shock of the failure of the 1918 spring offensives followed by defeat on the Western Front in late summer and fall; four years of privation caused by the blockade; the manifest overextension of German industry by the Hindenburg-Ludendorff Plan; and the desperate strategic situation occasioned by the collapse of the Second Reich's allies (Turkey, Bulgaria, and Austria Hungary) in October 1918.¹¹

---

7 The RAF did sponsor an official history of British air activities during the First World War, but that effort seems to have had the aim of justifying its existence as an independent service rather than uncovering useful lessons of air power's employment in World War I, as was the case with the German official histories.
8 Admittedly, for at least a portion of the 1920s, the RAF's continued existence as an independent service remained in question, as both the Royal Navy and the British Army attempted to regain the portions of air capabilities they had lost in 1917 with the creation of the RAF.
9 Air Ministry, "Results of Air Raids on Germany Carried out by British Aircraft, January 1st–September 30th, 1918," D.A.I., No. 5 (A.IIB, October 1918), Trenchard Papers, RAF Staff College, Bracknell, D-4.
10 This was, of course, a reference to Napoleon's comment about the importance of morale.
11 Significantly, that part of Germany where revolution broke out in its most virulent form was Bavaria, traditionally one of the most conservative parts of the Second Reich. But it was also the most threatened by the collapse of Austria-Hungary and the advance of Allied armies through the Balkans and over the Alps.

These factors indicate that the German revolution had occurred only in extremis. Indeed, if they demonstrate anything, it was how resilient the modern state actually is. Thus, the pre–World War II argument that the revolutions of 1917 and 1918 had proven the vulnerabilities of the modern state to strategic bombing in fact had done no such thing. Nevertheless, a memorandum that RAF's commander-in-chief, Air Marshal Sir Hugh Trenchard, circulated about the possibility of a war with France suggests how entrenched such beliefs had become by the late 1920s. Trenchard argued that "the policy of hitting the French nation and making them squeal before we did was a vital one – more vital than anything else."[12]

Certain elements of the RAF's senior leadership found these arguments attractive as a reflection of the general contempt in which British officers held civilians, including their own. Sir Henry Wilson – chief of the Imperial General Staff in the early 1920s before his assassination by the Irish Republican Army – had casually dismissed his political superiors throughout the First World War as a bunch of "old frocks." Moreover, the outbreak of revolution throughout Central and Eastern Europe at the end of the First World War suggested to many officers that civil society simply did not have the staying power of military organizations.[13]

By the early 1930s, the RAF under Trenchard's leadership had evolved a set of doctrinal assumptions that emphasized the psychological impact of air bombardment on an enemy.[14] By the mid-1930s, such thinking was having a substantial effect on Britain's politicians – best exemplified by Stanley Baldwin's comments in the House of Commons that not only would the bomber always get through but that the only response

---

[12] Quoted in Webster and Frankland, *The Strategic Air Offensive against Germany*, vol. 4, *Appendices*, appendix 2, "Memorandum by the Chief of Air Staff and Comments by his Colleagues," May 1928.

[13] What such arguments entirely missed was the fact that revolution had broken out in the military first before it spread to civilian society and that Europe's civilian societies, admittedly dragooned by their governments, had endured enormous privations and losses throughout the course of the war.

[14] Trenchard put his ideas in blunt terms to the air staff in discussions in 1922 about the possibility of a war with France: "I would like to make this point again. I feel that although there would be an outcry, the French in a bombing duel would probably squeal before we did. That was really the first thing. The nation that would stand being bombed [the] longest would win in the end." Webster and Frankland, *The Strategic Air Offensive against Germany*, vol. 4, Appendix 1, "Minutes of a Conference Held in the Room of the Chief of Air Staff," Air Ministry, 19 July 1923.

to such attacks would be counter-bombardment of the enemy nation.[15] Only the Chamberlain government's intervention in 1937 for the wrong reasons – that fighters were cheaper than bombers – led to an emphasis on the former over the latter. Ironically, creation of an effective Fighter Command resulted in an air defense system that flew in the face of the RAF's basic assumptions about strategic bombing, as well as those of many politicians.[16]

Meanwhile, notwithstanding its claims about the efficacy of bombing in damaging the enemy's morale, the RAF's senior leadership paid little attention to the key question of how its bombers were going to find the targets that would allow its bombers to attack an enemy population or industry. In the early 1930s, Arthur Tedder, the future air marshal and Dwight Eisenhower's deputy at SHAEF (Supreme Headquarters Allied Expeditionary Forces), always more realistic than his colleagues, replied to a question about how the RAF would find targets at night by commenting: "You tell me!"[17] There was also solid evidence available from RAF peacetime exercises conducted in the late 1930s that indicated how difficult finding and identifying targets would be in a future war. Commenting on bombing exercises conducted at night in 1937, the assistant chief of the air staff admitted: "It remains true, however, that in the home defense exercise last year, bombing accuracy was very poor indeed. Investigation into this matter indicates that this was probably due very largely to [the] failure to identify targets rather than to fatigue."[18]

Admittedly, most senior RAF officers assumed that strategic bombing in the future would be conducted during daylight hours. Nevertheless, given European weather conditions for most of the year, visual sighting of intended targets, including cities, was simply not in the cards. That was certainly the conclusion the Germans had drawn from exercises at home, as well as the Condor Legion's combat experiences in the Spanish Civil War. In contrast, the RAF's leadership ignored all of the available evidence on the baseless assumption that accurate navigation

---

[15] Baldwin's remarks quoted in Keith Middlemas and John Barnes, *Baldwin* (London, 1969), p. 735.
[16] In 1924, the air staff stated that "as a principle... the bombing squadrons should be as numerous as possible and the fighters as few as popular opinion and necessity for defending vital objects will permit." Public Record Office, PRO 20/40, Air Staff Memorandum 11A, March 1924.
[17] Quoted in Guy Hartcup, *The Challenge of War* (London, 1967), p. 126.
[18] PRO AIR 2/2598, Air Ministry File, 541137 (1938).

and bombing would not be a problem. Thus, even those interested in and supportive of the concept of direct attack on an enemy's population did little to push for development of navigational or blind-bombing technology.[19] As the British scientist R. V. Jones notes in his memoirs, he found himself

> astonished by the complacency that existed regarding our ability to navigate at long range by night. The whole of our bombing policy depended on this assumption, but I was assured that by general instrument flying, coupled with navigation by the stars, Bomber Command... could find pin point targets in Germany at night and that there was not any need for any such aids.... I was not popular for asking why, if this were true, so many of our bombers on practice flights in Britain flew into hills.[20]

Spain might have provided salient lessons if British airmen had paid attention to the air operations occurring there. That conflict indicated that bombing attacks aimed at breaking an enemy's morale would face a difficult task.[21] That was *not* the lesson the British learned. Instead, the attitude seems to have been that the war in Spain represented a conflict between two technologically primitive sides despite the fact that the Germans, the Italians, and the Soviets all sent significant numbers of modern aircraft to the fight.[22]

What is surprising is how little British or, for that matter, American airmen learned from the Battle of Britain, which would seem to have had direct applicability to the campaigns they would soon wage against the Third Reich. Neither air force recognized that the Battle of Britain had reconfirmed the lesson of World War I: *air superiority was an ironclad prerequisite for the success of any strategic air campaign.* Fighter Command not only had brought the German daylight offensive to a halt in September 1940, but by April and May 1941 British night fighters, equipped with radar, were imposing unacceptable losses on German

---

[19] In fact, the RAF failed to recognize the position of navigator as an integral member of bomber crews until late 1941. Until then navigation was assigned higgledy-piggledy to the pilots. Webster and Frankland, *The Strategic Air Offensive against Germany*, vol. 1, *Preparations*, p. 111.
[20] R. V. Jones, *The Wizard War* (New York, 1979), pp. 45–46.
[21] That was certainly the conclusion that some, but not all, Germans drew from their experiences, especially from the impact of the bombing of Guernica.
[22] The Germans, not surprisingly, learned the most, given their emphasis on serious lessons learned, but then they were active participants. For the influence of their experiences on the development of close air support, see Williamson Murray, "German Close Air Support," in Benjamin Franklin Cooling, ed., *Close Air Support* (Washington, DC, 1990).

bombers.²³ Moreover, analysis of major *Luftwaffe* bombing attacks on British cities indicated no serious loss of production because of a collapse in morale. For example, only approximately 5 percent of production was lost following major attacks on Hull and Birmingham in 1940 and 1941, and that drop lasted only for a short period.²⁴

Nevertheless, the reaction of Air Marshal Charles Portal, the RAF's new commander-in-chief, and Arthur Harris to the late December 1940 bombing of London encapsulates the attitude of many in the RAF's senior leadership at the beginning of the British bomber offensive. The air marshals assured one another that while the British with their "stiff upper lip" could take any amount of bombing, the Germans would not be able to stand up to heavy bombing.²⁵ The basic assumption, then, was that given an equivalent assault, similar to what the *Luftwaffe* was imposing on London, Germany would crack.

The Americans looked more carefully than the British at the German defeat in the Battle of Britain, but that is not to suggest they learned much that would prove of value in their daylight campaign against precision targets in Nazi Germany.²⁶ Instead, their conclusion about the *Luftwaffe*'s failure in the Battle of Britain emphasized the weaknesses of its bomber formations: German bombers were too lightly armed; they flew at too low an altitude; and their formation flying was weak. But the inability of *Luftwaffe* fighters to protect the bomber formations received little attention.

There was, however, one major strategic lesson the British and Americans did draw: air war was going to involve far greater numbers of fighters and bombers than they had estimated during the interwar period. Both air forces now began great programs of expansion that would affect the

---

[23] Basil Collier, *The Defence of the United Kingdom* (London, 1957), pp. 279–280. R. V. Jones indicates in his memoirs that by March 1941, the combination of distorting the beams and the coincident development of British night fighters equipped with airborne radar had largely blunted the German night-bombing offensive. Jones, *The Wizard War*, p. 179.

[24] Brereton Greenhous, Stephen J. Harris, William C, Johnston, and G. P. Rawling, *The Official History of the Royal Canadian Air Force*, vol. 3, *The Crucible of War, 1939–1945* (Toronto, 1994), p. 586.

[25] The exact opposite was the opinion of the German leadership: they believed the disciplined German population could stand up to air attack while the "liberalistic" British could not. Horst Boog, Werner Rahn, Reinhard Stumpf, and Bernd Wegner, *Das Deutsche Reich und der Zweite Weltkrieg*, vol. 6, *Der Globale Krieg, Die Ausweitung zum Weltkrieg und der wechsel der Initiative, 1941–1943* (Stuttgart, 1990), p. 442.

[26] Murray, *Luftwaffe*, p. 60.

course of the war, particularly in 1943 and 1944.[27] By then, as Verrier, has noted, American factories were turning out four-engine bombers "like cans of beans."[28] The British, considering the limitations of their economy, did almost as well. Both efforts required an enormous expansion not only of the production base but also of the maintenance and supply systems, the training establishments for aircrew and ground crew, and operational training units.[29]

The Preparation of German Air Defense

In sharp contrast to the Americans and British during the interwar period, German airmen developed a more realistic picture of what future air war would look like. Perhaps the best explanation for the realism in *Luftwaffe* doctrine lay in the fact that because of the Treaty of Versailles, Germany possessed no air force. In its absence, General Hans von Seeckt, an air enthusiast, created a cell of German airmen within the general staff, the members of which examined air matters until the creation of the *Luftwaffe*, first in clandestine form in 1933 and then in overt form in 1935. That cell took an active part in reviewing the actual lessons of the First World War – what actually had happened, not what German airmen wished had happened.[30] As a result, Germans had a realistic basis on which to build their preparations for the next war.

The initial statement of the German approach to air warfare did not appear until 1935 with the publication of *Die Luftkriegführung (The Conduct of the Air War)*, largely written by the *Luftwaffe*'s first chief of staff, General Walther Wever, regarded by many as the most brilliant staff officer in the army in the pre-Hitler period.[31] Unfortunately for the

---

[27] Ibid., pp. 92–104.
[28] Verrier, *The Bomber Offensive*, p. 326.
[29] Murray, *Luftwaffe*, pp. 92–104. Significantly, in 1941 Bomber Command turned no less than 14 of its operational squadrons into training units to expand the base for future expansion. Verrier, *The Bombing Offensive*, p. 126.
[30] Because they had no aircraft, German pilots brought into the *Reichswehr* (renamed *Wehrmacht* in 1935) had plenty of time to study the lessons of the last war.
[31] To create the *Luftwaffe*, the German Army transferred a significant number of officers to the new service in the first years of the *Luftwaffe*'s buildup. After the Second World War, a number of *Luftwaffe* senior officers complained that these were largely rejects. The fact that the army offered Göring a choice between General Erich von Manstein and Wever to be the new service's chief of staff, while Albert Kesselring was also among those seconded to the German Air Force, suggests that such postwar views represent an attempt to explain away the reasons behind the *Luftwaffe*'s defeat in the war. At the time, neither Göring nor Wever complained about the quality of the officers whom the army had made available.

Luftwaffe, Wever would die in an aircraft accident in 1936.[32] None of his successors brought the same intellectual and leadership qualities to the post.

The Conduct of the Air War represented a broader approach to air war than the doctrines evolving in Britain or the United States.[33] It not only lodged air power solidly within the joint arena but it also stressed that the political and operational context of the war should determine the use of air power,[34] noting explicitly that "The nature of the enemy, the time of year, the structure of his land, the character of his people, as well as one's own military capabilities" would determine how a nation might employ air power most effectively.[35]

For the Germans especially, this meant that, in terms of a war on the Continent, support for the ground campaign through interdiction, air superiority, and close air support were all crucial missions. It was all very well for air-power theorists in Britain and the United States to talk about destroying enemy cities and industrial power, but for Germany, such efforts as attacking Paris, Warsaw, or Prague would prove counter-productive if the *Wehrmacht* were to lose Silesia or the Rhineland.[36] Still, the *Luftwaffe* did take strategic bombing seriously as a mission that, in certain circumstances, might be a major mission for German air power. And unlike the Americans and the British, the Germans prepared far more seriously to execute that mission. In the end, the more realistic appreciation of air power's potential contribution explains why and how the *Luftwaffe* would make such an impressive contribution to the opening campaigns of the Second World War, compared with the dismal showing of its opponents.

---

[32] The accident was entirely Wever's fault. He failed to flight-check his aircraft properly before he took off, and the flap locks remained in place.

[33] It is still more applicable to air war than the basic doctrinal manuals produced by the United States Air Force, the 1990s version of which the author described as "See Jane fly. See Spot bomb."

[34] For a discussion of *Luftwaffe* doctrine as enunciated in *Die Luftkriegführung*, see Williamson Murray, *Luftwaffe* (Baltimore, 1985), pp. 9–10.

[35] Oberkommando der Luftwaffe (OKL, the Luftwaffe high command), *Die Luftkriegführung* (Berlin, 1935), paragraph 11.

[36] One of the great myths of Second World War historiography is the argument that the *Luftwaffe* was not interested in strategic bombing. The fact that the Germans had developed blind-bombing devices, long-range escort fighters, and a pathfinder force before the onset of war indicates that the Germans were far better prepared to conduct a strategic bombing campaign than their opponents. But in the early years of the war, none of the contending air forces had the slightest idea of the force structures, production requirements, or tactical capabilities required to conduct such a campaign.

Nevertheless, there was one glaring weakness in the German preparations for an air war. As with the army, virtually all of the *Luftwaffe*'s preparations aimed at conducting an offensive war that would carry the conflict to the enemy.[37] Thus, unlike the British under Dowding's stewardship at Fighter Command, the Germans at the beginning of the war had no conception of an approach that would incorporate developing technologies, particularly radar, fighters, and anti-aircraft guns, into a coherent air defense system. Instead, the German fighter force almost exclusively focused on offensive operations over the enemy's airspace. Radar was used until 1943 exclusively in a ground-control-intercept mode with radar sites controlling individual fighters, rather than the systematic approach the British used.

If there were a consensus among the Germans concerning air defense of the Third Reich in the years immediately preceding the war, it lay in the belief that Flak (anti-aircraft artillery[38]) alone could defend Germany's industry and cities. As a 1940 manual expressed it, Flak was the "decisive element in air defense" and "of the greatest importance for the defense of one's airspace."[39] This belief partially reflected technological developments in high velocity anti-aircraft guns in the last years of the First World War. After the war, given their lack of aircraft, the Germans placed great emphasis on further developing this technology.[40] Experience in Spain against relatively slow and low-flying aircraft reinforced the assumption that anti-aircraft artillery could handle whatever air challenge survived German air attacks on the enemy's air force.[41]

There were two additional weaknesses in the *Luftwaffe*'s preparation for war. First, like the army, the *Luftwaffe*'s senior leadership displayed little interest in logistics or intelligence beyond immediate tactical intelligence. The least competent officers in that service's general staff handled the problems of both intelligence and logistics. Underlining the *Luftwaffe*'s cavalier attitude toward these two aspects of air power, *Die Luftkriegführung* included no sections on either logistics or intelligence but closed with the note that sections dealing with those aspects of air power would be written later. They never were. Significantly, only Field Marshal Erhard Milch possessed some sense of the larger logistical

---

[37] For the offensive nature of German air-power conceptions, see particularly Boog et al., *Das Deutsche Reich und der Zweite Weltkrieg*, vol. 6, pp. 478, 549.
[38] *Fliegerabwehrkanone* (Flak), the air defense artillery.
[39] Boog et al., *Das Deutsche Reich und der Zweite Weltkrieg*, vol. 6, p. 438.
[40] Denied to them in 1919 by the Treaty of Versailles.
[41] Boog et al., *Das Deutsche Reich und der Zweite Weltkrieg*, vol. 6, pp. 437–439.

problems the Reich would face in fighting a world war and particularly the great danger that Germany would incur in bringing the United States into the conflict with its immense economic and industrial productive base.[42]

Meanwhile, in estimating the military potential of Germany's opponents, the performance of the *Luftwaffe*'s intelligence branch was appallingly bad even by the standards of that discipline.[43] Reinforcing the incompetence of German military intelligence was a deep strain of racial superiority that drove Nazi decision making and estimates of enemy strength. In the early war years, the German military's operational and tactical virtuosity and the failings of their opponents enabled its forces to evade the consequences of these weaknesses. But as the war continued, logistical and intelligence weaknesses were to exacerbate the *Wehrmacht*'s growing numerical inferiority on the war's battlefields.[44]

The Night Bomber Offensive, 1940 and 1941

British bombing efforts got off to a rocky start with the initiation of hostilities on 3 September 1939. Almost immediately, the RAF discovered that its government would not allow it to follow its preferred path of strategic bombing attacks against the Reich, its industries, or its population. The only bombers permitted to fly over German territory carried large bundles of propaganda leaflets, which Harris derisively described as providing the German population with toilet paper for the war's first year. The outcome of the few lethal bombing operations the government allowed the RAF to launch against the German fleet was disastrous. British bombers achieved nothing because the Chamberlain government's fear of killing civilians prohibited attacks even on warships tied up to wharves. Meanwhile, the second daylight raid against Kiel ran into a swarm of *Luftwaffe* fighters, which shredded the bomber formation. So much for the idea that RAF bombers could protect themselves against enemy fighters in

---

[42] In the early 1930s, Milch had visited the United States and focused on U.S. manufacturing centers on both coasts. Thus, he was not one to underestimate America's potential, as were most of the *Wehrmacht*'s other senior leaders.

[43] For a general discussion of the undervaluing of intelligence and its concomitant underestimation of enemy capabilities, see Horst Boog, "Higher Command and Leadership in the German Luftwaffe, 1935–1945," in Alfred F. Hurley and Robert C. Ehrhart, eds., *Airpower and Warfare: Proceedings of the Eighth Military History Symposium* (Washington, DC, 1979).

[44] Boog et al., *Das Deutsche Reich und der Zweite Weltkrieg*, vol. 6, p. 545.

daylight.⁴⁵ Whatever attacks Bomber Command would eventually launch against German targets would now obviously have to come at night.

Night leaflet missions during the appalling winter weather of 1939–1940 should have suggested there would be real problems in even identifying targets in Germany, much less hitting them accurately. It did not. On 10 May Winston Churchill replaced Neville Chamberlain as the prime minister. On the same day, the massed divisions of the *Wehrmacht* came west. The first three days of the advance of the German panzer divisions to the Meuse produced a series of major traffic jams on the narrow, winding roads of the Ardennes.⁴⁶ The RAF had no interest in such non-"strategic" targets. Instead, Bomber Command attacked "precision" targets lying in the Ruhr and other industrial sites in western Germany.

Meanwhile, in London, as the War Cabinet became aware of the momentum of the German advance between 10 and 15 May, it debated whether to unleash Bomber Command from the severe restrictions that the Chamberlain government had imposed on it.⁴⁷ On 15 May 1940 the Churchill government ordered the command to begin attacks on military targets throughout Germany, including oil refineries and marshaling yards.⁴⁸ At the conclusion of the meeting, Field Marshal "Tiny" Ironside, chief of the imperial general staff, noted in his diary: "I never saw anything so light up the faces of the RAF when they heard that they were to be allowed to bomb the oil refineries of the Ruhr.... They have built up their big bombers for this work, and they have been keyed up for the work ever since the war began. Now they have got their chance."⁴⁹

The problem was that the evidence was already at hand that Bomber Command's crews had no chance of hitting "precision targets." On 19 March 1940 a force of 50 RAF bombers had attacked the German seaplane base at Hörum on the island of Sylt in the North Sea, a target readily

---

⁴⁵ The RAF would launch several daylight raids deep into Germany with Lancasters in 1942 and 1943 but suffered unacceptable losses in achieving anything of significance. Only the Americans with their deep belief in daylight precision bombing would persist in the face of huge losses. In the end, however, only the appearance of the P-51 fighter, an aircraft capable of taking the B-17s all the way to Berlin, enabled the U.S. Army Air Forces to continue its daylight strategic bombing effort.

⁴⁶ For the extent of these traffic jams, see the pictures in Karl-Heinz Frieser, *Blitzkrieg Legende: Der Westfeldzug, 1940* (Stuttgart, 1995), p. 134.

⁴⁷ It was during this period that the Germans achieved their breakthrough on the Meuse, which led to their decisive victory over the Allied left wing and the collapse of Britain's position on the Continent.

⁴⁸ Public Records Office, PRO CAB 64/7, War Cabinet Meeting, 15 May 1940.

⁴⁹ Edmund Ironside, *The Ironside Diaries, 1937–1940*, ed. by Roderick MacLeod and Denis Kelly (London, 1962), p. 309.

identifiable by its shape and only a short distance across the North Sea. Of the attacking crews, 41 claimed they had identified and bombed the target. Aerial reconnaissance a few days later, however, revealed that the attack had inflicted no discernible damage on the target.[50] In other words, despite the aircrews' claims of success, none had managed to drop their bombs within a discrete area, easily identifiable by its location on the shores of the North Sea.

That stark evidence had little effect on the thinking of the RAF's senior leaders. On 28 April Bomber Command's new leader, Air Marshal Sir Charles Portal, sent a report to the air staff arguing that "if the [oil] plants proved to be as self-destructive as reported, Bomber Command could do 'immense damage' with its existing force."[51] Three months later Portal was still asserting that his bombers could hit oil targets and that the Reich's oil refineries would be "seriously damaged by a relatively light scale of attack."[52] For over a year, Bomber Command persisted in its "precision" campaign against German industrial, transportation, and petroleum targets. Meanwhile, the evidence continued to bubble up from below to indicate that the bombers were simply not hitting their targets. In November 1940, a conference of group navigators concluded that at least 65 percent of bombers dispatched were failing to hit their targets.[53]

Nevertheless, the following month Portal, now chief of the air staff, insisted to the chiefs of staff that 50 percent of the bombers could not only find but also hit targets "as small and unilluminated as oil plants."[54] Still, many within the RAF were already arguing for a campaign directed against the German population. As the deputy director of plans on the air staff suggested immediately after the German invasion of Denmark and Norway: "We know the brittleness of German morale [and thus should launch night raids] directed towards the moral and psychological factor."[55] In December 1940 the Ministry of Information assured the British population that the Germans could "not stand a quarter of the

---

[50] Webster and Frankland, *The Strategic Air Offensive against Germany*, vol. 1, *Preparation*, p. 140.
[51] Ibid., p. 141. It is not entirely clear whether Portal was being dishonest or oblivious during the period 1940–1941. Whichever, he was indeed making claims that were extraordinarily at odds with the realities in terms of Bomber Command's accuracy.
[52] Ibid., p. 151.
[53] Ibid., p. 216. The hope was that "the accuracy of night bombing [would] differ little from daylight bombing." However, it is also worth noting that there were also major problems with the accuracy of daylight bombing.
[54] Ibid., p. 216.
[55] Quoted in Greenhous et al., *The Crucible of War*, p. 536.

bombing" that Britain's population was then suffering in the night attacks of winter 1940.⁵⁶

In fact, the British were not even coming close to hitting targets accurately. German reports for the period May to July 1940 indicate that British bombs were spread over the Reich, in effect hitting more trees and cows than their intended targets. The first raid on the Ruhr on 15 May 1940 killed one dairyman in Cologne and wounded two people in Münster.⁵⁷ The problem was the British had not developed significant technological aids to help guide crews to their targets. As the official historians of the British strategic bombing campaign, Sir Charles Webster and Noble Frankland, noted:

> Thus, navigation remained largely a matter of observation, and by this means it was assumed that the majority of the night bombers would somehow or other arrive very close to their targets. Dilatory discussions about the need for technical aids such as radar and the Air Position Indicator did take place from time to time, but a general inertia overcame all significant progress until its serious consequences excited concern in Downing Street, and that did not happen until two years of war had passed.⁵⁸

The "general inertia" to which the official historians refer was aggravated by what one can only term the troglodytic refusal of a number of senior RAF leaders to believe that bombers required technological aids to find targets at night. In his memoirs R. V. Jones contrasts the eagerness with which Fighter Command under Dowding had embraced science and technology, with the lack of interest in Bomber Command in those areas: "Up to this time [summer 1941] it had been difficult to persuade Bomber Command to take science seriously."⁵⁹ As an historian of strategic bombing has noted, "when the Bomber Command missing rate started to get into the double figures, *then* its chiefs got interested in the scientific war of wits; but not before."⁶⁰

One might have thought that a close examination of the difficulties the Germans were having in hitting targets in Britain at night, even with the aid of *Knickebein*, would have suggested the need for technological aids

---

⁵⁶ Ibid., p. 541.
⁵⁷ Ibid., p. 537.
⁵⁸ Webster and Frankland, *The Strategic Air Offensive against Germany*, vol. 1, p. 205.
⁵⁹ Jones, *The Wizard War*, p. 210.
⁶⁰ Verrier, *The Bomber Offensive*, p. 148.

to help the bombers. Yet Arthur Harris, at the time the deputy chief of air staff, noted the following in an astonishing memorandum:

> Are we not tending to lose our sense of proportion over these German beams?... We use no beams ourselves but we bomb just as successfully as the Germans bomb deep into Germany.... I do not agree that these beams are in fact a serious menace to this country, or that they have proved to be in the past. They are simply aids to navigation, and it is within our experience that such aids are not indispensable to the successful prosecution of bombing expeditions.[61]

In August 1941, the RAF's illusions came crashing down. In early summer, Lord Cherwell, Churchill's scientific advisor and long a supporter of the bombing effort, directed D. M. B. Butt of the Cabinet Secretariat to examine the question of bombing accuracy. Butt studied more than 600 bombing photographs taken by British bombers in June and July that had attacked targets in France and Germany to ascertain the degree of the accuracy of their bombing. The official historians sum up his conclusions thusly:

> Mr. Butt concluded that of all the aircraft recorded as having attacked their targets, only one-third had gotten within five miles of them. The percentage of success, however, varied greatly with the geographical position of the target, the state of the weather and the intensity of the anti-aircraft defences. Over the French ports, for example, he calculated that two-thirds of the aircraft reported to have attacked the target had actually been within five miles. Over the Ruhr the proportion was reduced to *one-tenth*.... In full moon, two-fifths of the aircraft reported to have attacked their targets had, according to Mr. Butt's calculations, got within five miles of them. Without a moon the proportion fell to one fifteenth. These proportions only applied to those aircraft which claimed to have attacked their targets. If the total number of aircraft despatched was considered, the proportion would have been reduced by *another third*. [my italics][62]

The RAF's initial response to the Butt Report was largely negative. The commander of Bomber Command noted that "I don't think at this rate, we could have hoped to produce the damage which is known to have been achieved."[63] His direct subordinate, Air Vice Marshal Carr, commander of 4 Group, argued that "the lack of a photograph of the precise target should not be regarded as conclusive proof that the aircraft

---

[61] Quoted in Jones, *The Wizard War*, p. 169.
[62] Webster and Frankland, *The Strategic Air Offensive against Germany*, vol. 1, p. 178.
[63] Quoted in ibid., p. 179.

failed to attack its proper objective" – an astonishing rejection of clear evidence to the contrary.[64]

The episode demonstrates one of the great differences between the British and the Germans in regard to adaptation. While Hitler, as we shall see, overruled his military on numerous occasions, he did so largely on the basis of personal intuition and almost never on the arguments of civilian scientists or technologists. However, although Churchill never directly overruled his military advisers, he was certainly willing to include scientists and technologists in the discussions about fundamental issues. In this case, he forced the RAF and Bomber Command to pay serious attention to the Butt Report. The prime minister made it clear to Portal that the report represented "a very serious paper, and seems to require your most urgent action."[65] With "action this day" marked on the memorandum, Portal could not afford to ignore the prime minister's comments. The RAF now had to embrace technological change, whether its leaders were comfortable with new ideas or not.

Several individuals outside the air staff and Bomber Command had already raised the possibility of using long-range fighters as a means to resume daylight bombing in the face of the *Luftwaffe*'s daylight defenses. The first of these, not surprisingly, was Dowding, who had a nose for what was technologically possible. In March 1940, he pressed the air staff for developmental work on such a fighter. He met the following response from the assistant chief of air staff:

> It must, generally speaking, be regarded as axiomatic that the long-range fighter must be inferior in performance to the short-range fighter.... The question had been considered many times and the discussion had always tended to go in circles.... The conclusion had been reached that the escort fighter was really a myth. A fighter performing escort functions would, in reality, have to be a high performance and heavily armed bomber.[66]

In May 1941, Churchill himself expressed interest in the possibility of developing such a fighter. Portal condescendingly responded that long-range escort fighters could never hold their own against short-range fighters. There was, of course, no technological basis for that view. Instead,

---

[64] Quoted in ibid., p. 179. For the full Butt Report, see Webster and Frankland, *The Strategic Air Offensive against Germany*, vol. 4, appendix 13, "Report by Mr. Butt to Bomber Command on His Examination of Night Photographs," 18.8.41.
[65] Winston S. Churchill, *History of the Second World War*, vol. 4, *The Hinge of Fate* (Boston, 1951), p. 250.
[66] PRO AIR 16/1024, Minutes of the 20th Meeting of the Air Fighting Committee, held at Air Ministry, Whitehall, 12.3.40.

it more probably reflected Portal's desire to ensure that the government would not force the RAF to devote significant resources to a program that his prewar assumptions suggested the RAF did not need.[67] Churchill's response was that such a view closed "many doors."[68] As usual, he was right. The RAF had simply closed off an avenue of approach without any significant engineering or technological exploration, on the basis of prewar assumptions.[69] One might note that in late 1943 the *Luftwaffe*'s Research and Development Branch similarly assured the German Air Force's leadership that a long-range fighter "was a technical impossibility," just a few months before the P-51 arrived to shatter the *Luftwaffe*'s day-fighter force in the skies over Germany.[70]

Unable to conduct daylight bombing without incurring prohibitive losses, Bomber Command instead turned to an "area" bombing campaign – an effort to "dehouse" the population while the German people were still in their homes. Unfortunately, in 1941, Bomber Command could not even perform area bombing with much effectiveness. Following an attack on 1 October 1941 aimed at Karlsruhe and Stuttgart, German reports indicated British bombers were over "Aachen, Eupen, Malmédy, Coblenz, Neuwied, Kreuznach, Frankfurt am Main, Wiesbaden, Limburg, Darmstadt, Mainz, Worms, Trier, Offenburg, Saarfels, Nuremberg, Erlangen, Bamberg, Bayreuth, Coburg, Pegnitz, Aschaffenburg, Schweinfurt, Würzburg, Regensburg, Weiden, and Chemnitz."[71]

At least now, Bomber Command could no longer ignore its inability to find even large targets at night. One of its first responses led to a major expansion of its Operational Research Section. From this point on, Bomber Command's leadership, pushed by Churchill and Lord Cherwell, would examine scientific and technological problems through realistic analysis rather than prewar assumptions that had largely rested on hope.[72]

---

[67] In fact, the American and Japanese naval air forces were conducting a race to develop long-range fighters to extend the range of their carrier aircraft.
[68] Webster and Frankland, *The Strategic Air Offensive against Germany*, vol. 1, p. 177.
[69] The U.S. Army Air Corps and later the Army Air Forces would prove to be just as blind in their belief in the myth – already contradicted by the evidence of the first two years of the Second World War – of the ability of great formations of B-17s and B-24s to defend themselves against any defenses the Germans could throw up against them.
[70] Verrier, *The Bomber Offensive*, p. 310.
[71] Webster and Frankland, *The Strategic Air Offensive against Germany*, vol. 1, p. 185.
[72] As the former chief of staff of the U.S. Army, General Gordon Sullivan, noted on a number of occasions: "Hope is not a method." There were times that Bomber Command's Operational Research Center was used simply to buttress the arguments and assumptions of the command's leaders.

Despite the evidence that Bomber Command was inflicting relatively little damage on the Germans and that matters would not improve until it achieved significant improvement in bombing accuracy, the campaign had to continue for political reasons. In 1941, it was the only means available for the British to punish the Germans for the terrible suffering they had inflicted and were continuing to inflict on Europe's captive populations. Moreover, for most in Britain, the bombing campaign appeared the only way to pay back the Germans for the damage they had inflicted on Britain in 1940 and 1941.[73] In retrospect, the cost may appear to have been excessive, but dispassionate after-the-fact analysis misses the political demands of the time.

Even so, that cost confirms that the British in 1941 were receiving a most inadequate return on investment. A single raid on 7 November 1941 underscored what weather and the Reich's air defenses could inflict on attacking bombers. Out of a force of 400 bombers, the British lost 37, nearly 10 percent. Certain targets exacted even heavier loss percentages: aircraft attacking Berlin lost 12.5 percent, Mannheim 13 percent, and the Ruhr Valley 21 percent.[74] Unless Bomber Command could find means to lower its losses and improve its effectiveness, it confronted the real possibility Britain's political leaders would siphon substantial portions of its strength to other tasks such as the war in the Mediterranean or long-range patrols into the Atlantic to battle the U-boat menace.[75]

The German Response

As was typical of the German "way of war," the *Luftwaffe* focused almost exclusively on the immediate military problems confronting the Reich during the first two-and-a-half years of the war. Through summer 1941, the conquest of Poland, and Western Europe, and then the Battle of Britain, including the nighttime Blitz, absorbed its energies and focus. The long-term threat of British bombing disappeared in the fog of a

---

[73] Noble Frankland commented in his summary of the Combined Bomber Offensive that "The British are not such a placid people as they try to imagine. Cornered and wounded, they became very dangerous and with virtually one accord, through Bomber Command... they sprang at the throat of their seemingly invincibly superior opponent." Noble Frankland, *The Bombing Offensive against Germany* (London, 1965), p. 100.

[74] Webster and Frankland, *The Strategic Air Offensive against Germany*, vol. 1, pp. 185–186.

[75] It is now clear that British leaders would have done well to do precisely the latter, given the success that U-boats were currently enjoying.

seemingly endless string of operational victories on the Continent and in the Mediterranean. In June 1941 the *Luftwaffe*'s chief of staff, General Hans Jeschonnek, greeted the invasion of the Soviet Union with delight. Nevertheless, the fact that his service possessed fewer bombers in June 1941 than were in its front-line squadrons at the beginning of the May 1940 campaign against Western Europe suggests how badly the *Luftwaffe* was preparing for its major commitments in the invasion of the Soviet Union.[76]

In summer 1940, the *Luftwaffe* began to respond to the nightly sorties of British bombers into German airspace. In July it established the 1st Night Fighter Division in Brussels under General Joseph Kammhuber, a bomber pilot who had been shot down during the French campaign but who had returned to duty after the armistice with Vichy France. His command consisted of a hodgepodge of units, including day fighters (Bf 109s and Bf 110s) and Do 17 bombers. Initially, the new air defense system relied on acoustical detection in combination with searchlights. The first long-range Würzburg radar sets, devoted exclusively to air defense, did not arrive until October 1940. Moreover, none of Kammhuber's aircraft possessed airborne radar in the fall of 1940. The overall strength of the night defense force at the end of 1940 suggests how little effort the *Luftwaffe* was putting into the 1st Night Fighter Division: 165 aircraft (the table of organization called for 195 aircraft) and 173 crews. Only 104 of those aircraft were in commission (in flyable condition), while only 61 of the crews had qualified as combat ready.[77]

Ironically, in one of the few areas where the Germans enjoyed some success in late 1940 and 1941 – night-fighter intruder operations against British bomber bases – Hitler stepped in and ordered them stopped. Apparently, the *Führer* felt that shooting down British bombers over their bases would have no psychological impact on the German people.[78] Thus, the German defensive system was largely a hit-or-miss affair. But with the British unable even to locate cities most of the time, the teething troubles of the new defensive system did not appear particularly troublesome to either the *Luftwaffe* leaders or those of the Reich.

---

[76] Overall there had been little change in the *Luftwaffe*'s force structure between May 1940 and June 1941. In May 1940, the Germans had possessed 1,711 bombers; in June 1941, they possessed exactly 200 fewer. See Table XII, "German Aircraft Strength May 11, 1940 and June 21, 1941," in Williamson Murray, *Luftwaffe* (Baltimore, 1985), p. 83.
[77] Boog et al., *Das Deutsche Reich und der Zweite Weltkrieg*, vol. 6, p. 484.
[78] He was to continue to have such attitudes well into 1944. Murray, *Luftwaffe*, p. 130.

Thus, Germany's air defense capabilities grew only slowly from 1940 through the end of 1941, particularly since the high command's attention focused almost exclusively on what was happening in the war against the Soviet Union. As the Würzburg radar sites slowly came on line, German air defenses largely depended on a combination of searchlights, radar where available, anti-aircraft artillery, and night fighters, the last still not making a particularly impressive showing. In effect, there was no overall system of night defense in place, while a number of headquarters controlled the units deployed to support the night defense of the Reich.

By the end of 1941, Kammhuber possessed a larger but not significantly more effective force of night fighters: 302 aircraft, 150 in commission; and 358 aircrew, only 155 of whom were combat ready.[79] By this point he had also extended a series of ground control intercept (GCI) boxes from Holland south across Belgium almost to northern France – a line the British dubbed the Kammhuber Line. Nevertheless, the combination of the few night fighters, the short- (*Freya*) and long-range (*Würzburg*) radars, searchlights, and massive deployments of high-velocity anti-aircraft artillery was beginning to inflict increasing losses on the attacking British bombers, which, combined with the losses from weather and accidents, were bringing Bomber Command's loss rates close to the level of "unacceptable."

One continuing weakness in the "German way of war" lay in the military's poor management of the signals and radar technicians who undergirded the Reich's efforts in electronic warfare. This reflected in part the complexity of Germany's high-quality electronic equipment, but the more significant factor was that German leaders regarded technical work as not being related to combat and hence not deserving of the highest quality manpower. Aggravating the situation was the fact that Hitler had banned amateur radio in the mid-1930s because of his fear dissidents would utilize it to work against the regime. Thus, the pool of those experienced in radio and electronics was smaller in Nazi Germany than in Britain or the United States.[80]

But the problem with the German night-fighter defenses was not just a matter of senior leaders making bad decisions. Kammhuber was clearly a part of the problem. His relationship with Germany's scientific and technological communities does not appear to have been particularly good. The initial establishment of the Kammhuber Line represented a

---

[79] Boog et al., *Das Deutsche Reich und der Zweite Weltkrieg*, vol. 6, p. 492.
[80] Jones, *The Wizard War*, p. 244.

technological achievement of the first order, but the failure to develop an "identification friend or foe" (IFF) capability would eventually rob the system of much of its usefulness, while Kammhuber's investment in it made him less than willing to try new ideas. In simple terms, Kammhuber was a "control freak." In 1942, he turned down a proposal to build a wooden night fighter similar to the Mosquito used by the British with such success because, he argued, it might not display well on the Würzburg radars and thus would hinder control from the ground.[81]

"Bomber" Harris Arrives

In February 1942 Air Marshal Sir Arthur Harris assumed command of Bomber Command. Few other commanders in the Second World War equaled Harris's bloody-minded approach to war. Outspoken, contemptuous of others, within or outside of his service, who held contrary views, Harris was one of the most controversial senior officers in the war. Max Hastings has drawn a wonderful portrait of "Bomber" Harris:

> Sir Arthur Harris, as he now became, possessed something of the earthy, swaggering ruthlessness of an Elizabethan buccaneer. A broad man of medium height, his piercing eye gave him immediate presence in any company.... He gave no sign of fearing God or man, and in Washington [where he served for a short period in 1941] his outbursts of frankness left behind a trail of savaged American sensitivities.... His dry, cutting, often vulgar wit was legendary throughout the RAF, as was his hatred of the British Army and the Royal Navy.... He seemed to like the ogre-ish role that fortune had cast for him. His contemporaries called him 'Bert,' but his crews called him 'Butcher,' 'Butch' for short. His subordinates at High Wycombe were deeply in awe of him, and there was little scope for dissent in his councils. He was a man of startling directness, and his temper cannot have been improved by the ulcers from which he suffered throughout the war.[82]

Harris summed up his bombing philosophy with the comment that "[i]n Bomber Command we have always worked on the principle that bombing anything in Germany is better than bombing nothing."[83] He was not an innovator or a man of clear judgment, but he was certainly the right choice to restore Bomber Command's position in British strategy in the

---

[81] Greenhous et al., *The Crucible of War*, p. 609.
[82] Hastings, *Bomber Command*, p. 135.
[83] Webster and Frankland, *The Strategic Air Offensive against Germany*, vol. 3, *Victory* (London, 1961), p. 82.

face of its dismal showing thus far in the war.[84] Whether he was the man to lead the command in 1944 and 1945, when it possessed substantially new technologies as well as improved operational and tactical capabilities, is for the reader to judge.

As he assumed his new duties, Harris enjoyed a number of advantages his predecessors had not. The command was finally receiving heavy bombers in quantity: the Short Stirlings and particularly the Halifaxes and Lancasters, which provided an immense increase in capabilities. But equally important was the fact that the British were gaining an edge in the battle of the electronic war and technology.[85] The aircraft industry now began to equip bombers with *Gee*, a navigational device that used the intersection of radio beams from different stations in March 1942. The device afforded British bombers greater positional accuracy than had been the case with dead reckoning or celestial navigation.

Above all, Harris brought drive and leadership to a command suffering from a collapse in morale. Perhaps most important was the fact that Harris understood his command's limitations. There would be no more talk of "precision" targets, which he derisively described as "panacea" targets. Given the threat of German defenses and difficulties in identifying targets, Harris carefully picked the initial targets. In early March 1942, using *Gee*, Bomber Command struck the Renault armament factory outside of Paris, which it devastated, destroying more than 40 percent of the plant's machine tools.[86] Over the next two months of attacks on the Ruhr, there was no comparable success because of German defenses and the thick industrial haze that hung over the region, which obscured even urban areas the size of the Ruhr's cities.

However, at the end of March, using newly developed incendiaries, Bomber Command struck the ancient city of Lübeck near the Baltic Sea, not because of its industrial importance but because, as Harris suggested

---

[84] As the official historians note: "[Harris] had, after all opposed the introduction of the incendiary technique, the creation of the Pathfinder Force and the development of the bomb with which the Möhne and Eder dams were breached. He had confidently supposed that the Battle of Berlin could win the war, and he had declared that Bomber Command would be operationally incapable of carrying out the French railroad campaign." Ibid., p. 80.

[85] That is the persuasive conclusion of Gebhard Aders, *History of the German Night Fighter Force, 1917–1945* (London, 1978), p. 81.

[86] Webster and Frankland, *The Strategic Air Offensive against Germany*, vol. 1, pp. 387–388.

in a letter to the air staff, it was "built more like a fire-lighter than a human habitation."[87] Although the city lay beyond the range of *Gee*, it was on the coast and easy to identify. Moreover, its position on the Baltic coast allowed Harris to do an end run around the Kammhuber Line through Denmark, thus avoiding much of the German air defenses. The attack pulverized the city. At the end of April, the command struck Rostock, a city similar to Lübeck and also close to the Baltic Sea. The first two attacks largely failed, but a third wrecked the city and also inflicted major damage on the Heinkel factory lying on its outskirts.[88]

But Harris's major triumph of 1942 came with his attack on Cologne at the end of May.[89] By scratching together every aircraft in his command and expropriating most of the bombers assigned to its operational training units, he assembled 1,000 aircraft. On the evening of 30 May, a great armada of 1,046 British bombers set out to attack the Rhineland city. Daylight reconnaissance photographs taken on the following day indicated "heavy and widespread" damage. Three-hundred acres of damage had occurred in the city center. The damage was "on a much larger scale than any previously inflicted on a German city."[90] Moreover, Bomber Command lost only 37 bombers – a surprisingly low loss rate, considering the inexperience of many of the air crews. Equally important the raid achieved much propaganda value not only for the British but also for those suffering under German occupation.

Harris attempted to replicate the Cologne success a few nights later with another thousand-plane raid, this time against the industrial city of Essen. While the aircraft losses were less than those suffered during the Cologne attack, the raid was an abysmal failure. So inaccurate was the bombing that the *Oberkommando der Wehrmacht (OKW)* appears to have believed that the main attack was aimed at Duisberg and Oberhausen

---

[87] Ibid., p. 391.
[88] The damage included the destruction of a substantial portion of the jigs for the He 219, the major hope for the German night-fighter force, thereby delaying its production for a considerable period of time.
[89] There was considerable worry before the raid throughout the Bomber Command about the possibility of midair collisions between the bombers. However, the command's Operational Research Section was able to calculate that casualties would be fewer by concentrating the bomber stream of 1,000 aircraft into a small window of time, thus saturating the defenses; even with such a concentration of bombers, there would be only slight possibilities of air-to-air collisions.
[90] Quoted from the original reports in Webster and Frankland, *The Strategic Air Offensive against Germany*, vol. 1, p. 407.

rather than Essen.[91] For the rest of the year, the command failed to achieve further successes on the scale of Rostock and Lübeck, much less Cologne.

There would be no more thousand-bomber raids for the rest of the year because such efforts threatened to wreck Bomber Command's operational training units. Moreover, even though air defenses remained low on the Reich's list of military priorities, the combination of weather, antiaircraft fire, German radar, and fighters imposed a loss rate on British bombers that flirted with the category of unacceptable losses. Despite steadily increasing production, Bomber Command was barely able to maintain a strength of 500 bombers in its front-line units. Losses for 1942 were 1,404 aircraft shot down with a further 2,724 damaged by enemy action.[92] Of the new four-engine bombers reaching front-line squadrons, Bomber Command lost no fewer than 228 Stirlings, 249 Halifaxes, and 202 Lancasters.[93]

The heavy losses forced major tactical adaptations as well as technological innovations, some driven by the command itself, others forced on it from the outside. In the latter category, Harris set up a "pathfinder" force despite his strenuous objections to the idea in August 1942.[94] Once it was a reality, however, Harris appointed one of the most innovative and ferocious air commanders of the war, D. C. T. Bennett, to its command. Bennett was one of the few senior leaders in the RAF to have flown on active operations early in the war,[95] and continued to fly on active operations even after taking command. Throughout the war, he would fly his Mosquito to watch the performance of his pathfinders in bombing

---

[91] Ibid., p. 411.
[92] Webster and Frankland, *The Strategic Air Offensive against Germany*, vol. 2, *Endeavour*, p. 91.
[93] Public Records Office, AIR 22/203, War Room Manual of Bomber Command Operations, 1939–1945, compiled by Air Ministry War Room (Statistical Section), p. 9.
[94] For discussions on the formation of the pathfinder force as well as Harris's initial opposition, see Hastings, *Bomber Command*, pp. 191–192; and John Terrain, *The Right of the Line: The Royal Air Force in the European War, 1939–1945* (London, 1985), pp. 499–502.
[95] D. C. T. Bennett was shot down over Norway in early 1942 and then walked to Sweden to return to active duty. He commented sarcastically about his fellow group commanders in Bomber Command that they had not been "fortunate enough to be permitted to operate themselves [because of their rank and position]." Webster and Frankland, *The Strategic Air Offensive against Germany*, vol. 2, p. 433. Harris commented on Bennett in the following terms after the war: "his own intellectual powers made him impatient with slower and differently constituted minds, so that some people found him difficult to work with. He could not suffer fools gladly, and by his own high standards there were many fools." Quoted in Terraine, *The Right of the Line*, p. 502.

German cities and then would return home ahead of them to critique the crews mercilessly on their return.

The most important tactical rather than technological change was Bomber Command's increasing success in flooding the Kammhuber Line by concentrating the bomber stream in both time and space. It also tended to concentrate the bombing within a narrow framework, which provided those on the ground with less time to respond to the damage that British HE (high-explosive) bombs – of increasing weight – and incendiaries inflicted. The result was that German defenses, Flak as well as fighters, had only a relatively short window in which to deal with the attacking force.

Improved German air defenses forced other adaptations on the bombing force: British bombers no longer flew deep penetration raids during periods of full moon because the light made them too visible to the night fighters. The pathfinder force also received the first of an increasingly effective set of target indicators to guide the main force. Moreover, the RAF's 80 Wing was beginning to employ increasingly sophisticated electronic countermeasures against the German night defenses. These included jamming, both airborne and land-based, as well as direct interference with communications between German night-fighter pilots and their controllers.[96] By March 1943, Bomber Command represented an entirely new force compared with a year earlier, not only with the arrival of heavy bombers but also in terms of its tactical and technological sophistication.[97] As Harris suggested in his memoirs, "At long last we were ready and equipped."[98]

The Scientific War, the War of Production, and the German Response: 1942

Because of certain weaknesses in their electronics industry, the British had developed centimetric radar, while the German scientists had developed decimetric radars, which demanded higher technological capabilities and

---

[96] Ironically, well into 1942, substantial portions of the RAF opposed the utilization of electronic countermeasures for fear that the Germans would use such methods against British defenses even though the Royal Navy and the German Navy were utilizing jamming extensively against each other, including during the Channel dash by the German battle cruisers, the *Scharnhorst* and the *Gneisenau*. See Jones, *The Wizard War*, p. 289.
[97] For a discussion of Bomber Command's position at the beginning of 1943, see Hastings, *Bomber Command*, p. 194.
[98] Marshal of the RAF Sir Arthur Harris, *Bomber Offensive* (London, 1947), p. 144.

engineering but provided a clearer picture.[99] Interestingly, the Germans appear to have believed that radar on the centimetric wavelength would not work. As late as November 1942, a senior German scientist, Dr. Wilhelm Runge, the chief of the Telefunken Laboratories, commented that one could achieve little in the centimetric spectrum – and "only at great cost." Several weeks later, the Germans recovered an *H2S* device (which provided British navigators with a radar picture of the ground) and, to their astonishment, discovered that it was working on the centimetric spectrum[100] Thus, to a certain extent, Göring was justified in his comment that the cause of the increasing disadvantage under which the *Luftwaffe* was working was the result of German scientists having "too little in their thick heads."[101] Because of their choice to use the centimetric portion of the spectrum of radio waves, the British were able to develop airborne radars with less drag and weight than the German equivalents; moreover, it allowed them to develop an airborne radar, *H2S*, that tracked ground features.

Already by March 1942, the Bomber Command had introduced *Gee*, (a navigational device that allowed navigators to plot the position of a bomber through intersecting radio beams). In December 1942, *Oboe* (a more sophisticated navigational device) became available. *Oboe* provided both "a higher degree of accuracy than *Gee*" and "could thus be used as a blind bombing or blind marking device.[102] *H2S* then came into limited use in January 1943. In addition, the RAF had begun jamming German electronic signals in October 1942.[103] Moreover, the British had developed an IFF system before the war that allowed their ground radar operators to identify Allied aircraft, an especially important capability in terms of preventing British night fighters from attacking their own bombers. However, the Germans had failed to develop such a system through 1943, which exacerbated problems for their radar operators in guiding night fighters onto their targets.[104]

[99] Which is one of the reason the German signals intelligence, operating off the *Graf Zeppelin* dirigible in the English Channel in summer 1939, had been unable to detect British radar. They were looking in the wrong part of the electromagnetic spectrum – a clear case of mirror imaging.
[100] Aders, *History of the German Night Fighter Force*, p. 74.
[101] Boog et al., *Das Deutsche Reich und der Zweite Weltkrieg*, vol. 6, p. 556.
[102] Webster and Frankland, *The Strategic Air Offensive against Germany*, vol. 1, p. 317.
[103] Aders, *History of the German Night Fighter Force*, p. 79.
[104] The 9/11 Report, in one of its major insights, identifies the disaster as being the result of a lack of "imagination" on the part of all too many of those involved in the intelligence

Equally important was the advantage British scientific intelligence had gained in understanding the electronic parameters that were driving the technology of German radars. The first step toward gaining this advantage lay in a brilliant piece of scientific intelligence. With the help of low-level photographic reconnaissance, R. V. Jones, whom we have met before, identified a Würzburg site at Bruneval on the French side of the channel. Jones then persuaded the army, the Royal Navy, and the RAF to cooperate in launching a joint airborne raid with a seaborne extraction.[105] Despite a few small glitches, the raid succeeded, and the paratroopers brought out a complete *Würzburg* set. The British gained an enormous amount of scientific intelligence from that success.[106] R. V. Jones points out:

> So what had we gained? A firsthand knowledge of the state of German radar technology, in the form in which it was almost certainly being applied to our principal objective, the German night fighter control system. We now knew the extreme limits of wavelength to which Würzburg could be tuned, and that it had no built-in counter either to jamming or to spurious reflectors; moreover, it seemed that German radar operators were probably less able than our own. Besides giving us an estimate of the German rate of production and a knowledge of the German quality of design and engineering, it had provided us with the equivalent of a navigational 'fix' in confirming the dead 'reckoning' in our intelligence voyage into the German defenses.[107]

Most disastrously from the German point of view was the fact that neither Hitler and Göring nor the German high command took the nighttime threat seriously. Consequently, in late 1941 the night-fighter force found a number of its pilots and units redeployed to serve as close air support for German forces on the Eastern Front or to support Axis operations in the Mediterranean. The emphasis in German strategy remained firmly on

---

efforts before the event. In this case, a lack of imagination was clearly at work among both *Luftwaffe* leaders and scientists in the air defense effort. For the German lack of IFF capability, see Jones, *The Wizard War*, p. 287.

[105] The War Office, however, was not willing to allow the RAF radar technician, who accompanied the paratroopers to dismantle the Würzburg antenna and other electronic gear, to wear an army uniform and receive an army service number. Had the raid failed, the Germans would have immediately identified him as possessing the information about what the British were after. Jones, *The Wizard War*, p. 238.

[106] An unintended effect was the fact that since the Bruneval site had been unprotected, the Germans then placed extensive barbed-wire entanglements and trenches around all of the sites, which thus made them much easier for the British to identify. Jones, *The Wizard War*, p. 246.

[107] Ibid., p. 245.

the offensive war on the periphery – the east and the Mediterranean.[108] To wage that war, the *Luftwaffe* needed bombers, not night fighters. Left at the bottom of production priorities, the night-fighter force had to make do with a hodgepodge of the leavings. Meanwhile, a rising tide of losses in the night-fighter force – 31 in February 1942; 43 in March; 64 in April; 68 in May and June; and 107 in July – ensured the end strength of night fighters in both crews and aircraft would not grow to meet the steadily increasing threat.[109]

The one aircraft that might have made a major difference, the He 219, designed especially for the night-fighter role, ran into production difficulties as the result of damage inflicted on the Heinkel factory by Bomber Command's raid on Rostok in 1942. Thereafter, it failed to receive the priorities it deserved. The Reich's leadership was no more forthcoming with respect to the larger framework of night defense against the bomber offensive. In October 1942, Kammhuber asked for an additional 600 Würzburg radars and 150,000 more men. Göring exploded, exclaiming that the *Luftwaffe* would find it cheaper "to attack the British directly than to build up this gigantic organization."[110]

But there was a larger problem with German adaptation, and that was the result of two strategic factors. The first was the failure of the Germans to mobilize the economies of the occupied nations beginning in summer 1940.[111] The swift victories in Western Europe led the Nazi leaders to believe they had won the war.[112] Consequently, it was not until the Germans were finally stopped in front of Moscow in December 1941 that they got serious about utilizing the resources and industrial power

---

[108] Even in the midst of the desperate fighting over December 1941 and January 1942, as the Germans struggled to save Army Group Center from collapse, Hitler's focus was already on resuming the offensive in summer 1942 against Soviet forces defending the Volga and the Caucasus.

[109] Greenhous et al., *The Crucible of War*, p. 662.

[110] Ibid., pp. 661–662.

[111] One of the great myths of the Second World War has to do with the argument that the Germans failed to mobilize their economy in depth before the war because of their so-called *Blitzkrieg* strategy. In fact, in September 1939, the German economy was close to breaking under a strain that resulted from the Nazi regime's devoting close to 18 percent of GDP to military spending. The increases that the Germans were able to achieve after 1941 in military production were almost entirely a result of their ability to mobilize the European continent for the purposes of the Reich. For a discussion of these issues, see Murray, *The Change in the European Balance of Power*, chap. 1.

[112] The operations officer of the Armed Forces High Command (the OKW), Colonel General Alfred Jodl, commented in a memorandum on 30 June 1940: "To all intents and purposes, the war is won; all we have to figure out is how to win it."

that were now available to them in the conquered European countries. Their opponents, having been caught behind the power curve in 1940 and 1941, approached the mobilization of their economies in a far more ruthless fashion. In the sector of aircraft production, for example, the British and Americans, partially drawing on their prewar overestimations of *Luftwaffe* strength and production capabilities, set in motion massive production targets and provided the resources to meet most of them.[113]

In effect, the Anglo-American powers recognized that they were now engaged in a massive air battle of attrition against the Germans and that it would be aircraft production and the training of pilots and ground crews to support that production in the long run that would win the air war.[114] The results would not be fully evident until early 1943, but by then the Western Allies enjoyed a massive edge in aircraft production of all types over the Germans, even considering what the Pacific theater or the Soviets might siphon off. Meanwhile, the German leadership scoffed at American production claims. Typically, Göring casually dismissed reports about American industrial potential with the comment that the Americans "could only produce cars and refrigerators."[115]

The second strategic error lay in the failure of German leaders to make serious operational and strategic choices.[116] The fact was that in 1941 and 1942 they were waging massive offensive ground and air campaigns against the Soviet Union, an offensive holding action in the Mediterranean, and an offensive effort with their U-boats to cut the supply lines to Britain.[117] Thus, preoccupied with the tactical and operational problems confronting them on the periphery in those three great campaigns and unimpressed by the seeming ineffectiveness of British nighttime raids, the Germans missed the gathering threat that Bomber Command represented. The defeat in front of Moscow in December 1941 did result in

---

[113] For a discussion of these and associated issues dealing with aircraft production, see Murray, *Luftwaffe*, pp. 60, 92–104.
[114] There was some irony in this recognition because the prewar air theorists had argued that air war would prevent the attrition that had characterized the First World War. In every respect, they were wrong, because both on the ground and in the air, the Second World War was won by massive battles of attrition, in which, as Napoleon had suggested, God was invariably on the side of the big battalions.
[115] Asher Lee, *Göring: Air Leader* (New York, 1972), p. 58.
[116] Gerhard Weinberg's *A World at Arms: A Global History of World War II* (Cambridge, 1994) is particularly good on this.
[117] Both Gerhard Weinberg, the foremost historian of the Second World War, and this author have argued strongly that the U-boat campaign represented a disastrous misuse of resources, particularly given the Reich's other commitments.

a considerable effort to increase overall production, but the *Luftwaffe* now had to compete for industrial resources with an army that had lost much of its equipment in the disastrous winter campaign of 1941–1942 against the Soviets. Field Marshal Milch did succeed in upping German production by 4,000 aircraft in 1942. But that number paled in comparison to what Anglo-American production achieved during 1942. In fact, the Germans were losing the production race at an increasing rate.

The attacks against Lübeck and Rostock disturbed a few staff officers in the air defense business, while Goebbels raged in his diary about the destruction of German art by British barbarians.[118] In the aftermath of Bomber Command's thousand aircraft raid on Cologne, *Luftwaffe* leaders initially claimed a major success in terms of bombers shot down, but they underestimated the size of the attacking force by 50 percent. However, British propaganda and the damage on the ground soon told another story, as Hitler pointedly noted to the *Luftwaffe*'s chief of staff, Hans Jeschonnek. On June 3, Hitler received Jeschonnek in a furious mood. He ridiculed the *Luftwaffe*'s estimates, as well as its efforts to "gloss over or to describe what was a catastrophe as a defensive victory." In his conversation with the chief of staff, Hitler made several points fraught with significance for the future of the night defense effort. First, he underlined that the only reply to such "terror" attacks would have to be retaliation against British cities. He then pointed out that the Cologne raid represented an attempt by the British to establish a second front by aerial means.[119] However, as Bomber Command failed to achieve further major successes in 1942, the impact of the Cologne raid faded from Hitler's mind. Until early 1943, the Führer remained largely focused on Operation Blau (Blue), the drive to Stalingrad and the Caucasus, and thereafter the collapse of the Stalingrad front – not on the battle against Bomber Command.

The one resource the Germans continued to provide in abundance for the night defenses ironically was anti-aircraft artillery. By the end of 1941, the *Luftwaffe* had recognized that Flak was the least effective

---

[118] Josef Goebbels, *The Goebbels Diaries, 1942–1943*, trans. and ed. by Louis Lochner (New York, 1948), pp. 154–155, 186. Goebbels also noted: "Nevertheless it can't be overlooked that English air raids have increased in scope and importance, and that if they can be continued for weeks along these lines, they might quite conceivably have a demoralizing effect on the German population." *The Goebbels Diaries*, p. 160.

[119] *Kriegstagebuch des Oberkommandos der Wehrmachts*, 1942, vol. 2, part 2, ed. by Andreas Hillgruber (Stuttgart, 1982), entry for 3.6.42, p. 400. See also Nicolaus von Below, *Als Hitlers Adjutant, 1937–1945* (Mainz, 1980), pp. 311–312.

defensive measure in its arsenal against high-flying aircraft. As each Bomber Command raid crossed the Kammhuber Line and then engaged a major German population center, it met massive barrages from the high-velocity 88-mm, 105-mm, and 128-mm guns that made up the *Luftwaffe*'s anti-aircraft force. These batteries expended ammunition at a prodigious rate. Unfortunately for the Germans, the results were more visually and aurally spectacular than effective. For example, the 88-mm Flak 36 weapon required an average expenditure of 16,000 plus shells to hit – not necessarily bring down – a single bomber flying at high altitude.[120] Part of the problem was that muzzle velocities had increased little since 1918, when anti-aircraft fire was relatively effective. However, the speed and altitude of aircraft had increased enormously, which made them targets that were far more elusive.[121]

Nevertheless, throughout the war the Germans continued to expand their Flak forces at a furious pace. From 791 heavy Flak batteries in 1940, antiaircraft forces expanded to 967 in 1941, 1,148 in 1942, and 2,132 in 1943, with more to come in 1944. A conservative estimate would put the number of heavy antiaircraft weapons firing into the skies over the Reich by 1944 at 15–20,000 and the number of soldiers supporting this effort at well over half a million, even after one has made allowance for the Hitler Youth and various other nonmilitary personnel engaged in the Flak effort – the former, of course, could have performed far more useful tasks for the Reich.[122]

This effort to build up the anti-aircraft force not only represented an enormous expenditure of industrial resources diverted from the production of night fighters, not to mention the support of the ground forces; the volume of fire loosed against the attacking bombers also used up huge amounts of ammunition to little purpose.[123] Ironically, in view of the German belief in their technological sophistication, no one in the Reich's scientific or technological spheres possessed the imagination to push for the development of proximity fuses, which American industry was already producing in 1943.

Yet, in September 1942, Göring decreed the formation of 900 more heavy and 750 more medium and light Flak batteries, along with 200

---

[120] And that was the weapon with which most Flak batteries were equipped. Friedhelm Golücke, *Schweinfurt und der strategische Luftkrieg, 1943* (Paderborn, 1980), p. 156.
[121] Boog et al., *Das Deutsche Reich und der Zweite Weltkrieg*, vol. 6, p. 553.
[122] Golücke, *Schweinfurt und der strategische Luftkrieg*, p. 153.
[123] Much of that Flak ammunition consumed large quantities of aluminum, a key component in the production of aircraft.

more searchlight batteries. The driver behind this effort to increase the Flak forces was clearly Hitler.[124] Goebbels recorded in his diary in February 1943 that Hitler aimed at "expanding the Flak to a great extent" in the hope that "by late fall 1943 the territory of the Reich would possess Flak to such an extent that to fly through this Flak belt will represent an improbability, not to say impossibility. Even were the Flak seldom to hit its target, the enemy pilot would think three times before flying through it."[125]

Hitler's own experience in the First World War clearly influenced his decision making, particularly his belief in the efficacy of artillery, but his attitudes also reflected the pressure brought to bear on him by Goebbels and the Nazi *Gauleiters* (district party leaders), who believed that the sound of anti-aircraft guns blasting away at the British bombers reassured the population and kept up German morale.[126] All of this missed the reality that night fighters were more than twice as effective as Flak artillery despite their small numbers.[127] Nevertheless, Goebbels attacked the *Luftwaffe* in April 1943 at a meeting of *Gauleiters* from western Germany with the argument that it was simply not providing the Reich's cities with sufficient anti-aircraft guns for their defense.[128] Thus, because of the pressures from the uninformed in high political positions, the Reich's night air defense priorities would remain out of kilter to the war's end.

The Ruhr and Hamburg: Bomber Command on the Edge

In March 1943, Bomber Command began a major effort to take out the Ruhr with a series of major attacks on its industrial cities. It was now at last able to deal out devastating damage that was to have a major impact on the Reich's industrial output. Concerning the latter, the official historians of Britain's strategic bombing effort estimate that Bomber Command's attacks were sufficient to reduce the industrial output by

---

[124] For Hitler's demand that the *Luftwaffe* place more emphasis on Flak in its armaments programs, see Bundes Archiv/Militärarchiv (BA/MA), RL 3/60, Besprechungsnotiz nr 46/42, 6.3.42, Karinhall, Göring, Milch, Jeschonnek, v. Brauchitsch.
[125] Goebbels's diary entry for 22 February 1943, quoted in Boog, et al., *Das Deutsche Reich und der Zweite Weltkrieg*, vol. 6, p. 554.
[126] One of the major indirect effects of the British nighttime bombing offensive was that it caused the Germans to expend huge resources on men, material, and military capabilities in building up defensive capabilities that the Germans could have used far more effectively on the ground on the Eastern Front or, after June 6, 1944, in Normandy.
[127] Boog et al., *Das Deutsche Reich und der Zweite Weltkrieg*, vol. 6, p. 555.
[128] Goebbels, *The Goebbels Diaries*, entry for 19 April 1943, p. 322.

one-and-a-half months – a notable achievement but far short of what prewar theorists had predicted. It was equally important in terms of Allied morale and that of the occupied countries:

> It also meant that, for the first time, Germany herself, in contradistinction to her armies abroad, began to pay the price for the fearful deeds which she had perpetrated, and was yet to perpetrate, against others.... It also marked the beginning of a famous Battle in the course of which Bomber Command was to show itself capable of not only achieving an occasional victory, as had previously been the case, but a whole series of consistent and pulverising blows among which the failures were much rarer than the successes.[129]

An account of the 5–6 March 1943 raid on Essen suggests the enormous strides the command had made since its first blundering attacks in May 1940, nearly three years earlier:

> Five *OBOE* Mosquitoes of 109 Squadron led the attack.... The, five, spaced out over forty minutes under *OBOE* control, first dropped yellow indicator flares 15 miles short of Essen to mark the route inward. The night was clear, but haze shrouded the town. Over Krupps, purely on *OBOE* signals, the five then in turn dropped red indicators. Meanwhile at one- and two-minute intervals, 22 *H2S* pathfinders – Stirlings and Halifaxes – acted as 'backers-up'. They first reinforced the yellow markers along the approach route and then, over the target area, aimed green indicators (plus some explosive and incendiaries) at the red indicators dropped by the Mosquitos.
> Led by other *H2S* pathfinders, the main force followed in three waves. Their instructions were to bomb the red indicators, or, if these were invisible, the green. First the Halifaxes put in an attack which lasted 18 minutes. Then, with this still in progress, the Stirlings and Wellingtons delivered a ten minute assault. Finally as the last Halifaxes were departing, the Lancasters streamed in, to add a further ten minutes of death and destruction. In each case the bomb load was one-third high explosive (some fused for long delay) and two third incendiary.... The whole violent incursion took little more than the planned 40 minutes – a concentration that overwhelmed both the active and the passive defenses.[130]

Recent research by Adam Tooze indicates that the raids on the Ruhr were even more successful than historians have thought. In effect, the damage that Bomber Command's raids dealt to the Ruhr's infrastructure,

---

[129] Webster and Frankland, *The Strategic Air Offensive against Germany*, vol. 2, pp. 94, 108.
[130] Denis Richards, *The Hardest Victory: RAF Bomber Command in the Second World War* (London, 1994), pp. 168–169.

especially its transportation network beginning in March 1943, brought what had been a steady increase in German armaments production to a sudden halt.[131] By disturbing the Ruhr's transportation network, Bomber Command was able to slow the output and distribution of coal and steel, which were the essential commodities on which increases in production absolutely depended.[132] Even more to the point:

> Reading contemporary sources, there can be no doubt that the Battle of the Ruhr marked a turning point in the history of the German war economy, which has been grossly underestimated by post-war accounts.... In the summer of 1943, the disruption in the Ruhr manifested itself in a so-called 'Zulieferungskrise' (sub-components crisis). All manner of parts, castings and forging were in short supply. And this affected not only heavy industry directly, but the entire armaments complex.... The Ruhr was the choke point and in 1943 it was within the RAF's grip. The failure to maintain that hold and to tighten it was a tragic operational error. The ongoing disaster that Speer and his cohorts clearly expected in the summer of 1943 was put off for another year.[133]

The great difficulty for the British was that reliable economic analysis was still in its infancy. Of all the air forces in the interwar period, only the U.S. Army Air Corps had made some effort in this respect, but that analysis had focused almost exclusively on the American economy in the belief that an enemy's economy would work in the same fashion.[134] In any case, given their contempt for scientific advice, one wonders how willing Harris and his staff at Bomber Command would have been to listen to economic analysts suggesting what they should bomb. Still, the conundrum that confronted Bomber Command's leaders, as it has all airmen, lay in the fact that the actual impact of air attacks does not

---

[131] Because the Eighth Air Force had managed to launch relatively few raids on German industry by July 1943, the major slowdown in the growth of military production was clearly the result of Bomber Command's efforts. For the halt in the production increases in the German war economy, see Adam Tooze, *The Wages of Destruction: The Making and Breaking of the German War Economy* (New York, 2006), p. 600.

[132] And the production and distribution of coal formed the essential backbone of the economy: without increases in coal production and its distribution throughout the Reich, steel production could not rise; increases in electrical production would stop; and increases in synthetic fuel, synthetic rubber, and ammunition would not be possible.

[133] Tooze, *The Wages of Destruction*, pp. 597, 598, 601.

[134] That analysis led the Americans to miss the fact that the German electrical network was a major weak link in the Reich's war economy because it was working at nearly full capacity. However, since the American electrical industry possessed substantial excess capacity, American analysts missed a major opportunity to damage the German economy in 1943.

become clear until after the war is over – in the case of British attacks on the Ruhr, not until more than 60 years had passed.

Throughout this period, Bomber Command remained a sledgehammer rather than a rapier. Beyond the range of *Gee* and *Oboe*, Bomber Command was still very much the prisoner of weather conditions over Europe as well as those over the target. Even the introduction of H_2S, an airborne radar that allowed the bombers to identify major ground features such as lakes and rivers, was of little help in the depths of the Continent. Two major raids in spring 1943 on the Skoda works in Czechoslovakia achieved nothing. The first raid mistook an insane asylum for the works, while the second in May achieved an excellent bombing concentration in open fields to the north, because the markers had gone down too far from the target.[135]

On the other hand, a spectacular raid in mid-May suggested what might be possible for the command in the future. Both tactical and technological adaptations played major roles in the famous dams' raid, led by one of Bomber Command's most famous pilots, Guy Gibson.[136] Harris opposed the idea when the air staff first proposed it, but when ordered to put the raid together, he provided full support. The effort depended on a specialized bomb designed by Barnes Wallis, one of the war's most innovative designers of aerial weapons, and capable of cracking concrete-encased dams 100 feet thick at their base, extraordinary flying skills, and new tactics. This is an important point because Harris often strenuously opposed ideas imposed from the above, but then when forced to comply, unlike so many military leaders and bureaucrats throughout history, he made every effort to make the concept work.

Executed after only three months of workup by what soon would be the most famous unit in the RAF, 617 Squadron, Gibson's force of 19 Lancasters, attacking at low level, took out the Möhne and Eder dams. During the pinpoint attack, Gibson, flying above and using his VHF radio, provided the attacking bombers with vectors to the target. At one moment, he even flew beside an attacking Lancaster to draw anti-aircraft fire to his aircraft. The tactic of having an aircraft control the bombing visually and by voice to provide guidance to the follow-on bombers soon became known as the "master bomber." Nevertheless, the cost was

---

[135] Richards, *The Hardest Victory*, pp. 133–134.
[136] For a wonderful thumbnail sketch of Gibson's career in the RAF and Bomber Command, see Max Hastings, *Warriors: Extraordinary Tales from the Battlefield* (London, 2005), chap. 10.

heavy – eight Lancasters shot down and most of the rest damaged. And the raid damaged only slightly the most important target, the Sorpe dam.[137] In a narrow sense, the raid was a failure because it did not destroy the Sorpe dam and because of the heavy losses the Germans inflicted on the attacking bombers. But in developing new tactical ideas, the raid represented a major breakthrough. Moreover, Harris kept the squadron in its specialized, elite status, and as the official historians suggest, "this single squadron changed the operational possibilities which were open to the force."[138]

Bomber Command had now achieved the capability to strain German defenses to the breaking point, especially as the *Luftwaffe*'s air defense adaptations lagged behind British innovations. Over much of western and central Germany and near the German coasts, British bombers stood a good chance of getting their bombs relatively close to the target. Pathfinder marking with ground target indicators when there was relatively little cloud cover or through the clouds with massive sky markers – nicknamed "Christmas trees" by the watching Germans – was becoming increasingly sophisticated and effective. Moreover, the introduction of Mosquitos acting as pathfinders, with their range, speed, and ability to fly at high altitudes, allowed the British to extend *Gee*'s range ever deeper into Germany, while the introduction of night intruders caused the Germans increasing difficulties.[139]

Yet, even with these successes, Bomber Command's losses flirted with defeat. In 43 major attacks between March 1943 and the end of June, it lost 872 bombers with a further 2,126 damaged. Despite these losses,

---

[137] For the dams' raid, see Webster and Frankland, *The Strategic Air Offensive against Germany*, vol. 2, pp. 168–178; Terraine, *The Right of the Line*, pp. 537–542; Guy Gibson, *Enemy Coast Ahead* (London, 1946); and Paul Brickhill, *The Dam Busters* (London, 1951).

[138] Webster and Frankland, *The Strategic Air Offensive against Germany*, vol. 2, p. 168.

[139] Unfortunately, the intruders in 1943 were the much inferior Beaufighters, which were not nearly as effective as the Mosquito night fighters would have been, but Fighter Command did not want to risk losing its new radar sets on the Mosquitos over German-held territory. Nevertheless, the mere fact that the Germans knew that British night fighters were stooging around in the skies over Germany added to the psychological pressures on the night-fighter crews. Again, the secondary and unintended effects may have been more important than the actual successes. Webster and Frankland, *The Strategic Air Offensive against Germany*, vol. 2, pp. 140–141. The Mosquito was undoubtedly the most versatile aircraft of the war: it acted as a long-range reconnaissance aircraft, a night fighter, a pathfinder, a high-level strategic bomber, a low-level bomber, and an intruder.

the command's front-line strength rose from 593 in February to 787 in August – a reflection of the massive production and crew training programs the British had set in motion in summer 1940.[140] At this point, the British introduced another major technological innovation – "Window" – and with it were able to launch one of the most devastating raids of the Second World War.[141] Even before gaining access to German radar technology, as a result of the Bruneval raid in February 1942, the British had divined that they could create spurious echoes in German radar receivers by using strips of aluminum cut to a length that mimicked the return a bomber would give.[142] That both the radar sets on board the night fighters and those on the ground supporting the Flak and GCI sites used the same frequency meant that the same length of aluminum strip would render the entire German air defense system ineffective. But fears that the Germans might then turn around and use this capability against British defenses delayed the introduction of "Window" for eighteen months.[143] In retrospect, the delay may not have been a bad thing because its use earlier would have forced the Germans to alter their night defenses radically.

In late July 1943, Bomber Command launched a massive assault on Hamburg, the first use of "Window."[144] The codename for the operation was Gomorrah, a most suitable title. The city resided prominently on the Elbe estuary, a target easily identified by *H2S* given the easily recognizable radar returns off the Elbe estuary. With the help of a massive deployment of "Window," Bomber Command's first attack on 24 July blinded German defenses. Because both German ground and airborne radar were on the same wavelength, "Window" in effect blinded the entire air defenses of Hamburg. Intercept operators of "Y" Service in Britain, the intelligence organization that monitored German radio transmissions, listened to the rising levels of frustration among German controllers, GCI radar operators, and radar intercept operators in the night fighters, none of whom

---

[140] Webster and Frankland, *The Strategic Air Offensive against Germany*, vol. 2, pp. 110–111.
[141] "Window" was the code name for what we today term as "chaff," the use of aluminum strips to confuse and disable an enemy radar system.
[142] Jones, *The Wizard War*, p. 288.
[143] For a detailed examination of the delay in utilizing "Window," see ibid., chap. 33.
[144] One of the factors that led to the British decision to use "Window" was the fact that the defection of a German night fighter to Britain in May 1943 confirmed that German radar, airborne and ground, both utilized the same wavelength. The British had determined the wavelength of German ground radars through the means of the Bruneval raid. Greenhous et al., *The Crucible of War*, p, 694.

could make sense of their radar screens that indicated the approach of tens of thousands of bombers.[145] On 25 and 26 July, American B-17s then struck various targets in the Hamburg area, further adding to the damage and the difficulties confronting German firefighting forces on the ground.

On the evening of 27 July, a second great RAF raid occurred. In this case, nearly every condition was perfect. The weather was warm and dry. There was little or no cloud cover. "Window" worked as effectively as it had in the first raid. A substantial portion of Hamburg's fire service was off on the city's western side fighting smoldering coke and coal fires caused by earlier attacks. Those raids had also substantially damaged Hamburg's water system. Finally, the first pathfinders put their markers down in the middle of the largest lumberyard in Europe, where timber imports from the Baltic arrived in Germany.

The results were devastating.[146] The combination of the markers and kiln-dried lumber created a massive fire in the city center that acted as a huge beacon for the follow-on bomber crews. A massive firestorm soon began. Within 20 minutes, the city's center exploded. Further bombing spread the firestorm to the northeast, as the phenomenon of "creep back" occurred (the tendency of bomber crews to drop their loads earlier and earlier). Temperatures reached nearly 1,000 degrees centigrade; winds in the city's center were 300 to 400 miles an hour. By the next morning, the fire had burned out an enormous four-mile square in Hamburg's center, with considerable damage to nearby areas. Most of the city's utilities were out of commission; transportation systems no longer functioned; and the raid destroyed 250,000 of Hamburg's 450,000 houses.[147] This was area bombing with a vengeance. The official count was that 41,800 Germans died in the firestorm or from the bombing, but the number may well have been higher.[148] Bomber Command, however, was not finished. Two days

---

[145] Aileen Clayton, *The Enemy Is Listening* (London, 1980), p. 269.

[146] For the most complete account of the course and effects of the attack, see Martin Middlebrook, *The Battle of Hamburg: Allied Bombing Force against a German City in 1943* (London, 1980).

[147] Out of 122,000 apartments in Hamburg, the raids damaged or destroyed 40,000, and out of 450,000 houses, 250,000. It knocked out of commission 75 percent of the city's electric works, 60 percent of its water system, and 90 percent of its gas works. The immediate falloff in industrial production was considerable: 40 percent for major firms and 80 percent for medium and small concerns. OKW Wehrwirtschaftsstab, "Erfahrungen bei Luftangriff," von Oberst Luther, Wwi O/wk Kdo X, 15.1.44, National Archives and Records Service (NARS) T-79/81/000641.

[148] Greenhous et al., *The Crucible of War*, p. 696. Middlebrook's estimate is lower. Middlebrook, *The Battle of Hamburg*, p. 272. See also Hans Rumpf, *The Bombing of Germany* (London, 1963), pp. 82–83.

later, a third great raid achieved major destruction without a firestorm, so that casualties were considerably lower. A fourth raid in early August ran into bad weather and achieved little.

Bomber Command achieved this frightening success at little cost. The missing rates of its four raids on Hamburg were 1.5 percent, 2.2 percent, 3.5 percent, and 4 percent, considerably under what its bombers had suffered during the Battle of the Ruhr.[149] Nevertheless, the rise in losses reflected a surprisingly quick recovery for German defenses. The destruction was the "greatest" success Bomber Command would achieve until Dresden. And rumors of its terrifying results coursed through the Reich in succeeding weeks.

During the next three months, Bomber Command struck cities throughout western and central Germany with some success. On the night of the Eighth Air Force attack on Schweinfurt and Regensburg (17 August 1943), the British attacked the research station at Peenemünde, where the Germans were developing the V-1 cruise missile and the V-2 ballistic missile. New and improved markers and marking techniques contributed to the raid's success.[150] However, by now a radical reorganization had led to a substantial and rapid recovery of the night-fighter force. Thus, even with their late arrival on the Baltic, German night fighters were able to shoot down 40 British bombers out of an attacking force of 597 (a 6.7 percent loss rate) with 37 damaged.[151]

The German Response and the Battle of Berlin

Even the increasing damage that Bomber Command was inflicting on the Reich's cities and industry in spring 1943 had failed to wake German leaders from their torpor in regard to the night defense of the Reich. Hamburg, however, came as a terrible shock.[152] For the first time, senior leaders had to recognize the extent to which the British night bombing threatened Germany's strategic position. Goebbels could not believe the first reports he received about the firestorm on 27 July.

> Kaufman gave me a first report on the effect of the British air raid. He spoke of a catastrophe that simply staggers the imagination. A city of a million

---

[149] Webster and Frankland, *The Strategic Air Offensive against Germany*, vol. 2, pp. 155–156.
[150] For a discussion of the raid, see ibid., pp. 282–284.
[151] Ibid., p. 284.
[152] Hitler was at times furious at the damage inflicted on the Ruhr and Hamburg, and not surprisingly, Göring's prestige collapsed. But no fundamental changes in policy or emphasis occurred.

inhabitants has been destroyed in a manner unparalleled in history. We are faced with problems that are impossible of solution.... He spoke of about 800,000 homeless people who are wandering up and down the streets not knowing what to do. I believe Kaufman has lost his nerve somewhat in the face of this undoubtedly exceptional situation.[153]

Speer informed Hitler that six more raids on the scale of the second night attack on Hamburg would "bring Germany's armaments production to a halt." The *Führer*, ever the optimist, replied that Speer would straighten things out.[154] For the short term, Hitler was correct, not because Speer was wrong in his estimate but because the RAF's success in attacking Hamburg depended on peculiar circumstances not likely to be replicated: a period of warm dry weather; the blinding of German defenses; and the city's location on the Elbe, which made its location easily identifiable to the *H2S* radar sets in the bombers. The Hamburg success, therefore, was misleading, because such conditions would rarely occur over the course of the remainder of the war.[155]

Tactically and operationally, the Germans responded quickly.[156] Earlier, in spring 1943, as Bomber Command swamped the Kammhuber Line, a number of *Luftwaffe* officers had suggested scrapping the whole concept of night defense. Major Hajo Herrmann, a former bomber pilot, proposed concentrating day fighters directly over the target. They would use searchlights as well as the reflected light from the burning city below to attack the bombers – a measure of how serious the situation appeared to these officers.[157] These "wild-sow" tactics represented a desperate expedient because they would throw large numbers of day-fighter pilots against British bombers at night and in sometimes appalling conditions. They achieved some success, but the losses to the single-engine fighter forces made the wild sow tactics a dubious expedient.

The Peenemünde attack underlined the weakness of the wild-sow tactics. German controllers, misled by a Mosquito feint at Berlin, concentrated the fighters and most of the night fighters over Berlin. Antiaircraft gunners then proceeded to blast away at the steadily increasing

---

[153] Goebbels, *The Goebbels Diaries*, p. 419.
[154] Albert Speer, *Inside the Third Reich* (New York, 1970), p. 284.
[155] Only three more times in the war would great firestorms occur: Dresden and Tokyo being the two obvious cases, and Kassel in October 1943.
[156] For the extent of the give-and-take of additional technological aids on both sides of the contest, see Greenhous et al., *The Crucible of War*, p. 704.
[157] Tag-und Nachtjagd, "Besprechungsnotiz," Nr. 63/43 am 27.6.43, Obersalzberg, Albert Simpson Historical Research Center: K 113.312-2, v. 3.

number of German fighters over Berlin, which they mistook for British bombers, while the fighters fired off recognition symbols at each other. The evening's proceedings then ended with a major pileup of aircraft landing on the Brandenburg-Briest airfield.[158] (A few night fighters, not fooled by the action over Berlin, had turned north to arrive over Peenemünde as the last wave of bombers was attacking.)

Other *Luftwaffe* officers suggested more radical changes to the tightly controlled system of the Kammhuber Line. Shortly before Hamburg, Göring's staff requested better radar sets to support a pursuit force that would not be tied to GCI sites but would be guided into the bomber stream and then fly directly along with it shooting down bombers.[159] If the Germans calculated the route of British bombers correctly, the "tame-sow" approach had far better prospects because it would place large numbers of trained night fighters in the bomber stream for substantial periods of time. By mid-August, both the wild-sow and the tame-sow tactical approaches were in place. In the case of the Peenemünde raid, the German night fighters got there late but in sufficient numbers to savage the last wave of bombers over the target and on their way home. Nevertheless, even as the Germans adapted, they confronted new threats. Toward the end of August 1943, the British began conducting nighttime intruder attacks with Mosquito night fighters.[160]

The Germans also moved quickly to counter the problems raised by the introduction of "Window." Here chance played an important role.[161] In summer 1943, German scientists had been developing a new airborne radar set, the *SN2*, which operated on a longer wavelength than those employed by German fighters at the time. Although it picked up its target

---

[158] For Milch's reaction to this less than distinguished effort, see "Der erste grosse Einsatz der 'wilden Sau,' Auszug aus der G.L.-Besprechung am 20.8.43 im RLM," Albert F. Simpson Historical Research Collection: K 113.312–2, v. 3.

[159] BA/MA, RL 3/54, Der Reichsminister der Luftfahrt und Oberbefehlshaber der Luftwaffe, Br. 21, Nr. 8731/43, 21.7.43, Betr.: "Sofortmassnahmen für Verfolgungsnachtjagd über grössere Räume."

[160] Greenhous, *The Crucible of War*, p. 714.

[161] In book one of *On War*, Clausewitz notes that "It is now quite clear how greatly the objective nature of war makes it a matter of assessing probabilities. Only one more element is needed to make war a gamble – chance; the very last thing that war lacks. *No other human activity is so continuously or universally bound up with chance* [my italics.] And through the element of chance, guesswork and luck come to play a great part in war." Carl von Clausewitz, *On War*, trans. and ed. by Michael Howard and Peter Paret (Princeton, 1975), p. 85. Interestingly, the greatest military historian of all, Thucydides, is equally insistent on the dominant role of chance in war in his *History of the Peloponnesian War*.

at relatively longer ranges, the Germans were about to stop its development because it also possessed the disadvantage of an excessive minimum range. However, SN2's different wavelength enabled it to pierce the "Window" clouds of aluminum strips to pick up British bombers. Not surprisingly, the *Luftwaffe* began a crash program to equip its night fighters with SN2 sets.[162] Ironically, at the same time, the production of new night fighters continued to lag.

One other major adaptation in terms of equipment occurred in summer 1943 that was to have a devastating impact on British losses in the Battle of Berlin.[163] Front-line German squadrons began installing upward firing cannons, called *Schräge Musik*, located immediately behind the crew positions.[164] This allowed night fighters to approach bombers from below and behind, where all the British bombers had a blind spot. By aligning his aircraft under and slightly behind the bomber's wing, a night-fighter pilot could blast the bomber's engines and vulnerable fuel tanks. The only possibility of survival for the bombers was instantaneous, violent aerial maneuvers. In most cases, by the time the British crews realized they were under attack, it was already too late. Exacerbating the problem for the British in winter 1943–1944 was the fact that RAF intelligence remained ignorant of the new German night-fighting tactic, largely because debriefing officers refused to believe the few reports they had been receiving from bomber crews that German night fighters were firing upward while flying underneath the bombers.[165]

Still, German leaders, military as well as civilian, continued to shy away from the realization that night fighters represented the only antidote to Bomber Command's offensive by their ability to inflict an unacceptable level of losses on its bombers. Throughout 1943 German bomber production continued at a higher level than night fighters – a reflection of the leadership's focus on supporting the operational fight both in the Mediterranean and the east, and its desire to pay the British back in

---

[162] Bill Gunston, *Night Fighters* (New York, 1976), pp. 103–104.
[163] Some of the losses in the Peenemünde raid are attributable to night fighters equipped with the *Schräge Musik* cannons. Richards, *The Hardest Victory*, p. 200.
[164] See particularly the clear discussion of the *Schräge Musik* tactics in Martin Middlebrook, *The Nuremberg Raid* (New York, 1974), pp. 278–279.
[165] Moreover, many of the crews refused to believe that the violent explosions they could see as German night fighters quite literally blew British bombers out of the sky, followed by a flaming path to the ground, represented the destruction of a bomber. As a result, the rumor spread throughout Bomber Command that the explosions they were seeing were shells fired up into the sky by the Germans to affect the morale of crews.

kind.¹⁶⁶ It was above all the latter that fathered the German failure to defeat the British night offensive. Ironically, not until late 1943 did fighter production as a whole receive as high a priority as production of U-boats, which the Allies had already defeated in May 1943.

Hitler's response reflected the instincts that had driven him throughout his career: to strike back. He commented to his military aides immediately after the Hamburg catastrophe: "Terror can only be broken by terror." Attacks on German airfields, he added, made no impression on him, but the destruction of Germany's cities was another matter. "The German people demanded reprisals."¹⁶⁷ Hitler also ordered continued emphasis on the buildup of the Reich's Flak forces, a dead-end that siphoned off resources and manpower from more vital areas. Even Field Marshal Milch, normally clear headed, commented to his staff at the height of the Battle of the Ruhr that retaliation was the only means available to stop the bomber offensive. Göring, ever the sycophant, fully supported Hitler's desire for retaliation over defense.¹⁶⁸ A conversation between the *Reichsmarschall* and Milch is most revealing in this regard. To Milch's argument that the Germany needed a greater emphasis on air defense, Göring commented that "When every city in Germany had been smashed to the ground, the German people would still live. It would certainly be awful, but the nation had certainly lived before."¹⁶⁹ Echoing Hitler in October 1943, he commented that the German people did not care whether the *Luftwaffe* attacked British airfields; rather, "All they wished to hear when a hospital or a children's home in Germany is destroyed is that we have destroyed the same in England; then they are satisfied."¹⁷⁰

The *Führer*'s emphasis on retaliation rather than air superiority led the Germans down the path to disaster. The *Luftwaffe* and the army were

---

¹⁶⁶ The important point here is that the Ju 88 was used as both a bomber and a night fighter, while the other bombers and night fighters competed for engines, aluminum, and production facilities.

¹⁶⁷ "Hitler zur Frage der Gegenmassnahmen zur Beantwortung der allierten Luftangriffe," 25.7.43, Albert F. Simpson Historical Research Center: K 113.312-2, v. 3.

¹⁶⁸ In a conversation with Reichsmarschall Göring, Fritz Sauckel commented: "The only argument that makes an impression on a racial cousin [the British] is that of retaliation." BA/MA, RL 3/61, "Stenographische Niederschrift der Besprechung beim Reichsmarschall am 28.11.43 in Karinhall."

¹⁶⁹ Ibid.

¹⁷⁰ Heimatsverteidigungsprogramm 1943, "Besprechung beim Reichsmarshall am 7.10.43, Obersalzburg, Fortsetzung," Albert F. Simpson Historical Research Center: K 113.312-2, vol. 3.

both about to produce their own retaliation weapons: the V-1 and the V-2. The former was probably marginally cost-effective, in that it was to tie down substantial British resources in 1944. However, the latter, while a triumph of German engineering, made no sense at all. The German Army had viewed the V-2 as a large artillery piece – an astonishing commitment of resources to what was in the end a large shell with a circular error of probability (CEP) of an area equivalent to the city of London.[171] The U.S. Strategic Bombing Survey estimated that in the last year of the war, the resources devoted to the "revenge weapons programs were equal to the production of 24,000 fighter aircraft."[172] The foremost historian of the V-2 program has estimated that it consumed the equivalent of one-fourth of the resources the United States expended on the Manhattan Project.[173] This represented an enormous misallocation of resources, especially when one considers that the program overloaded the instrument and electrical component industries, both crucially important to the production of the radars used by night fighters.

The recovery of the German air defenses after Hamburg reflected the difficulties under which the British were operating as much as the effectiveness of the German defenses. In retrospect, both sides were on the brink of defeat. It was the British who suffered the immediate consequences of their weaknesses – a situation aggravated by Harris's decision to launch a campaign to defeat Germany before the invasion of Western Europe. But in the long run the Germans would suffer the greater defeat.

Unrealistic expectations at the higher levels added to Bomber Command's burden. Six Group even instructed its crews that the reason for evasive maneuvers was not "to lose" the enemy fighter but to present "a difficult target" for the enemy, while allowing the bomber's gunners clear fields of fire.[174] Even more disastrously, Harris completely disregarded the advice of Portal's chief scientific adviser, R. V. Jones. The latter suggested that a substantial number of Bomber Command's losses were occurring over the main targets, particularly in the last attacking waves as night fighters arrived. He suggested that the command could lower its losses by reducing the size of raiding forces and thus their time

---

[171] For an outstanding examination of the V-2's history and capabilities, see Michael Neufeld, *The Rocket and the Reich, Peenemünde and the Coming of the Ballistic Era* (Washington, DC, 1994).
[172] U.S. Strategic Bombing Survey, "V-Weapons (Crossbow Campaign)," Military Analysis Division, Report # 60, January 1947.
[173] Neufeld, *The Rocket and the Reich*, p. 273.
[174] Greenhous et al., *The Crucible of War*, p. 715.

over target. Moreover, by increasing the number of raids on a given night, the British would be able to confuse and mislead the German controllers. Harris would have none of it. He wanted large raids that could deal out punishment on Hamburg's scale. In retrospect, successes would be all too few, and Harris's emphasis on massive city-busting raids would cost the command dearly.[175]

Adding to the difficulties of Bomber Command in the Battle of Berlin was the fact that the Germans had caught up in the electronic side of the conflict.

> Laus equipment based on the Doppler principle was being added to fighter and Flak-control Würzburgs to penetrate Window. Beyond that, Bernhardine and Uhu – direct data-link systems employing, respectively, a coded ticker-tape and visual display on the A1 screen to give the position of the bomber stream were past the experimental stage.... Tinsel, the jammer aimed at the enemy's high frequency commentary, had been neutralized by the simple introduction of more powerful radio transmitters.... These were in addition to Bumerang, Flamme, Flensburg, Naxos, Naxburg, Rosendaal, and Korfo equipment – which began to appear during the winter 1943–1944 and enabled *Luftwaffe* signals intelligence to detect, plot and in some instances home in on Bomber Command's *Oboe*, IFF, Monica, and *H2S* transmissions.[176]

In early November 1943 Harris penned a note to Churchill in which he underlined his future strategy. He listed 19 major German cities that his command had largely destroyed, 19 as seriously damaged, and a further nine as damaged. He then drew the conclusion "that the Ruhr is largely 'out,' and that progress has been made towards the elimination of the remaining essentials of German war power." His crucial assumptions came at the end:

> I feel certain that Germany must collapse before this programme, which is more than half concluded already, has proceeded much further. We have not much further to go. But we must get the USAAF to wade in in greater force. If they will only get going according to plan and avoid such diversions as Ploesti... we can get through with it very quickly.
> We can wreck Berlin from end to end if the USAAF will come in on it. It will cost us between 400–500 aircraft. It will cost Germany the war.[177]

---

[175] Ibid., p. 719.
[176] Ibid., p. 734.
[177] The memorandum is filled with a number of faulty assumptions. The USAAF (US Army Air Forces) was in no position to wade in because it had just suffered a series of disastrous defeats in October 1943 in the daytime skies over the Reich. Moreover, it was incapable of bombing at night. Germany's cities and economy to the east of the

Heavily influenced by RAF Air Marshal Trenchard's pronouncements of the prewar period, Harris was clearly looking to achieve a decisive, war-winning victory over the Germans with his command with only minor help from the Americans.

There was substantial opposition on the air staff to Harris's proposed campaign against the German capital. The one solid supporter was the air staff's chief of intelligence, Air Vice-Marshal F. F. Inglis, not the first in a long line of military intelligence officers in the Second World War to base estimates on hope and what they believed others wanted to hear.[178] But while a significant number of the air staff opposed the campaign to destroy Berlin, no one was willing to bring Harris to heel, especially considering his close relationship with Churchill and the widespread popularity Bomber Command's leader enjoyed among the British population.

The problem was Berlin as a target – it lay at a great distance from British bomber bases. Winter weather on the route to and over the German capital was invariably appalling. Equally important, the capital was beyond the range of British navigation devices. The size and dispersion of the city, along with the lack of easily recognizable landmarks, made it extraordinarily difficult to achieve the concentrated bombing inflicted on Hamburg in July 1943. In fact, the weather over Berlin from November 1943 through February 1944 was so bad that RAF reconnaissance aircraft could take pictures of the damage on only two occasions. Quite simply, the conditions for anything approaching another Hamburg did not exist.

The offensive against Berlin opened in November 1943 with four major raids on the German capital. British losses in these raids were surprisingly low. They cost only 4 percent of the bombers dispatched, with an overall loss rate for the month of 3.6 percent. But the loss rate was misleading. In fact, the weather was so bad that on several occasions, German fighters could not even take off to intercept the bombers – much to Goebbels's outrage.[179] Accompanying the low loss rate was a general lack of concentrated bombing.

Ruhr were not in nearly as bad shape as Harris was suggesting, while German defenses were more formidable than he was willing to admit. His bomber units were soon to discover just how wrong he was on the last point. Harris's letter to the Air Ministry's public relations branch at this time makes clear his emphasis: "[The real objective is] the obliteration of German cities and their inhabitants.... [Our] aim is the destruction of German cities, the killing of German workers and the disruption of civilised community life throughout Germany." Greenhous et al., *The Crucible of War*, p. 725.

[178] Greenhous et al., *Crucible of War*, p. 732.
[179] For the loss rates for British bombers, see Murray, *Luftwaffe*, pp. 204–210.

Goebbels, the *Gauleiter* for Berlin, had ordered not only the evacuation of a million of Berlin's population but had also overseen extensive preparations throughout the capital to preclude that another Hamburg or Kassel would occur. Still the damage was extensive. After one major raid, the propaganda minister noted in his diary:

> Devastation is again appalling in the government section as well as in the western and northern suburbs. The workers quarters in the Wedding and the region along Wolgast street are especially hard hit. The state playhouse and the Reichstag are aflame, but fortunately we are able to localize those fires.... Hell itself seemed to have broken loose over us. Mines and explosive bombs keep hurtling down upon the government quarter. One after another of the most important buildings begins to burn. As I look out on the Wilhelmplatz after the attack, the gruesome impression of the evening before is even heightened.[180]

Nevertheless, the German night defenses were gradually getting a handle on the threat. With either Berlin or cities deep in central Germany as targets, night fighters, supported by an increasingly effective control system, took a rising toll on the attackers despite RAF countermeasures. During fall 1943, control of the night fighters evolved into a running commentary by the chief German controller as to the course and progress of the bombers. He was then able to vector the tame-sow fighters to radio beacons now located throughout Germany whence they could move into the bomber stream. As the system settled down, the Germans became increasingly adept at feeding fighters directly into the bomber stream.

The rushed development of a number of electronic devices significantly aided the night fighters. The first step was to monitor IFF transmissions to determine the course of the bomber stream. When the British turned off their IFF signals over enemy territory, German scientists developed new devices that picked up other radio signals from the bombers.[181] British scientists had developed a device, codenamed "Monica," to warn

---

[180] Goebbels, *The Goebbels Diaries*, pp. 522–523.
[181] Disastrously, a rumor circulated throughout Bomber Command that the continued use of IFF would block out German radar transmissions. As a result, in direct contravention to orders, some crews left their IFF transponders on, which allowed the Germans to track not only them but the bomber stream as well. R. V. Jones had warned about the dangers of leaving the IFF on over German territory, but this met little response until an Ultra intercept warned that the Germans were indeed homing in on the IFF transmissions from bombers. "At first there was some disbelief in Bomber Command headquarters, which I had accused of the immoral practice of encouraging brave men to clutch at false straws in their hour of greatest danger...and I was particularly critical of the Operational Research Section which, as scientists, should have been more objective." Jones, *The Wizard War*, pp. 388–390.

bombers that the radar on German fighters had picked them up. Unfortunately for the British, the Germans captured the device early in the battle from a crashed bomber and turned it. With the "Flensburg" apparatus, night fighters could home directly onto bombers using "Monica." In addition, the Germans provided fighters with a device called "Naxos," which homed in on *H2S* transmissions.[182]

Yet, the Germans also continued to pay for their failure to provide the resources and skilled manpower necessary to build an effective production system for the radar systems on which the night-fighter force depended. Of the 300 *SN2* sets manufactured by early November 1943, *Luftwaffe* maintenance crews managed to fit only 49 sets to night fighters, of which only 12 were operationally ready by the month's end. It was not until January that Telefunken production facilities began turning out relatively reliable sets – a mark of how far behind the British the German electronics industry had become.[183]

Moreover, much of the production of night fighters continued to be of obsolete aircraft such as the Bf 110, the Do 217, and the Me 210. Astonishingly, when General "Beppo" Schmidt, Kammhuber's successor, asked for substantial increases in the electronic devices on which the night fighters depended, he received the answer that, except for the *SN2* radar, all the rest had a low production priority.[184] The German response to Hamburg in every area had been reactive with little thought given to long-term requirements. As the German fighter ace Adolf Galland noted after the war, "Our command allowed the enemy to dictate the necessary defensive measures instead of countering actively with original measures planned with foresight."[185] The larger issue was that at the operational and strategic levels of war, statesmen and generals must live in the future because it is there that they can have their greatest impact. They must think in terms of what the enemy might do as much as what he is doing today. The German leadership failed to do that in almost every case.

Not all of the combat adaptations were German. The British began to use imitative deception. Fake controllers provided inaccurate directions to the night fighter, first operating from Britain and then airborne over the Continent in specially built Lancasters.[186] When that no longer worked,

---

[182] Air Ministry, *The Rise and Fall of the German Air Force* (London, 1948), pp. 278–279.
[183] Aders, *History of the German Night Fighter Force*, p. 123.
[184] Greenhous et al., *The Crucible of War*, p. 769.
[185] Adolph Galland, *The First and the Last* (London, 1955), pp. 197–198.
[186] Ibid., p. 123.

the British jammed the range of frequencies German controllers used.[187] Clearly, technological adaptation to the actual conditions of combat was occurring at an increasingly swift pace on both sides, but at least during the Battle of Berlin, the Germans held the lead.

By January 1944, German night fighters were flying out over the North Sea to intercept the incoming bombers.[188] Their success that month forced the British to take drastic action. Raid planning became more complex with a number of spoof raids launched along with the main effort to deceive the defenders. Pathfinders no longer laid out route markers to guide the bombers, nor did ground markers (incendiary devices) any longer indicate turning points for the bomber stream. Such marking devices had revealed each raid's direction to German fighters as well and thus drew them directly into the bomber stream. While such British adaptations helped keep losses down, they also increased navigation errors and decreased bombing accuracy. In effect, Harris lost the Battle of Berlin in January 1944, although like Haig on the Somme and Passchendaele, he persisted in the campaign past any reasonable point. There is a point where maintenance of the objective becomes self-defeating – needlessly subjecting one's own forces to slaughter.

During most of February 1944, Bomber Command launched attacks on western and central Germany to keep its losses under control. However, at the end of March, the British launched two heavy raids deep into Germany. Both suffered exceedingly heavy losses. On March 24, an attack on Berlin lost 73 bombers for a missing rate of 9.1 percent.[189] One week later, the British attacked Nuremberg in the most disastrous raid of the war. Not only were the weather conditions perfect for the night fighters – with bomber contrails lit up by the moon – but the raid's course was particularly unimaginative, in fact, flying directly over one of the German night-fighter beacons. By the time the raid was over, Bomber Command had lost 108 bombers, 61 on the attack leg and 47 on the flight out. The Halifaxes of 4 Group had a particularly bad night, losing 20.6 percent of the aircraft dispatched.[190] As a fitting end to the night's wretched events, a number of the attacking aircraft bombed Schweinfurt.[191]

---

[187] Middlebrook, *The Nuremberg Raid*, pp. 32–33.
[188] Air Ministry, *The Rise and Fall of the German Air Force*, p. 200.
[189] Webster and Frankland, *The Strategic Air Offensive against Germany*, vol. 2, *Endeavour*, p. 207.
[190] Middlebrook, *The Nuremberg Raid*, pp. 161, 277, 330.
[191] Ibid., pp. 204–207.

Thus, in the last week of March Bomber Command lost 190 bombers (7 more in an attack on Essen). Over the course of the five months of the Battle of Berlin, Harris's command had lost 1,128 bombers.[192] His estimate that the command would lose only 500 bombers was off by 225.6 percent. As Bennett of the pathfinders commented in an interview after the war, the Battle of Berlin "had been the worst thing that could have happened to the Command.[193] The official historians of the British strategic bombing effort note: "The implication was equally clear. The German fighter force had interposed itself between Bomber Command and its strategic objective."[194] For Harris, the actualities of combat were finally clear: Bomber Command needed the "provision of night fighter support on a substantial scale."[195]

The German night fighters had achieved a major tactical success, but at a heavy cost. Between January and March 1944, the *Luftwaffe* lost no fewer than 15 percent of the night-fighter sorties launched. Admittedly, many of those were the result of weather and the exhaustion of the crews, but only desperation enabled the Germans to continue the battle despite such losses.[196] But although the writing was on the wall, the *Luftwaffe*'s leadership appears not to have understood what had produced their success or its fragility. Meanwhile, even as the night-fighter force was gaining its success against Bomber Command, the American Eighth Air Force was launching huge daylight raids into Germany, accompanied by long-range fighters. The raids targeted the German aircraft industry and forced the *Luftwaffe* into a massive battle of attrition to protect its production base. In March 1944 P-51s accompanied a major raid all the way to Berlin. Cumulative pilot losses in the *Luftwaffe*'s day-fighter force from January to May were devastating and eventually cost the Germans daylight air superiority over not only Western Europe but Central Europe as well.[197]

The response to the massive American daylight assault again underlines the short-term, shortsighted approach the Germans were still taking to addressing the problems raised by Bomber Command's attacks. As early

---

[192] See table XLI in Murray, *Luftwaffe*, p. 210.
[193] Interview with D. C. T. Bennett, RAF Staff College Bracknell, conducted by Group Captain R.A. Mason. For the impact on the air crews in the command, see particularly Hastings, *Bomber Command*, chap. 11.
[194] Webster and Frankland, *The Strategic Air Offensive against Germany*, vol. 2, p. 193.
[195] Ibid., p. 193.
[196] Greenhous et al., *The Crucible of War*, p. 746.
[197] For a discussion of this battle and its losses on both sides, see Murray, *Luftwaffe*, pp. 223–232.

as April 1943, the Germans had begun throwing their night fighters into the daylight battle against American B-17s.[198] This penchant continued throughout 1943 into 1944. During the Schweinfurt and Peenemünde raids on 17 and 18 August 1943, the *Luftwaffe* lost 30 night fighters, 21 of them in daylight operations against the Americans. The employment of scarce night fighters in such operations was shortsighted enough in 1943. But in the first months of 1944, confronted not only by American B-17s and B-24s but by Eighth Air Force fighters as well, the German night-fighter force suffered unsustainable losses of irreplaceable aircraft and air crews.[199]

The Denouement: Overlord and the Transportation Plans

The Battle of Berlin ended with the March 1944 Nuremberg raid. In fact, even had Harris wished to continue the battle, he could not have. The Allied invasion of the Continent, Operation Overlord, was scheduled to occur within the next two months, and the Supreme Commander Allied Expeditionary Forces, General Dwight Eisenhower, had demanded control over the strategic bomber forces, American as well as British. He wanted the strategic bomber forces to execute the plan devised by his deputy, Air Marshal Sir Arthur Tedder, to destroy the French transportation network in western and northern France and thereby make the movement and logistical support of German forces resisting the invasion difficult, if not impossible. Both American and British bomber barons strongly resisted Eisenhower's demand, but in the end they lost: Churchill and Roosevelt were not about to risk the success of the invasion to indulge airmen who thus far in the war had promised more than they had delivered.

The critical nodes in the French rail transport network were the marshaling yards. Here Harris attempted to wheedle out of his assignment by suggesting to Churchill that Bomber Command was far too blunt an instrument to attack such targets successfully and that the collateral damage from such night raids would kill tens of thousands, if not hundreds of thousands, of Frenchmen. Churchill almost bought Harris's argument, but a series of six Bomber Command test raids in March 1944 proved

---

[198] In this intercept, Göring forbade the use of night-fighter pilots who had reached twenty victories in daylight operations against the Americans. "Ultra, History of US Strategic Air Force Europe versus German Air Force," June 1945, SRH-013, p. 59.

[199] See Murray, *Luftwaffe*, pp. 211, 224–232.

Harris wrong. Harris had argued that the raids would require a full Bomber Command effort, when, in fact, as Tedder's chief scientist Solly Zuckerman pointed out, even a relatively small number of bombers could produce the required effects.[200]

Using *Oboe* and new marking techniques, the raids succeeded beyond anyone's expectations.[201] With the pathfinder force doing the marking and using new instruments and markers, and with a master bomber controlling the effort to keep "creep back" to a minimum and only enough bombers to destroy the target, Bomber Command, to the surprise of its commander, proved itself superior to Eighth Air Force's daylight bombers in attacking and destroying precision targets. Here the crucial advantage was *Oboe* because targets in France were well within its range. Thus, pathfinders could find their targets with relative ease and mark them accurately for follow-on bombers. In addition, the Battle of Berlin had pulled the *Luftwaffe*'s night fighters as well as the bulk of the Flak forces deep into Germany, so that these destructive raids confronted minimal air defenses and consequently suffered only light losses. Bomber Command's six attacks in March against French marshaling yards were a great success – the attack on Vaires hit a load of mines next to a *Waffen SS* troop train. The resulting explosion added to the bombing and wrecked the yard completely, in addition to killing 1,200 of Hitler's murderous fanatics on the troop trains.[202]

The transportation plan, in which Bomber Command carried the heaviest load, played a major role in the success of Operation Overlord (codename for the invasion of Europe). The weight of bombs dropped suggests the extent of the command's effort. In March 1944, Harris had devoted 70 percent of the sorties flown to targets in Germany. In April, with its focus on France, the command dropped 34,000 tons of bombs on transportation targets as against only 14,000 dropped in Germany. The totals for May and June were 28,000 and 52,000 tons, respectively.[203] Bomber Command's losses were minimal, at least in comparison to what it had suffered in the preceding Battle of Berlin.

The *Luftwaffe*'s response to the destruction of the French transportation system was virtually nil. On 1 April, *Luftflotte Reich* (Air Force

---

[200] Solly Zuckerman, *From Apes to Warlords* (London, 1980), p. 234.
[201] Webster and Frankland, *The Strategic Air Offensive against Germany*, vol. 3, *Victory*, p. 27.
[202] Greenhous et al., *The Crucible of War*, p. 794.
[203] Webster and Frankland, *The Strategic Air Offensive against Germany*, vol. 3, *Victory*, p. 39.

Reich) received control of all air defense assets over Germany. However, *Luftflotte 3* (Third Air Force) remained in control over France and the Low Countries, and there was little coordination between the two commands.[204] In effect, the Germans still failed to think in terms of an integrated continental air defense, rather than separate area defenses determined by the old frontiers. Thus, only rarely did the night fighters from the *Luftflotte Reich* intervene against attacks on the French railroad system, while *Luftflotte 3* possessed only small numbers of night fighters to counter Bomber Command's attacks. Perhaps most seriously, the *Luftwaffe*'s high command failed to draw a coherent picture of what the attacks on the French railroad network presaged.[205]

By the end of May, the massive Allied bombing campaign against the French transportation network had achieved enormous success. A *Luftwaffe* intelligence report of 3 June 1944 underlines the extent of the damage the campaign had inflicted on the lines of communications the *Wehrmacht* would need in its efforts to repel the invasion:

> In Zone 1 [France and Belgium], the systematic destruction that has been carried out since March of all important junctions of the entire network – not only of the main lines – has most seriously crippled the whole transport system (railway installations, including rolling stock). Similarly Paris has been cut off from long distance traffic, and the most important bridges over the lower Seine have been destroyed one after the other. As a result... it is only by exerting the greatest efforts that purely military traffic and goods essential to the war effort... can be kept moving.... The rail network is to be completely wrecked. Local and through traffic is to be made impossible, and all efforts to restore the services are to be prevented. This aim has so successfully been achieved – locally at any rate – that the *Reichsbahn* [German Railway] authorities are seriously considering whether it is not useless to attempt further repair work.[206]

Of the 37 major targets that Tedder's planners assigned to Bomber Command, Harris's forces had "sufficiently damaged 22 to require no more attention until further notice" and had "severely damaged" the

---

[204] For further discussions of these issues, see Greenhous et al., *Crucible of War*, pp. 797–800.

[205] Part of the problem was undoubtedly a reflection of the pressure Eighth Air Force was exerting on the *Luftwaffe* over the Reich. That represented the immediate and terrible danger, while the attacks on marshaling yards in France represented events in an important but peripheral theater, at least to *Luftwaffe* commanders.

[206] Air Historical Branch, "Air Attacks against German Rail Systems during 1944," Luftwaffe Operations Staff/Intelligence, No. 2512/44, "Air Operations against the German Rail Transport System during March, April, and May 1944," 3.6.44.

rest.[207] In retrospect, the transportation plan did not succeed in preventing the *Wehrmacht* from holding the Allies up in Normandy for two months, but it did ensure that the Germans could win neither the battle of the buildup nor the massive battle of attrition that ensued in Normandy.[208]

Throughout the summer of 1944, Bomber Command focused on supporting the great battle in Normandy, both by continuing its suppression of the French railroad network and by conducting direct attacks on German front-line positions to enable British forces in eastern Normandy to break out. The former continued to add to the supply woes of *Wehrmacht* forces, but the latter failed dismally. At least Bomber Command managed to keep most of its bombs on the German side of the line, which was not true of the American Eighth Air Force.[209] With the breakout in early August from the beachhead, Allied forces flooded across France to the German frontier. Ironically, the success of the transportation plan had created a logistical wasteland. Anglo-American ground forces were now on the wrong side of that desert, a fact that goes far toward explaining the stalemate that settled over the Western Front in mid-September 1944.

The Allied ground victory in Normandy and the subsequent liberation of France and Belgium fundamentally changed the air equation in favor of Bomber Command. The *Luftwaffe* lost much of its early-warning system, which relied on radar sites and radio intercept stations along the French coast. Moreover, the British almost immediately established *Oboe* stations in eastern France, on the German frontier, so that this crucial navigation and blind-bombing aid could now range deep into the Reich. In response, the *Luftwaffe* could mount its defensive response only over German territory, which gave the night fighters and their controllers less time to respond, exposing British bombers to attack for a shorter period. At the same time, the American daylight offensive was making two important contributions to the night offensive. In achieving air superiority over Central Europe, Eighth Air Force's fighters had not only wrecked the German day-fighter force but, as noted earlier, had

---

[207] Quoted in Greenhous et al., *The Crucible of War*, p. 805.
[208] The one missing link in the transportation plan was the barge traffic down and across the Seine, which Allied air power largely failed to interdict. For a clear discussion of the impact of the transportation plan on German logistics during the Normandy campaign, see Russell A. Hart, *Clash of Arms: How the Allies Won in Normandy* (Boulder, CO, 2001), pp. 226–227, 371–372, 382, 387–390.
[209] Not once but twice Eighth Air Force's bombers dropped bombs on American troops in support of Operation Cobra, the second time killing more than 100 American soldiers, including Lieutenant General Lesley McNair.

imposed heavy losses on the night fighters as well, since the *Luftwaffe*'s high command continued to commit some of its night fighters to the day battle.[210]

By early September, Bomber Command had largely recovered from the savage beating that its squadrons had suffered in the Battle of Berlin. During the five-month period between the end of March and the end of August, the command suffered only light losses in its forays against targets in occupied France, while flying fewer and less dangerous missions into Germany.[211] As a result, the experience level of its crews climbed substantially, and larger numbers of Lancasters and Mosquitos reached operational squadrons. Not surprisingly, the relatively light losses led to a substantial improvement in morale – which Overlord's success further improved.

By September 1944, Bomber Command represented the fruition of five years of steady adaptation to the challenges of night bombing and those raised by increasingly sophisticated German defenses. Anthony Verrier has outlined the range of these improvements in marking targets alone that by the fall of 1944 made Bomber Command not only a terrible weapon of destruction but also one that could achieve considerable precision in its attacks:

Oboe Sky Marking
Blind Oboe sky marking – Main Force normally approaches in the same direction as the Oboe run in and bombs sky markers at 165 mph with zero wind velocity on bomb sight.

Oboe Ground Marking
Blind Oboe ground marking backed up as necessary with Target Indicators of different colour. Main Force aims preferably at Oboe Target Indicators.

Controlled Oboe
Oboe Target Indicators are assessed by Master Bomber who instructs Main Force by Radio Telephone and sometimes backs up Oboe markers with further Target Indicators of distinctive colour.

8 Group Visual
Similar to controlled Oboe (though may be used beyond Oboe range with H2S or eyesight). Master Bomber visually assesses Oboe markers and re-marks visually.

---

[210] For the impact of the daylight American offensive on the *Luftwaffe* and particularly its fighter pilots, see Murray, *Luftwaffe*, pp. 223–232.
[211] In February 1944, Bomber Command lost 5 percent of sorties dispatched; March, 3 percent; April, 2 percent; May, under 3 percent; June, 2 percent; July, 2 percent; August, 1.2 percent; September, 2 percent. Verrier, *The Bomber Offensive*, p. 292.

H2S Ground Marking
Similar to Oboe ground marking, but, because H2S is less accurate, more initial markers are put down and backers up aim at mean point of impact. Main Force aim at this backing-up and not at H2S marking.

H23S Sky Marking
Similar to Oboe sky marking.

H2S Newhaven
A form of 8 Group Visual. Starts in the same way as H2S [ground marking] but flares are also dropped. Pathfinder Force visual markers then mark aiming point visually.

Musician Newhaven
Same as H2S Newhaven but with initial proximity marking by Oboe.

5 Group Visual
Flares and proximity marking followed by visual dive marking with the offset modification.[212]

In the last three months of 1944, Bomber Command dropped a greater tonnage of bombs than it had dropped in all of 1943.[213] Against Duisberg alone, in a single day the command dropped as great a weight of bombs as the *Luftwaffe* had dropped on London to that point in the war.[214] Meanwhile, Bomber Command's long-time opponents in the German air defense system, while at times able to put up considerable resistance, were essentially crippled. Not only had they lost warning time, but the fuel on which night fighters depended was only available in small amounts. On the night Bomber Command destroyed Dresden, the lack of fuel grounded almost all the night fighters. Moreover, with hardly any fuel at all, the *Luftwaffe*'s training establishment could no longer produce aircrews to replace those killed or maimed by Mosquito night intruders, appalling weather conditions, or the exhaustion of prolonged combat.

On 25 September 1944, as a result of the Octagon Conference in Quebec, operational control of the Allied bomber forces returned to Harris and Carl A. Spaatz.[215] Eisenhower and Tedder could now only request support or provide advice as to the target sets they felt to be the most deserving of attack. Surveying the damage done to the French transportation network and the difficulties inflicted on the *Wehrmacht*'s ability to support the battle in Normandy, Tedder's planners as well as his chief

---

[212] Verrier, *The Bomber Offensive*, pp. 292–293.
[213] Webster and Frankland, *The Strategic Air Offensive against Germany*, vol. 3, p. 184.
[214] Ibid., p. 66.
[215] Greenhous et al., *The Crucible of War*, p. 832.

scientist Solly Zuckerman proposed a massive assault by all of the Allied air forces, tactical as well as strategic, on the German transportation system. Using the direct evidence of the rapid decrease in traffic flow in France after the attacks began in April 1944, they argued that the collapse of the German war economy would ensue in relatively short order. The records indicated that attacks on the marshaling yards on the Franco-German-Belgian frontier had caused a precipitous fall in the shipment of coke and coal to the Ruhr.[216]

Not surprisingly, Tedder and Zuckerman ran into opposition – and not only from Harris and Spaatz but also from Air Commodore S. O. Bufton, chief of the air staff's directorate of bomber operations. Harris opposed the plan aimed at the Reich's transportation system, because he aimed to return to his area-bombing attacks.[217] Spaatz, on the other hand, wished to give additional emphasis to the campaign against the Reich's petroleum industry, attacks that were already having a major impact on the *Wehrmacht*'s ability not only to fight but to train.[218] Enigma decrypts buttressed Spaatz's case. They indicated a progressive collapse of the German petroleum industry, a finding that helped to keep Eighth Air Force's commanders focused on this critical target set.[219] Interestingly, Bufton, with increasing support from Portal, believed attacks on Germany's oil infrastructure represented the best possible use of Bomber Command. Portal summed up his attitude by warning Tedder that "it would be dangerous to apply wholesale to Germany the lessons of France" – in other words, do not pay attention to the evidence.[220] In retrospect, those arguing for an emphasis on the German petroleum missed the fact that such attacks were largely going to hurt the *Wehrmacht*'s mobility, while attacks on the transportation system were going to cause the collapse of the German war economy.

---

[216] Zuckerman, *From Apes to Warlords*, pp. 300–301.
[217] Harris was in favor of continuing under Eisenhower's command because he believed he would run into less opposition to his approach to bombing than were he to be placed back under the control of the air ministry and Portal.
[218] For a discussion of the impact of the campaign against Germany's petroleum industry, see Murray, *Luftwaffe*, pp. 258–259.
[219] The intelligence officer at Eighth Air Force who handled Ultra reported after the war that the intercepts, indicating that shortages were general and not local, convinced "all concerned that the air offensive had uncovered the weak spot in the German economy [which] led to exploitation to the fullest extent." PRO 30/20/16, Ansel E. M. Talbert, Major, U.S. Army Air Corps, "Handling of Ultra at Headquarters Eighth Air Force."
[220] Webster and Frankland, *The Strategic Air Offensive against Germany*, vol. 3, p. 65.

What astonished Zuckerman was the fact that none of the senior airmen and intelligence officers in both Eighth Air Force and Bomber Command displayed any inclination to examine the evidence of the French railroad records. "And at the time it did not seem strange to me, although it does now, that neither Bufton nor his opposite numbers in Bomber Command and in the American air Forces ever wanted to examine the German or French records. So far as they were concerned, the hard evidence which now lay even more strongly behind our plan could not match the *a priori* assumptions and wishful thinking that lay behind their alternative strategies."[221] The best that Tedder could achieve was an agreement that Bomber Command and Eighth Air Force would cooperate in the transportation campaign. Harris agreed to use the *Reichsbahn*'s marshaling yards as the aiming point for his command's great area-bombing raids on cities. Spaatz agreed that when weather prevented Eighth Air Force from bombing petroleum targets, his bombers would attack transportation targets.

Harris's position was less defensible than Spaatz's, especially when one considers the improvements that had occurred in Bomber Command's ability to hit precision targets even in bad weather over the course of the previous two-and-a-half years. Nevertheless, Harris proceeded on his own path. In October, when the command dropped twice as great a tonnage on Germany as any other month of the war, it devoted hardly any tonnage to oil or transportation targets. Harris's return to area bombing represented direct disobedience of the new directive sent by the air ministry. In it the air staff laid down that the "first priority" was to be the campaign against oil; second, of equal importance, was to be the German transportation system.[222] While the directive mentioned counterair and support for land operations, nowhere did it directly suggest that area bombing of what was left of Germany's cities was to be a major priority.

There now took place a furious fight between Portal and Harris. As the official historians admit, "[n]evertheless, the increased conviction and clarity with which the air staff presented their case did not have a corresponding effect upon Sir Arthur Harris, with the result that what had previously been a difference of opinion now became a serious dispute. Nor was this dispute ever resolved, and there can be no doubt that it diminished the effectiveness of Bomber Command in the final phases of

---

[221] Zuckerman, *From Apes to Warlords*, p. 303.
[222] Webster and Frankland, *The Strategic Air Offensive against Germany*, vol. 3, *Victory*, p. 63.

the war."²²³ In the end, Harris won out after a long exchange of letters, in which Portal came close to ordering that Bomber Command switch its effort to the oil campaign and in which Harris virtually dared Portal to fire him.²²⁴

Tedder's objective was clearly to focus the immense resources of Bomber Command, Eighth Air Force, Fifteenth Air Force, and the Allied Tactical Air Forces on destroying the transportation network on which the continued functioning of the Reich's war economy depended. Postwar figures confirm how effective the transportation campaign was in strangling the German war economy, even in its truncated form. It had an almost immediate impact on German transport. From mid-August 1944 on, the loading of railroad cars plummeted. During the week ending 19 August, the *Reichsbahn* loaded and dispatched 899,091 cars; by the week of 28 October, that figure had fallen to 703,580 cars; and by 23 December, the number had fallen to 547,309, despite the heavy demands from German forces attacking in the Ardennes (the Battle of the Bulge). By December 1944, the marshaling capacity of German rail yards had declined to 40 percent of normal; by February 1945, it had reached 20 percent. The Battle of the Bulge confirmed that the air offensive against the transportation system was not yet able to prevent the *Wehrmacht* from executing military operations.²²⁵

But the strategic impact of the bombing offensive was far broader. By early January, its attacks "had reduced the available capacity for economic traffic in Germany to a point which could not hope to sustain, over any period of time, a high level of military production."²²⁶ The loss of transportation gradually strangled the economy by disorganizing the flow of those elements crucial to further production of weapons and ammunition.²²⁷ Under such conditions, neither planning nor actual production could take place in an orderly fashion.

---

²²³ Ibid., p. 77.
²²⁴ The exchange of letters and opinions is admirably summed up by the official historians: see ibid., pp. 75–94.
²²⁵ USSBS, "The Effects of Strategic Bombing on German Transportation," Report No. 200, Washington, DC, 20 November 1945, p. 1.
²²⁶ Ibid., p. 3.
²²⁷ For a fuller examination of the impact of the transportation campaign on the German war economy and the arguments among the senior Allied commands during this period, see the excellent work by Alfred C. Mierzejewski, *The Collapse of the German War Economy, 1944–1945: Allied Air Power and the German National Railway* (Chapel Hill, NC, 1988).

The collapse of coal transportation suggests the extent of this situation. In January 1944, the Essen division of the *Reichsbahn* loaded an average of 21,400 cars daily. By September 1944, that daily total had dropped to 12,000, of which only 3,000 to 4,000 were long haul. By February 1945, Allied transportation attacks had virtually cut the Ruhr off from the rest of Germany. The *Reichsbahn* often had to confiscate what little coal was loaded just to keep locomotives running. Underlining the impact of transportation attacks was the state of coal production and stocks in the Ruhr between August 1944 and February 1945. Despite the fact that coal production fell drastically from 10,417,000 tons in August to 4,778,000 tons in February, stocks in Ruhr collieries rose from 415,000 tons to 2,217,000 tons; the stocks of coke similarly rose from 630,000 tons to 3,069,0004.[228] The Ruhr was quite literally buried in coal, but German railroads could no longer transport coal or coke even to local industries, much less to those in the rest of Germany.

The figures suggest that had Bomber Command focused its effort on the transportation plan beginning in October 1944, the German war economy might well have collapsed a month or two earlier than it did and might also have prevented the *Wehrmacht* from deploying the forces and the supplies that made possible the Ardennes offensive of December 1944. Bomber Command certainly possessed the precision and combat capabilities to inflict enormous damage on the Reich's transportation network. While two months does not appear to represent much time, it is well to remember that the Third Reich, even in its death throes, was killing off tens of thousands of European civilians every day the war continued, while the battlefronts, east, west, and south, were killing tens of thousands more. Bomber Command's greatest failure may have been the failure of its leader to adapt to the new capabilities and context that could have enabled it to bring the war to a conclusion months earlier than May 1945. But Harris, deeply influenced by his past and the culture of the RAF in which he trained and worked before 1939, refused to adapt and thereby ignored the possibilities.

Conclusion

The most significant influence on the way the opposing sides adapted had to do with how they viewed the past. On the German side, Nazi arrogance

---

[228] USSBS, "The Effects of Strategic Bombing on German Transportation," Report No. 200, Washington, DC, 20 November 1945, p. 3.

and racial prejudice compounded a national belief that the defeat in 1918 had resulted from the Jews and communists stabbing an unbroken and undefeated army in the back. Nothing could have been further from the truth. The reality was that a willful and arrogant German leadership had taken on the whole world, including, at the end, the United States and, not surprisingly, had lost. Yet, in the Second World War, German leaders again took on the whole world, except that this time they managed to get the Americans involved earlier and at far greater cost to themselves.[229] On the strategic level, the Germans repeated every mistake they had made in the previous conflict with even more disastrous consequences. No matter how carefully they may have analyzed the tactical and operational lessons of World War I, that effort could not outweigh the disastrous results of strategic myopia – a myopia which the German government had encouraged and fostered right from the beginning of the interwar period.[230]

On the British side, prewar governments proved contemptuous of the idea that strategic factors should actually govern the behavior of their state in the 1920s and 1930s.[231] The result was the disaster of the Munich Conference in September 1938, which wrecked the European balance of power and led directly to the catastrophes of the opening years of World War II. Ironically, Winston Churchill, the politician-strategist who understood history the best in Britain, came to power only after his predecessors had squandered nearly every strategic advantage the British and their French allies possessed. At that point, despite the series of disasters that overwhelmed Britain's allies on the Continent, Churchill intuitively understood that the strategic calculus would not allow the United States and the Soviet Union to remain aloof from the struggle, although the fact that Germany would willfully draw both powers into the European conflict in 1941 must have surprised even him.

---

[229] In this regard, while Hitler made the decision to declare war on the United States, the senior naval leaders had urged him to make such a declaration throughout the summer of 1941, while no one in either the army or *Luftwaffe* voiced the slightest opposition to the decision. As Gerhard Weinberg has pointed out, because German military leaders believed they had lost World War I because the Jews and communists had stabbed the army in the back, from their point of view, the United States had not played a major role in the events of 1918.

[230] In this regard, see particularly Holger H. Herwig, "Clio Deceived, Patriotic Self-Censorship in Germany after the Great War," *International Security*, Fall 1987.

[231] For a discussion of these issues, see Murray, *The Change in the European Balance of Power*, chap. 2.

In any case, Churchill had to make war with the military instruments he found in the United Kingdom. And the RAF, with its contempt of history, waged a war at night that paid little heed even to its own experiences. In September 1917, Lieutenant Commander Lord Tiverton of the Royal Naval Air Service had reported to the Air Board that "experience has shown that it is quite easy for five squadrons to set out to bomb a particular target and for only one of those five ever to reach the objective, while the other four, in the honest belief that they have done so, have bombed four different villages which bore little, if any, resemblance to the one they desired to attack."[232] Without the memory of its own past as an anchor, too many RAF commanders simply believed that their prewar assumptions would prove valid. Thus, they refused to enlist even technology in their quest to prove that "the bomber would always get through."

Once Bomber Command's leadership was disabused of that notion, the contest between its bombers and the *Luftwaffe*'s night-fighter defenses revolved around how leading figures, civilians as well as military, viewed technology. And here, the manner in which individual leaders came to think about war and technological developments during the prewar period influenced to a great extent how they adapted to the actual conditions of the conflict. On the German side, three factors were of crucial importance. First: the German leadership, and not just Hitler, thought in terms of an offensive war – one focused largely on the ground. Here traditional German military culture as well as the Reich's position on the Continent played a major role.

Second: one should not underestimate the role of Nazi ideology, with its aggressive *Weltanschauung*, in the German response to Bomber Command's challenge. The idea of focusing primarily on a defensive stance against the swelling night offensive was anathema to the Nazi approach. Thus, well into 1943, the production of night fighters and the technological support they required took a back seat to virtually every other military requirement. The production of bombers siphoned off substantial resources from the nighttime as well as the daytime struggle. But even more deleterious were the V-1 and the V-2 programs. From the clear vantage point of the twenty-first century, these production choices appear bizarre, but in reality, they fit within a thoroughly understandable

---

[232] Quoted in Group Captain R. A. Mason, "The British Dimension," in *Airpower and Warfare*, ed. by Alfred F. Hurley and Robert C. Erhard (Washington, DC, 1979), pp. 30–31.

intellectual framework, given the assumptions undergirding Nazi decision making.

Third: equally important was how German leaders viewed their scientific community; scientists and technologists, in the German view, were simply technicians who were supposed to do what they were told. Science was the servant of the military rather than an originator. While the Germans made some impressive technological adaptations during the course of the war at night, there were a number of astonishing gaps, the most obvious being the failure to develop IFF or proximity-fused antiaircraft shells. Substantial numbers of German scientists disappeared into the military, where their contributions to the war effort would prove minimal. Thus, there was none of the partnership that characterized Fighter Command's relations with some of Britain's leading scientists. One might also note that a major failure in the German approach to modern war was a belief in the inherent superiority of German technology.

On the military side of the equation, the German capacity to adapt also displayed major weaknesses. The entire German approach to war emphasized the tactical and the purely operational.[233] Thus, there was simply no focus on the long term. In the period 1940 through 1942, this was particularly dangerous, because the Germans simply wished away the long-term implications of British efforts to build up Bomber Command. The ridicule that Goebbels heaped on Anglo-American production figures reflected not just the propaganda minister's attitude but that of Germany's military leaders as well. By the time of the Battle of Berlin, the American daytime assault was already ripping the guts out of the *Luftwaffe*, while in the west, Anglo-American forces were gathering for the great cross-channel invasion. And here the Germans failed miserably to counter the assault on the French transportation network that ensured Overlord's success.

Finally, the Nazi state's top-down style of leadership helped sustain the Kammhuber Line long after it had lost utility, delaying a more effective use of available technology. That allowed the British to maximize their capabilities by concentrating the bomber stream in time and space, which in turn minimized the limited potential of the German night-fighter force. Reinforcing the failure to adapt was a consistent pattern of analytic failure on the part of the *Luftwaffe* general staff and within Kammhuber's staff as well. To a considerable extent, this reflected an emphasis on the

---

[233] "Purely operational" underlines that logistics and intelligence did not factor into the German equation.

present rather than on the long view. Moreover, with strategy the purview of Hitler alone, there was no corporate memory capable of focusing on the rising level of threat that Bomber Command represented. Hitler, at least, recognized that the May 1942 raid on Cologne represented a significant warning signal, but his attention soon wandered back to the Eastern Front, while others simply went back to business as usual. The raids on Essen beginning in March 1943 should have represented a wake-up call; they did not. By the time of the Hamburg raids in late July 1943, it was already too late, even considering the recovery in late 1943.

On the British side, Bomber Command's adaptations to the actuality of combat reveal some considerable ironies. The complete inability of its bombers to hit anything at night, which marked its campaign over the course of its first two years, may have been a blessing in disguise. Nevertheless, the influence of prewar assumptions and the refusal to acknowledge a significant problem with navigation at night, even in periods of bad weather, are astonishing. As suggested earlier, the one advantage the British enjoyed in this regard lay in the ability and willingness of the political leadership to force the RAF's leaders to pay attention to the Butt Report. Still, sprinkled throughout Bomber Command's conduct of the war was an attitude that the theory must be right and damn the facts. It took the direct interference of Churchill and Lord Cherwell to force the Butt Report on a most unwilling air staff and senior leadership of Bomber Command.

When Harris assumed command in February 1942, he envisioned no other path but that of area bombing. That stubborn commitment persisted even after technological improvements made other and better options possible. In retrospect, Harris's ruthless, driving leadership was a major factor in keeping the night-bombing offensive going. Nevertheless, that same personality severely inhibited his staff's ability to adapt to the conditions that his crews were confronting. Moreover, much of the RAF's senior leadership was clearly wedded to the prewar assumption that bombing the enemy's population was the surest means to break his morale and defeat him. While area bombing may have been the only operational approach possible through mid-1943, it was not the only approach thereafter. Having almost wrecked his command in the Battle of Berlin, Harris was astonished to discover that it was capable of precision attacks in March 1944 that he had argued were not possible.

Yet when control of the command reverted to him in September 1944 after the success of Overlord, Harris immediately returned to his earlier area-bombing campaign. His refusal to acknowledge the effectiveness of the campaign against the French railroad network and its potential applicability to its German counterpart conformed to a pattern clearly set in the prewar period and during the first year of the war: if the evidence suggested that the assumptions were incorrect, then one need only ignore the evidence. Undoubtedly, the massive battering that Bomber Command dealt out to Germany's cities in the last eight months of the war contributed to the German collapse in the spring of 1945. However, in view of the capabilities that Bomber Command enjoyed by mid-1944, one cannot help believing that the collapse might have come sooner, had Harris developed a more imaginative and adaptive approach to the bombing of Germany.

The price paid for such single-mindedness came in the lives of Bomber Command's aircrews, the proportionate losses of which in almost every respect rivaled the losses of British officers and NCOs in the First World War. Out of every 100 airmen who flew with Bomber Command during the war (and that number includes those who flew during its last eight months, when the command was at its largest and when it suffered its fewest losses), more than 50 percent were killed on operations and *fewer than one-quarter* survived the war uninjured and without time in German POW camps. That was the terrifying bill paid by the British nation during the long, dark course of Bomber Command's campaign from 15 May 1940 to 7 May 1945.

7

The 1973 Yom Kippur War

In many respects, the outcome of the Yom Kippur War was as much a surprise to military analysts and pundits as the stunning victory the Israel Defense Forces (IDF) had gained in the Six-Day War five years earlier. In October 1973, the Egyptian and Syrian armies caught Israel's military forces by surprise, not so much because the Arabs misled Israeli intelligence as to the timing of the offensive but because the Arab armies displayed tactical capabilities with which no one in Israel had credited them and that for a time seemed to threaten the existence of the Jewish state.[1]

Under the pressures of combat in adverse circumstances, the Israelis made significant combat adaptations in a short period. Despite, or

---

[1] That was certainly the impression of Minister of Defense Moshe Dayan for a short period on the first and second days of the Arab offensive. At times, Dayan appears to have believed Israeli forces might not only lose the Golan but also suffer a massive defeat in the north that would threaten the existence of the state.

I am indebted to Brigadier General Dov Tamari, Israel Defense Force (IDF, retired), Brigadier General Shimon Naveh (IDF, retired), and Ms. Ofra Gracier for their extraordinarily generous efforts in making the arrangements for a series of interviews with senior Israeli officers, who were in various critical positions during the Yom Kippur War. These interviews took place during a visit to Israel in October and early November 2000. In addition, these three friends arranged a staff ride of the Golan Heights for the author, which was of inestimable value in assessing the events that took place there in October 1973. They contributed immensely to the questioning of the officers who provided most of the insights in this chapter. Moreover, when necessary, they provided translation and greater specificity in my discussions with the various generals whom I interviewed during my visit to Israel. Whatever faulty interpretations are contained in this chapter are my own and not those of whom I interviewed.

perhaps because of, their initial setbacks, they adapted in some areas with considerable agility and turned the tables on their opponents. However, what makes this case study so interesting lies not only in the areas in which the Israelis successfully adapted but also in the areas where they found it more difficult, if not impossible, to adapt. The causes of their failures may be even more important to thinking about war in the future than the reasons underlying their successes.

This chapter begins by examining the military and strategic background, then turns to the planning and preparations for war, followed by a discussion of the war's conduct and the adaptations that did or did not take place during military operations. As with previous chapters, the purpose is not to write another history of the Yom Kippur War but rather to examine the processes and difficulties of change and adaptation under the pressures of combat. Given the war's relatively short duration, it is not surprising the Israelis encountered substantial difficulties. The task is to examine how in some areas they managed to adapt with considerable alacrity, while in others they failed almost completely.

The Israeli Military through to the Six-Day War

The Israeli State formed its military institutions in response to the conflict that broke out immediately upon its founding in 1948. Confronted with the resistance of Palestinian irregulars as well as the conventional military forces of their Arab neighbors, the Israelis created a viable state and its military institutions in the midst of a war for survival.[2] Despite Israel's overwhelming victory in the ensuing conflict, its Arab neighbors refused to recognize its existence but turned instead to guerrilla warfare, while building up their military forces for a renewed conflict. Thus, in the early days of their independence, the Israelis were almost always under attack from Arab guerrillas, while at the same time they had to establish conventional military forces to defend themselves against a major attack.[3]

---

[2] In many respects in 1947 and 1948, the Israelis confronted problems similar to those the American colonists faced in their war of independence against the British in creating military institutions out of nothing. The difference was that during their war of independence, the Americans held almost unlimited space to defend their claim to independence, while the Israelis possessed almost no space; and when the American Revolution was over, only the Indians remained to threaten American independence.

[3] The immediate neighbors were obviously Egypt, Syria, Jordan, and Lebanon, but for substantial periods of Israel's existence, Saudi troops have been deployed near its frontiers. In the 1973 war, units from Iraq, Morocco, and Libya participated in the fighting against the Israelis.

In 1955, these difficulties increased when the Egyptians and other Arab states began to receive substantial military aid from the Soviet Union. Given the multiple threats, the Israelis created a military system based on a small active military with the ability to mobilize virtually the state's entire male population to flesh out its ground forces. This military system demanded the IDF have sufficient time to mobilize before the outbreak of major combat operations. But Israel's lack of geographic depth – the distance between the West Bank territories and Tel Aviv on the Mediterranean was barely eight miles – intensified worries about whether it could mobilize in sufficient time to protect the homeland without suffering disastrous casualties and irreparable damage to its infrastructure.

In 1956, Israel, hoping to dampen Egypt's support of terrorism, formed an ad hoc alliance with Britain and France, both of which were seeking to regain control of the Suez Canal and overthrow Gamal Abdel Nasser, Egypt's dictator. In the ensuing war, Israeli brigades smashed through Egyptian defenses and drove almost to the Suez Canal after destroying Egyptian forces in the Sinai, while British and French military operations barely managed to gain a foothold on the canal's northern edge. Despite the Israeli success, most commentators excused Egypt's defeat on the grounds that its army had faced attacks from two directions. The Israelis eventually relinquished their hold on the Sinai in return for the demilitarization of the peninsula and the introduction of United Nations (UN) forces into the demilitarized areas.

What the demilitarization of the Sinai gave the Israelis was warning time.[4] It certainly did not give them any greater strategic depth. But they now possessed the warning time to mobilize their forces, should the Egyptians choose to remilitarize the Sinai. In 1967, that warning time provided the Israelis with the time needed. In May, in response to proddings from the Soviets that the Israelis were about to attack Syria, Nasser deployed substantial forces into the Sinai. At the same time, he demanded that the UN pull out its observers from the Sinai.[5] As Egyptian forces flooded

[4] I am indebted to Brigadier General Dov Tamari (IDF, retired), deputy division commander in Major General Avraham Adan's Division in the Yom Kippur War, in an interview in Tel Aviv, 24 October 2000, for this point. The position of deputy division commander is similar to that of assistant division commander in the U.S. Army, but the Israeli position carries more independence and authority than is the case with assistant division commanders in the U.S. Army. During a short period of the war, General Tamari received command of a portion of Adan's division, which he fought as a small division.

[5] To this day, it remains unclear as to why the Soviets instigated the crisis. In the end, it was probably a combination of incompetence and what one recent commentator has described as "the tendency of communist decision makers to be influenced by their own

toward Israel and the UN withdrew, the Israelis mobilized and deployed from the Negev to Gaza, preparatory to undertaking offensive military operations.

For the next three weeks, there was a standoff as diplomats desperately sought a peaceful solution. The Israelis integrated and retrained their reservists, as they prepared to strike. On the other side of the hill, Egyptian commanders were unclear as to whether they were to undertake offensive operations – which was certainly the desire of the feckless crowds in Cairo – or defend the Sinai. The muddle at the highest levels served only to demonstrate the fact that senior officers were selected more for their political and ideological loyalty to Nasser's regime than for their military competence.[6] Moreover, few Egyptian officers or soldiers had trained or prepared to fight in Sinai's desert wastes. Caught up in Nasser's propaganda trumpeting that Egypt was on the verge of destroying Israel, few senior military leaders or their subordinates undertook the detailed and rigorous business of preparing seriously for war, especially a defensive war.

In the ensuing conflict, the Israelis launched a devastating surprise blow that destroyed the Egyptian Air Force at its bases. An offensive by three Israeli divisions into the Sinai immediately followed the air attack.

---

propaganda on imperialist and Zionist perfidy..., magnifying the threat Israel really posed to Syria." Nasser does not appear to have wanted war, and his instructions to the Egyptian Army were that it was to conduct defensive operations but be prepared for offensive operations. The actions and pronouncements coming out of Cairo, however, suggested that the Egyptians were intent on war. Michael B. Oren, *Six Days of War: June 1967 and the Making of the Modern Middle East* (Oxford, 2002), pp. 55–60.

[6] The difficulties that Arab armies have confronted over the past six decades have had little to do with the bravery of their individual soldiers but have rather been the result of, first, the fact that Arab societies and culture have been unwilling to support the kind of discipline that modern military organizations have demanded, since their invention in the seventeenth century in Western Europe; and second, the reality that tyrannies of all colors have found it difficult to reconcile the need for professional competence at the highest levels of their military organizations with their [own] political survival. In the latter case, the danger for tyrannies is that military institutions led by competent commanders possess the ability to overthrow the tyrant. Such was certainly the attitude of Saddam Hussein and his advisers in all three major wars that Iraq fought between 1980 and 2003. For the development of military effectiveness in the West, see Williamson Murray and MacGregor Knox, "Thinking about Revolutions in Warfare," in MacGregor Knox and Williamson Murray, eds., *The Dynamics of Military Revolution: 1300–2050* (Cambridge, 2001), chap. 1. For the problems Arab nations have confronted in developing effective military institutions, see Colonel Norvell B. de Atkins, U.S. Army (retired), "Arab Armies," unpublished paper, October 2002. For the role of culture in military effectiveness, see Williamson Murray, "Does Military Culture Really Matter?" *Orbis*, Winter 1999; and Williamson Murray, "Military Culture Does Matter," *Strategic Review*, Spring 1999.

However, they had no operational objective beyond exploiting tactical surprise to destroy Egyptian forces lying to their front in Sinai. Nor was there an operational headquarters to coordinate the movement of the three divisions as the campaign unfolded. In the end, the lack of operational control did not matter. In a matter of hours, not days, the three Israeli thrusts shattered the Egyptian Army, much as the German drive across the Meuse had shattered the French Army's equilibrium on 13 May 1940. Just as the French observer Antoine de Saint Exupéry described the collapse of the French army in 1940, so might one describe the Egyptian Army's collapse in 1967:

> The tank detachments that move easily across the countryside because no tanks oppose them produce irreparable damage even though the actual destruction they cause is apparently superficial – the capture of local command staffs, severed telephone lines, burning villages. [The tanks] play the role of those chemical agents that destroy not the organism as a whole, but its nervous system. Throughout the landscape across which [they] have swept like lightening, the [Egyptian] army, even if it appears almost intact, has ceased to be an army. It has been transformed into separate clots. Where an organism existed, there remains only a collection of disconnected organs. Between the clots – however combative the men may be – the enemy moves as he wishes. An army that is nothing more than the numerical sum of its soldiers ceases to be effective.[7]

Accompanying their devastating victory over the Egyptians, the Israelis wrecked the Jordanian Army, conquered the West Bank as well as the old city of Jerusalem, and blasted the Syrians off the Golan Heights. The Israeli ground attacks used a number of approaches. In the northern Sinai, General Israel Tal's division broke through Egyptian positions at Khan Unis and then smashed through defensive positions at Sheikh Zuweid to the west in operations executed almost entirely by armored forces.[8] Further south, Ariel Sharon's division attacked the Kusseima-Abu Ageila position. It drove armored thrusts from the north and west (behind the Egyptians), supported by infantry to clear enemy trench lines, while Israeli paratroopers attacked and silenced Egyptian artillery. Sharon's division possessed bare equality against its dug-in opponents, the 2nd Egyptian Division.[9] When the Israeli attacks went in, they were supported by 80 artillery pieces, the din of which disguised their movements. Sharon's

---

[7] Antoine de Saint Exupéry, *Pilote de guerre* (New York, 1942), pp. 94–95.
[8] Oren, *Six Days of War*, p. 179.
[9] The 2nd Division possessed seven infantry battalions, 140 artillery pieces, and 130 tanks, and Sharon's Division, eight infantry battalions, 140 guns, and 130 tanks.

headquarters orchestrated this combined-arms operation with a synchronized night attack that destroyed the Egyptian position and opened the way for a drive on the Mitla Pass and Suez Canal.[10]

Meanwhile, on the Jordanian front, Israeli paratroopers stormed Jerusalem's Old City. Finally, on the war's last day the IDF seized the Golan in an infantry-armor assault, supported by artillery. Air superiority made possible close air support and interdiction strikes that pounded Arab formations and enabled all of the ground operations conducted by the Israelis. When the dust settled, the Israelis had been successful on every front. For the Arabs, there was no avoiding the reality that an army consisting of Jews, a group despised by Arab society over the course of the previous 13 centuries, had destroyed the military organizations on which they had lavished such great resources.[11]

Yet, despite the Israeli success, there were difficulties. In some areas, Egyptian, Syrian, and Jordanian soldiers had fought with great tenacity. Tal's lead battalion had suffered heavier casualties than it would suffer in the Yom Kippur War: the battalion commander was killed, the S-3 and three out of four company commanders wounded, and almost the entire command element wiped out.[12] But most important, there had been no overall control of Israeli forces at the operational level.

The high command seems to have thought it would be best for Israeli forces to halt short of the Suez Canal but failed to communicate that intention to the division commanders. Thus, the divisions ended up in reaching the canal simply because it was there, rather than through operational or strategic design. No one at the political and higher command levels seems to have thought through the strategic and operational, much less the political, implications of occupying a line along the Suez Canal. As Sharon suggests about the resulting situation – one that he had done so much to create: "So it was that without any long-range thinking being done about the situation, our soldiers found themselves on the Suez Canal."[13]

---

[10] Oren, *Six Days of War*, pp. 181–182. For a more detailed examination of the combined-arms battle with rather primitive, but useful, maps, see also Ariel Sharon with David Chanoff, *Warrior: An Autobiography* (New York, 1989), pp. 191–200.

[11] In fact, the victory reflected the fact that Israel, dominated by Jews from Europe, was a Western state with Western military institutions, while the Arabs still faced the enormous challenge presented by a civilization that the West had created over ten centuries and that they were being asked to adapt to in less than a century.

[12] Interview with Major General Haim Erez (IDF, retired), brigade commander, Sharon's Division, Yom Kippur War, Israeli Armored Museum, 1 November 2000.

[13] Sharon, *Warrior*, p. 229.

Fallout from the Six-Day War

After the catastrophe to Arab arms, a conference of Arab political leaders at Khartoum enunciated their response to military defeat. However, their "three no's" – no recognition, no peace, and no negotiations – confronted the Egyptian government with a number of unpalatable realities, not the least of which was the fact that the Israelis were on the banks of the canal. Nasser's refusal to deal with the Israelis led the Egyptians into a blind alley. With the loss of revenues from the Suez Canal and the problem of replenishing Egypt's arsenal, devastated by the Six-Day War, the Egyptians were forced into increasing dependence on the Soviet Union to replenish their devastated arsenal. Meanwhile, Nasser's insistence on continued confrontation with the Israelis committed the Egyptian military almost immediately to action of some kind, which, within two weeks of the ending of the Six-Day War, led to shelling of Israeli positions along the Suez Canal.

On the opposite side, the Israelis possessed little more strategic insight. Not surprisingly, their overwhelming victory resulted in what one might best term a case of "victory disease." As Prime Minister Golda Meir commented, "the mere thought of the Egyptian army crossing the canal is an insult to intelligence."[14] Certainly, the Israeli general public and political leaders carried away from the Six-Day War a sense that their enemies were incapable of putting together coherent and effective military operations.[15]

Moreover, most Israelis regarded the IDF's victory as having at last provided the Jewish state with the strategic depth it had lacked in the first two decades of its existence. What was lost in such thinking was the fact that its regular forces were now deployed far from Israel's heartland and their mobilization base. In effect, gaining geographic depth meant the loss of warning time, for Israeli forces were now directly at the enemy's doorstep and far from their own military bases.[16]

But this failure to understand the strategic consequences of holding on to the Sinai was only one of the symptoms of "victory disease" within the

---

[14] Sharon, *Warrior*, p. 265.
[15] Interview with Brigadier General Iri Kahn, (IDF, retired), company commander, reserve paratroop battalion, Yom Kippur War, Tel Aviv, 28 October 2000. General Kahn, who at the time was a reserve paratrooper, suggested Israeli paratroopers trained as if their future opponents "would be as good as you are." Nevertheless, despite the considerable losses that occurred during the War of Attrition, "the impression of the Six-Day War never wore off."
[16] I am indebted to General Dov Tamari for this point.

Israeli military. The IDF failed to carry out a rigorous, careful lessons-learned examination of the Six-Day War.[17] Historians often accuse military institutions of studying and preparing for the last war, which is supposedly why they do badly in the next. In fact, they rarely, if ever, carry out a careful lessons-learned analysis of the last war. Like most human organizations, militaries tend to examine what makes them look good rather than what calls their success into question.[18] For the most part, they are content, particularly if successful, to rest on their laurels and, if unsuccessful, to search for excuses to explain away their ineptitude or ineffectiveness.[19]

Thus, the Israelis were hardly unique when they failed to examine coherently what had worked and why, and what had failed and why.[20] As the G-3 of Southern Command during the Yom Kippur War put it, a large number of mistakes occurred throughout the Six-Day War, which saw "no substantial conduct of brigade level operations, but instead was at best a bunch of disjointed battalion-level actions." In effect, there was "no professional analysis of the war, no willingness to look at the IDF's organization, training, structure, or tactics." To discover the lessons of recent combat experience, one needed, in his words, "a culture of asking questions"; instead, the IDF focused on answers and solutions in the narrowest sense.[21] Thus, throughout the six years between the Six-Day

---

[17] Arial Sharon, in his not-always-reliable memoirs, claims that as chief of training in the aftermath of the war, "I began to study the war intensively, going over each of the battles and each of the battlefields with the individual commanders, refighting the actions with them in an effort to draw as many lessons as possible from their experiences." Sharon, *Warrior*, p. 208. The evidence does not support his claim.

[18] In fairness, one should note that most military cultures do not create a caste of generals and admirals open to criticism from below or outside the organization on how their forces have performed.

[19] This was the case with the French Army during the interwar period. For that failure, see Robert Allan Doughty, *The Seeds of Disaster: The Development of French Army Doctrine, 1919–1939* (Hamden, CT, 1985), pp. 72–90.

[20] A substantial portion of the lessons-learned process is to *learn* from the examination of what had happened in the last war. The Israeli tank hero of the Yom Kippur War notes in his memoirs: "There was no doubt, I thought, that the T-55s were more advanced than our tanks, especially when it came to night firing. We knew it from the Six-Day War, but little attention had been paid to the fact." Avigdor Kahalani, *The Heights of Courage: A Tank Leader's War on the Golan* (Tel Aviv, 1987), p. 49.

[21] Moreover, the process of developing lessons is, more often than not, flawed. After the Yom Kippur War, the Israelis did make extensive efforts to gain lessons from their experiences by holding a series of conferences with commanders. But Adan comments in his memoirs about the effort: "Worst of all, the men presented events both as they saw them and as they wanted to see them. Much information was lost because of the superficial nature of the conference." Major General Avraham (Bren) Adan, *On the*

War and the Yom Kippur War, there was little willingness to consider how the enemy could have behaved and might behave in the future.[22]

Without an overall lessons-learned examination of what had actually happened, the Israeli high command drew the lessons with which it was most comfortable.[23] The armored units appeared to have achieved the most spectacular successes in the Six-Day War, a perception that resulted in their receiving the greatest attention and resources in the postwar period.[24] Sharon's combined-arms destruction of the 2nd Egyptian Division received less interest and analysis than it deserved. Thus, IDF leaders emphasized armored formations rather than combined-arms warfare in the run-up to the Yom Kippur War.

But perhaps the most significant weakness to result from the IDF's general failure to conduct a lessons-learned analysis was that the Israelis did not come to grips with the problems of conducting war at the operational level. Instead, they focused on the tactical problem of controlling brigades, battalions, and companies, rather than on controlling multidivisional forces in a larger campaign or in thinking through the problems of developing a campaign design appropriate to Israel's strategic objective and the operational contexts within which tactical actions would be fought.[25] This criticism is not to suggest that the Israelis failed to conduct their small-unit training at the same high levels as before the Six-Day War. If anything, the experiences of small-unit leaders in combat, officers

---

Banks of the Suez: An Israeli General's Personal Account of the Yom Kippur War (Novato, CA, 1980), p. 465.

[22] Interview with Brigadier General Shai Tamari (IDF, retired), G-3 Southern Command, Yom Kippur War, Tel Aviv, 27 October 2002.

[23] One Israeli officer noted to me that "the IDF had not analyzed the Six-Day War in a professional manner. The IDF was rather good at learning short-term lessons because they involved improvisation, something most Israelis were rather good at. No one sat down after the war to analyze the large number of mistakes that had taken place. There was no willingness to look at organization, training, structure, or tactics." Interview with General Shai Tamari, Tel Aviv, 27 October 2000.

[24] Even after the Yom Kippur War was over, the Israeli tank commander Avigdor Kahalani could write in his memoirs the following about his experiences of fighting on the Golan Heights: "Artillery has always seemed to me something we can win without, perhaps because it doesn't do much harm to tanks." Kahalani, *The Heights of Courage*, p. 32.

[25] This weakness would show up throughout the fighting in the Sinai in the Yom Kippur War. At the start of the fight against the Syrians, there was not even a divisional battle but rather uncoordinated operations by two independent brigades, one of which fought at the company and platoon level rather than the battalion-brigade level, a factor that played a considerable role in its destruction during the first day of the Yom Kippur War. Conversations with Generals Naveh and Dov Tamari, Tel Aviv, 24 October to 2 November 2000.

as well as NCOs, raised training levels throughout the army, a factor that would prove of considerable importance in the next conflict.[26]

Contributing to the IDF's unwillingness, or inability, to come to grips with the experiences of the 1967 war was the fact that Israeli forces found themselves almost immediately thereafter engaged in what became known as the War of Attrition. The Egyptian Army conducted a series of increasingly heavy artillery bombardments on Israeli positions, often accompanying them with commando raids. Israeli ground forces replied with their own raids, some indeed leading to spectacular successes, while the Israeli Air Force reached ever deeper into Egypt with air raids.[27]

The heavy Egyptian bombardments in fall 1969 forced the Israelis to address the problems presented by their forward positions along the Suez Canal. In September, an Egyptian artillery bombardment killed ten and wounded 18 IDF soldiers. A month and a half later, a more intense bombardment killed 15 and wounded 34.[28] These were losses Israel's body politic was unwilling to sustain. The result was a serious debate within the IDF about how to defend Israel's strategic position in the Sinai and along the canal. Complicating the problem for the Israelis was the fact that their hold on the canal had hardened into a national consensus that the IDF should retain that posture until the Egyptians negotiated.[29]

The result of the debate was a compromise that combined both positional and mobile defensive schemes.[30] To minimize their exposure, the Israelis reduced their presence along the canal to an outpost line, the purpose of which was to warn of either an Egyptian raid or offensive. As one general noted: "These strong points never were planned to prevent a Canal crossing or serve as a defensive line. They were only a warning line."[31] Another Israeli observer suggested that the "Bar-Lev" Line[32] was designed "entirely within the tactical context of the War of Attrition and

---

[26] Interview with General Dov Tamari, Tel Aviv, 24 October 2002.
[27] Such as the raid on Green Island at the northern end of the Suez Canal and the December 1969 raid, in which the Israelis captured and successfully lifted out of Egyptian territory the components of the Soviet's newest air-defense radar. Martin van Creveld, *The Sword and the Olive, A Critical History of the Israeli Defense Force* (New York, 1998), p. 213; Sharon, *Warrior*, p. 233.
[28] Adan, *On the Banks of the Suez*, p. 43.
[29] As one of the Israeli officers interviewed by the author put it: "The [Israeli] public's demand is always on the safety of its soldiers and low casualty rates, but that public has little interest in strategic issues or real military issues." Interview with General Kahn, Tel Aviv, 28 October 2002.
[30] For a fuller account of the debate, see Adan, *On the Banks of the Suez*, pp. 42–55.
[31] Ibid., p. 48.
[32] Nicknamed after Chaim "Kidoni" Bar-Lev.

was never meant to deal with the problems raised by a major Egyptian offensive."[33]

The difficulty lay in the fact that an Egyptian raid or a major offensive called for entirely different responses – in the former, retention of the Bar-Lev positions; in the latter, withdrawal to positions in the rear. Exacerbating the tension between holding and withdrawing was the fact that the outpost line cost Israel considerable resources, while the media's labeling the positions the "Bar-Lev Line" after the current chief of staff inevitably imbued it with the IDF's military prestige. Given the muddled thinking that had gone into the line, when war came, Israeli commanders held differing conceptions as to how the small garrisons should respond to waves of attacking Egyptian infantry.

But there was a larger problem, and that involved the defense of the Golan as well as the Sinai. Throughout its existence, the IDF had based its conception of war as well as its planning on the belief that it must take the offensive in any conflict. *The belief that it "must" had, by the early 1970s, hardened into a belief that it "would" take the offensive.* Thus, planning for military operations on the Golan and along the canal assumed the IDF would receive sufficient warning to mobilize and deploy the reserves needed to launch an immediate offensive.[34] For example, of the seven operation plans for the defense of the canal line, six involved the IDF's taking the offensive before the Egyptians. Two plans included amphibious operations to get around the surface-to-air missile belt the Egyptians had thrown up along the canal's west bank.

However, there seems to have been no strategic goal for these offensives, apart from simply gaining territory. Thus, there was neither a strategic nor operational end-state in the mind of those planning for a future war.[35] The sole defensive plan on the Suez front still assumed that the

---

[33] Interview with General Dov Tamari, Tel Aviv, 24 October 2000.
[34] Here Israel's geographic position, as in the case of Prussia and Germany in the nineteenth century, had an enormous influence over the predisposition of the IDF for the offensive. For a discussion of the influence of geographical position on strategy, see Williamson Murray and Mark Grimsley, "On Strategy," in Williamson Murray, MacGregor Knox, and Alvin Bernstein, eds., *The Making of Strategy: Rulers, States, and War* (Cambridge, 1994), chap. 1. For the influence of geographical position on Israel's strategy, see Michael Handel, "The Evolution of Israeli Strategy: The Psychology of Insecurity and the Quest for Absolute Security," in *The Making of Strategy*. See also Williamson Murray, "Some Thoughts on War and Geography," in Colin S. Gray and Geoffrey Sloan, eds., *Geopolitics, Geography and Strategy* (London, 1999).
[35] These observations are drawn from extensive interviews and discussions with General Dov Tamari, Tel Aviv and the Golan Heights, 24 October to 2 November 2000.

IDF would have four days of strategic warning and would thus possess three fully mobilized armored divisions when operations began. It visualized surrendering no territory but instead almost immediately launching a counteroffensive, the preparations for which Sharon had already taken in hand in the area just south of the area the Israelis would nickname the "Chinese Farm" during the fighting in October 1973.[36]

Planning was even more muddled on the Golan where the Israeli Northern Command had posited three alternative ground force commitments in case of war – a single brigade, a single division, and two divisions. Despite these different force levels, IDF planning visualized only one operation: an offensive into Syria toward Damascus.[37] Not surprisingly, there was no serious "red teaming" of the plans or of the enemy's alternatives. Facile assumptions drove not only the planning but also consideration of future operational possibilities.

In such an atmosphere, the assurances by the IDF's intelligence organizations that the Arabs would not launch a war because they recognized they could not defeat the IDF in battle seemed to make sense. But in accepting that proposition, the Israelis ignored Clausewitz's most basic principle that "war is not a mere act of policy but a true political instrument, a continuation of political activity by other means."[38] Thus, they missed the possibility the Egyptians and Syrians might have a political and strategic end-state in mind other than the absolute defeat of Israel's military forces.[39] Within that framework of political understanding, war was a distinct possibility, especially considering the willingness of the Soviet Union to supply the Arabs with the most up-to-date arms.

---

[36] Sharon claims in his memoirs that he was worried war was coming sooner than later during his stint as the commander of Southern Command. "What particularly concerned me in all this was the discipline with which the Egyptians conducted themselves. More officers were present than ever before [along the canal], and there was no question that their troops were acting purposefully, in accordance with specific training goals. Their movements were marked by determination and initiative, and even the details indicated meticulous planning.... A transformation had come over the Egyptians since the Six Day War. This was an enemy with a clear mission, concerned with analyzing its problems, finding solutions, and preparing thoroughly for its task. It was no longer the silk underwear army that we had broken five years earlier." Sharon, *Warrior*, p. 264.
[37] Interview and briefing with General Naveh, Golan Heights, 23 October 2000.
[38] Carl von Clausewitz, *On War*, trans. and ed. by Michael Howard and Peter Paret (Princeton, 1976), p. 86.
[39] In fairness to Israeli intelligence analysts, such goals had clearly been held by the Egyptian and Arab military and political elites during Israel's War of Independence in the late 1940s and in the run-up to the Six-Day War in 1967.

One must remember, of course, that military planning is almost always just an exercise. The Prussian general, Helmuth von Moltke, who won two decisive wars in the nineteenth century and fundamentally altered Europe's strategic map for three-quarters of a century, is reputed to have commented that plans are nothing, but planning is everything. Military planning prepares military forces to think about their alternatives as well as those of their opponents.[40] And when war begins, it provides an intellectual and force-structure framework for the deployment of forces. Moltke may have been exaggerating when he noted that no operational plan survives first contact with the enemy. But his point is that since one can never predict the context of future operations – the nature of the enemy's responses, the choices he will make, his aims, much less the war's political framework – one can never fully understand ahead of time what will confront one's forces in war. What is significant here is what Israeli planning suggests about the mind-set of Israeli military leaders and the intellectual preparation undertaken in the years and months before the Yom Kippur War.

Perhaps the greatest tragedy of the Yom Kippur War lay in the fact that it could have been avoided. In 1971, Anwar Sadat, who had assumed Nasser's position as Egypt's head of state after the latter's death, offered to begin serious negotiations with the Israelis that would involve peace and recognition in return for the Sinai. However, Bar-Lev, then the IDF's chief of staff, persuaded the political leadership to reject the offer, because the giving back of the Sinai would cause Israel to lose its strategic depth.[41] The chief of staff's position reflects an inability or unwillingness to recognize the political and operational consequences of the radical changes in the strategic and operational environment that had resulted from the Six-Day War. It was not that the Israelis were operationally derelict – in fact, their principal military faults were tactical – but rather they allowed operational desiderata to override strategic objectives.

On the morning of 6 October 1973, Israeli intelligence finally recognized that the Arabs were about to attack. Prime Minister Golda Meir refused to authorize a preemptive strike by the air force because of the possible political ramifications, but she did authorize the mobilization of a portion– but only a portion – of the reserves in the midst of the High Holidays. Thus, the processes of mobilization and deployment began at

---

[40] This is not to deny that logistic planning and phased deployment plans do not have considerable importance in preparing forces for the movement to contact.
[41] Interview with General Dov Tamari, Tel Aviv, 24 October 2000.

the last moment, while small forces on the front lines waged a desperate struggle not only to hold but also to survive.

The Opposing Sides

The opposing forces possessed a number of strengths and weaknesses. Of all the forces involved in the Yom Kippur War, the Egyptians had undergone the greatest improvement from their debacle of 1967. A combination of defeat, the War of Attrition, and a real emphasis on professionalism had weeded out much of the dead wood in the officer corps by October 1973. Sadat appears to have been one of the few dictators in history comfortable enough with his position to tolerate competence among his senior military commanders.[42] Moreover, and perhaps most important, the Egyptian president developed a strategy with limited political goals that took into account not only the strengths and weaknesses of his own forces but also the IDF's weaknesses as well – and therein lay his strategic wisdom.

The Egyptian plan involved a massive crossing of the Suez Canal by a combined-arms force. The breadth of the attack would prevent the Israelis from launching a counterattack of sufficient strength to stop the Egyptians from building a defensive perimeter. Moreover, the defensive perimeter would not reach beyond the range of the protecting SAM (Surface to Air Missile) shield on the canal's west bank, which would prevent the Israeli Air Force from intervening decisively in the ground battle. The units that were to seize the east bank would consist of a mixed force of infantry and armor, with the former equipped with thousands of Sagger antitank missiles. In addition, Egyptian commandoes would land by helicopter behind Israeli defensive positions to plant mines and establish Sagger ambushes to attack Israeli armor as it deployed forward. Sadat's aim was to seize and hold the east bank and, if operations went well, a portion of the Sinai, to unlock the political stalemate.

To achieve that aim, the Egyptians deployed 200,000 troops in two armies: the Second in the north with 110,000 soldiers and the Third in the south with 90,000. All together, attacking forces consisted of five infantry divisions, two mechanized infantry divisions, and two armored

---

[42] For a discussion of the Egyptian military leadership at the time of the Yom Kippur War, see Edgar O'Ballance, *No Victor, No Vanquished: The Yom Kippur War* (San Raphael, CA, 1978), pp. 20–21. One of the few dictators willing to tolerate competence from his military leaders and, to a high degree at that, was unfortunately Adolf Hitler.

divisions (the latter in reserve and under the control of the Egyptian general headquarters or GHQ). More than 1,000 tanks would support the attacking infantry divisions.[43] The Egyptians planned their offensive in meticulous detail with particular attention to the engineering aspects of crossing the canal, destroying the embankments the Israelis had built, and constructing the bridges over which their main forces would deploy. Nevertheless, there were weaknesses.

Above all, the Egyptians, while trained to higher standards than in 1967, could not match the Israelis in their level of training or in their ability to adapt to a rapidly moving battlefield. Once the battle spiraled out of control and situations arose for which they had not prepared, the Egyptians were likely to run into difficulties. The great question mark was whether they could adapt to rapidly altering circumstances on the battlefield as well as in the strategic environment.

Like the Egyptians, the Syrians had received a massive infusion of Soviet military aid in the aftermath of 1967. By October 1973, they possessed approximately 1,100 tanks, including T-62s, 2,000 artillery pieces, over 60 SAM batteries, including ten of the new SAM-6s, and large numbers of ZSU anti-aircraft guns.[44] Syria's strategic objectives remain less clear than those of the Egyptians, largely because of the obsessive secretiveness of Assad's regime since the war. Nevertheless, the Syrian plan appears to have been no more than a straight-out bash aimed at knocking the Israelis off the Golan. And it is clear that their offensive possessed no *Schwehrpunkt* – no operational goal other than pushing the Israelis back.

Covered by a SAM umbrella and after a massive artillery bombardment, three Syrian mechanized divisions were to conduct a first-wave assault with two armored divisions in reserve. Unlike the Egyptians, the Syrians had not worked out how to coordinate infantry and armor. Thus, over the first days of the war, the Israeli defenders largely had to contend with Syrian tanks and armored personnel carriers and not with Syrian infantry armed with Saggers (antitank missiles).[45] Although small-unit training in the Syrian Army had improved, in no sense were its troops or officers expected to display initiative or be capable of adapting to unexpected combat situations.

On the other side, the IDF's air force and navy depended largely on professionals, but their ground forces required the mobilization of trained

---

[43] Van Creveld, *The Sword and the Olive*, p. 221.
[44] O'Ballance, *No Victor, No Vanquished*, p. 36.
[45] Interview with General Dov Tamari, Tel Aviv, 24 October 2000.

reservists. In the Yom Kippur War, those reservists performed effectively for two reasons. First, they received consistent, continuous, and rigorous training. Second, many, if not most, were veterans of the War of Attrition and the Six-Day War (some were also veterans of the 1956 War and the War of Independence). Moreover, the IDF that went to war in October 1973 was larger and considerably better equipped – and in some respects better trained, although combined-arms training had atrophied – than in 1967. But the hurried mobilization, the commitment to combat in uncertain circumstances, and in some cases a lack of familiarity with new equipment created problems that had not been present in 1967.

Perhaps the largest difficulty confronting the Israeli ground forces was the fact that nearly all their commanders remained focused on the tactical level of war, in other words, on brigade- and battalion-level combat. They had grown up in an army that had fought the War of Independence in company- and battalion-sized formations, the 1956 War in battalion- and brigade-sized formations, and the Six-Day War in brigade- and division-sized formations. The IDF was an army in which nearly all officers, certainly senior commanders, had combat experience, and combat experience was what the IDF valued most. There was little interest in book learning or thinking about the theoretical side of war. Most senior officers believed that experience in combat was enough.

Not surprisingly, then, professional military education received short shrift in the army's vision of preparing for future war. As one commentator has noted:

> [At the staff college, the students] did precious little serious reading and almost no writing – with the result that, compared with their colleagues in other countries, they remained almost entirely unfamiliar with the history of their own profession, Israeli military history specifically included.... [T]he highest course was the battalion commanders' course. Thus, officers beyond that grade could serve their last fifteen years without any formal instruction – which actually happened to General ["Dado"] Elazar (who served as chief of staff from 1972 to 1974). As General [Israel] Tal once told a visiting French writer, in the IDF senior officers advanced by 'natural selection.'[46]

As a result, the senior leadership was woefully unprepared for handling the higher levels of command beyond the world of tactics and battalion and brigade leadership – in other words, the operational level of war. Neither in their understanding of operational design nor in their ability to control formations larger than a division were Israeli senior officers

---

[46] Van Creveld, *The Sword and the Olive*, pp. 168–169.

intellectually or experientially prepared for the challenges that the coming war would present.

Additional factors in Southern Command exacerbated these deficiencies. Its commander, Major General Shmuel Gonen, would have two reserve division commanders under him who had recently been his superiors, Ariel Sharon, who had only in late summer relinquished Southern Command, and Avraham Adan, who as the commander of the Armored Corps was about to give up that command and retire to the reserves.[47] But it was the deficiencies in the intellectual preparation of senior officers that cost the IDF and the Israeli nation the greatest number of casualties.

In the end, the Israelis were caught in a position where none of their assumptions about warning or possible responses to an Arab buildup or Arab capabilities turned out to be true. This was a reflection of their failure to educate as well as train their officer corps. Above all, Israeli arrogance and underestimation of their potential opponents were the primary drivers that undermined the validity of Israeli assumptions about future war. They were also to be the primary cause of the heavy losses their front-line units would suffer over the course of the war.

But that is only a part of the story. Equally important was the fact that those examining the possibility of future war failed to take into account how the strategic and political framework might distort operational assumptions or those that they were making about warning.[48] By 4 October the evidence was available to conclude that the Egyptians and Syrians were about to attack. Nevertheless, in the face of mounting evidence, the intelligence chiefs refused to alter their estimate of the situation.[49] By the morning of 6 October, they had changed their tune, but there remained considerable hesitation among the politicians and senior

---

[47] Since the Yom Kippur War, the IDF has ceased the practice of moving senior commanders to become commanders of reserve divisions, largely as a result of the fallout from Gonen's unfortunate relations with his subordinates, who had been his superiors just months before.

[48] The G-3 of Northern Command, Major General Uri Simchoni (IDF, retired), commented to the author that the IDF fervently believed his command would receive forty-eight hours to mobilize. "All our plans were phased in twelve and twenty-four hour segments leading up to full readiness in 48 hours. That assumption was *WRONG*" (General Simchoni's emphasis). Interview, Tel Aviv, 31 October 2000.

[49] Van Creveld, *The Sword and the Olive*, p. 223. Part of their reluctance has to do with the fact that the Israelis had ordered a partial mobilization the previous May on the basis of ambiguous indicators that turned out to be false. Mobilizations were expensive, both to the IDF and to the Israeli economy, and there was an upcoming election scheduled for the end of November. Another mobilization, seemingly to no purpose, would have cost the ruling coalition votes.

military leaders about what the intelligence meant. The warning that the Arabs would attack that day came at 0430 hours, but the decision to mobilize four reserve divisions, instead of a full mobilization of all the reserves, did not come for at least another four hours, only six and a half hours before the Egyptians and Syrians struck.

The prime minister, Golda Meir, turned down a proposal that the air force launch a preemptive air strike to destabilize and disrupt the final deployments of the Egyptian and Syrian armies. The obvious basis for Meir's decision was that she wanted to avoid giving the impression that the war was the result of Israeli actions. Here, as with the delays on the morning of 6 October in ordering full mobilization, the strategic context, political necessity, and human foibles determined the operational framework within which the Israeli military would have to operate in the war's opening moments.[50] These were factors that serious professional military education might, at least, have prepared the IDF's generals to address and might have mitigated the extraordinary difficulties that were soon to befall them. No doubt the military was partly responsible in this respect, but equally at fault was the failure of Israel's leaders to give their commanders reasonable guidance.

Learning on the Battlefield: The War of Atonement

The Arab attack did not catch all of Israel's military leaders by surprise.[51] But most senior officers, if worried at times, were unwilling to challenge the intelligence estimates. As a result the normal command appointments

---

[50] Such a state of affairs should not have surprised any student of Clausewitz, who in the 1820s commented on a plan for a potential Austro-Prussian War: "War is not an independent phenomenon but the continuation of politics by different means. Consequently the main lines of every major strategic plan are *largely political in nature*, and their political character increases the more the plan applies to the entire campaign and to the whole state.... [T]here can be no question of a *purely military* evaluation of a great strategic issue, or of a purely military scheme to solve it." Quoted in Peter Paret, *Clausewitz and the State* (Princeton, 1976), pp. 379–380.

[51] Haim Erez, who would command one of Sharon's brigades, was assigned to the staff college as an instructor in the immediate period before the war. (He also held the position of brigade commander of a reserve formation). He recalled listening to a lecture in early October 1973 by one of the IDF's senior intelligence officers. The briefing provided a detailed and, in retrospect accurate, picture of the deployment and lay down of Egyptian forces, but the conclusion of the briefer was that the Egyptians would not attack. Erez's sense was, however, quite different; he immediately called his senior staff officers and battalion commanders and ordered them to remain close to their phones because of his feeling that something was up. Interview with General Erez, Israeli Armor Museum, 1 November 2000.

proceeded. Sharon gave up his position as commander of Southern Command at the end of summer 1973, while in early October Avraham Adan was about to retire from his position as commander of the Armored Corps. Moreover, the commander of the regular armored division stationed in the Sinai was on the brink of surrendering his command to another officer. Thus, the war broke on an IDF organizationally as well as intellectually unprepared for war. At 0800 hours on the morning of 6 October, two Phantom jets roared at low level over central Israel to warn the population that something was afoot.[52] Almost immediately thereafter, the mobilization processes began, this time instead of by radio by soldiers going from house to house because of the Yom Kippur High Holidays.[53]

Overall direction of the conduct of the war resided in the IDF's general headquarters in Tel Aviv. Providing that direction and making the crucial strategic and operational choices were Defense Minister Moshe Dayan, the hero of the 1956 War and the Six-Day War, and Chief of Staff General Elazar. Because of their positions, both bore the largest share of responsibility for the fact that the Arab attack caught the IDF by surprise. Thereafter, they and their subordinates at general headquarters effectively handled the large number of problems associated with the mobilization of Israel's reserves under the most trying of circumstances. They then guided the movement of those forces to the combat theaters with considerable skill.

What they did not provide was overall long-range strategic and operational guidance for the conduct of the war. Thus, they stood aside while their subordinates, particularly on the Suez front, undertook a number of seriously flawed actions that resulted in needlessly heavy losses and casualties.[54] By not providing a context or "commander's intent" within which their subordinates could make decisions, they allowed the generals on the scene to issue orders that were to have the most serious of operational and political consequences.[55] There is, however, another side of

---

[52] Van Creveld, *The Sword and the Olive*, p. 224.
[53] With not only the radio and television stations but also the entire country shut down in observance of the High Holidays, the mobilization proceeded relatively smoothly. The problem was that, without the warning time that the IDF had always assumed would be available, there was a desperate need to send mobilized units to the front, whether they were ready or not.
[54] Interview with General Dov Tamari, Tel Aviv, 31 October 2000.
[55] In particular, the decisions to mount a crossing of the canal on 14 October and then to allow Adan's drive to Suez City, virtually to surround the Egyptian Third Army, and proceed with the first steps toward that army's destruction came close to destroying the

the coin. The major failure of guidance preceded the outbreak of hostilities. Once forces were engaged, interference with field commanders by a headquarters distant from the fight confronted serious obstacles and entailed serious risks. In the event, the rapidity with which the battle developed afforded little time to acquire and analyze the information necessary to make significant changes in tactical arrangements, even had Tel Aviv desired to do so.

The Northern Front

The commander of Northern Command, Major General Yitzhak Hoffi, had worried in the late summer about major Syrian deployments near the Golan Heights. In response, he strongly lobbied Dayan and Elazar for major reinforcements. They finally gave him the army's elite 7th Armored Brigade, ironically the only brigade trained to cross the Suez Canal.[56] The senior officers of that brigade conducted a staff ride of the Golan on 23 September under their commander, Avigdor Yanosh Ben-Gal.

The 1st Battalion of the 7th Armored Brigade, under the future tank hero, Lt. Col. Avigdor Kahalani, began arriving on 26 September, and at first came under the command of the "Barak" Brigade, led by Yizhak Ben Shoham.[57] The last battalion of the 7th Brigade would not straggle onto the Golan until 6 October in the hours immediately before the Syrians struck with virtually no time to adjust to its surroundings. By that time, Northern Command had divided the Golan between the two brigades, which together possessed approximately 177 tanks: the "Barak" Brigade receiving responsibility for the southern portion of the heights and the 7th Brigade responsibility for the northern section.[58] Against the two Israeli armored brigades, the Syrians brought more than 1,400 armored fighting vehicles to the fight.[59] Interestingly, in terms of the lack

---

possibility of an eventual peace treaty between Israel and Egypt, which Sadat's limited offensive had created. In the end there was to be no Israeli strategic response or even analysis of the challenge that the Egyptians and Syrians were mounting.

[56] According to one former general, the 7th Brigade was selected because the politicians refused to mobilize a reserve brigade with elections looming at the end of November. Interview with General Simchoni, Tel Aviv, 31 October 2000.

[57] In his somewhat unreliable and eccentric history of the IDF, van Creveld identifies the commander of the "Barak" Brigade as Benyamin Shoham. Van Creveld, *The Sword and the Olive*, p. 229.

[58] Interview with Major General Yitzak Hoffi, IDF retired, commander Northern Command, Yom Kippur War, Tel Aviv, 27 October 2000.

[59] Herzog, *The War of Atonement*, p. 127.

of operational focus in Northern Command, and the IDF in general, the two brigades remained directly under Northern Command with no divisional headquarters to coordinate their defense of the Golan or to keep track of the battle once it began. The division commander, Rafael Eitan, assigned to Northern Command, would not assume control of the Golan Heights and the battle until morning 7 October.[60]

Thus, the two brigades fought their battles as independent forces with little or no coordination. In the north, Yanosh Ben-Gal fought his brigade as a brigade, careful to keep sufficient reserves, barely, in hand to counter possible breakthroughs. Kahalani's memoirs indicates that Ben-Gal orchestrated a brigade-level battle in which he kept his battalion and company commanders informed of the overall battle that was occurring in the north.[61] Still, the 7th Brigade barely hung on in the face of persistent, almost suicidal attacks by waves of massed Syrian tanks. Kahalani's battalion in particular dealt out terrible punishment to the Syrians.

By the time the Syrians had exhausted themselves on the afternoon of 7 October in the northern Golan, their attacking divisions had lost between 200 and 300 armored fighting vehicles. Their lack of imagination and coordination in their attacks helped the Israelis considerably. To all intents and purposes, they had launched an all-armor attack. What few infantry participated found themselves closed up in Soviet-manufactured armored personnel carriers. At least for the first two days, when the Israelis were most vulnerable with few infantry to cover their tanks and little preparation to fight a combined-arms battle, the Syrians were deluging Israeli positions with artillery fire, while launching mass tank attacks, but their infantry remained virtually absent from the fight.

On the southern portion of the Golan, things did not turn out so well for the Israelis. The commander of the "Barak" Brigade, Ben Shoham, was an inspirational, popular commander. However, he proved incapable of conducting a brigade-level fight. Admittedly, his brigade had more

---

[60] Kahalani, *The Heights of Courage*, p. 75.
[61] Ibid., pp. 6–92. What is indeed surprising is the fact that none of the three general histories of the war available in English provide a clear description of the fighting that occurred in the northern Golan over the course of the first several days. Van Creveld has the 7th Brigade arriving on the afternoon of 6 October (when in fact virtually all of its tanks were in position), while Herzog and O'Ballance, the latter drawing largely from Herzog's account, describe the battle as if Kahalani were in charge. Van Creveld, *The Sword and the Olive*, p. 229; O'Ballance, *No Victor, No Vanquished*, pp. 127–135; and Chaim Herzog, *The War of Atonement: The Inside Story of the Yom Kippur War, 1973* (London, 1975), pp. 79–82.

ground to defend than the 7th Armored Brigade, and that ground was less defensible.[62] At the start of the battle, Ben Shoham seems to have believed that the Syrians were incapable of launching a major offensive and, once the fighting started, that it was simply another border clash.[63] Whatever his assumptions, he spread his brigade across the length of the southern Golan, where it fought as companies and platoons rather than as a brigade. At first, Ben Shoham's tanks had considerable success. Even when the Syrians began to break through, the Israelis inflicted heavy losses on them by using lateral roads and paths. But in the end, by attempting to defend everything, the "Barak" Brigade defended nothing.

By late afternoon on 6 October, the brigade's cohesion began to collapse, and the Syrians were able to drive deep onto the plateau of the southern Golan. With no reserves available, Ben Shoham drove down the Tapline road on the evening of 6 October, where his command section soon ran into Syrian tanks driving northwest along the road. There was already a Syrian brigade of 50 tanks to his rear.[64] By then he had lost control of his brigade. One source estimates that it was down to 15 tanks by the early morning hours of 7 October, while the Syrians still had approximately 450 tanks remaining in the southern sectors of the Golan with what appeared, at least to Dayan, as an open road to Galilee.[65]

But the fight had also exhausted the Syrians. During that night their forces hunkered down and failed to take advantage of the desperate situation in which the Israelis found themselves. There are a number of explanations for the Syrians' failure to exploit their advantage. Perhaps the extent of their success remained unclear; perhaps the heavy losses they had sustained in breaking the "Barak" Brigade made their commanders cautious; perhaps the desperate resistance of the Israelis to their front deterred them; perhaps simple inertia and an inability, or unwillingness, of Syrian officers to display initiative accounted for their failure to act; or

---

[62] The operations officer of Northern Command, Simchoni, suggested to the author that he and his commander General Hoffi considered that the Northern Golan was the more important operational and strategic area, and consequently they had given the 7th Brigade less territory to defend. But the largest factor appears to have been the competence of the brigade commander. Interview with General Simchoni, Tel Aviv, 31 October 2000.
[63] This at least is van Creveld's explanation. Van Creveld, *The Sword and the Olive*, p. 229.
[64] Herzog, *The War of Atonement*, p. 85.
[65] Ibid., p. 84.

perhaps some or all of these factors combined to stop them.[66] Clausewitz provides an equally plausible explanation:

> Each of the thousands [who make up an army] needs food and rest, and longs for nothing so much as a few hours free of danger and fatigue. Very few men... are able to... feel beyond the present moment. Only these few, having accomplished the urgent task at hand, are left with enough mental energy to think of making further gains – gains which at the time may seem trifling embellishments of victory, indeed an extravagance.[67]

Meanwhile, Northern Command had little it could do during the first eight hours of the fighting. It was too far from the battle to coordinate the desperate fighting taking place on the Golan. Nor did it possess any additional forces until the reserves began arriving. Eitan's divisional headquarters would not be able to assume control until the morning of 7 October, while the first reserves did not reach the theater until 2000 hours on 6 October.[68]

All Northern Command could do at that point, according to its operations officer, was to shovel arriving reserve units up onto the Golan into a situation that remained murky and largely uncertain, particularly in the south where command and control had broken down with the destruction of the "Barak" Brigade. Thus, Northern Command ordered the first arriving reserve armored battalion to move up to the Tapline road and then find and hold the Syrians. In fact, it found the Syrians far sooner than expected, almost across the Golan Heights, and was almost immediately wrecked. During the night, more reserve units arrived from their depots: all, except for infantry without armor personnel carriers, immediately moved forward to stabilize the desperate situation. By midday on 7 October, Northern Command had begun to get a handle on unfolding events. The insertion of a division commander onto the Golan helped, but it took Eitan much of the day to grasp the overall situation and then

---

[66] Interview with General Simchoni, Tel Aviv, 31 October 2000.
[67] Clausewitz, On War, pp. 263–264.
[68] Interestingly, General Simchoni suggested to the author that the mobilization process had been far too bureaucratized and that, in some areas, it broke down at the start. It certainly did not provide for immediate reinforcement of the hard-pressed forces engaged in heavy combat on the frontiers. Only the fact that Israelis in general recognized that war could occur at any time allowed their initiative and willingness to find ad hoc solutions to overcome a cumbersome process. Interview with General Simchoni, Tel Aviv, 31 October 2000.

assert control over the chaos that characterized much of the situation on the southern Golan.[69]

By the afternoon of 7 October, the Israelis had sufficient forces on the Golan to hold the Syrians, although the fighting remained intense along the Tapline road. But the situation that had characterized the evening of 6 October, which had led Dayan on the morning of 7 October to suggest the IDF might have to abandon the entire Golan and defend Israel along the Jordan River Valley, was no longer so desperate.[70] Syrian losses, which had been horrific over the course of the first day, continued to mount, while Israeli reinforcements were beginning to flood onto the Golan.

Almost immediately, Israeli commanders at the higher levels – those not actually engaged in the fighting – began to consider counterattacking and driving the Syrians off the Golan. That night, Elazar, Bar-Lev, and Dayan made the key operational decision of the war. Because the Sinai lay between the Egyptians and Israeli territory, the threat in that theater was less immediate. Thus, they decided that Hoffi would get the high command's last reserve division to address the more direct threat to Israeli territory.[71] By 8 October, the Israelis were able to begin a major counterattack. In the center Major General Dan Laner's division halted the last of the Syrian attacks and then cleared the enemy from the central Golan, while Kahalani in the north halted the last major Syrian attack – this one with T-62s led by Assad's brother.[72] Meanwhile, from the south, Major General Moshe Peled's division drove up from the south and pushed the Syrians back from positions they had seized overlooking the Sea of Galilee.

By the time the Israeli counterattacks went in, the Syrians had clearly shot their bolt. By Wednesday morning on 10 October, the three Israeli divisions were back at the prewar Purple Line, dividing Israeli-held territory from Syria. Altogether, the Syrian Army had lost 867 tanks on the Golan along with vast amounts of other military equipment.[73] The

---

[69] Interview with General Simchoni, Tel Aviv, 31 October 2000.
[70] Herzog, *The War of Atonement*, p. 99.
[71] Dayan, who was not always stable, seems to have suggested that the IDF might have to abandon the Golan, but by the time Bar-Lev had visited Northern Command's headquarters, the fighting on the Golan was beginning to look up from the Israeli point of view. Herzog, *The War of Atonement*, p. 116.
[72] Interview with General Hoffi, Tel Aviv, 27 October 2000.
[73] Herzog, *The War of Atonement*, p. 127.

commander of Northern Command later claimed that the Israelis captured more than 350 Syrian tanks on his front, which Israeli repair shops and conversion sites eventually repaired.[74]

With the Golan cleared, the Israeli high command then decided to continue the offensive with a three-division thrust toward Damascus. There were to be two major thrust lines, with an additional effort by the Golani Infantry Brigade to regain positions lost on Mt. Hermon in the war's first days. The rationale seems to have been strategic and political – a belief that an offensive aimed toward Damascus would force the Syrians to seek a cease-fire. Given that the Israelis also wished to deliver a major blow against the Egyptians before agreeing to a cease-fire, it is difficult to accept that rationale at face value. Perhaps the most reasonable explanation is that the Syrian successes on 6 October, which had threatened for a time to drive the Israelis off the Golan, so shocked Israel's political and military leaders that the real reason for the offensive was a desire for revenge, that most human of emotions, as Thucydides underlined long ago.

The offensive did gain territory and certainly placed Damascus under threat. Israeli forces drove approximately ten to 15 miles into Syria but then came to a halt. At the strategic level, however, that "success" did not persuade the Syrians to seek an armistice, although it did have the unintended effect of leading them to press the Egyptians to do something more than just hold on to the territory they had gained along the canal. At an operational level, the three-division offensive simply pushed into Syrian territory. The operational concept, if there were one, aimed at best at gaining territory rather than destroying more of the Syrian Army. The casualty figures suggest how little was gained at what cost. During the first two days, the Israelis suffered heavy casualties as a percentage of the two brigades engaged in defending the Golan. However, in aggregate, the counterattacks that drove the Syrians off the Golan and the subsequent offensive into Syrian territory toward Damascus suffered heavier casualties, although spread across a larger number of units.[75]

Tactical and Operational Adaptation on the Golan

In terms of tactical adaptation, the Israelis did not have to do much over the first several days in the north because the failure of the Syrians to mount a true combined-arms attack played to Israeli strengths. With

---

[74] Interview with General Hoffi, Tel Aviv, 27 October 2000.
[75] Interview with General Simchoni, Tel Aviv, 31 October 2000.

a solid grasp of basic, tank-on-tank tactics and command of the high ground against an opponent who was not particularly skilled, the Israelis slowly improved their combined-arms effectiveness at the tactical level. The problem was that this improvement had to come on the battlefield and could only be acquired at considerable cost.[76]

The dogged Syrian resistance after 10 October in defending their own territory only aggravated the impact of the weaknesses in combined-arms tactics on the Israeli side. Moreover, those commanding the offensive into Syria remained largely in the dark as to what was happening on the tactical level. In effect the feedback loops failed, so that those at brigade and division level found it difficult to understand what was happening at the sharp end and what kind of resistance their troops were actually running into.[77]

In the north, however, the real difficulties in adaptation, came at the operational level. The problems stemmed from a number of causes: a failure to prepare intellectually or organizationally for war at this level; the lack of any headquarters capable of conducting war at the operational level; and the pressures of combat as well as the organizational framework of the IDF, which made it almost impossible to address longer-range issues. The first issue, the failure to prepare intellectually, this chapter addressed earlier. The gap between tactics and operations had a number of serious consequences in organizational terms. The first consequence, and perhaps the most serious, was that there was no headquarters at the beginning of the war to handle even the lower-level, tactical conduct of the battle: the two brigades on the Golan could not even turn to a divisional headquarters to coordinate their defensive operations. As the G-3 of Northern Command suggested to the author, the higher one went in the Israeli command, the greater was the gap in the ability to handle the situation.[78]

When on the second day the Israelis managed to get a divisional headquarters up to the Heights to coordinate the 7th Brigade and what was left of the "Barak" Brigade, two reserve divisions began arriving. Northern Command thus had to act as the operational command, even though it had made no preparation to serve in that role before the war. However, it served more as a tactical rather than an operational headquarters. Before the war it had not even run a command-post exercise with its units; thus,

---

[76] Interview with General Simchoni, Tel Aviv, 31 October 2000.
[77] Interview with General Kahn, Tel Aviv, 28 October, 2000.
[78] Interview with General Simchoni, Tel Aviv, 31 October 2000.

it had virtually no conception of what it would take to run a battle of the magnitude that erupted on the Golan. The command's G-3 suggests that its battle and resource management was mostly poor, "without concept or system."[79] It could only shovel reserve units up onto the Golan throughout the first night in the hope that somehow they would stem the Syrian tide.

That lack of foresight created a nightmarish scene within Northern Command's headquarters with officers screaming into phones, reading maps, giving orders, and only a few listening. There were, however, some efforts to learn or extend the operational focus of the command. A number of retired officers, who no longer possessed reserve assignments but who had experience in the north, arrived at Northern Command's headquarters. The command's operations officer persuaded Hoffi to establish an advanced planning cell on the second day under the former head of Israeli intelligence, Major General Aharon Yariv, who was at the time the head of the Jaffe Center at Tel Aviv University. The group's task was to begin planning for the next day and think through the emerging situation and the possibilities open to the Syrians as well as Israelis.[80] They made important contributions to the conduct of the battle after the third day, but the ad hoc nature of the group suggests a great deal about the universal lack of intellectual and organizational preparation in the prewar period.

In a tactical sense, particularly in the early days of the Syrian offensive, the Golan's defense was a magnificent achievement. Tactical adaptation then allowed the Israelis to mount a successful, but costly, counterattack that drove the Syrians off the Golan and pushed them back along the road to Damascus. But the defense of the Golan was seriously flawed by the lack of coherent operational concepts and preparations, either organizational or intellectual, and by flawed assumptions from the strategic down to the tactical levels, which made recovery difficult.

Under the desperate pressures of combat, the Israelis found it almost impossible to adapt to the operational conditions confronting them, largely because of their failure to prepare intellectually in the prewar period and their unnecessary underestimation of what their potential opponents might be capable of accomplishing. The unimaginative, seemingly aimless offensive into Syria suggests a failure to think seriously

---

[79] Interview with General Simchoni, Tel Aviv, 31 October 2000.
[80] Interview with General Simchoni, Tel Aviv, 31 October 2000.

about the larger strategic framework within which the Israelis were fighting the war. In the end, battalion and brigade commanders and their men, rather than the operational commanders above them, won the war on the Golan.

The Southern Front: The First Days

From the beginning of the fight along the Suez Canal, things began to unravel at every level. Perhaps the most serious flaw in Israeli preparations lay at the level of Southern Command's headquarters.[81] The appointment of Shmuel Gonen to command two officers, who had been his superiors in the immediate past, represented a serious enough handicap, even if the individuals concerned had been the most altruistic of generals. They were not. Equally serious, Gonen possessed neither the personality nor the intellectual breadth to handle the complex problems of command at the operational level in a desperate and uncertain situation.

The report of a postwar commission that studied the causes of the Yom Kippur catastrophe characterized Gonen in the following terms:

> [Gonen] did not prepare a detailed operational plan, and he did not see to it that an operational order was issued and reached the commanders of his troops. He did not ascertain whether his forces had arrived in full and were deployed in the manner required for the operation.... When the battle began, he conducted it without an effective control system or staff work; he refrained from taking personal command of his troops, and consequently did not know firsthand what was happening on the battlefield. He took crucial decisions in moving an Ugda [division] from one sector to another hastily and without ascertaining by every possible means the objectives, as defined to him by the chief of staff [of the IDF] as a condition for moving the division. He frequently changed the objectives of divisions and gave them new ones without providing his forces with information concerning our own or the enemy's forces. He caused a gradual erosion of the objective and of the method with which he charged the chief of staff, being impatient for a quick canal crossing before the essential conditions for such a decisive step had been created.[82]

The postwar judgment is not entirely fair, for others also bear significant responsibility for the troubles in Southern Command. Nevertheless,

---

[81] Admittedly, there were also organizational problems. As one Israeli officer commented, "the command was structured for peace, not war, and there was neither the ability nor the willingness to alter the command's structure under the pressures of war." Interview with General Shai Tamari, Tel Aviv, 27 October 2000.

[82] Quoted in Adan, *On the Banks of the Suez*, pp. 154–155.

Gonen proved incapable of handling the extraordinary operational and tactical difficulties that confronted the Israelis along the canal.

The plans Gonen inherited from his predecessor did not help matters. Sharon believed the IDF would be able to hold an Egyptian offensive near the canal and with the forces available in the Sinai go over to an offensive without waiting for the reserves.[83] Sharon also appears to have believed that the IDF should abandon the Bar-Lev Line immediately if the Egyptians attacked but rejected the arguments of those who argued for at least a 48-hour pause before beginning any counterattack to allow the reserves to arrive. At the least, had Sharon been in command, he would most probably have taken the forces immediately available in the Sinai and launched them in a solid blow, with an operational emphasis on hitting the Egyptians where they were most vulnerable.[84] Gonen accepted Sharon's overly optimistic planning but disregarded the former's advice to abandon the outpost line along the canal in the face of a major attack. Moreover, Gonen never understood Sharon's willingness to allow the Egyptians to move into the Sinai, where an Israeli counterattack might have unbalanced them and created opportunities for operational exploitation. Finally, Gonen's underestimation of the capabilities of the Egyptian enemy led him to attack everywhere.[85]

The initial challenges confronting Southern Command, as the Egyptian offensive broke on their positions at 1350 on 6 October, were (1) what should be done with the outposts along the canal, (2) what was the likely objective and nature of the Egyptian offensive, and (3) how should the IDF respond? The first challenge presented a relatively easy solution: withdraw the garrisons as quickly as possible once it became clear that the

---

[83] Adan commented to the author that Sharon's plans in retrospect were largely unrealistic and could not have been implemented given the conditions that actually existed along the canal in October 1973, but that the major difference between Gonen and Sharon was that the latter would have very quickly adapted to what was actually happening on the battlefield as well as the actual context, such as the fact that the IDF had been caught by surprise. He would not have attempted to impose his view on reality as Gonen was to do consistently during his period in command. Interestingly, in light of that comment, it is worth noting that Adan and Sharon have remained bitter enemies since the 1973 War, if not before. Interview with Major General Avraham Adan, IDF retired, commander of the Adan Division, Yom Kippur War, Tel Aviv, 27 October 2000.

[84] Given the Israeli underestimations of their opponents and their lack of preparations to fight a combined-arms battle at the tactical level, it is entirely conceivable that they might have suffered an even more disastrous defeat than the one they suffered in the first couple of days of fighting on the Suez front. Given the strength and deployment of the Egyptian forces, this was a distinct possibility.

[85] Interview with General Shai Tamari, Tel Aviv, 27 October 2000.

Egyptians were launching major offensive operations. However, Southern Command dithered, unsure of what it should do, and left the garrisons in place.[86] The other two challenges were more difficult because the lack of warning time, which the Israelis had assumed they would have, meant reserve forces would not begin arriving until the next day and would not be in complete formations until 8 October.

Here, Southern Command under Gonen's leadership acted without reflection. It launched the regular armored division stationed in the Sinai in a series of uncoordinated, all-armor attacks aimed at breaking through to the strong points, while at the same time it failed to give any orders for the garrisons to pull out. As a result, Avraham Mandler's division suffered prohibitive losses in these attacks in its efforts to reach the Milano and Qantara strong points on the Bar-Lev Line. Israeli armor with no accompanying infantry lost 17 of 21 tanks. By the morning of 7 October, the Sinai armored division was down to 110 tanks out of its establishment of 290, with nothing to show for its heavy losses.[87]

Nevertheless, these setbacks seem to have made little impression on Gonen or Southern Command's staff. By late afternoon on 7 October, the first reserve units began dribbling into its area of responsibility. In Tel Aviv, Dayan favored going over to the defensive, while Elazar, misinformed as to Adan's attitude, favored a limited offensive to set up the possibility of a crossing operation. Given the desperate situation on the Golan, the Israeli high command had already made the operational decision to place the emphasis on the north. Gonen himself seems to have exercised little self-discipline in the tactical sphere. Remaining at his headquarters far from the fighting, he assumed his forces were not having serious difficulties in the tactical arena, when in fact the Egyptians were butchering Mandler's tanks with tank fire from the west bank and Sagger antimissile fire from the east bank.[88] Few of these tactical realities appear

---

[86] Here the initial uncertainty about what was occurring along the Suez Canal, magnified by Israeli assumptions about the Egyptians, confronted Gonen with a conundrum: if this were not a major offensive but rather a series of raids, then withdrawing the garrisons from the Bar-Lev Line would cause a political crisis in Israel and most probably would have ended his career. On the other hand, if it were a major offensive, then leaving the garrisons in place would ensure their destruction.

[87] Adan, *On the Banks of Suez*, pp. 29, 83.

[88] Adan suggested to the author that Mandler had argued against a resumption of Israeli attacks on the evening of 7 October, but in the confusion that characterized Southern Command's planning, Gonen paid him no attention. Interview with General Adan, Tel Aviv, 27 October 2000.

to have been passed along to the reserve forces hustling down the roads of Sinai.[89]

But serious errors at the operational level soon aggravated the tactical problems the Israelis were facing. Over the evening of 7 October, a series of separate meetings between Gonen and his division commanders took place under the most hurried and careless of circumstances.[90] Elazar weighed in with Gonen, but by the time the night played out, no one had a clear idea of what was supposed to happen. Adan believed his orders were to sweep south from Qantara, abandoning the canal garrisons to their fate, while Sharon remained in reserve. On the other hand, Sharon appears to have thought he was to take his division rapidly to the south and attempt a crossing near Suez City (over Egyptian bridges) that his division was to capture.

Southern Command, however, appears to have been under the impression that Adan and Sharon would sweep through the Egyptians and seize the enemy's bridges in a number of places so that Israeli tanks could cross to the west bank, despite the fact that they were too heavy to cross on the Soviet-manufactured bridges the Egyptians had emplaced.[91] What Gonen did *not* do was to concentrate the combat power of the three divisions now available to him in a striking force to counterattack at least one segment of the Egyptian crossing forces. Thus, the Israelis fought the battles on 7 October as a series of small unit actions to relieve the outposts on

---

[89] Nor, of course, was there time for such experiences to be absorbed except by the survivors. But things were going dreadfully wrong, and there was no system in place for the Israelis to pass lessons learned from the survivors to those who were yet to engage in battle.

[90] Adan describes his meeting with Gonen in the following terms: "I had to fight my way through scores of male and female soldiers crowded in [Southern Command's] bunker and its corridors. Some were wrapped in blankets, taking naps, while others sat on stairs, talking. I saw the familiar faces of friends and colleagues, but also noticed many outsiders and visitors. The place was a mess; you could barely find your own feet. Looking at maps and listening to transceivers, I tried to follow reports from our forces along the front, but in vain. So deafening was the noise in the room and so distorted the sound from the radio that it was impossible to understand anything. It was a frustrating and depressing situation." Adan, *On the Banks of the Suez*, p. 95.

[91] As Sharon points out in his memoirs: "[t]he idea that we might fight our way through to the canal in the south and find intact Egyptian bridges there was based on the merest wishful thinking. And even if we did, we knew that the Egyptian bridges were constructed for the lighter Soviet-made tanks and would not support ours." There is, however, not the slightest evidence that Sharon, or anyone else for that matter, pointed this out to Gonen. Sharon, *Warrior*, pp. 301–302.

the Bar-Lev Line, the garrisons of which should have withdrawn at the first signs of a major Egyptian offensive.

On 8 October, Gonen again responded with only a portion of his force.[92] Moreover, he communicated to his subordinates a completely unrealistic picture of what was happening, of the enemy's capabilities, and of the possibilities open to the Israelis, but a picture that nonetheless drove his assessments and decisions.[93] As Adan suggests in his memoirs, "Gonen... neglected realistic approaches, failing to take measures really needed to deal with the actual situation. Eventually, this led him to issue additional orders, irrelevant to the situation on the battlefield."[94] Intelligent discourse over the nature of operational and tactical choices simply was not taking place; quite literally nothing more was occurring than a dialogue of the deaf.

What was *not* considered (except possibly in Dayan's mind) was the possibility of a tactical and operational withdrawal back to the Sinai passes, so that the Israeli reserves could come up and fully integrate into their combat units.[95] Such a move would also have allowed the Israelis to fight a mobile tank battle, if and when the Egyptians moved out from the canal, a battle, moreover, that would have taken place beyond the coverage of the Egyptian air defense system. But Israeli military leaders, most still blinkered by their previous successes against Arab armies, refused to take the time to rethink their assumptions, the reconsideration of which might have led to the realization that they were facing an entirely new situation and context.[96] Instead, they rushed to take aggressive

---

[92] Interview with General Erez, Israeli Armor Museum, 1 November 2000.
[93] This picture is largely drawn from Adan, *On the Banks of the Suez*, pp. 91–103.
[94] Adan, *On the Banks of Suez*, p. 111.
[95] Adan's memoir argues that Southern Command was not wrong in deciding to launch its attack on 8 October: "Should the IDF have attacked quickly on 8 October, even though the reserves were still far from being in full force or organized? In my view – yes. Under the circumstances as we understood them and in line with our basic assumptions, there was not one of the southern front commanders who recommended waiting until we could build up strength and organize fully. Everyone believed that we had to take the initiative from the Egyptians as soon as possible." What Adan does criticize was the failure then to adapt Israeli actions to the reality of the tactical situation. Ibid., p. 163.
[96] Only Israel Tal of all the Israeli generals grasped at the beginning that this was going to be a different kind of war from the 1956 and 1967 conflicts. Tal commented to General Dov Tamari on the morning of 6 October: "Listen, don't think about offensive operations. We are in a worse situation than in 1948. We must think only of defensive operations." Interview with General Dov Tamari, Tel Aviv, 31 October 2000.

actions that were irrelevant to the situation at hand, their inbred aggressiveness perhaps amplified by their frustration over the surprise the Arabs had achieved.[97]

Adan began his drive to the south at 0800 on 8 October with only four artillery tubes in support, the rest of his artillery still bottled up in the traffic jams on the roads leading from Israel to the western Sinai.[98] At first, his division appeared to advance without serious opposition. But as Israeli armor moved within range of Egyptian defenses along the canal, losses rose dramatically. Adan's deputy division commander, Brigadier General Dov Tamari, observed the division's movement from a helicopter that was serving as a communications link between Adan and Southern Command (the Egyptians appear to have succeeded in jamming much of the Israeli command net). He soon recognized the difficulties into which the division's lead units were getting.[99]

But worse was about to happen. Gonen now pulled Sharon out of his reserve positions in the center and sent his division hurtling south. In so doing, the latter pulled away from Adan's division even as it was running into difficulties. Moreover, Sharon refused to release one of his battalions to Adan as ordered and actually pulled the unit off key terrain features, thus abandoning positions that would cost the Israelis a high price in blood and material to retake later in the war.[100] Up on the canal, Adan found his division in serious straits by late afternoon. His tank battalions, which had already suffered heavy casualties during the day, were under attack from the west by the Egyptian 2nd Infantry Division and from the south by the Egyptian 16th Infantry Division. Adan ordered a retreat; by that time, he had lost nearly 70 tanks out of the 170 he had possessed when the day began.

---

[97] Adan's criticism of Gonen actually encapsulates the attitudes of most Israeli senior leaders in Southern Command in their evaluation of their commander during the first days of the war: "Gonen, although in real trouble, never stopped having optimistic hopes that were clearly unrealistic and irrelevant. He burned with a desire to bring about a change in his difficult situation – and fast!" Like all too many commanders in history, Gonan desired to impose his picture and conceptions on reality, rather than adapt that picture and those conceptions to the actual situation. Adan, *On the Banks of the Suez*, p. 111.

[98] Ibid., p. 119.

[99] Interview with General Dov Tamari, Tel Aviv, 24 October 2002.

[100] Sharon does not mention the incident in his memoirs, but Adan does. Testimony from Israeli officers interviewed by the author indicates that Adan is correct in his criticism. The fact that Sharon was still holding up publication of the official history of the Yom Kippur War as late as 2000 suggests that he had something to hide. Adan, *On the Banks of the Suez*, pp. 133, 157.

Throughout the fighting on 8 October, Southern Command exercised no coherent control over the three divisions under its command but rather issued orders that became increasingly out of touch with what was happening on the battlefield. In effect, "[t]here was no common language between GHQ [in Tel Aviv] and Southern Command, and certainly none between Southern Command and the divisions in the field."[101] One of the results of the consistently unrealistic orders issuing from Southern Command was that commanders in the field such as Adan, not to mention Sharon, paid decreasing attention to the orders from above, a situation that tensions between the division commanders fighting the Egyptians only served to aggravate.[102]

The experience on 8 October finally awoke Elazar to the difficulties occurring on the Suez front. He ordered Southern Command to discontinue its counterattacks and wait for the Egyptians to attempt a breakout. Late that afternoon, Sharon received orders to turn his division around and return to the center. On 9 October, disobeying his orders, as he was to do repeatedly throughout the war, Sharon proceeded to launch a series of attacks and learned the same hard lesson that his fellow division commanders had already learned. On that day, his division lost more than 50 tanks, while the divisions on his flanks, although at times under heavy attack from the Egyptians, lost only 15 each. But one of Sharon's efforts, a reconnaissance patrol, did gain one valuable piece of information: there was an open seam between the Second and Third Egyptian Armies, precisely at the point where, in the prewar days, the Israelis had established the means to make a canal crossing.[103]

Late on 9 October, perhaps one of the most important Israeli decisions occurred at General Headquarters. After considerable argument between the minister of defense and the chief of staff, the Israeli leadership decided that Gonen was incapable of running Southern Command under the pressures of the Egyptian offensive. Dayan forced Elazar to place Chaim Bar-Lev, the former chief of staff, in charge of the command, although he did agree to leave Gonen as his deputy instead of removing him entirely from the scene. On 10 October, Bar-Lev arrived to assume command.[104]

---

[101] Ibid., p. 116.
[102] Interview with General Dov Tamari, Tel Aviv, 24 October 2000; and interview with General Avraham Adan, Tel Aviv, 27 October 2000.
[103] Adan, *On the Banks of Suez*, pp. 190–191.
[104] It does speak well of Gonen that he agreed to continue the fight as deputy commander of Southern Command under Bar Lev.

Thus far, there had been little adaptation during the movement of reserves across the Sinai and then the hastily mounted operations. Each reserve division, first Adan's and then Sharon's, had mounted its attack with no information as to what had caused Mandler's heavy losses, while Southern Command, instead of acting as an information bridge, busied itself in issuing irrelevant orders. Now with the order to halt offensive operations, division commanders had their first real opportunity to begin the processes of adaptation. Southern Command, even with the changeover to Bar-Lev, seems to have played little role in these efforts at tactical adaptation. Rather, each division adapted on its own.

During the fighting on the east bank that ensued during the next week, Adan gathered his brigade and battalion commanders every evening for an intensive session on (1) what each had learned during the day, (2) how they could best adapt to the conditions they were confronting, and (3) how the division could better accomplish its mission during the coming day.[105] In addition, Adan established a small forward-command post from which he could direct the battle, while his deputy, Brigadier General Tamari, ran the main headquarters – his aim being to get a better feel for what was actually happening and the tactical framework in which events were taking place.[106]

Quickly, under the pressures of combat, the Israelis reknit the framework of a combined-arms approach to combat. Here the presence of numerous veterans who not only had trained under the concept of combined arms but who also had fought in the Six-Day War within a combined-arms framework helped restore a sensible tactical framework. But as one officer noted, it took nearly five days to work out the tactics of employing infantry, armor, and artillery together in a coherent and combined-arms fashion to handle the Sagger antimissile threat. Meanwhile, everyone was screaming for infantry and paratrooper units.[107] In this process of readaptation, the lull along the canal front after the first four days of intense fighting aided the Israelis considerably.

Meanwhile, the Israelis were driving on the northern front and achieving gains that appeared to pose a threat to Damascus and the stability of the Syrian regime. Israeli expectations were that their offensive in the north would force the Syrians to seek an armistice and pressure the

---

[105] Interview with General Dov Tamari, Tel Aviv, 24 October 2000; and interview with General Adan, Tel Aviv, 27 October 2000.
[106] Interview with General Adan, Tel Aviv, 27 October 2000.
[107] Interview with General Shai Tamari, Tel Aviv, 27 October 2000.

Egyptians to accept a halt to the fighting. It did nothing of the kind. Instead, the Syrians placed great pressure on the Egyptians to come out from under their protective umbrella of SAMs and launch their forces directly against the Israelis in the desert spaces of the Sinai.

On 14 October, the Egyptians responded to the Syrian demands for help. Their two armored divisions, which had remained on the west bank of the canal in reserve, crossed to the east bank and moved out into the Sinai beyond the cover of the air defenses. The move, done to maintain Arab solidarity, played into Israeli hands. This was the battle the IDF had been hoping for, a mobile battle of armored formations killing each other at maximum range.[108] The Israeli Air Force was also able to throw its weight onto the scale now that the Egyptian armor had moved beyond the cover of the SAM belt. But the main victory went to Israeli tanks. Brigadier General Avraham Mandler had been mortally wounded the day before, his place taken by Brigadier General Kalman Magen, who had been about to take command of the Sinai armored division at the beginning of October.[109] Altogether the Egyptians lost more than 250 tanks in the fighting against Israeli armor, while the Israeli aircraft destroyed a motorized force of the Egyptian Third Army moving south from Suez City toward Sharm al-Sheikh.[110]

The Sinai Front: The Israeli Counterattack

The Egyptian attack on 14 October saved the Israelis from the possibility of a serious military defeat. Over the previous several days, they had debated whether to launch a major counteroffensive across the canal at the place where Sharon's reconnaissance unit had found the gap between the Egyptian Second and Third Armies. Apparently, they reached the point where they decided to attack whether the Egyptians struck out from the canal or not.[111] Ironically, the Egyptian move came the day

---

[108] Apparently, Elazar displayed considerable anger that the Egyptians had not been allowed to advance deeper into the Sinai where they could have been destroyed more completely. But Adan commented to the author that because the IDF had spent no time in practicing mobile defense at either the tactical or operational levels, such an approach would have been difficult to pull off, although he did think both his division and Sharon's could have done it. Interview with General Adan, Tel Aviv, 27 October 2000.

[109] Adan, *On the Banks of the Suez*, pp. 230–231.

[110] Van Creveld, *The Sword and the Olive*, pp. 233–234.

[111] The decision appears to have been largely driven by Elazar, who argued in the cabinet that a crossing of the Suez Canal was the only way the Israelis could force the Egyptians

before the Israeli D-Day. Not only did the Egyptian offensive result in severe casualties that substantially attrited their armor, it also moved most of their reserves over to the east bank, leaving few forces on the west bank. In effect, nothing could have better improved the prospects for the coming Israeli counteroffensive.

However, on the negative side, Israeli planning and organizational thinking displayed the same weaknesses at the operational level that had plagued them thus far in the war. While considerable adaptation had taken place at the tactical level, little had changed in terms of improving the thought processes at the operational level. The crossing attempt would involve two divisions, Sharon's and Adan's, with no operational headquarters to coordinate the movement and the fighting. Ironically, the one command that had practiced crossing the canal was the 7th Armored Brigade, which had moved to reinforce the Golan Heights in late September and early October. After the heavy actions it had fought in stopping the Syrians on the northern section of the Golan, it was in no position to return to the Sinai.[112] Southern Command's headquarters was to coordinate the operation, but as had been true throughout the fighting, it remained a distant and uncertain observer. Like Gonen, Bar Lev never visited the front to gain a firsthand impression of what was happening.[113]

Without a coordinating headquarters, Sharon and Adan fought their own fights with little coordination or cooperation. But the most serious weakness in the Israeli operation lay in the planning. Southern Command assigned four distinct missions to Sharon's division: (1) make the breakthrough to the canal, (2) drive the forces of the Egyptian Second Army northward to widen the corridor, (3) make the crossing of the canal, and (4) bring up the bridging equipment that would make possible the movement of Israeli forces across the canal.[114] The Adan Division's one

---

to agree to a cease-fire. Dayan, however, argued that the Israelis should first approach the Egyptians. In retrospect, given Sadat's aims, the Israelis could probably have gained a cease-fire. Elazar won out, one would guess, largely on the unwillingness of the civilian ministers to overrule the chief of staff. Interview with General Dov Tamari, Tel Aviv, 24 October 2000.

[112] Interview with General Dov Tamari, Tel Aviv, 24 October 2000.

[113] Dayan appears to have been the only senior leader above division commander to visit the front regularly to gain an impression of what was happening. Adan, *On the Banks of Suez*, p. 234.

[114] Sharon in his memoirs presents the plan for crossing the canal as his entirely: "That night approval came to cross the canal. With that I presented my plan to Bar Lev, and the headquarters staff had it approved. My division would break through the Egyptian

assigned mission, on the other hand, was to prepare itself for operations on the other side of the canal.[115] Thus, Sharon had received multiple missions. Not surprisingly, he focused on the one that appealed the most to his aggressive nature – namely, the crossing of the canal. Meanwhile, he left to one of his brigade commanders, Amnon Reshef, the task of driving the Egyptians back from the corridor. Sharon's lead elements had little difficulty in reaching the canal, but here again the focus even on the brigade level was fuzzy. Erez had the mission to clean up the east bank in front of his force, begin crossing the canal, and pull the crossing equipment up to the canal.[116]

However, Reshef's brigade ran into a buzz saw of Egyptian resistance, as it attempted to push elements of the Egyptian Second Army back to the north away from the narrow corridor. Furious fighting ensued after the Israelis had reached Egyptian positions. By morning, Reshef had lost nearly 60 tanks of the 100 with which he had begun the battle.[117] Moreover, he made little progress in pushing the Egyptians to the north, while a monumental traffic jam built up in the narrow corridor opened by the Israelis.[118] Luckily for them, the Egyptians remained largely in the dark as to the aim of the IDF's counterattack. But Sharon at last had to ask that someone from outside his division take over responsibility for protecting and policing the main road leading to the canal.[119]

lines [*step 1*], secure a corridor to the canal [*step 2*].... Once the paratroopers had secured the area [on the other side of the canal – *step 3*], a pontoon bridge would be laid and... the great preconstructed rolling bridge would be towed into place and pushed across [*step 4*]." Sharon, *Warrior*, p. 311.

[115] Adan suggested that both his and Sharon's divisions attack together to create a wide enough corridor to ensure that the bridging equipment and the crossing force could cross immediately upon reaching the canal, but he was overruled in favor of having Sharon's division by itself push through to the canal. Adan, *On the Banks of the Suez*, pp. 255–256.

[116] Interview with General Erez, 1 November 2000.

[117] Adan, *On the Banks of the Suez*, p. 269.

[118] Adan describes the traffic jam in the following terms: "The Akavish axis was the only paved road leading from Tassa to the crossing zone. It was narrow – no more than 3.5 to 4 meters wide – and flanked on both sides by heavy dunes. Hundreds of vehicles loaded with fuel, ammunition, and engineering equipment were stuck bumper to bumper on the road for 20 km, totally jamming the axis. At various points along the road, vehicles that had tried to pass the traffic jam were stuck in the sand." Needless to say, the entire traffic jam was enormously vulnerable to Egyptian air attack or an Egyptian attack from the north, which explains why Reshef was willing to take such heavy losses in attempting to drive the Egyptians back to the north. Adan, *On the Banks of Suez*, p. 270.

[119] Sharon could not bear to admit in his memoirs that Adan was the most sensible choice for that task. Sharon, *Warrior*, p. 313.

During the ferocious fighting that followed, the Israelis engaged in fractious debate within the Southern Command's command structure, to a considerable extent reflecting the lack of a clear operational concepts, no clear lines of authority, and the command's unwillingness to grapple with what was actually happening in the front lines. Once on the banks of the Suez, Sharon immediately initiated a crossing operation with paratroopers assigned to his division. He reinforced those light units with tanks, ferried across by pontoon rafts. Those initial moves certainly made sense. What did not make sense was Sharon's unleashing of a portion of the tanks to raid the Egyptian positions on the west bank. Over the course of 16 October, that force drove 20 kilometers into Egyptian positions and destroyed four SAM sites, as well as a battalion of ten tanks and 25 armored personnel carriers.[120] But they returned to the bridgehead almost completely out of fuel and ammunition. If that raid were not enough to alert the Egyptians, Golda Meir announced to the Israeli parliament that Israeli tanks were operating on the canal's west bank – a report that Egyptian journalist Mohamed Hassanein Heikal got into Sadat's hands almost immediately after the Israeli prime minister had completed her speech.[121]

While a small force of Sharon's tanks was raiding on the west bank, the positions along the corridor came under increasing pressure from the Egyptians who were still in the dark about Israeli intentions. Nevertheless, they were certain that something really big was afoot. Thus, the Egyptian Second Army put increasing pressure on the corridor and was even able to cut it at times, while interdicting much of the road with sporadic artillery fire. Adan's division had to commit some of its forces to reopening the Tirtur and Akavish roads, while Sharon's forces cleared the area known as the Chinese Farm. As Adan suggests in his memoirs, despite the fact that the two divisions were now committed side by side to driving the Second Army back from the corridor, "coordination between Sharon and me was not good."[122]

In fact, it was not until the paratroopers arrived that the Israelis were able to begin clearing the area north of the corridor in the early morning hours of 17 October. At the same time, paratroopers on the west bank undertook to push the Egyptians back from the bridgehead where they

---

[120] Adan, *On the Banks of the Suez*, p. 273.
[121] The Egyptian high command had already received reports of Israeli tanks on the west bank but had disregarded those reports as simply indicating a raid (which was what Sharon had launched). But Meir's pronouncement immediately energized Sadat.
[122] Adan, *On the Banks of the Suez*, p. 279.

had already massed nearly 150 artillery pieces to interdict the rafts and Israeli efforts to complete their first bridge. Meanwhile, the Egyptian Second Army launched its 25th Armored Brigade in an effort to achieve what it had failed to do the previous day. It ran straight into a massive tank trap, where the Israelis destroyed 50 to 60 T-62s against a loss of one tank to a Sagger antimissile and two more damaged in a minefield laid in the prewar period.[123] The problem that now confronted the Israelis, as the survivors of the 25th Armored Brigade retreated to the north, was how to get Adan's division across the canal so that it could conduct an operational-level maneuver to destroy the Egyptian air defenses (the SAM belt) and trap a significant portion of the Egyptian Army on the canal's western bank.[124]

Those exploitation operations flowed more smoothly than had the canal crossings for a number of reasons: first, the Egyptians failed to act with dispatch, even when it was clear the Israelis were on the west bank of the Canal in strength.[125] But the larger reason was that once in the clear on the west bank, the Israelis were back within their comfort zone of divisional operations. While two divisions, Adan's and Magen's, participated in the drive south, they did not need a higher headquarters to coordinate their operations against negligible Egyptian forces.

Meanwhile, Sharon had ambitions of surrounding the Egyptian Second Army, but his division had been badly shot up, and there was no Israeli general in his area with whom he could quarrel. The mobile operations served to bring out the great weakness of the Egyptian Army: its inability to react to swiftly moving Israeli units and a fluid situation in which commanders had to make decisions without waiting for instructions from above. As the Third Army Commander reported to the Egyptian Minister of War,

> Sir the situation is fluid, the enemy is breaking through. The commander of the 113th Brigade is behaving like a frightened rabbit and is at the HQ of the 6th Division... [thirteen] kilometers from his units. Enemy tanks are

---

[123] Ibid., p. 303.
[124] Adan comments in his memoirs: "The real problem was not to get tanks across quickly, but to transfer formations ready for prolonged combat in order to launch an offensive and penetrate deep into the other side. The only brigade not involved in battle that day, [Erez's] brigade with its thirty-eight tanks, was in fact already on the west bank, but it, too, had no fuel." Ibid., p. 307.
[125] Part of this had to do with strategic and political arguments in the highest levels of the Egyptian high command. Sadat settled the argument by decreeing that most of the Egyptian forces would remain on the east bank of the canal to ensure the political goals for which he had embarked on the war.

annihilating his artillery.... Unfortunately, I have to deal with liars. The brigade commander is not leading his men through the wadi but is sitting at km 109.... May God ease our burden![126]

In the end, by breaking the first cease-fire arranged by the United Nations, Adan's division managed to surround the Egyptian Third Army. For the most part, it represented a textbook case of armored exploitation. However, an inexcusably careless operation to take Suez City marred its success. Spurred by Southern Command, which ordered the operation as long as it did not lead to "a Stalingrad situation," Adan threw paratroopers into the city.[127] Almost immediately they came under withering fire that trapped a portion deep within the city and inflicted heavy casualties. It represented a nasty end to a nasty war that had resulted in terrible casualties for the IDF and the nation of Israel.

Tactical and Operational Adaptation on the Suez Front

In the end, the IDF had seemingly redeemed its reputation on the Suez front by what appeared at the time as a brilliant canal crossing followed by an exploitation that trapped virtually all of the Egyptian Third Army on the east bank of the canal. Yet a closer examination of the record raises troubling questions not only about the IDF's preparation for the war in the widest sense but also about its ability to adapt when confronted with entirely new and challenging problems, particularly at the operational level. *In the largest sense, the Israelis displayed a senior leadership culture that utterly ignored unity of command and mutual support, failed effectively to seek or use tactical intelligence about how the enemy was fighting, and repeatedly indulged in what can only be called insubordination.*

The processes of tactical adaptation in the south mirrored those that occurred in the north, although perhaps at a slower pace. The initial operations – first by Mandler's Division on 6 and 7 October, then by Adan's Division on 8 October, and finally by Sharon's Division on 9 October – were a disaster both tactically and operationally. At the tactical level, the IDF paid an even heavier price for its lack of combined-arms training and preparations during the prewar period than its units paid on the Golan Heights.

---

[126] Adan, *On the Banks of the Suez*, p. 388.
[127] Ibid., p. 409.

What underlines one of the most troubling weaknesses of Southern Command and the IDF is the fact that clearly there was no agency or means, even in an informal sense, to convey to the arriving reserve formations that combat against the Egyptians had undergone order-of-magnitude changes. Thus, each one of the armored divisions along the canal repeated the same experiences and dismal results. It is one thing to experience heavy losses in confronting an unexpected situation at the outbreak of a conflict. But it is another to repeat the same mistakes day after day even if different units are making the errors.

The great weakness in the IDF's tactical preparations for war lay in its lack of emphasis on combined-arms training at every level. Adan notes the impact of this failure on the infantry units that were eventually attached to his division:

> The major weak point of the attacking forces lay in the infantry troops who were rushed to the division. These infantry forces were neither equipped for nor trained in combined combat with armor. Not only were [they] not organic to the division, but they themselves consisted of companies that had joined up on the battlefield, without being acquainted with one another.... In short, neither their equipment nor their vehicles, neither their training nor their inclinations fitted them for armored action.[128]

To a certain extent, adaptation at the front could offset those failures in preparation – undoubtedly helped by the experiences of so many Israeli soldiers in the previous wars fought by the IDF. But the bill for tactical adaptation came in blood, especially on the Suez front where it came in the first actions of the war and continued almost to the end. Here, adaptation took place at the tactical level thanks to the skill and initiative of the tankers, infantrymen, and gunners, the officers, NCOs, and enlisted. They received insufficient help from their superiors and from the IDF as an organization of controlled violence.

What could not be overcome were the failures to prepare commanders and staffs for war at the operational level. Initiative and flexibility could not make up for the lack of education and conceptualization. What started off as a dysfunctional organizational structure at Southern Command remained a dysfunctional structure throughout the war that was incapable of providing operational-level guidance to its division commanders. These commanders in turn, with little clear guidance from above, waged their separate fights, often with unconscionable and unseemly squabbling. And

---

[128] Ibid., p. 430.

there was no intermediate corps-level operational command to coordinate the fight.

To paraphrase a point that Barry Watts and this author have made elsewhere, military organizations that do not realistically prepare for war in peacetime have a difficult time adapting to the actual conditions of war.[129] Because the Israelis at least trained rigorously at the tactical level, they were able to adapt quickly to the actual conditions they confronted, although at considerable cost. At the operational level, they were not nearly so successful; only the mistakes of their opponents, who were even less prepared to wage an operational-level campaign, prevented a serious defeat of the IDF and allowed the Israelis to gain a modicum of success, but at a heavy price.

---

[129] Barry Watts is one of the most sophisticated military analysts of this generation. Unfortunately, much of his work has not been published for reasons of classification or because it has aimed at influencing specialized audiences within the defense community.

8

Conclusion

Adaptation and the Future

> *Politically, too, we rushed into the business with our usual disregard for a comprehensive political scheme.... The coordinating of Arabian politics and the creation of an Arabian policy should have been done at home – it could only have been done successfully at home. There was no-one to do it, no-one who had thought of it, and it was left to our people in Egypt to thrash it out, in the face of tremendous opposition from India and London, some sort of wide scheme which will, I am persuaded, ultimately form the basis of our operations with the Arabs.*[1]
>
> Gertrude Bell, letter, April 29, 1916

The Strategic Environment

At present, the United States confronts the most complex and uncertain international environment in its history.[2] For the first time since the collapse of the Soviet Union, an economic and political competitor, the People's Republic of China, appears to have the capacity to challenge America's dominance in the long term. The Middle East is in even greater turmoil than it has been at any time since the collapse of the Ottoman Empire at the end of the First World War, a turmoil that the youth bulge throughout the area can only serve to exacerbate.[3] Moreover, adding

---

[1] Gertrude Bell Archive, letter, April 29, 1916, Newcastle University, Robinson Library, http://www.gerty.ncl.ac.uk/ (accessed 16 June 2009).
[2] The document U.S. Joint Forces Command, "The Joint Operational Environment," Norfolk, VA, November 2008, forms the basis for the following discussion on the emerging strategic environment.
[3] One of the lessons in history is that excess population of the young, combined with periods of rising expectations, represents a recipe for revolutions and periods of major conflict. Both are present in other areas of the world beside the Middle East, but the possibility of

to the difficulties that failing states have represented in the past is the possibility that a number of significant "national entities" – among others, Pakistan, Mexico, North Korea, and Nigeria – could collapse, bringing with their demise the kinds of troubles that Yugoslavia's disintegration in the early 1990s brought to the Balkans and Europe.

In the immediate future, the strategic and political results of American interventions in Afghanistan and Iraq remain uncertain. The collapse of the Russian economy concurrently with a fall in energy prices several years ago led to a major crisis between Russia and Ukraine over the transshipment of gas supplies on which much of Europe depends. In 2008, the invasion of Georgia by the KGB mafia that runs Russia raises serious questions about the reliability of that nation. At present, the world's energy supplies are more uncertain than they have been at any time since the Second World War, while recent perturbations in the financial markets have shaken the global economy in a fashion that has not occurred since the Great Depression of the early 1930s. Adding to those uncertainties is the fact that a technological and information revolution is occurring at a pace never before seen in history, with consequences in the political, social, and military spheres that are difficult to predict.[4]

Such an international environment obviously carries with it serious implications for the U.S. military. It suggests that the threats to American interests, as well as those of its allies and partners, will range across the spectrum of conflict from peacekeeping to peace enforcement to midlevel conventional conflict, all the way to deterrence in the best case, and, in the worst case, war at the high end. Thus, the ability to adapt at every level of war from the tactical to the strategic and political would seem to be more important to the American polity and its military than at any time since 1941. Unfortunately, there is going to be no simple path for the preparation of the U.S. military to fight the wars of the future.[5]

That range of threats means that U.S. military forces will inevitably find themselves committed to areas shaped by vastly differing cultural and

---

revolution and conflict in that region carries with it the threat to a substantial portion of the world's oil supplies.

[4] For a discussion of the implications of such revolutionary changes for the social and political framework within which wars have taken place, see the introductory and concluding chapters in MacGregor Knox and Williamson Murray, eds., *The Dynamics of Military Revolution, 1300–2050* (Cambridge, UK, 2000). See also William H. McNeil, *The Pursuit of Power: Technology, Armed Force, and Society since AD 1000* (Chicago, 1982).

[5] And those wars will inevitably occur. For a discussion of the nature of the coming century, see Colin S. Gray, *Another Bloody Century: Future Warfare* (London, 2005).

historical frameworks. Thus, the success of American interventions, or the adroit avoidance of unnecessary interventions, will require understanding not only the fundamental nature of war but also the complex contexts within which such conflicts might take place. The great difficulty for present and future American military leaders is that they cannot predict where, against whom, or when they will find themselves involved in major military operations. Nor can they predict with any degree of accuracy the kind of conflicts and missions in which they will find themselves.

For the present, the United States cannot afford the luxury of preparing its forces for one particular form of war, whether that form be conventional or insurgency. Nor can it dismiss the period after the end of active military operations as someone else's problem. The ability to adapt to the unforeseen conditions and contexts of the future becomes of even greater importance in the effectiveness of military forces than was the case in the twentieth century.[6]

Moreover, straining the capabilities and ability of U.S. military forces are several factors of considerable importance in thinking through the employment of military forces. *First*, in a fashion unprecedented since World War II, the United States will have to project its military power across the two great oceans that surround it.[7] Admittedly, that reality represented a major problem throughout the Cold War, but the difference now is that the United States may well not have access to the extensive infrastructure of bases in both Europe and the Pacific that has existed since 1943. The return of U.S. forces to North America presages the emergence of a more complex set of logistical problems, which will make the projection of military power more difficult. *Second*, sophisticated and cheap weapons are becoming increasingly available on the world's arms

---

[6] On the ability of military forces to adapt to new circumstances, the problems that confronted the Royal Navy, Royal Marines, and British Army in the Falklands is a good example of military adaptability at its best. For excellent discussions of the campaign and the adaptations that were required, see the following works, among others: Max Hastings and Simon Jenkins, *The Battle for the Falklands* (New York, 1984); Lawrence Freedman, *The Official History of the Falklands Campaign*, vol. 2, *The 1982 Falklands War and Its Aftermath* (London, 2005); and Admiral Sandy Woodward and Patrick Robinson, *One Hundred Days: The Memoirs of the Falklands' Battle Group Commander* (London, 1988).

[7] In the 1980s, a number of historians and pundits criticized the American military for its overemphasis on logistics, while at the same time comparing it with the *Wehrmacht*'s minimal logistical footprint. What they missed was the problem the United States confronted in projecting military power across two great oceans and then fighting campaigns on the other side of the world. The American high command had no choice but to emphasize logistics.

markets and thus could be available to relatively weak states as well as nonstate actors, actors who may wish to deny access to particular areas of interest to the United States. *Third*, it is unlikely that any future opponent of the United States will allow U.S. and Allied military forces unhindered access to crisis areas, as Saddam Hussein's Iraq was to do on not one but two occasions. *Fourth*, unlike past wars in which the U.S. homeland was inviolate, today the nation is vulnerable to cyber and terrorist attacks that could have major consequences not only politically but militarily as well.

This, then, is the strategic and political conundrum within which the U.S. military will have to operate. If anything, such environments will demand an even greater ability to adapt to the actual conditions of a conflict than has been true in the past. The future will demand that commanders, their staffs, and their subordinates adapt swiftly not only to the kaleidoscope of conflict at the sharp end but also to the cultural, political, and social framework within which such conflicts take place. Moreover, the institutions that sustain and guide the military forces of the United States, providing everything from operational capabilities to operating concepts, are the slowest to recognize the need for change or the problems raised by the particular enemies the United States will confront in the twenty-first century.

Adaptation: The Problem

As the first chapter suggested, similar factors drive successful innovation in peacetime as drive successful adaptation in war. Both require imagination and a willingness to change; both involve imagination as to the possibilities and potential for change; and both demand organizational cultures that encourage the upward flow of ideas and perceptions as well as direction from above. Particularly important is the need for senior leaders to encourage their staffs and subordinates to seek out new paths. Both involve intellectual understanding as well as instinct and action. As Clausewitz notes, "in our view even junior positions of command require outstanding intellectual qualities."[8] Thus, it would seem that education of the force and preparation of its leaders should become as important as the training regimens of the services and the joint forces.

Among other qualities, curiosity about new possibilities is crucial to successful change and adaptation. In effect, the organizational culture of

---

[8] Carl von Clausewitz, *On War*, trans. and ed. by Michael Howard and Peter Paret (Princeton, 1976), p. 111.

particular military organizations formed during peacetime will determine how effectively they will adapt to the actual conditions they will face in war. Equally important is how honest they prove to be in examining past lessons and the results of war games and exercises.[9] As Barry Watts and the author pointed out, "a related hypothesis is that military organizations which have trouble being scrupulous about empirical data in peacetime may have the same difficulty in time of war."[10] How willing peacetime organizations are to encourage initiative and independent thinking will also play a major role in how adaptive they will prove under the psychological demands of combat.

Yet, there are substantial differences between innovation and adaptation. In peacetime, time poses few significant challenges to the innovator; he may lack significant resources, but he has time to form, test, and evaluate his ideas and perceptions. The opposite is true in war. There, those involved in combat usually possess a plethora of resources, but time is not one of them; those pursuing serious changes in doctrine, technology, or tactics in the midst of a conflict have only a brief opportunity to adapt. Adding to their difficulties is the fact that as their organization adapts, so, too, will the enemy.[11] Moreover, in peacetime those who will innovate in the emerging strategic environment will have to consider indeterminate opponents who, more often than not, represent an idealized, rarely changing depiction of potential enemies.[12] In war, however, the enemy is real, and as a human entity, he, too, adapts to the conditions he confronts and, more often than not, in a fashion that may be largely

---

[9] What is astonishing, given its importance to military effectiveness, is how little time and effort military historians have devoted to serious research and examination of military culture. The period between the two world wars has a number of outstanding works devoted to the study of innovation, but virtually none examining the issues involved in the formulation of particular military cultures, including the subcultures of the particular services.

[10] Barry D. Watts and Williamson Murray, "Military Innovation in Peacetime," in Williamson Murray and Allan R. Millett, eds., *Military Innovation in the Interwar Period* (Cambridge, 1996), p. 414.

[11] The most graphic example of this phenomenon is the case of the French Army, which had significantly changed its offensive doctrine over winter 1916–1917 but then ran into the reality that the Germans had made equally radical changes in their defensive doctrine by inventing the system of defense in depth. See Chapter 3 of this work for further discussion of this issue.

[12] Red teaming is supposedly a method of presenting a realistic depiction of the enemy, but for the most part, military organizations have not taken it seriously. See Williamson Murray, "Red Teaming: Its Contribution to Past Military Effectiveness," DART Working Paper #02-2, Hicks and Associates, September 2002; and "Thoughts on Red Teaming," DART Working Paper #03-2, Hicks and Associates, May 2003.

unexpected by his opponents. Thus, adaptation demands constant, unceasing change because war itself never remains static but involves the complexities thrown up by humans involved in their attempt to survive.

This monograph has examined a number of historical case studies on the problems that military organizations have confronted in adapting. The critic might well argue that past adaptations have little to do with the current and future difficulties the American military will confront in the twenty-first century. In terms of answers to specific problems, they are largely correct. History can only point toward uncertain paths to the future.[13] It cannot provide answers to specific problems. At best, it can suggest the kinds of questions that military organizations and their leaders need to ask before and as they attempt to change.

But it is the asking of the right kinds of questions that is the essential first step to any successful adaptation to the problems raised by a particular conflict. Historical understanding can lead, if properly used, to a questioning of the faulty assumptions with which military organizations have entered a conflict. Nor should one forget that when the assumptions are flawed, the approaches and adaptations they suggest and the direction they provide will invariably prove dangerously irrelevant.[14] Only the right questions can lead to successful adaptations. There are a number of wildcards in the framework of adaptation. Among them are two crucial factors: *first,* all going-in assumptions are faulty to some degree. Therefore, one must assume the need to adapt to the actual conditions and the actual enemy. *Second,* when and who asks the questions matters. In the period from 1964 to 1968, there were a number of officers at every rank who were asking the right questions. But because Johnson, McNamara, and Westmoreland did not, things did not change.

Here it is particularly germane to remember Michael Howard's comment that military organizations almost always get the next war wrong. Thus, it is paramount that military leaders determine the nature and character of the war on which they have embarked. As Clausewitz suggests in *On War:* "No one starts a war – or rather, no one in their senses ought to do so – without first being clear in his mind what he intends

---

[13] On the subject of what history suggests about the future, see Williamson Murray, "History, War, and the Future," *Orbis,* Fall 2008.
[14] It became clear as early as summer 1915 to some British commanders that prolonged artillery bombardment had no chance of success unless concentrated in density. Unfortunately for British soldiers, Haig refused to recognize this reality until 1918. Quite simply, he never encouraged his subordinates or staff to question the basic tactical approaches that he found congenial.

to achieve by that war and how he intends to conduct it.... This is the governing principle which will set its course, prescribe the scale of means and effort which is required, and make its influence felt throughout down to the smallest operational detail."[15] In fact, Clausewitz is being ironic, because few cases in history have featured political and military leaders who managed to figure out beforehand the kind of war on which they are actually embarking. Nor have most shown much willingness to alter their perceptions and assumptions in the face of reality – at least until defeat and disaster have stared them in the face.

And if Professor Howard is correct, then political and military leaders must be willing to challenge their most closely held assumptions, if they are to adapt.[16] The inability to recognize that one has failed to understand the kind of war on which one has embarked or that one has miscalculated the balance of forces in a fundamental fashion, has in the past inevitably presented the greatest of difficulties, and this will be true in the future as well. Adaptation requires that political and military leaders determine not only the tactical, operational, and technological parameters of the conflict but also its strategic and political ones. The latter will invariably prove the most difficult because it requires leaders to question their most cherished beliefs.[17]

On the military side of the equation, most leaders will find themselves and their subordinates encumbered with their intellectual and historical baggage. Adaptations must come not only in the technological and warfighting spheres where the American military have proven consistently superior to any and all opponents since the end of the Cold War but also in areas of cultural, political, and intellectual spheres. The American conventional "way of war" proved devastating in confronting Saddam Hussein's ill-trained, ill-disciplined, and technologically inferior forces.[18] It is unlikely, however, that America's opponents in coming decades will

---

[15] Clausewitz, *On War*, p. 579.
[16] See, in particular, Michael Howard, "The Use and Abuse of Military History," *Journal of the Royal United Services Institute*, February 1962.
[17] Admittedly, the task of military leaders at the strategic level is to provide coherent, intelligent advice as to the possibility of the means available to achieve the ends desired. As a result, they too must play a role in debates about strategic policy, and if they do not, because they are either unwilling or unable, then they are abdicating their responsibility.
[18] For a short history of the conventional war, see Williamson Murray and Robert H. Scales, Jr., *The Iraq War: A Military History* (Cambridge, MA, 2003). For the war from Saddam's skewed perspective, see Kevin Woods with Michael R. Pease, Mark E. Stout, Williamson Murray, and James G. Lacey, *The Iraqi Perspectives Report* (Annapolis, MD, 2006).

prove so foolish as to challenge the United States and its military forces in the arena of conventional military operations. Certainly, the lesson would appear to be crystal clear: do not challenge the United States in areas where its conventional military power can dominate the battle space.

In the sequel to the insurgency that followed the destruction of Saddam's conventional military forces, the U.S. effort possessed serious flaws. At the sharp end of combating a growing numbers of insurgents, U.S. soldiers and marines proved extraordinarily adaptable to the conditions on the street that they faced.[19] However, at the higher level of command, the story was not so positive. One brigade commander commented to the author on his 15-month experience from July 2003 to September 2004 in the following terms:

> Too many leaders (both civilian and military) at the highest level [brigade commander and above] or those positioned in staffs at operational headquarter or in strategic executive branch positions were excessively involved in what was happening in tactical units at the expense of developing a long-term strategy and operational concept to implement it.... There was little conception of the operational art at CJTF-7.[20] Units initially occupied zones that transcended local government boundaries.... Military units were more or less distributed evenly across Iraq, even though it soon became apparent that the heart of the insurgency lay in the Sunni Triangle.... Shortage of forces, lack of vision, or lack of will prevented a more permanent presence in the area and an effective plan to deal with Fallujah until after it had become a symbol for the insurgency.... Movement of Coalition forces to consolidated bases should have been contingent upon the creation of effective local security forces. By leaving early, we ceded portions [of the countryside] to the insurgents.[21]

In the end, the most important attribute of military effectiveness is the ability to adapt to the actual conditions of combat and the conflict.[22] There is also a direct connection among peacetime preparation, the willingness to innovate in an imaginative fashion, and the culture of military organizations and their ability to adapt when they confront the actual

---

[19] The clearest discussion of the adaptations at the intermediate levels of command to the problems raised by the insurgency is Peter Mansoor, *Baghdad at Sunrise: A Brigade Commander's War in Iraq* (New Haven, 2008).
[20] Combined Joint Task Force-7.
[21] Colonel Peter Mansoor, e-mail to the author.
[22] Interestingly, the three authors of the introductory guidance essay in the three-volume study on military effectiveness failed to address this issue; see Allan R. Millett, Williamson Murray, and Kenneth Watman, "Military Effectiveness: Historical Dimensions of the Problem," *International Security*, Summer 1986.

conditions of wartime employment. Those military organizations that display imagination and a willingness to think through the changes that occur in the tactical, operational, and strategic levels in peacetime have in nearly every case been those that have shown a willingness and ability to adapt and alter their prewar assumptions and preparations to reality.[23] Of course, military organizations can learn through the experiences gained by killing their own members. German commentators at the end of the Battle of the Somme noted how much the British had learned over the five months of the battle. But the cost of that learning, some 400,000 casualties and 120,000 dead, would seem to have been excessive.

In effect, in Iraq, too many U.S. senior military leaders at the higher levels learned how to deal with the insurgency over an extended period of time – time which allowed the insurgents to sink their roots down into fertile soil – rather than by drawing on their preparations, mental and otherwise, from peacetime.[24] To a considerable extent, their performance in the first year of the insurgency was almost as if there were no applicable lessons from America's experiences in Vietnam, much less from Iraq's own history.[25] Thus, when there is no ability to recognize the patterns from a military organization's own experience, the direct result is a repetition of the same mistakes and errors. It is as Yogi Berra noted, "déjà vu all over again."[26]

---

[23] There is an important and growing literature on the problems associated with military organizations and innovation in peacetime. Among the best are the following: Thomas C. Hone, Norman Friedman, and Mark D. Mandeles, *American and British Aircraft Carrier Development, 1919–1941* (Annapolis, MD, 1999); Harold R. Winton and David R. Mets, *The Challenge of Change, Military Institutions and New Realities, 1918–1941* (Lincoln, NE, 2000); David E. Johnson, *Fast Tanks and Heavy Bombers: Innovation in the U.S. Army, 1917–1945* (Ithaca, NY, 1998); Stephen Peter Rosen, *Winning the Next War: Innovation and the Modern Military* (Ithaca, NY, 1991); and Harold R. Winton, *To Change an Army: General Sir John Burnett-Stuart and British Armored Doctrine, 1927–1938* (Lawrence, KS, 1988).

[24] After his return to the United States, Major General Buff Blount, commander of the 3rd Infantry Division during the invasion of Iraq, was highly critical of much of the senior civilian and military leadership in Iraq during the initial months of occupation, the general ignorance of Iraq, Arab culture, and the unwillingness to recognize that an insurgency was building. But then General Blount had spent no less than six years in Saudi Arabia in various capacities.

[25] For the British experience in Iraq in 1920, which the American experience would almost exactly replicate 83 years later, see Lieutenant General Sir Aylmer L. Haldane, *The Insurrection in Mesopotamia, 1920* (London, 1922, reprinted 2005).

[26] American philosopher-baseball player Yogi Berra; attribution to "Berra, Yogi," in Elizabeth Knowles, ed., *The Oxford Dictionary of Modern Quotations*, Oxford Reference Online, http://www.oxfordreference.com/views/ENTRY.html?subview=Main&entry=t93.e157 (accessed April 27, 2009).

Perhaps the most fundamental lesson of the U.S. experience in Vietnam had been that U.S. forces could not win the war in the long run; only the indigenous South Vietnamese forces could win the war, because they knew the countryside, the enemy, and, above all, the nature of the struggle. Yet, having seen Ambassador Bremer and the Coalition Provisional Authority dismiss the remnants of the Iraqi Army and police forces, U.S. forces assumed the effort to police Iraq with inadequate troop strength, while making only minimal effort to rebuild both the local police and Iraq's armed forces.[27] A participant in the initial efforts to rebuild the Iraqi military recalled to this author in an e-mail in 2004:

> The base structure was an extraordinarily bad plan. Under the concept decided upon by [American advisers] at the MOD [Ministry of Defense], all bases would be run by a civilian staff from the MOD. That staff would consist of twenty-three personnel per base. Their only duty would be to supervise the contractors who would provide ALL services – building maintenance, sewer, water, chow, ambulance, fire, ranges, roads, etc. . . .
>
> When I joined CMATT [Coalition Military Advisory Training Team], the Ministry of Defense had hired twenty Iraqis (after six months of screening). By March 2004 that number was up to forty. They said they needed 300 to start the ministry in June. Didn't look like they would make it. Very bureaucratic, civil service process for vetting and hiring Iraqis. For the most part, it did not seem to include any input from the Iraqis themselves.
>
> Funding was a constant issue – and over peanuts. For instance DOD [the U.S. Department of Defense] withheld $78 million needed for base construction for almost six months. [Major General Eaton, U.S. Army, head of the advisory effort] told them that every day they withheld after January 1, 2004, meant at least one day delay in completing the bases needed to house the forces graduating from boot camp. . . . When the Pentagon finally approved the $78 million, [it] put a stop on the next wave of $238 million. Apparently, someone in the Pentagon felt that they could supervise the construction much better in a couple of hours from Washington than the guys in Iraq could in eighteen hours a day. . . .
>
> I took over in January [2004] with two bases open, one about to open, and then a need to open one about every twenty days for months. We had no SOPs, no TTPs [tactics, techniques, and procedures], no test of the concept, no reliable contractors, no training program. And apparently no one in the MOD thought this was a problem because NO action had been taken in any of these areas. . . .

---

[27] One of the clearest lessons of the war in Vietnam is that only indigenous forces can defeat an insurgency. Thus, while there were reasons for the decision to disband the Iraqi Army in May 2003 – this author happens to disagree with them – the lackadaisical approach to building a new military over the course of the next several years represented an astonishing error in judgment.

There was NO communications system between myself and the bases. The only one that CMATT and the army battalions possessed was the one between CMATT and the few advisers out there. Since the advisers did not share a compound with the Iraqi Army or the base people, we had no reliable communications. I resorted to having my base managers open a Yahoo account and use the local internet café twice a day to communicate with us in Baghdad.[28]

Adaptation and Technology

As the first chapter suggested, the major factor in the increasing importance of adaptation to the effectiveness of military organizations has been the appearance of technology over the course of the past century and a half. That proposition has certainly proven attractive to the American military, especially in the past 50 years. For a number of pundits in the 1990s, it seemed as if technological advances would provide a silver bullet to escape the difficulties that have pervasively handicapped the employment of military forces throughout the centuries. In the period before the campaigns in Afghanistan and Iraq, some senior officers at the highest levels argued that advances in computing power and the advent of an ever-widening variety of precision weapons would allow American forces to see all potential targets and then destroy them in an area of 200 miles by 200 miles – in effect, a box that worked out to 40,000 square miles. Moreover, the argument went even further: the sophistication of technological systems available to the American military would allow their forces to remove friction from the battlefield.[29]

The experiences of Afghanistan and Iraq have dissipated that fog of willful ignorance about the fundamental nature of war, not to mention of historical experience.[30] In fact, throughout the twentieth century, with the possible exception of the advent of nuclear weapons, technology has been an enabler and driver of change rather its determinant. Even more important than technology in innovation and adaptation has been the creation of military cultures amenable to careful historical and experiential learning, honest analysis, and imaginative, realistic thinking about the future possibilities of weapons systems.

---

[28] E-mail from Colonel T. X. Hammes, USMC (retired), to the author.
[29] For the foremost exposition of this extreme view, see Admiral William A. Owens with Ed Offley, *Lifting the Fog of War* (New York, 2000).
[30] For a brief discussion of the timelessness of the fundamental nature of war, see Joint Forces Command, "The Joint Operational Environment," part 1.

It is worthwhile to remember that in the invasion of France and the Low Countries in 1940, French tanks were distinctly superior in a technological sense to the amalgam of obsolete German and Czech armored fighting vehicles that the *Wehrmacht* possessed.[31] On the other hand, the first-line tanks the Germans possessed in 1944 were distinctly superior to those possessed by the Anglo-American armies. Yet at the same time, the Sherman tank possessed a huge advantage over the *Wehrmacht*'s Tiger and Panther tanks because of its maintainability. The larger point is that the Allies, especially the Americans and the Soviets, understood far better than the Germans the crucial point that *dependability* and *ease of maintenance* are major factors in combat effectiveness.[32] In other words, they had adapted in the largest sense to the age of the internal combustion engine, and the Germans had not.

On the other hand, the crucial point to remember in terms of the German victory over the Western allies in May-June 1940 is that it was an adaptable, coherent, combined-arms doctrine that allowed the Germans to overwhelm their opponent in a brilliant six-week campaign. It was not the technology of the tank per se that provided them with the margin of victory. Above all, the Germans folded the armored fighting vehicle into a concept of war that placed an understanding of combat itself as the determinate for thinking about future war, not technological advances such as weapons systems.[33] As *Truppenführung* ("Troop Leadership"), the German army's basic doctrinal manual, noted in its introductory paragraph:

> [1.] War is an art, a free and creative activity founded on scientific principles. It makes the highest demands on the human personality. 2. The conduct of war is subject to continual development. New weapons dictate ever-changing forms. Their appearance must be anticipated and their influence evaluated. Then they must be placed in service quickly. 3. Combat situations are of unlimited variety. They change frequently and suddenly and seldom can be assessed in advance. Incalculable elements often have a decisive influence. One's own will is pitted against that of the enemy. Friction and errors are daily occurrences.... 10. The decisive factor, despite technology

---

[31] In this regard, see particularly the comparison of weapons systems possessed by the Germans and their Allied opponents in Karl-Heinz Frieser, *Blitzkrieg-Legende: Der Westfeldzug 1940* (München, 1995), pp. 46–52.

[32] This was particularly important for the American military that confronted the enormously difficult problem of having to project its military power across two great oceans.

[33] The misunderstandings about the nature of German doctrine during the Second World War lie in the overemphasis on the tank rather than the tactical system of war, which was responsible for the *Wehrmacht*'s early successes.

Conclusion   317

and weaponry, is the value of the individual soldier.... The emptiness of the battlefield requires soldiers who can think and act independently, who can make calculated, decisive, and daring use of every situation.[34]

What matters in technological adaptation as well as technological innovation is how well new and improved technologies are incorporated into effective and intelligent concepts of fighting: it is not the technological sophistication that matters, it is the larger framework. German radar technology throughout the early years of the Second World War was clearly more sophisticated technologically than that possessed by the British. Yet, as Chapter 5 suggested, the incorporation of radar into a systemic approach to air defense provided the British with an enormous advantage in their ability to defend the British Isles from air attacks – an approach that the Germans would not finally hit on until the Allied bombing of Hamburg in July 1943 forced them to adapt their entire air defense system to an entirely new approach.[35]

As Alan Beyerchen has noted in regard to peacetime innovation (his comments are equally applicable to wartime adaptation):

> British technological innovation was the outcome of the interaction of technical and operational innovation, and the changed context meant new parameters for both in turn. [Air Marshal Sir Hugh] Dowding and [Sir Henry] Tizard, a military man and a scientist with the same goals, were the two figures who understood earliest and perhaps best how radar was transforming the context of combat. Their actions blurred the boundaries between technical and operational change, as each pressed for operational development and innovation that would spur technical advance. As new devices became available, they availed themselves of the possibilities, but they did not rely on technical innovation to alter procedures and thinking.[36]

One final note on technological adaptation is in order. A crucial piece of the puzzle for successful adaptation lies in the willingness of senior military leaders to reach out to civilian experts beyond their narrowly focused military bureaucracies. No matter how expert senior officers may be in technical matters, they can rarely, if ever, be masters of the technological

---

34 Bruce Condell and David T. Zabecki, *Truppenführung: On the German Art of War* (Boulder, CO, 2001), pp. 17–18.
35 Until that point in the war, the Germans had used radar in its ground control intercept (GCI) mode in which each radar site controlled a single fighter. This minimized the ability to concentrate large numbers of fighters against the large, concentrated formations of bombers that the British sent over to attack German cities. See Chapter 6 for further discussion of these issues.
36 Alan Beyerchen, "From Radio to Radar," in Murray and Millett, eds., *Military Innovation in the Interwar Period*, p. 286.

side of the equation. Thus, real openness to civilian expertise in the areas of science and technology must form a crucial portion of the processes of adaptation.[37]

In the Second World War, it was that openness that does much to explain the Anglo-American success in not only in the operational but also the intelligence sphere. Scientists such as R. V. Jones bridged the gaps that existed between the world of science and that of operations and, in Jones's case, the bridges among science, operations, and intelligence.[38] The British and the Americans were willing to use civilians to the fullest in spurring on the processes of adapting technological changes to operational and tactical needs. Their success depended on using those outside the bureaucracy to their fullest, while the German military, for the most part, regarded expertise outside of the narrow confines of their operational and tactical worlds as something that only needed to be ordered around to provide the needed answers.

It is clear that we live in an era of increasingly rapid technological change. The historical lesson is equally clear: U.S. military forces are going to have to place increasing emphasis on realistic innovation in peacetime and swift adaptation in combat. This will require leaders who understand war and its reality as well as the implications of technological change. Imagination and intellectual qualities will be as important as the specific technical and tactical details of war making. The great challenge here is how to inculcate those qualities widely in the officer corps.

Adaptation at the Strategic Level

The need for adaptation at the strategic level may represent the easiest to recognize but the most difficult to accomplish. To paraphrase Clausewitz, everything in strategic adaptation is simple, but the simplest thing is difficult.[39] Simply put, strategic change at the highest level requires confronting a number of unpalatable realities. Those realities *must* lead

---

[37] Here there is a problem in that the services have their own scientific and technological bureaucracies that can be prone to the "not invented here" syndrome. This is not necessarily a new phenomenon because the P-51, which was an American design with a British Rolls-Royce engine, came close to falling between the cracks, because it had no clear parentage in the bureaucratic world of 1942–1943.
[38] R. V. Jones's memoirs, *The Wizard War* (New York, 1979) represents one of the great contributions to our understanding of the interrelationships among science, technology, operations, and intelligence over the course of the Second World War.
[39] The original sentence in Clausewitz reads "Everything in war is very simple, but the simplest thing is difficult." Clausewitz, *On War*, p. 138.

statesmen and military leaders to challenge their most basic assumptions. The appallingly bad conduct of German strategy in both world wars suggests a flight from unpalatable strategic realities into a universe of pure military operations.[40]

The first challenge lies in the political realities of strategy itself. "War, therefore, is an act of policy."[41] Yet, as because war always finds itself driven by politics, its purposes and goals will inevitably find themselves influenced by internal as well as external factors. And because it is a human endeavor, human weaknesses, fears, passion, and anger will contribute to both political goals and their interplay with strategy. Neither should we underestimate the capacity of sheer incompetence, ignorance, or overweening pride to influence, if not drive, the political as well as the military goals for which a nation fights a war.

By November 1914, it had become apparent to the chief of the Prussian Great General Staff, General Erich von Falkenhayn, that Germany could not win the First World War. His advice to Chancellor Bethmann Hollweg was that Germany needed to make some sort of compromise peace, preferably with czarist Russia, but with France as well, if necessary.[42] The chancellor's reply was an outright refusal.

> For the first time in German history, a chancellor was asked by a chief of the general staff to take charge, to make the necessary political decisions, and to end the war.... Now in November [the chancellor, Theobald von Bethman Hollweg] again declined to face reality, and informed Falkenhayn that he was prepared to fight to the bitter end, no matter how long it might take. By rejecting the advice of the only person who had a clear appreciation of Germany's strategic situation at the end of 1914, Bethman Hollweg became morally culpable for the continuing slaughter.[43]

Yet, it is not difficult to understand his position. To admit to the German public that the Reich could not win the war after all the heavy

---

[40] The nature of German post–World War II memoirs underlines this point in spades. As Gerhard Weinberg has commented, German memoir literature by the generals might have followed a more realistic track in its analysis of the war had it led to the following conclusion: "If the Führer had only listened to me, the war would have lasted another six months, and the Americans would have dropped the atomic bomb on Berlin."
[41] Clausewitz, *On War*, p. 87.
[42] Holger H. Herwig, *The First World War: Germany and Austria-Hungary, 1914–1918* (London, 1997). In fairness to the chancellor, Falkenhyn's proposals for ending the war quite simply had no chance of being achieved, given German actions in the first four months of the conflict. Herwig, pp. 116–117.
[43] Ibid., p. 116.

casualties the conflict had already entailed (perhaps upward of 300,000 dead) would have led almost immediately to the fall of the monarchy and perhaps to a revolution that would have overturned the Wilhelmine Empire's entire social fabric and political order.[44]

In effect, by December 1914, the decision to embark on the First World War by invading Belgium (and thus bringing Britain immediately into the conflict), the so-called Schlieffen Plan, had closed off the alternative of a compromise peace except for continuing the conflict in the hope that something else might turn up instead of defeat. In a real sense, the Germans had reached a dead-end strategically before the war had hardly begun. The battle cry of *Weltmacht oder Niedergang* ("world power or defeat"), which echoed throughout right-wing German circles, represented a political drive that could only end in one result, since the mantra of "military necessity" over all other concerns, including the political, moral, and strategic, meant that Germany would soon be fighting a war against all the other major powers, including the United States.[45]

Similarly, senior officials in the Johnson administration recognized by late 1967 that virtually all the assumptions that had driven the U.S. decision to intervene in the Vietnam conflict were turning out to be faulty.[46] Politically, it appeared to the president and his advisers that any decision to withdraw would lead to disastrous electoral results. In the end, it took the political smashup of the Tet Offensive to awaken the administration in Washington into addressing the basic strategic question of whether Vietnam was worth the effort. But by that point, it was too late for the administration to change course.

Even when the new Nixon administration took over in 1969, the question of how to extradite the United States from a conflict that was proving increasingly divisive at home proved extraordinarily difficult to resolve. In fact, the American intervention and how it was handled had created new and complex strategic conundrums that offered up no simple and easy solutions. Only major changes in the international

---

[44] Ibid., chap. 1.
[45] On the pernicious role of pure "military necessity" and the trumping by that concept of political and strategic factors by the German military, see Isabel Hull's study of German strategic policy before and during the course of the First World War: *Absolute Destruction: Military Culture and the Practice of War in Imperial Germany* (Ithaca, NY, 2007).
[46] Among other works, see H. R. McMaster, *Dereliction of Duty: Lyndon Johnson, Robert McNamara, the Joint Chiefs of Staff, and the Lies That Led to Vietnam* (New York, 1997).

environment – particularly the explosive split between China and the Soviet Union – allowed the Nixon administration to execute a withdrawal that kept America's reputation relatively intact.

Yet, one should not believe that strategic adaptation over the course of a conflict cannot exercise a powerful and, in some cases, beneficial outcome. Perhaps the two best examples, Abraham Lincoln and Otto von Bismarck, come from the nineteenth century, with the successful adaptations to the ever-changing strategic and political frameworks those leaders confronted. There were, of course considerable differences in personality and background: the first was a quintessential American politician, the second an autocrat; but the essential point is that both were students of history and both were extraordinarily good judges of their opponents as well as their supporters. Both adapted their strategic framework to fit the overall political and military realities of the conflicts in which their nations were involved. And in both cases, that strategic framework shifted as either they adapted their assumptions to reality or as new possibilities opened up.

In the case of the former, Lincoln's initial conception was that it would take a few easy victories to return the great majority of Union sympathizers in the South to the old flag. By the summer of 1862, however, the realities of the battlefield and Southern resistance had altered Lincoln's understanding of the political and strategic landscape sufficiently for him to issue the Emancipation Proclamation, which not only ended all hope of reconciliation but was a straight-out declaration of war on the South's economic and political system.[47] General Ulysses S. Grant, himself a skillful strategist and evaluator of the political scene, put the factors behind the gradual but radical adaptation of Union strategy to the realities of the war accurately in his memoirs:

> Up to the battle of Shiloh, I as well as thousands of other citizens believed that the rebellion against the Government would collapse suddenly and soon, if a decisive victory could be gained over any of its armies. Donelson and Henry were such victories. An army of more than 21,000 men was captured and destroyed. Bowling Green, Columbus and Hickman, Kentucky, fell in consequence, and Clarkesville and Nashville, Tennessee, the last two with immense amounts of stores, also fell into our hands. The Tennessee and Cumberland Rivers, from their mouths to the head of navigation, were secured. But when confederate armies were collected which

---

[47] For the evolution of Lincoln's strategy, the best place to start are James McPherson's works, in particular, *Battle Cry of Freedom: The Civil War Era* (Oxford, 2003); and his *Tried by War: Abraham Lincoln as Commander-in-Chief* (New York, 2008).

not only attempted to hold a line farther south, . . . but assumed the offensive and made such a gallant effort to regain what had been lost, I gave up all idea of saving the Union except by complete conquest.[48]

The result was what one historian has accurately described as the "hard war," best characterized by the signs left by Sherman's troops in their march to the sea, which derisively renamed the Southern villages through which they passed "Chimneyvilles," an accurate description of what they left behind.[49] Throughout his presidency, Lincoln maneuvered with great care through the shoals of a republican constitution, while ensuring the continued loyalty of the war Democrats to the cause of the Union. The latter factor led him to appoint a number of war Democrats to important commands during the war, most of whom, with the exception of Major General John A. "Black Jack" Logan, proved less than impressive on the field but who were essential to keeping the pro-war coalition together until the Confederacy collapsed.

Bismarck's strategic goal at the beginning of his tenure as Prussia's chancellor was straightforward: internally, to solve the constitutional impasse between his king and the *Reichstag*, and externally, to achieve for Prussia the dominance over the northern German states. To achieve the latter aim, he was perfectly willing to allow the Austrians to create a *condominium* over the south German states, which after all possessed a Catholic population, one characterized by the values of *schlamperei* (sloppiness) in contrast to good solid values of Prussia's Protestants.[50]

But Austria refused to cooperate, and Bismarck found himself involved in an unwanted war, the Seven Weeks' War of 1866, which quickly resolved itself after the crushing defeat administered by Graf von Moltke's armies to those of Austria.[51] The quick peace that followed – quick enough to rob Prussia's generals of a parade down Vienna's thoroughfares, a decision for which they never forgave Bismarck – allowed Prussia to establish direct control over northern Germany and a loose alliance

---

[48] Ulysses S. Grant, *Personal Memoirs of U.S. Grant*, vol. 1 (New York, 1885), p. 368.
[49] Mark Grimsley, *The Hard Hand of War, Union Military Policy toward Southern Civilians, 1861–1865* (Cambridge, 2008).
[50] For an outstanding account of Bismarck's political and strategic policies and how he adapted his strategy to the actual conditions he confronted, see Marcus Jones, "*Via Victoribus*: Bismarck's Quest for Peace in the Franco Prussian War, 1870–1871," in Williamson Murray and James G. Lacey, eds., *The Making of Peace, Rulers, States, and the Aftermath of War* (Cambridge, 2009).
[51] For the most recent book on the Seven Weeks' War, see Geoffrey Wawro, *The Austro-Prussian War: Austria's War with Prussia and Italy in 1866* (Cambridge, 1996).

with the southern German states now that Austria was excluded. Within a matter of months, he discovered that this settlement remained impermanent: the French were dabbling extensively in southern German affairs, while all too many in Vienna regarded the settlement of 1866 as impermanent.

Bismarck then instigated the Franco-Prussian War (1870–71), which solved the problem of the south German states by creating the *Kaiserreich*, which only the "Iron Chancellor" himself was capable of running.[52] Bismarck's external efforts appeared complete, and unlike all too many victors in war, he appeared to be content to leave the roulette table with his winnings. However, in 1875, fearing the extraordinarily quick recovery of the French, he considered war for a short period. Yet his own fears about the unintended and unpredictable consequences of another war, as well as the clear warnings from the other major European powers that they would not stand aside, led Bismarck to reconsider. For the next decade and a half, he was content to manipulate the European scene from Berlin peacefully, understanding that any further conflicts on which Germany might embark would entirely undo the political work that he had created.

In both cases, Lincoln and Bismarck displayed the ability to adapt their strategic and political assumptions and perceptions to the actual strategic landscape before them. What makes them extraordinary is how they adapted. Both understood history in the best sense of the word: both listened, observed, and judged those who worked for them shrewdly; both understood the political and strategic environment as one that never remained static but was always in flux; both intuitively understood that there were second- and third-order effects that resulted from their actions; and both were willing to accept and learn from their mistakes. And finally they rarely, if ever, reinforced failure.[53]

Successful strategic adaptation also has to do with the ability to understand the other. As Sun Tzu suggested more than two millennia ago, "If you know the enemy and know yourself, you need not fear the results of

---

[52] For the origins and course of the war, see Michael Howard's magisterial account, *The Franco-Prussian War* (New York, 1969). For an excellent study of the war itself, see Geoffrey Wawro, *The Franco-Prussian War: The German Conquest of France, 1870–1871* (Cambridge, 2003).

[53] The performance of Anglo-American leaders to estimate and adapt their strategic vision to reality is also worthy of note, but it is at least the opinion of this author that while both leaders were great strategists, neither Churchill nor Roosevelt came up to the extraordinarily high standards set by Lincoln and Bismarck.

a hundred battles."⁵⁴ Strategic adaptation requires both an understanding of where the observer stands as well as a sense of the nature of the opponent or opponents.

In both world wars, the Germans never understood their own weaknesses, much less the nature of the powers ranged against them despite the fact that their adversaries were either Europeans like themselves or their offspring (the United States) from the same tree. Hitler's *Weltanschauung* and naturally that of his followers, including the *Wehrmacht*'s senior leaders, rested on a belief in the inherent inferiority of other races and nationalities. There can be no other explanation for the fact that the German military had its most complex codes, supposedly undecipherable, read by its enemies for the second straight great war. But even more humiliating to the German belief in their racial superiority, the Soviets were able to use *maskirovka* (deception) from Stalingrad on to disguise the location of every single one of their major offensives through to the end of the war.⁵⁵ Until the American historian Colonel David Glantz uncovered the extent of the German failure to adapt their intelligence procedures in the face of consistent mis-estimates, the memoirs of the defeated generals ascribed their troubles on the Eastern Front to Soviet materiel and manpower superiority.

Yet the ability of American policy makers in estimating the "other" correctly and then adapting their strategy to follow a more realistic course has not exactly been a story of consistent success in the period since the Second World War. The obdurate refusal of not only Douglas Macarthur but also most senior leaders in Washington in 1950 to estimate the Chinese strategic threat correctly is a case in point. So, too, was the general inability to recognize the deadly combination of Vietnamese nationalism with the political and social fanaticism of the French Revolution.⁵⁶ The latter proved to be a particularly dangerous misapprehension of

---

⁵⁴ Sun Tzu, *The Art of War*, trans. by Samuel B. Griffith (Oxford, 1971), p. 84.
⁵⁵ The one case where this was probably not true was the last great Soviet series of offensives that broke the back of German resistance in Poland, East Prussia, and Silesia. By that point in the war, it should have been obvious to the meanest intellect where the Red Army was going to strike.
⁵⁶ A number of the Viet Minh leaders had received their education at French schools in Vietnam where they imbibed the heady language and political philosophy of the French Revolution. Interestingly, many of the founding leaders of the North Vietnamese regime have chosen to write and speak in French as their language of intellectual discourse rather than in Vietnamese. In terms of true revolutionaries, Ho Chi Minh was a founding member of both the French and Vietnamese communist parties as well as a high-ranking member of the Soviet and Chinese communist parties.

Conclusion

the ideological and historical roots of the North Vietnamese leadership. Instead of historical analysis as a path to understanding the nature of America's opponents, strategic adaptation fell back on the nostrums of American political science with its emphasis on ahistorical and homogenized approaches such as game theory and signal sending – approaches that had virtually no effect on a North Vietnamese leadership infused with the zeal of the French Revolution.[57]

Operational and Tactical Adaptation

In an age of instrumented combat ranges and innovative computer simulations, it would seem that adaptation to the conditions that military forces will confront on the battlefields and the conflicts of the twenty-first century would pose less of a problem than was the case in the twentieth century. Yet everything that we have seen in the ongoing struggles in Iraq and Afghanistan suggests that the problems associated with adaptation in the past will remain with us for the foreseeable future. For one thing, the fundamental nature of war is not going to change. And *friction*, that annoying ability for things to go wrong, will find new ways to bedevil the human condition, especially under the conditions and pressures of combat.[58] Above all, technical simulations will not be able to model the reality that the enemy is attempting to kill and destroy those who are attacking him. As Clausewitz notes, in such conditions of brutality, fear, uncertainty, and death, "it is the exceptional man who keeps his powers of quick decision intact."[59]

Combat in nearly every case will still involve the occupation of ground, and the occupation of ground means that U.S. forces will come up against not only adaptable enemies but also, in most cases, social, cultural and historical contexts that will be entirely foreign to their conceptions and

---

[57] Some of the war gaming, such as the series of SIGMA war games in 1964, rested on historical, ideological, and cultural understandings of the North Vietnamese leadership, but those at the top, particularly Secretary of Defense Robert S. McNamara, had no desire to change the strategic drift that was leading the United States straight toward an ill-thought-out intervention. McMaster is particularly good on this; see his *Dereliction of Duty*. And in terms of his background, Ho Chi Minh was a member of *four* revolutionary communist parties: his own, the French (a founding member), the Soviet, and the Chinese.

[58] As CFLCC's (Coalition Forces Land Component Command) intelligence chief commented in the midst of the March 2003 invasion of Saddam's Iraq, "I am drowning in information." This reality will continue to plague efforts to adapt at the operational and tactical levels: what matters is not sheer mountains of information but real insight into what has occurred and is occurring.

[59] Clausewitz, *On War*, p. 113.

understanding of the world. In the words of Major General Robert Scales, U.S. Army (retired), "the military today must not only understand technology but also the cultural environment in which that technology will be employed."[60] Here adaptation becomes far more difficult than simply adapting to the conditions of combat, which the case studies discussed earlier indicate will be difficult enough. In the arena of wars, with the omnipresence of the media and where political concerns now matter at the tactical level, adaptation to the cultural framework will become an essential element in military effectiveness. Adapting to cultural and political factors in organizations devoted to the use of violence in the settlement of international disputes will, by itself, represent a knotty, difficult problem.

As with adaptation at the strategic level, adaptation at the operational and tactical levels requires a thorough and honest evaluation of one's opponent. On May 1, 1942, the Japanese carried out a series of war games that evaluated their proposed attack on Midway as well as their overall operational design for follow-on campaigns. In evaluating the performance of the chief umpire for the games, the leading historian of the Battle of Midway, Gordon D. Prange, notes:

> [Admiral Matome] Ugaki presided with a firm hand, and carried through this grandiose scheme [for upcoming operations] with a sunny lack of realism. As he sincerely believed that no situation could exist in which the Japanese would not be in complete control, he allowed nothing to happen which would seriously inconvenience the smooth development of the war games to their predestined conclusion. He did not scruple to override unfavorable rulings of other umpires.[61]

Unfortunately for the Allied cause in the Pacific in 1942, the U.S. Navy proved equally capable of underestimating its opponents despite what should have been a wakeup call at Pearl Harbor. At the Battle of Savo Island two months after Midway, the Allies lost four heavy cruisers (one Australian and three American, with a fifth American heavy cruiser badly damaged) despite the possession of radar that should have provided the task force an enormous tactical advantage over the enemy in night fighting.[62] The raiding Japanese force of heavy cruisers suffered only

---

[60] Murray and Scales, *The Iraq War*, p. 251.
[61] Gordon D. Prange, *Miracle at Midway* (New York, 1982), p. 31.
[62] The after-action report on the battle identified one of the factors that caused the disaster as the "misplaced confidence in the capability of the radar pickets." For a concise description of the battle, see Richard B. Frank's outstanding, *Guadalcanal: The Definitive Account of the Landmark Battle* (New York, 1990).

minimum damage, with 129 sailors killed in action; the Australian-American fleet, on the other hand, had lost 1,077 sailors. Admiral Richmond Kelly Turner, the naval commander of the amphibious forces at Guadalcanal, would characterize the defeat in the following terms:

> The Navy was still obsessed with a strong feeling of technical and mental superiority over the enemy. In spite of ample evidence as to enemy capabilities, most of our officers and men despised the enemy and felt themselves sure victors in all encounters under any circumstances.... The net result of all of this was a fatal lethargy of mind which induced a confidence without readiness, and a routine acceptance of outworn peacetime standards of conduct. I believe that this psychological factor as a cause of our defeat, was even more important than the element of surprise.[63]

It would not be for another two months of fighting and continued heavy losses in battles around the Solomon Islands before U.S. naval forces would be able to take on the Japanese with some hope of success. All the technological superiority in the world meant virtually nothing until U.S. commanders, the skippers of the warships, and the crews had improved their training and preparation to the point where the capacity to adapt became second nature. Their peacetime training had not forced them to reach that level; neither had their contempt for their Japanese opponents allowed them to adapt tactically and conceptually to the war they were fighting in the Solomons. It was only when photos of burned-out ships and oil-soaked dying sailors hit home that the U.S. Navy formed the wartime culture that allowed it to handle the Japanese in the tropical seas of the southern Pacific.

Concluding Thoughts

> *Other officers told me how they had seen the Hussars charging into the Jerry tanks sitting on the tops of their turrets more or less with their whips out. 'It looked like the run-up to the first fence and the point-to-point,' the adjutant described it. The first action was very typical of a number of those early encounters involving cavalry regiments. They had incredible enthusiasm and dash, and sheer exciting courage which was only curbed by the decreasing stock of dashing officers and tanks.*[64]
>
> Robert Crisp, North Africa, 1942

It is all too easy to suggest that the American military needs to be more adaptive and imaginative in the twenty-first century. How to do so is the

---

[63] Quoted in Frank, *Guadalcanal*, p. 123.
[64] Robert Crisp, *Brazen Chariots* (New York, 1960), p. 32.

real question. Again, the answer is a simple matter, but its realization represents extraordinary difficulties because it involves changing military cultures that have evolved over the course of the past century. And cultural change in large organizations represents an effort akin to altering the course of an aircraft carrier.[65] There is no doubt that profound cultural changes have occurred in the American military as a result of our experiences of Afghanistan and Iraq. Those changes and the realism about combat and conflict will remain embedded as long as the officers who experienced them control the culture. Nevertheless, that culture is one the day-to-day experiences of war, combat, and training form. And as was the case with the experiences of the Vietnam War, time will wash out those experiences of the recent past in Iraq and Afghanistan. This time, it would be doubly tragic if there were not a change in the fundamental view of how officers view their profession.

In 1996, this author wrote the following words about what was necessary to encourage a more fruitful innovation in the officer corps of the American military. There is no reason not to repeat them in reference to preparing America's military to adapt to the wars that will inevitably follow Afghanistan and Iraq:

> One needs to rethink professional military education in fundamental ways. A significant portion of successful innovation in the interwar period depended on close relationships between schools of professional military education and the world of operations.... [A]ny approach to military education that encourages changes in cultural values and fosters intellectual curiosity would demand more than a better school system: it demands that professional military education remains a central concern *throughout the entire career of an officer*. One may not create another Dowding and manage his career to the top ranks, but one can foster a military culture where those promoted to the highest ranks possess the imagination and intellectual framework to support innovation [and adaptation].[66]

---

[65] I am indebted to Lieutenant General Paul Van Riper, USMC (retired), for this point.
[66] Williamson Murray, "Innovation Past and Future," in Murray and Millett, eds., *Military Innovation in the Interwar Period*, p. 327.

Index

Abu-Ageila, 266
Académie Française, 26
Adan, Major General Avraham, 269n21, 278, 280, 291–298, 299(nn115, 118), 300–303
adaptation. *See also* technology
  ancient world and, 38–43
  assumptions and, 6, 29–31, 49, 85, 96, 197, 213, 258, 260, 310–311, 313, 319, 323
  battlefield analysis and, 15, 57, 63, 117, 125–131, 145
  bureaucracies and, 18, 21–22. *See also* bureaucracies
  civilian experts and, 159, 167–169, 259, 317–318
  cultural framework and, 22, 24–29, 31, 35–36, 72, 79, 119, 147, 265n6, 325–327
  enemy and, 18, 38, 309–311, 316, 321, 324–327. *See also* World War I
  history of, 2–3, 44–55
  innovation, relationship to, 3, 5, 308–309, 312
  lessons learned analysis and, 56, 65, 85, 95, 98, 115, 121n5, 269–271, 292n89, 296, 309
  military-civil revolution and, 50
  operational, 197, 306, 311, 318, 325–327
  political, 57, 306, 311, 321, 323, 326
  reality versus assumptions and, 6, 15, 37–38, 66–67, 70, 79, 85, 96, 193, 197, 258, 311, 323
  strategic, 29, 309, 311, 318–325
  tactical, 4, 50, 52–53, 62, 64, 89, 98, 109–110, 115, 122, 125, 197, 231, 306, 309, 311, 318, 325–327
  training and, 131–137, 151, 327
  warrior societies and, 44–45
Adler (Eagle), Operation, 177
Adolphus, Gustavus, 46
Adrianople, Battle of, 43
Afghanistan, 306, 315, 328
Agincourt, Battle of, 45
Alexander the Great, 26, 39
Allenby, Field Marshal Sir Edmund, 96
Alma, Battle of, 50
American Civil War
  adaptation and, 4, 33–34, 50–53, 321–322
  assumptions and, 33, 321
  command competence and, 28
  dispersal of forces and, 14
  grand strategy in, 33–34
  Grant, U.S. and, 12–13, 321
  lessons learned and, 56
  mobilization and, 51, 53
  projection of power and, 54
  riverine navy and, 53
American Revolution, 263n2
Amery, Leo, 60
Antietam, Battle of, 33, 52

329

Arab culture, 265, 267
Arausio, Battle of, 40
Arras, Battle of (1917), 103–104
Asquith, Herbert, 82
Assad, Hafez al, 276
Atlanta, siege of, 52
Atlantic, Battle of, 188–192
Augustus, Caesar, 41
Austerlitz, Battle of, 14
Australia, 115–116
Austria, 123
Austria-Hungary, 54, 199
Austro-Hungarian Empire, 29, 95n61
Austro-Prussian War, 55, 322–323

Baldwin, Stanley, 156, 200
Balkans, 87, 306
Barbarossa, Operation, 66, 147–150, 225, 260
   Red Army, purges of, and, 27–28, 68
   Stalingrad and, 226
   winter campaign of 1941 and, 149, 226
Bar-Lev, Major General Chaim, 274, 285, 295–296
Bar-Lev Line, 271–272, 290–291, 293
Beams, Battle of the, 23
Beaverbrook, Lord (William Maxwell Aitken), 165–166
Beck, General Ludwig, 122–123
Belgium, 82, 250, 319
Ben-Gal, Colonel Avigdor Yanosh, 281–282
Ben Shoham, Yizhak, 281–283
Bennett, Air Vice Marshal Donald, 220, 246
Bensusan-Butt, David Miles, 211
Bentley Priory, 158, 183
Berlin, 183, 214, 241, 246
Berlin, Battle of (air), 238, 241–243, 248–251, 259–260
Beyerchen, Alan, 156
Bismarck, Otto von, 32, 54–56, 321–323
Blenheim, Battle of, 47
Bletchley Park, 169, 177, 191–192. *See also* Ultra
Blount, Major General Buford, 14n35, 313n24
Bock, Field Marshal Fedor von, 136–137
Boer War, 61, 80
Bohemia, 124

Bonaparte, Napoleon, 7, 14, 26–27, 49, 81n21
Brauchitsch, General Walter von, 130, 166
Bremer, Ambassador L. Paul III, 314
Britain. *See also* British Army, British Expeditionary Force, Royal Air Force, Royal Navy
   air defense and, 155–159, 170, 176–177, 194
   appeasement policy and, 156
   British Foreign Office and, 19
   civil bureaucracy and, 23, 186–187
   Crimean War and, 50
   intelligence services and, 23, 168–169, 177, 186–187, 191–192, 233, 238
   interwar period and, 66, 155–159, 199–200, 257–258
   military bureaucracy and, 21–22
   modern governmental finance and, 47, 49
   political leadership and, 155–156, 158, 162, 194n147, 200, 214, 257, 260
Britain, Battle of, 161–167
   adaptation and,
      British, 181, 185, 193–194
      German, 180, 182, 193, 195
   aircraft technology and, 154, 156, 186, 188
   intelligence and, 168–171, 179–182, 184, 186–187, 191–195
   London, targeting of, and, 184–185, 187
   night offensive and, 186–188
   opening phase of, 174–177
   planning for, 167–173
   radar and, 156, 158, 170, 178–180
   radio navigation and, 167–168, 174, 186–187
   RAF, assault on, and, 178–185
   strategic framework and, 187–188
British Army and,
   anti-intellectualism and, 83
   armored forces and, 15, 65, 107–108
   command, failures of, and, 95
   culture of, 95, 98
   lessons-learned analysis and, 85, 95, 98, 121n5
   professionalism, lack of, and, 60
British Expeditionary Force, 20
   armored warfare and, 107–108, 116

battlefield analysis and, 64–65, 95, 111
casualty rates and, 78, 95
defensive tactics and, 112–113
Flanders and, 85, 105–109
leadership of, 95, 111, 116–117
logistical difficulties and, 116
Somme, Battle of the, and, 95–99
tactical adaptation and, 64, 89, 115
Bruchmüller, Lieutenant Colonel Georg, 22
Bruneval, 223, 233
Brusilov Offensive, 95n61
Bulgaria, 199
Bulge, Battle of the, 255–256
bureaucracies
  combat analysis and, 21
  culture of, 21
  decision making and, 23
  human nature and, 24
  leadership in, 22
  nature of, 18–19
  technology and, 19–20

Caesar, Julius, 26
Cambodia, 72
Cambrai, Battle of (1917), 108–109
Canada, 115–116
Carr, Air Vice Marshal Sir Charles Roderick, 211
Carthage, 40
Catton, Bruce, 51n41
Chamberlain, Colonel Joshua Lawrence, 13
Chamberlain, Neville, 158, 173, 201, 207–208
Charteris, Brigadier General John, 107
Chemin des Dames, 103–104, 113, 138
Cherwell, Lord (Frederick A. Lindemann), 23, 211, 213, 260
Chickamauga, Battle of, 54
China, People's Republic of, 24, 305, 324
Churchill, Sir Winston, 82–83, 155, 189, 208
  Britain, Battle of, and, 167–168
  leadership of, 22, 194n147, 257–258, 260
  Overlord, Operation, and, 247
  RAF bomber offensive and, 212–213
Clausewitz, Carl von, 9–10, 15–16, 26, 48
Coalition Provisional Authority, 19, 314
Cobra, Operation, 250n209

Cold War, 69–72, 307
Cologne, 219–220, 226, 260
combat
  analysis and battlefield reporting of, 11–12, 15, 21, 57, 63
  context of, 325–326
  experience and, 64, 95–96, 98, 112, 119
  nature of, 11
  psychological effect of, 9–12
  technology, impact of, and, 37–38, 59
command
  battlefield reporting and, 14, 21
  bureaucracies and, 20–21, 23
  competence and, 26–29, 95, 312
  culture of, 96
  decision making authority and, 13, 108–109
  effectiveness, elements of, and, 17
  individual attributes and, 28–29
  intellectual preparation for, 8–9
  nature of, 12
Cone, General Robert W., 15n38
Constantinople, 43n15
Coventry, 187–188
Crécy, Battle of, 45
Crimean War, 49–50
Czechoslovakia, 124, 128, 231

Damascus, 273, 286, 288, 296
Davis, Jefferson, 33n92
Dayan, Moshe, 262n1, 280–281, 283, 285, 291, 293, 295, 298(nn111, 113)
Denmark, 54, 163
Dogger Bank, Battle of, 60
Dönitz, Admiral Karl, 151, 171–172, 190–191
Doolittle, Lieutenant General James, 180n102
Dowding, Air Marshal Sir Hugh, 156–159, 171, 181, 183–184, 194n147, 212, 317
Dresden, 235, 252
Duisberg, 252

Eagle Day, 178–179
Eaton, Major General Paul, 314–315
Eder dam, 231
Edward III of England, 44
Egypt
  Armies
    2nd Egyptian Army, 295, 298–301

Egypt (*cont.*)
  3rd Egyptian Army, 295, 297, 301–302
  Attrition, War of and, 271–272, 275
  Brigades
    25th Armored Brigade, 301
  Divisions
    2nd Infantry Division, 294
    16th Infantry Division, 294
  government. *See* Gamal Abdel Nasser and Anwar Sadat
  Six-Day War and, 264–268, 275
  strategy and, 265, 273, 275–276, 301n125
  Yom Kippur War and, 262, 275–276, 278–279, 286, 290–295, 297–302
Eisenhower, General Dwight D., 201, 247, 252
Eitan, General Rafael, 282, 284
Elazar, Major General David, 277, 280–281, 285, 291–292, 295, 297(nn108, 111)
Emancipation Proclamation, 33–34, 321
Enigma, 16n44, 150, 253
Epanimondas, 39
Essen, 229, 260
Europe
  European way of war and, 48
  military organizations of, 57–61, 63–65, 79, 117, 119
  tribal warfare and, 44–45

Falkenhayn, General Erich von, 64, 93–94, 99, 101, 319
Fall Gelb, 65
Fallujah, Battle of (Nov. 2004), 13n32
Flanders, 85, 93, 105–109
Foch, General Ferdinand, 92
Forester, C. S., 75
Fourth Generation of War, 38
France
  Army. *See* French Army
  Crimean War and, 50
  interwar period and, 115
  levée en masse and, 48, 55
  military organizations and, 47–48
Franco-Prussian War, 55, 57–58, 323
Frankland, Noble, 210
Fredericksburg, Battle of, 52
Frederick the Great, 29

French Army
  adaptation and, 64, 100–101, 114–115
  Champagne offensive and, 91
  high command, failure of, and, 90–92, 125n18
  innovation and, 104
  Nivelle Offensive and, 64
  war, preparation for, and, 26, 115
French Revolution, 4, 48–49, 82, 324–325
Fritsch, General Werner von, 122–123
Frontinus, Sextus Julius, 42
Fuller, J. F. C., 65, 107–108

Galland, Major General Adolf, 244
Gallipoli, Battle of, 25, 80n16, 97
Gamelin, General Maurice, 26, 92
Gaza, 265
Gehlen, Major General Reinhard, 150
General Motors, 25
George, David Lloyd, 24–25
Georgia, 306
German Air Force (*Luftwaffe*), 129
  air defense and, 204–207, 232, 236, 243, 249–250, 252. *See also* German Air Force night fighters
  anti-aircraft artillery and, 206, 216, 226–228
  Britain, Battle of. *See* Britain, Battle of
  close air support and, 137–145, 223
  Condor Legion and, 138–139, 201
  doctrine and, 159–160, 170, 195, 205
  Enigma and, 169, 191
  France, Battle of, and, 164, 167
  intelligence and, 169–171, 179–182, 184, 206–207
  Kammhuber Line and, 216–217, 219, 236–237, 259
  leadership of, 204, 206, 246, 249, 259
  logistics and, 206–207
  mining operations and, 174
  morale and, 185
  night fighters and,
    air defense and, 215–217, 221, 228, 233, 235, 243, 245, 249, 250, 258
    daylight battles and, 247, 251
    radar and, 222, 238, 240, 243–244
    tactics and, 236–238, 246
  operational planning and, 170–172, 238
  Order of Battle and, 169
  Polish campaign and, 127, 140–143
  prewar preparation and, 137–140

Index

radio navigation and, 157, 167–168, 174, 186–187
Soviet Union, invasion of, and, 215
Spanish Civil War and, 138–139
technology and, 159, 215–218
training and, 252
war games and, 160
German armed forces (*Wehrmacht*), 166, 219
  after-action reporting and, 125–131, 142–144
  Austria and, 123
  combat effectiveness of, 145, 147, 253, 255, 316
  combined arms doctrine and, 316
  Czechoslovakia and, 124, 128
  innovation and, 147
  intelligence failures and, 148–150, 207, 324
  joint cooperation and, 171–172, 186, 188, 192
  leadership of, 125–131, 134, 151, 324
  Overlord, Operation, and, 250, 252
German Army, 125–127, 129, 131–137, 141, 148
  after-action reporting and, 142–144
  Armies
    Eighth, and, 124
    Twelfth, and, 124, 130
  armored warfare and, 123
  Army Group
    B, and, 136–137
  Condor Legion and, 138–139
  Corps
    XIX Panzer, and, 127–128, 143
  culture of, 57n57, 120, 145–146, 151–152
  Divisions
    8th Infantry, and, 130
    44th Infantry, and, 134
    88th Infantry, and, 134
    208th Infantry, and, 135–136
    2nd Light, and, 129
    7th Panzer, and, 128, 143–144
    10th Panzer, and, 136, 142–143
  doctrine and, 122
  draft and, 58n58
  general staff system and, 85, 103, 110, 121n6, 122, 146
  Harz exercises and, 122
  interwar period and, 119–125, 146–147

  leadership of, 66, 101
  military effectiveness of, 7, 145
  operational effectiveness and, 147
  political adaptation and, 57
  storm troopers and, 112, 114–116, 138
  strategic effectiveness and, 57, 147
  tactical revolution and, 13, 101–103
  training and, 124, 131–137
German Empire, 29, 32
  civilian leadership and, 34–35
  German General Staff, 21–22, 63–64, 83
  innovation and, 60
  military culture and, 35
  military leadership and, 63, 101, 109
German Navy (*Kriegsmarine*)
  Enigma and, 150, 191–192
  Norway, invasion of, and, 163
  radio traffic and, 168–169
  U-boat offensive and, 171–172, 225
  war planning and, 160–161
  weather ships and, 191–192
Germany. *See also* Prussia, German Empire
  German tribes, 40–41
  Kriegsakademie and, 145–146, 152
  military bureaucracy and, 22
  Nazi Germany, 28n80, 66
    Anschluss and, 123, 128
    armaments production and, 230, 236, 244, 255, 258
    armored warfare and, 123, 316
    Britain, Battle of. *See* Britain, Battle of
    bureaucracy of, 159
    economy of, 224–225, 230, 253, 255–256
    ideological motivation and, 126n19, 151, 257–258
    interwar period and, 120–125, 137–140, 146–147, 257
    leadership and, 238, 244, 258–259
    military culture and, 258
    political failures of, 186, 228
    rearmament and, 123, 126
    scientific community and, 159, 259
    Spanish Civil War and, 123, 138–139
    strategic difficulties and, 161–162, 186, 223–225, 235, 257
Gettysburg, Battle of, 13
Giambiastiani, Admiral Edmund P., 15n38
Gibson, Wing Commander Guy, 231
Glantz, Colonel David, 150n100, 324

Goebbels, Paul Joseph, 137, 226, 228, 235, 243, 259
Golan Heights, 266–267, 272–273
Gonen, Major General Shmuel, 278, 289–295, 298
Göring, Field Marshal Hermann, 159, 225
  anti-aircraft force and, 227–228
  Britain, Battle of, and, 170–171, 178, 180, 182–184
  RAF bomber offensive and, 222–224, 239
Gough, General Sir Hugh, 112
Grandmaison, Colonel Louis de, 81
Grant, General Ulysses S., 7, 10n24, 12–14, 28, 33–34, 53, 321
Gravellotte, Battle of, 57
Great Depression, 24
Great Leap Forward, 24
Greece, ancient, 27, 38–44
Guadalcanal, 327
Guderian, General Heinz, 6n12, 127–129, 142–143

Hackworth, Colonel David, 11
Haig, Field Marshal Sir Douglas, 20, 25, 34n97, 64, 70, 85–86
  Flanders and, 106–109
  Somme, Battle of and, 95–98
Halder, General Franz, 66n82, 148, 166
Halleck, Major General Henry, 28
Hamburg, 233–236, 260
Hamilton, General Sir Ian, 80n16
Hannibal, 40
Hapsburgs, 46
Harris, Air Marshal Sir Arthur, 23, 157, 203, 211, 217–221, 260–261
  Overlord, Operation, and, 247, 252–256
  strategy and, 240–242, 245
Heikal, Mohamed Hassanein, 300
Herodotus, 27
Herrmann, Major Hans-Joachim, 236
Himmler, Reichsführer Heinrich, 123n13
Hindenburg, Field Marshal Paul von, 21, 101
Hindenburg-Ludendorff Plan, 199
Hinsley, Sir Francis Harry, 168–169, 191
Hiroshima, 69
Hitler, Adolf, 66, 82, 123, 131, 151, 212, 216, 239
  air defense and, 226, 228, 236

Britain, interest in, and, 166–167, 171, 172n72, 183, 186, 215, 223
  leadership of, 258, 260
Hodges, Lieutenant General Courtney, 28
Hoffi, Major General Yitzhak, 281, 285, 288
Hollweg, Chancellor Theobald von Bethmann, 94n58, 319
Howard, Sir Michael, 9, 35, 86, 310–311
Hundred Years' War, 44–45
Hunter-Weston, Lieutenant General Sir Aylmer, 97–98
Hussein, Saddam, 27n74

Industrial College of the Armed Forces, 67
Industrial Revolution, 2–3, 37
  French Revolution, merging of, and, 82
  impact of, 49–50, 58–59
Inglis, Air Vice Marshal F. F., 242
innovation
  adaptation, comparison to, 2, 308–309, 312
  assumptions and, 5, 37, 313
  concept and doctrine development and, 5, 309
  empirical evidence and, 5, 309
  enemy and, 309
  history of, 44–48
  interwar period and, 119, 309n9, 328
  tactical, 38–39, 108, 313
  technological, 317
  training and education and, 12, 67, 328
interwar period, 57, 65–67, 115, 117, 119–125, 137–140, 146–147, 198–201, 203–204, 230, 257, 309n9, 328
Iraq, 6, 28, 31, 38, 42, 73, 265n6, 306, 312–315, 328
Iraq War, 13n32, 14n35, 15n38, 19
  assumptions, 31
  conventional war and, 72
  insurgency and, 31, 73, 313
  intellectual preparation for, 73
  tactics and, 73
Iraqi Freedom, Operation, 15n37
Iraqi Perspectives Project, 27n74
Ironside, Field Marshal William, 208
Israel
  alliances and, 264

Index

geographic depth and, 264, 268
military institutions and, 264–263
political leadership and, 268, 274, 286, 295
strategic depth and, 264, 268, 274
western civilization and, 267n11
Israel Defense Forces
   adaptation and, 262–263, 286–289, 290n83, 296, 298, 302–304
   assumptions and, 273, 278, 283, 288, 293
   Bar-Lev Line and, 271–272, 290–291, 293
   Brigades
      Barack Brigade, 281–284, 287
      Golani Infantry Brigade and, 286
      7th Armored Brigade, 282–283, 284, 287, 298
   combat pressures and, 262–263, 287–288, 295–296
   enemy, evaluation of, and, 278, 288, 290n84
   high command and, 267, 270, 280, 285–286, 291, 295
   Independence, War of, and, 277
   intellectual preparation and, 274, 278, 280, 287–289
   intelligence organizations and, 262, 273–274, 278–279, 288, 302
   Israeli Air Force and, 275–276, 297
   lessons learned analysis and, 269–271, 292n89, 296
   mobilization and, 264, 268, 274, 276–277, 279–280
   1956 War and, 264, 277, 280
   Northern Command and, 281–288
   operational effectiveness and, 266–267, 270, 272–274, 277–280, 282–283, 285–293, 297–298, 300–304
   organizational difficulties and, 269, 270n23, 280, 287–288, 289n81, 298, 303
   planning and, 272–274, 288, 290, 291n88, 298
   preparation for war and, 273, 280–282, 287–289, 290n84, 302–303
   professional military education and, 277–279
   Six-Day War and, 262–270, 274
   Southern Command and, 289–296, 298, 300, 302–303
   strategic effectiveness and, 267–268, 270–274, 278–281, 283n62, 286, 288–289
   tactical effectiveness and, 266, 270–271, 274, 277, 281, 286–288, 290–293, 296, 297n108, 298, 302–304
   training and, 269–271, 276–277, 302–303
   War of Attrition and, 271–272
   Yom Kippur War. *See* Yom Kippur War

Jackson, Lieutenant General Thomas, 7, 14n34
Japan
   Midway, Battle of, and, 17–18, 326
   Pearl Harbor, attack on, 32, 326
   Russo-Japanese War and, 80–81
Jena-Auerstadt, Battle of, 81n21
Jerusalem, 266–267
Jeschonnek, General Hans, 140, 215, 226
Jodl, General Alfred, 166, 170
Joffre, General Joseph, 90, 92
Johnson, President Lyndon Baines, 30–31, 310, 320
Joint Forces Command, 15n38
Joint Vision 2010, 16
Jomini, Baron Antoine-Henri de, 51n42
Jones, R. V., 23, 167–168, 174, 187, 202, 210, 223, 240–241, 243n181, 318
Jordan, 266
Josephus, Titus Flavius, 42
Julian, Emperor, 43
Jünger, Ernst, 100, 105, 112
Jutland, Battle of, 60

Kahalani, Lieutenant Colonel Avigdor, 281–282, 285
Kamikazes, 67n85
Kammhuber, General Joseph, 215–217, 224, 259
Keegan, John, 11
Keitel, Field Marshal Wilhelm, 166
Kennedy, Paul, 75
Kesselring, Field Marshal Albert, 174, 182–184
Khan Unis, 266
Khartoum Resolution, 268
King, Fleet Admiral Ernest, 7
Kitchener, Field Marshal Lord Herbert, 96
Knox, MacGregor, 18–19, 28n80
Königrätz, Battle of, 55

Korean War, 69
Kretschmer, Admiral Otto, 190
Krulak, General Charles C., 13
Kursk, Battle of, 149

Laffargue, Captain André, 91–92, 100
Landing Zone Albany, 30
Langemark, Battle of, 82
Laos, 72
Lee, General Robert E., 14n34
Leigh-Mallory, Air Vice Marshal Trafford, 175, 185
Leuctra, Battle of, 39
levée en masse, 48, 55
Liddell Hart, Basil H., 3n6, 57, 65
Lincoln, President Abraham, 33–34, 54, 321–323
Linebacker, Operation, 72
Logan, Major General John A., 322
Loos, Battle of, 25
Lossberg, General Fritz von, 98n76, 105
Low Countries, 131, 161
Lübeck, 219, 226
Ludendorff, General Erich, 21–22, 64, 83, 101–104, 110, 113, 115–116
Lusitania, 35
Lützen, Battle of, 46

MacArthur, General of the Army Douglas, 324
Magen, Brigadier General Kalman, 297, 301
Magersfontein, Battle of, 61
Manchuria, 61
Mandler, General Avraham, 291, 296–297, 302
Mangin, General Charles, 100
Manhattan Project, 240
Mansoor, Colonel Peter R., 31n87, 312n21
Marius, Gaius, 41
Marlborough, Duke of, 7
Marne, Battle of the, 82
Marshall, Brigadier General S. L. A., 11
Marshall, General of the Army George C., 7, 33
Mattis, Major General James, 14n35, 38, 98
Maurice of Orange, 46
McNair, Lieutenant General Lesley J., 250n209

McNamara, Secretary of Defense Robert S., 30, 310, 325n57
McNaughton, Robert, 30
McPherson, Major General James B., 14n34
Meir, Golda, 268, 274
Messines, Battle of, 106
Metz, siege of 1870, 55
Meuse-Argonne offensive of 1918, 115
Mexico, 306
Michael Offensive of March 1918, 86
Middle Ages, 44–45
Midway, Battle of, 17–18
Milch, Field Marshal Erhard, 206–207, 226, 239
Military Assistance Command Vietnam (MACV), 70
military organizations
  Arab societies and, 265, 267
  bureaucracy and, 35–36
  culture of, 72, 119, 308, 309n9, 312, 315, 328
  decision making in, 7, 9–10, 30
  history, lessons of, and, 66
  incompetence and, 24–29, 118
  intellectual preparation for war and, 8–9, 62–63, 70, 145, 152, 308, 328
  leadership of, 5, 29, 308, 311
  lessons-learned analysis and, 309
  military genius and, 26–27
  peacetime innovation and, 5, 66, 119, 309, 328
  staff colleges and, 56, 83
  technology, impact of, and, 37–38, 117
  three-block war and, 13
  tyrannical regimes and, 265n6
  war games and, 309
military profession, 38, 79, 118, 152, 328
Mitla Pass, 266
Modder River, Battle of, 61
modern warfare, 4, 78
  counterinsurgency and, 151
  decentralized command and control and, 12–13, 108, 122
  guerrilla warfare and, 263
  lethality of, 61–62, 78
  logistics and, 120
  maneuver warfare and, 137
  mechanization and, 122, 124
  nature of, 36

Index

problems of, 73
strategy and, 120
Moelders, Colonel Werner, 181n106
Möhne dam, 231
Moltke, Graf Helmut von, 54–56, 274, 322
Montgomery-Massingberd, Field Marshal Sir Archibald, 121n5
Moravia, 124
Munich Conference, 158, 257

Nagasaki, 69
Napoleon I. *See* Bonaparte, Napoleon
Napoleonic Wars, 19–20
Narvik, Battle of, 163
Nasser, Gamal Abdel, 264–265, 268, 274
Naveh, Brigadier General Shimon, 270n25
Nelson, Admiral Horatio, 60
New Zealand, 115
Nigeria, 306
Nile, Battle of, 60
Nimitz, Fleet Admiral Chester, 67n85
9/11 Commission Report, 154n2
Nivelle, General Robert, 100, 103–104
Nivelle Offensive, 64
Nixon, President Richard M., 320
Normandy, 250, 252
North Korea, 306
Norway, 163, 188
Nuremberg, 245, 247

Octagon Conference, 252
Ottoman Empire, 29, 305
Overlord, Operation, 247–256, 259
Oxford Political Union, 155

Pakistan, 306
Panama, 73
Park, Air Vice Marshal Keith, 175, 181, 183–185
Passchendaele, Battle of, 22, 25, 34n97, 78, 105–107
Pearl Harbor, 161n26
Peenemünde, 235–237
Peled, Major General Moshe, 285
Peloponnesian War, 17
Periander, 27
Persian Empire, 39
Pétain, Marshal Philippe, 90–91, 104, 114
Petersburg, siege of, 54
Philip II of Macedon, 39

Plan Dog memorandum, 32n90
Plumer, General Sir Herbert, 106
Poitiers, Battle of, 45
Poland, 124–131, 140–145
Portal, Air Marshal Sir Charles, 203, 209, 212–213, 253–255
Portugal, 20
Potomac, Army of the, 53–54
Prien, Lieutenant Commander Günther, 190
Prussia
European politics and, 32, 322
General Staff and, 54, 56
Kriegsakademie and, 57
military success, misconceptions of, and, 56
Schleswig-Holstein and, 54
technological revolution and, 54–55
Unification, Wars of, 57
War Ministry and, 22
Punic War, Second, 40

radar systems
development of, 156, 158, 175–180, 186, 188, 190, 317
(GCI) ground controlled intercept, 206, 216, 233, 237, 250
(H2S) British airborne ground scanning radar, 222, 229, 231, 233, 236, 241, 244, 251–252
(IFF) identification friend or foe, 217, 222, 241, 243, 259
(SN2) German airborne radar, 237–238, 244
(Window) Allied radar countermeasure, 233–234, 237–238, 241
Würzburg radar, 215–217, 224
radio navigation systems
development of, 167–168, 174, 186–187
(GEE) British radio navigation, 218–219, 222, 231–232
(*Knickebein*) German radio navigation, 168, 174, 186–187
(Oboe) British radio navigation targeting, 222, 229, 231, 248, 250–252
Raeder, Admiral Erich, 151, 163
Rawlinson, General Sir Henry, 96–97
Regensburg, 235
Reshef, Colonel Amnon, 299

Rhineland, 123
Richmond, siege of, 54
Rolling Thunder, Operation, 71
Roman Empire, 2–3, 41–43
Roman-Jewish War (AD 66–70), 42
Roman Republic, 40–41
Rommel, Field Marshal Erwin, 15, 16n44, 129, 143–144
Roosevelt, President Franklin Delano, 32, 68n88, 247
Rostock, 219, 224, 226
Royal Air Force (RAF)
  Air Ministry and, 23, 165, 168, 254–255, 260
  assumptions and, 199–201, 213, 241, 254, 258, 260–261
  Barking Creek, Battle of, and, 174
  Bomber Command and, 23, 34, 181
    adaptation and, 220–221, 231, 244–245, 251–252, 256
    Britain, Battle of. See Britain, Battle of
    innovation and, 220, 232–233
    leadership of, 217–221, 230–231, 240, 246, 254, 256, 260
    Operational Research Section and, 213, 219n89, 243n181
    Pathfinder Force and, 218n84, 220–221, 229, 232, 234, 245, 248, 252
    target accuracy and, 208–214, 219–220, 231, 248–249, 260
  Butt Report, 211–212, 260
  Condor Legion and, 201
  doctrine and, 155–157, 166, 181, 194, 199–200
  failures and, 5, 23
  fighter aircraft and, 156, 158–159, 162, 212–213
    night fighters and, 202, 222, 232n139, 237, 244, 246
  Fighter Command and, 157, 165, 178–185, 194, 201
  France, Battle of, and, 164–165
  interwar period and, 198–201, 203–204, 230
  leadership of, 156, 194n147, 199–201, 203, 209, 220, 258, 260
  navigation aids. See radio navigation and radar systems
  strategic bombing campaign and,
    area bombing and, 213, 234, 253–254, 260
    background of, 198–204
    Berlin, Battle of (air), 238, 241–243, 246, 248–251, 259–260
    Cologne and, 219–220, 226, 260
    daylight raids and, 207–208
    electronic warfare and, 216, 218, 221–222
    German air defenses and, 204–207, 215–217, 221, 233
    Hamburg and, 233–236
    incendiaries and, 218–219, 221, 229
    Kammhuber Line and, 216–217, 219, 221
    night bomber offensive and, 208–211, 213, 218–219, 222–223, 228–229, 231–236, 240
    oil campaign and, 253–255
    Overlord, Operation, and, 247, 250–256, 259
    radar and, 221, 223
    Ruhr Valley and, 228–232
    training and, 204, 220
    transportation campaign and, 247–250, 253, 256, 259
Royal Navy
  anti-submarine warfare and, 189–190, 194
  Britain, Battle of, and, 181
  combat philosophy of, 60
  Crete, Battle of, and, 173
  English Channel defense and, 173
  Norway, invasion of, and, 163
  Royal Naval Air Service and, 258
  tactics and, 60
Ruhr Valley, 228–232, 253, 256
Rumsfeld, Secretary of Defense Donald, 31
Rundstedt, Field Marshal Gerd von, 129
Rupprecht, Crown Prince, 113
Russia
  Brusilov Offensive and, 95n61
  Crimean War and, 50
  economy of, 306
  Russo-Japanese War and, 80–81
  World War I and, 87
Russian Revolution, 29

Sadat, Anwar, 274–275, 280n55, 297n111, 300, 301n125
Saint-Exupéry, Antoine de, 266

Index

Sassoon, Siegfried, 74
Savo Island, Battle of, 326–327
Scales, Major General Robert, 73
Scandinavia and, 163, 179, 188
Schepke, Lieutenant Commander Joachim, 190
Schleswig-Holstein, 54
Schmidt, Major General Joseph, 170, 179, 182, 184, 244
Schweppenburg, General Leo Geyr von, 57
Sedan, Battle of (1870), 55
Sedan, Battle of (1940), 6n11
Seeckt, General Hans von, 121–122, 138, 146, 204
Serbia, 87
Sevastopol, siege of, 50
Sharon, Ariel, 266–271, 273, 278, 280, 290, 292, 294–302
Shenandoah Valley, 34
Sheridan, General Philip Henry, 34
Sherman, General William Tecumseh, 14n34, 34, 53
Shiloh, Battle of, 10n24, 52
Simchoni, Major General Uri, 278n48, 281n56, 283n62, 284n68
Sinai Peninsula, 264–266, 268, 271–272, 274–275, 280, 285, 290–294, 296–298
Six-Day War, 262–270
Skoda Works, 231
Slim, Field Marshal Viscount, 12n28
Social Darwinism, 58n58
Solomon Islands, 327
Somalia, 73
Somme, Battle of the, 22, 25, 63, 78, 95–100
Sorpe dam, 232
Soult, Marshal General Jean-de-Dieu, 14n33
Soviet Union
   agricultural disaster and, 24
   Arab states and, 264, 268, 273
   bureaucracy and, 27–28
   Cold War and, 69, 71
   deception efforts and, 150, 324
   innovation and, 68
   invasion of. *See* Barbarossa, Operation
   Six-Day War and, 264, 268
Spaatz, General Carl A., 252–254
Spain, 20
Spanish Civil War, 123, 138–139, 201–202
Spanish Succession, War of, 49
Sparta, 39
Speer, Albert, 167, 230, 236
Sperrle, Field Marshal Hugo, 174, 182–184
Spion Kop, Battle of, 61
Spotsylvania Courthouse, Battle of, 53
Spruance, Admiral Raymond, 28–29
Stalin, Joseph, 27–28, 68
Stark, Admiral Harold, 32n90
Stonne, 6n11
St. Privat, Battle of, 57
strategy
   adaptation, costs of, and, 29
   bureaucracies and, 19
   grand strategy, formation of, 31–32
   modern war and, 120
Stülpnagel, Otto von, 122
Stumpff, General Hans-Jürgen, 174–175, 179
Sudetenland, 128
Suez Canal, 264, 267–268, 271, 275–276, 280n55, 281, 286, 289–303
Sulla, Lucius Cornelius, 41
Sun Tzu, 323–324
Sweden, 46
Switzerland, 44–45
Syria
   Six-Day War and, 264–267
   Yom Kippur War and, 262, 273, 276, 278–279, 281–288, 296–298

tactics
   air-to-air combat and, 181, 185
   American Civil War and, 50–53
   armored warfare and, 107–108, 116, 123
   artillery and, 87–90, 93–94, 108–110
   close air support, 137–145, 223
   combined arms, 62, 65, 106–108, 110n118, 116–117, 146, 267
   competence in, 25
   defense in depth and, 77, 86, 99, 102–104, 108, 117, 146
   dispersal of forces and, 13–14
   exploitation, 110, 116–117, 122, 146, 301–302
   history of, 13–14
   infantry and, 108–110
   maneuver and, 63, 116, 122
   phalanx and, 38–40
   reverse slope defense and, 93

tactics (cont.)
  revolution in, 13, 64, 101–104
  Roman legion and, 38–43, 46, 53
  strategic bombing and, 231
Tal, General Israel, 266–267, 277, 293n96
Tamari, Major General Dov, 264n4,
    270n25, 293n96, 294, 296,
    297n111
Tamari, Major General Shai, 270n23,
    289n81
technology. See also Industrial Revolution
  armored warfare and, 22–23, 316
  artillery and, 89, 206, 216, 226–227
  atomic weapons and, 69
  barbed wire and, 80, 83, 94, 96, 98
  civilian experts and, 159, 167–169, 259,
    317–318
  combat capabilities and, 58
  electronic warfare and, 216, 218, 221,
    241
  friction and, 17, 315
  gunpowder and, 45–47
  intellectual demands and, 73
  knowledge versus information and, 16
  medical revolution and, 58
  military revolution and, 58, 78
  multiple technologies, 37–38
  naval revolution and, 59
  nuclear weapons and, 69, 315
  pace of change in, 36–37, 47, 57–58,
    306
  peacetime innovation and, 2, 156,
    317
  radar. See radar systems
  radio navigation. See radio navigation
    systems
  railroads and, 54–55
  rifled weaponry and, 50–51
  submarines and, 193
  tactical problems and, 60
  telegraph and, 54, 59
  war, application to, and, 84n29
Tedder, Air Chief Marshal Sir Arthur, 201,
    247, 252–255
Tet Offensive, 31
Teutoburg Forest, Battle of the, 41n10
Thebes, ancient, 39
Thoma, General Wilhelm Ritter von, 123
Thrasybulus, 27
Thucydides, 17
Tizard, Sir Henry, 317
Tooze, Adam, 229

Torch, Operation, 33
Trafalgar, Battle of, 60
Travers, Timothy, 115
Trenchard, Air Marshal Sir Hugh, 200,
    242
Triandafillov, General Vladimir, 68
Tukhachevsky, Marshal Mikhail, 68
Turkey, 199
Turner, Admiral Richard Kelly, 327

Ukraine, 306
Ultra, 243n181, 253n219
United Nations, 264, 302
United States
  adaptation and, 4, 32–34, 50–53, 72–73,
    115, 310–315, 318, 320–328
  Afghanistan and, 6, 306, 315, 328
  civilian theorists and, 70
  Civil War. See American Civil War
  Cold War, 69–72, 307
  Division, U.S. Army
    1st Armored Division, 31n87
    101st Airborne Division, 70
  economy of, 230
  industrial potential of, 225, 227
  insurgency and, 31, 73, 312–313
  interwar period and, 66–67, 230,
    328
  Iraq and, 6, 31, 38, 42, 73, 306,
    312–315, 328
  logistics and, 307
  military bureaucracy and, 69
  professional military education and, 69,
    328
  projection of power and, 307
  twenty-first century strategic
    environment and, 305–308
  United States Air Force, 69, 71–72
  United States Army Air Corps, 230
  United States Army Air Forces, 208n45,
    241, 246–247
  Overlord, Operation, and, 248,
    249n205, 250, 253–255
  United States Marine Corps, 67
  United States Navy, 326–327
    innovation and, 67
    Naval War College and, 67
    Top Gun program, 72
  United States Strategic Bombing Survey,
    240
Upton, Brevet Major General Emory, 53,
    56

V-1 and V-2 missile, 235, 240, 258
Vansittart, Sir Robert, 19
Varus, Publius Quinctilius, 41n10
Verdun, Battle of, 63, 94, 100–101
Verrier, Anthony, 197–198, 204, 251
Versailles, Treaty of, 121, 123, 138, 204
Vietnam War, 29–31, 69–73, 313–314, 320, 324–325
Vimy Ridge, Battle of, 90–91

Wallis, Sir Barnes Neville, 231
war
  civilian theorists and, 70
  conduct of, 38
  conventional warfare and, 40, 48, 61, 69, 72–73
  defensive positions and, 52–53
  definition of, 1
  enemy response, framework of, 36, 274, 309–310
  friction and chance and, 16–18, 315, 325
  human nature and, 6–7
  intellectual preparation for, 8–9, 62–63, 67–71, 79, 110, 145, 152, 274
  levels of, 7
  modern warfare. *See* modern warfare
  nature of, 8, 57n57, 237n161, 307, 315, 325
  operational level of, 25, 38, 44, 117, 147, 151, 244, 308, 311
  political level of, 30, 69, 79, 120, 147, 274, 308, 311, 319, 321
  population, excess of the young and, 305n3
  psychological pressures of, 6, 8–11
  strategic level of, 29–30, 34, 44, 120, 147, 244, 311, 321. *See also* strategy
  study of, 57, 83, 119, 198, 277
  tactical level of, 38, 44, 52, 83, 117, 147, 309, 311. *See also* tactics
war gaming, 67, 148, 309, 325n57, 326
Waterloo, Battle of, 10n24, 14, 49
Watts, Barry, 304, 309
Webster, Sir Charles, 210
Weinberg, Gerhard, 257n229
Wellington, Duke of, 7, 10n24, 14, 19
Westmoreland, General William, 70–71, 310
Westphalia, Treaty of, 48
Wever, General Walther, 204–205
Wilhelm II, Kaiser, 32
Wilson, Field Marshal Sir Henry, 200
Wilson, Sir Horace, 23
Wolseley, Field Marshal Lord, 83
world strategic environment, 305–308
World War I
  adaptation and, 59, 76, 93, 96, 109, 115
  air power and, 104, 138
  anti-intellectualism and, 83
  armored warfare and, 107–108, 116
  artillery and, 87–94, 96–100, 108, 110
  assumptions and, 29, 85, 96
  Balkans Campaign and, 94
  battlefield reporting and analysis and, 21, 63–65, 80, 85
  British strategy and, 25
  Champagne offensive and, 91
  civil-military relations and, 76
  complex adaptive system and, 76
  enemy adaptation and, 76–77, 79, 83, 87, 103–104, 117–118
  Flanders and, 85, 93, 105–109
  gas warfare and, 35, 92–93
  infantry tactics and, 96–98, 100
  leadership and, 14, 21, 74, 80, 85, 98, 101, 118
  lessons learned and, 65, 115
  lethality of, 61–62, 74, 80
  maneuver and, 76, 78, 114n131
  Michael Offensive and, 86, 114, 138
  military incompetence and, 74
  mobilization and, 67, 84
  modern war and, 4, 78
  Napoleonic concepts and, 80, 86, 96, 107
  operational level of, 63–64, 75, 104, 113–114, 117
  political level of, 76, 79–80, 87, 96, 101
  prewar period, 61–62, 79–80, 89
  Spring Offensives of 1918 and, 78, 113–115
  strategic level of, 25, 34–35, 76, 80, 87, 96, 101, 113, 199
  tactical level of and, 62–65, 74, 76–79, 83, 85, 87–90, 104–110, 108, 117, 147, 151, 259
  technological revolution and, 59, 76–77, 84, 98, 117
  United States, entry into, 32, 93, 115
  unrestricted submarine warfare and, 32, 101n86, 172, 188

World War II
  adaptation and, 65, 147, 151, 156–158, 193–194, 231, 238, 259
  aircraft, long-range fighter, and, 212–213
  aircraft production and, 158, 165–166, 170, 194, 204, 224–227, 238–239, 244, 246, 258
  Britain, Battle of. *See* Britain, Battle of
  Czechoslovakia, 124, 128, 231
  daylight precision bombing and, 208n45, 234, 246–247, 250
  economies of belligerents and, 67, 224–225, 230, 253, 255–256
  French Air Force and, 164
  French campaign and, 137, 148, 163–164
  intellectual preparation for, 67–68
  intelligence operations and, 148–150, 169, 171, 191–193, 195
  logistical failures and, 148, 161
  Low Countries and, 161
  Mediterranean theater and, 224–225
  North Africa and, 15, 16n44, 33, 68n88
  operational level of, 125, 169, 193, 225
  Overlord, Operation and, 247–256
  Pacific theater and, 32
  Phoney War and, 162, 174
  Polish campaign and, 125–131
  political level of, 151, 214
  Scandinavia and, 163, 179, 188
  senior leadership and, 14, 193–195, 224–226
  Soviet Union, invasion of. *See* Barbarossa, Operation
  strategic level of, 32–33, 66, 68, 147, 151, 161, 167, 171, 192–193, 225, 257
  tactical level of, 66, 122, 125, 193, 225, 326–327
  U-boat offensive and, 161, 188–194, 225

Yariv, Major General Aharon, 288
Yom Kippur War
  Golan Heights and, 276, 281–289, 291, 298, 302
  intelligence and, 262
  Northern Front and, 281–289, 296
  Sinai Front and, 273, 297–302
  Sinai Peninsula and, 274–275, 280, 285, 290–294, 296–298
  Southern Front and, 289–297
  Suez Canal and, 275–276, 280n55, 281, 286, 289–303
  Suez Front and, 295–296, 302–304
Yugoslavia, 306

Zhukov, Marshal Georgy, 7
Zuckerman, Solomon, 248, 253–254